# A Year in the
# New Testament

## New Testament Chapter Summaries

Roger Hillis

2025: One Stone Press.
All rights reserved. No part of this book may be reproduced in any form without written permission of the publisher.

Published by:
One Stone Press
979 Lovers Lane
Bowling Green, KY 42103

Printed in the United States of America

ISBN 978-1-966992-02-8

All scripture references, unless otherwise noted, are taken from the New King James Version, copyright by Thomas H. Nelson, Inc., Nashville, Tennessee, 1979, 1980, 1982, 1993.
Used by permission.

1(800)428-0121 • www.onestone.com

## Introduction to "A Year in the New Testament"

Welcome to a year long study of the New Testament. This is a combined Bible Reading Program, along with some brief chapter summaries of each chapter of the New Testament.

There are 260 chapters in the New Testament. The design of the Reading Program is to read a chapter every day, five days per week. Fifty-two weeks in a year, times five chapters each week equals 260 chapters in a single year.

You have the freedom to read these chapters and summaries at your own pace. (You also have the freedom to not do this at all, of course.) My suggestion is that you read the chapter from the Bible first, then read my summary of the chapter. If you find it helpful, after that, you might consider reading the Biblical text again, after looking at the synopsis of each chapter.

I would remind you that the Bible is inspired while my summaries are not. I have tried not to "add to" or "take from" the Bible as I have attempted to organize and explain the sacred writings.

I have included three reading plans, described below, to get you through the entire New Testament in a single year. If you read a chapter every day, you will finish with 105 days to go. If you follow one of the schedules here, you should start on January 1 and finish the New Testament by December 31.

Some will want to use the extra two days each week to review. Some might use them to catch up on missed readings. You might have other Bible studies and reading plans that you are doing and those two extra days will give you time to study other things. Of course, that is entirely up to you.

I have to say that this has been one of the best things I have ever done for myself. This all started early in 2020 with the Covid-19 pandemic shutdowns. Being at home with some extra time, I wrote the material on the book of Revelation to share with the church and give some people, who also had some extra time, a challenging study that would keep their minds focused on the Bible. I got a really good response from several Christians who said they got a lot out of the study. So I decided it would be a good thing for me to write chapter summaries on the rest of the New Testament as well. It was such an encouragement for me as I got excited about going through the entire New Testament this way. I wish I had done this 40 years ago. It would have helped my understanding of the new covenant a lot. I hope some young preachers might be encouraged by this effort and take on a similar challenge because I believe it will really help them grow spiritually to write their own chapter summaries.

Because we are all different, I have developed three different approaches to using this study guide.

Plan 1 is a schedule that will allow you to read through the books in the order they are contained in the New Testament. You will study all four gospel accounts together, one right after the other, then Acts and then the letters from Romans through Revelation.

Plan 2 is a schedule I have often used in reading different versions of the New Testament. It spreads out the gospels and intersperses the other books throughout, ending with Revelation.

Plan 3 is an attempt to look at the books in an approximately chronological order. The life of Christ is first (all four gospels), then as we go into Acts, I have tried to insert the books/letters into Acts close to where they were written, then the general epistles and Revelation. Use any of these schedules or make up your own, if you desire. There is no right or wrong answer here. I just hope it helps you.

## Plan 1

Week 1 – Matthew 1-5
Week 2 – Matthew 6-10
Week 3 – Matthew 11-15
Week 4 – Matthew 16-20
Week 5 – Matthew 21-25
Week 6 – Matthew 26-28, Mark 1-2
Week 7 – Mark 3-7
Week 8 – Mark 8-12
Week 9 – Mark 13-16, Luke 1
Week 10 – Luke 2-6
Week 11 – Luke 7-11
Week 12 – Luke 12-16
Week 13 – Luke 17-21
Week 14 – Luke 22-24, John 1-2
Week 15 – John 3-7
Week 16 – John 8-12
Week 17 – John 13-17
Week 18 – John 18-21, Acts 1
Week 19 – Acts 2-6
Week 20 – Acts 7-11
Week 21 – Acts 12-16
Week 22 – Acts 17-21
Week 23 – Acts 22-26
Week 24 – Acts 27-28, Romans 1-3
Week 25 – Romans 4-8
Week 26 – Romans 9-13
Week 27 – Romans 14-16, 1 Corinthians 1-2
Week 28 – 1 Corinthians 3-7
Week 29 – 1 Corinthians 8-12
Week 30 – 1 Corinthians 13-16, 2 Corinthians 1
Week 31 – 2 Corinthians 2-6
Week 32 – 2 Corinthians 7-11
Week 33 – 2 Corinthians 12-13, Galatians 1-3
Week 34 – Galatians 4-6, Ephesians 1-2
Week 35 – Ephesians 3-6, Philippians 1
Week 36 – Philippians 2-4, Colossians 1-2
Week 37 – Colossians 3-4, 1 Thessalonians 1-3
Week 38 – 1 Thessalonians 4-5, 2 Thessalonians 1-3
Week 39 – 1 Timothy 1-5
Week 40 – 1 Timothy 6, 2 Timothy 1-4
Week 41 – Titus 1-3, Philemon, Hebrews 1
Week 42 – Hebrews 2-6
Week 43- Hebrews 7-11
Week 44 – Hebrews 12-13, James 1-3
Week 45 – James 4-5, 1 Peter 1-3
Week 46 – 1 Peter 4-5, 2 Peter 1-3
Week 47 – 1 John 1-5
Week 48 – 2 John, 3 John, Jude, Revelation 1-2
Week 49 – Revelation 3-7
Week 50 – Revelation 8-12
Week 51 – Revelation 13-17
Week 52 – Revelation 18-22

## Plan 2

Week 1 – Luke 1-5
Week 2 – Luke 6-10
Week 3 – Luke 11-15
Week 4 – Luke 16-20
Week 5 – Luke 21-24, Acts 1
Week 6 – Acts 2-6
Week 7 – Acts 7-11
Week 8 – Acts 12-16
Week 9 – Acts 17-21
Week 10 – Acts 22-26
Week 11 – Acts 27-28, Galatians 1-3
Week 12 – Galatians 4-6, Ephesians 1-2
Week 13 – Ephesians 3-6, Philippians 1
Week 14 – Philippians 2-4, Colossians 1-2
Week 15 – Colossians 3-4, 1 Thessalonians 1-3
Week 16 – 1 Thessalonians 4-5, 2 Thessalonians
Week 17 – Matthew 1-5
Week 18 – Matthew 6-10
Week 19 – Matthew 11-15
Week 20 – Matthew 16-20
Week 21 – Matthew 21-25
Week 22 – Matthew 26-28, Romans 1-2
Week 23 – Romans 3-7
Week 24 – Romans 8-12
Week 25 – Romans 13-16, 1 Corinthians 1
Week 26 – 1 Corinthians 2-6
Week 27 – 1 Corinthians 7-11
Week 28 – 1 Corinthians 12-16
Week 29 – 2 Corinthians 1-5
Week 30 – 2 Corinthians 6-10
Week 31 – 2 Corinthians 11-13, Mark 1-2
Week 32 – Mark 3-7
Week 33 – Mark 8-12
Week 34 – Mark 13-16, 1 Timothy 1
Week 35 – 1 Timothy 2-6
Week 36 – 2 Timothy 1-4, Titus 1
Week 37 – Titus 2-3, Philemon, Hebrews 1-2
Week 38 – Hebrews 3-7
Week 39 – Hebrews 8-12
Week 40 – Hebrews 13, James 1-4
Week 41 – James 5, 1 Peter 1-4
Week 42 – 1 Peter 5, 2 Peter 1-3, 1 John 1
Week 43 – 1 John 2-5, 2 John
Week 44 – 3 John, Jude, John 1-3
Week 45 – John 4-8
Week 46 – John 9-13
Week 47 – John 14-18
Week 48 – John 19-21, Revelation 1-2
Week 49 – Revelation 3-7
Week 50 – Revelation 8-12
Week 51 – Revelation 13-17
Week 52 – Revelation 18-22

## Plan 3

Week 1 – Matthew 1-5
Week 2 – Matthew 6-10
Week 3 – Matthew 11-15
Week 4 – Matthew 16-20
Week 5 – Matthew 21-25
Week 6 – Matthew 26-28, Mark 1-2
Week 7 – Mark 3-7
Week 8 – Mark 8-12
Week 9 – Mark 13-16, Luke 1
Week 10 – Luke 2-6
Week 11 – Luke 7-11
Week 12 – Luke 12-16
Week 13 – Luke 17-21
Week 14 – Luke 22-24, John 1-2
Week 15 – John 3-7
Week 16 – John 8-12
Week 17 – John 13-17
Week 18 – John 18-21, Acts 1
Week 19 – Acts 2-6
Week 20 – Acts 7-11
Week 21 – Acts 12-14, James 1-2
Week 22 – James 3-5, Acts 15, Galatians 1
Week 23 – Galatians 2-6
Week 24 – Acts 16-18, 1 Thessalonians 1-2
Week 25 – 1 Thessalonians 3-5, 2 Thessalonians 1-2
Week 26 – 2 Thessalonians 3, Acts 19, 1 Corinthians 1-3
Week 27 – 1 Corinthians 4-8
Week 28 – 1 Corinthians 9-13
Week 29 – 1 Cor 14-16, 2 Corinthians 1-2
Week 30 – 2 Corinthians 3-7
Week 31 – 2 Corinthians 8-12
Week 32 – 2 Corinthians 13, Romans 1-4
Week 33 – Romans 5-9
Week 34 – Romans 10-14
Week 35 – Romans 15-16, Acts 20-22
Week 36 – Acts 23-27
Week 37 – Acts 28, Colossians 1-4
Week 38 – Ephesians 1-5
Week 39 – Ephesians 6, Philippians 1-4
Week 40 – Philemon, 1 Timothy 1-4
Week 41 – 1 Timothy 5-6, Titus 1-3
Week 42 – Hebrews 1-5
Week 43 – Hebrews 6-10
Week 44 – Hebrews 11-13, 2 Timothy 1-2
Week 45 – 2 Timothy 3-4, 1 Peter 1-3
Week 46 – 1 Peter 4-5, 2 Peter 1-3
Week 47 – 1 John 1-5
Week 48 – 2-3 John, Jude, Revelation 1-2
Week 49 – Revelation 3-7
Week 50 – Revelation 8-12
Week 51 – Revelation 13-17
Week 52 – Revelation 18-22

Remember, of course, that you can follow any Bible reading schedule you want. There are lots of different plans out there and any of them can be used with these chapter summaries. The main thing is for you to read your Bible. May God richly bless you as you spend time with Him in His inspired message.

"For this reason we also thank God without ceasing, because when you received the word of God which you heard from us, you welcomed it not as the word of men, but as it is in truth, the word of God which also effectively works in you who believe" (1 Thessalonians 2:13).

"Blessed is he who reads and those who hear the words of this prophecy, and keep those things which are written in it; for the time is near" (Revelation 1:3).

Roger Hillis
rogerhillis1953@gmail.com

Dedication

*This book is lovingly dedicated to my parents Harry Jr. and June Hillis and my in-laws James and Audrey Capps.*

# The Gospel according to MATTHEW

## Matthew 1

"The book of the genealogy of Jesus Christ, the Son of David, the Son of Abraham" (Matthew 1:1).

Thus reads the first verse of the first book of the New Testament. Verses 1-17 trace the lineage of Jesus of Nazareth, starting with Abraham and concluding with Joseph, the husband of Mary who was the mother of the Messiah. Listed are 14 generations from Abraham to David, 14 generations from David to the Babylonian captivity, and 14 generations from Babylon until the Christ. There are a few individuals who are omitted so the numbers come out 14-14-14, as this would be easier to remember.

There are several key points that should be made about this genealogy.

Matthew traces the lineage through David's son, Solomon (verses 6-7) and the kings of Judah. Luke's lineage is followed through David's son, Nathan (Luke 3:23-38).

To show the importance of women in God's plan, there are four women who are mentioned, plus Mary. Tamar (verse 3), Rahab (verse 5), Ruth (verse 5) and the wife of Uriah (Bathsheba, verse 6) are all mentioned as part of Jesus' ancestry. Many people yet today believe that Christianity demotes women to an inferior station in life, but Jesus actually came to elevate women in the eyes of mankind. Women were not normally included in Jewish genealogies, but God, by inspiration, wanted to list these women who were ancestors of the Christ.

Another significant point to realize is that three of these women were Gentiles, which is interesting if not fully prophetic in the sense of Jesus providing universal salvation, not just for the Jewish people. One of the reasons Jesus came was to break down the middle wall of separation between Jew and Gentile. God had a specific purpose for creating the bloodline of Christ through Abraham's descendants (the Hebrew people or the nation of Israel), but once that purpose was fulfilled in Jesus, the dividing wall was removed forever.

Some of the Bible characters listed in Matthew 1 are quite prominent in the Old Testament narrative, while many of them are obscure or perhaps totally unknown, as far as any details of their lives are concerned. This shows us that someone can be really important in God's plan, even if other people know little or nothing about them.

The main purpose of Matthew's record is to show that Jesus of Nazareth was a physical descendant of Abraham. This would show the original Jewish readers that Jesus could be the Messiah. It doesn't prove that He is, only that He is from the right lineage. That's the primary point Matthew is trying to make.

Some facts about the birth of Jesus are found in verses 18-25. Other details are given in Luke 1-2. The angel Gabriel's visits with Zacharias and Mary, along with Mary's journey from Galilee to Judea for a three month period with Elizabeth are not included here. That's why it is so helpful to read all of the gospel accounts, to learn things from one that the other writers may not have included.

Engaged, but before they are legally married, Mary is "found with child of the Holy Spirit." Fornication was (and still is, of course) a serious sin in the first century. A young, unmarried woman who became pregnant, along with the male partner, was to be stoned to death, according to the Law of Moses (see Deuteronomy 22:23-24). Joseph did not want Mary to be publicly humiliated so he had decided to put her away quietly. Then an unnamed angel of the Lord appears to him and tells him the whole story. Joseph decides to do the right thing and carry on with the marriage. This fulfilled the Messianic prophecy of Isaiah 7:14, quoted here in verse 23. The baby is to be named Jesus, which means Savior.

## Matthew 2

Verse 1 tells us that Jesus was born in Bethlehem "in the days of Herod the king." That would be Herod the Great who ruled from 37-4 B.C. Early attempts to reconcile the world's calendars with the birth of Christ miscalculated the timing of the events and, as a result, rather than being born in the year 0, Jesus was actually born in around 4-6 B.C.

Wise men from the East (primarily the Medo-Persian Empire which had conquered the Babylonians in around 538 B.C.) come to Judea to see the Messiah in person. Some Bible versions refer to them as Magi. The Magi are from Media and they are special teachers to the Medo-Persian kings. They are highly skilled in philosophy, medicine and the natural sciences. They say that they have seen His star and have come to worship the one they call "the King of the Jews" (verse 2; see also verses 9-11). This deeply troubles Herod; he doesn't want any competition for the adulation of the people of Judea.

Herod calls together the chief priests and scribes of the Jewish people and asks them where the Messiah was supposed to be born. They quote Micah 5:2 and tell him that the Christ was to be born in the village of Bethlehem in Judea. (By the way, the Book of Mormon incorrectly says that Jesus was born in Jerusalem, one of thousands of inconsistencies in that man-made, not divine book.) After they inform Herod of the birthplace of Jesus, he tells the Magi and then asks them to come back and report to him after they have seen the Messiah, falsely claiming he wants to worship Him also.

They find Jesus and Mary, give them three gifts (that's where the common idea that there were three wise men comes from; the fact is we are not told how many of them there were), and then, warned by God, they return to their homes without reporting back to Herod.

God warns Joseph and Mary that Herod is going to try to kill the baby Jesus and tells them to take the family to Egypt for a period of time. Matthew includes a reference to this from Hosea 11:1 and applies it to Jesus, although it was not clear in the original that it was speaking of Him. Herod, infuriated by the Magi's failure to tell him where the baby was, takes matters into his own hands and issues a decree that all the male children in the town of Bethlehem and the surrounding region who are under the age of two should be put to death. Again, this indirectly fulfills a prophecy from Jeremiah 31:15.

After the death of Herod, an angel of the Lord appears in a dream to Joseph and tells him it is now safe to return from Egypt. Because Herod's son, Archelaus is reigning over Judea, Joseph decides to settle his family in the region of Galilee, to the north of Judea. They end up in a small village called Nazareth.

Verse 23 is a puzzle in some ways. There is no direct passage from the Old Testament that is quoted here word for word and that has caused some to claim that this is an error in the Bible. Let's consider the verse for a moment and see if we can make sense of it.

There are many Messianic references in the Old Testament. This is one that is more obscure than most and takes us back to a prophecy found in Isaiah 11, a highly Messianic passage. "There shall come forth a Rod from the stem of Jesse, And a Branch shall grow out of his roots" (Isaiah 11:1). That is talking about the Messiah. In English, it is harder to see the connection, but if we remember that the Hebrew Bible is written in the Hebrew language, it becomes clearer. The word translated as "branch" in the Isaiah passage is from a Hebrew word, NEZER. Do you see how that looks and sounds a little bit like NAZAR-eth? It is kind of a play on words, really, not a direct quote from the Old Testament that Matthew utilizes here to show a loose fulfillment in the early life of Jesus, growing up in Nazareth in Galilee as a descendant of David. Most of the other prophecies are easier to understand and see their direct fulfillment in the life of Christ. This one shows us that even small details in the Old Testament can often be linked to Jesus. He is like a branch (NEZER) that grows up and becomes known as a NAZARene.

## Matthew 3

The text now jumps forward almost 30 years. At the end of Chapter 2, Jesus was just a small baby/child. Now He is "about thirty years of age" (Luke 3:23). John the Baptist begins his public ministry as the forerunner of the Messiah and comes "preaching in the wilderness of Judea" (verse 1). In the Old Testament, this region of the world was known as Judah, named after the Southern Kingdom which in turn was named after one of the twelve sons of Jacob, but now it has been changed slightly to Judea. Judah was the tribe of Israel that Jesus was born into. (That's also where the word, Jew, originated during the time of the Babylonian captivity. "Jew" is a term applied to those from Judah/Judea.)

John's message was clear and simple. "Repent, for the kingdom of heaven is at hand!" After 400 years of no revelations from God (often called "The Silent 400 Years" or the period between the testaments), God finally breaks the silence. The long predicted kingdom that would be more powerful than any other is about to appear (Daniel 2:44). It was to be a spiritual kingdom, not an earthly one. It would live in the souls of all those who would pledge their allegiance to the Anointed One.

John's purpose as a forerunner to the Christ was to call the nation of Israel to repentance and to prepare the hearts and minds of the people for the coming of their Savior. Matthew quotes Isaiah 40:3 and applies it to John. The idea behind a forerunner is one who would go before a traveling ruler and announce his imminent arrival to the peoples through whose land the caravan would pass. Often, in the days before paved roads and interstate highway systems, an advance team would precede the company of the king to make certain they would have easy travel. Sometimes they would have to build roads through or around obstacles that might be in the path that the king and his entourage would be taking. John's job was to prepare the way for the arrival of the King of kings. He sought to bring the Hebrew nation (Israel) to repentance so that they would accept Jesus as the promised Messiah. In some lives, John succeeded. In others, he did not.

The physical description of John (verse 4) sounds much like that of the Old Testament prophet, Elijah (see 2 Kings 1:8). This was intentional, of course. Elijah was a prophet of God during a difficult and challenging time in Hebrew history. Ahab was king #8 in Israel, the Northern Kingdom. All of the kings in the North were wicked, without exception, but Ahab was especially evil. He was married to a woman named Jezebel, the daughter of Ethbaal, the king of the Sidonians, who worshiped a false god named Baal, not the one true God of heaven. This couple was a constant thorn in the side of Elijah as he tried to rally the people of Israel to follow the Lord. In many ways, Elijah's work foreshadowed that of John the Baptist. Malachi 4:5-6 predicted the coming of Elijah before the Messiah and this prophecy is said to have been fulfilled in the life and work of John the Baptist (see Matthew 11:11-14; 17:10-13; Mark 1:2; Luke 1:17). When asked if he was Elijah, John said he was not literally a reincarnated Elijah (John 1:21), but Elijah was a "type" or a shadow of John, in that the work they did for God was quite similar.

John accomplished his mission well (verses 5-6), even though many Jews did not end up accepting Jesus as the Christ. Re-read his sermon found in verses 7-12 and it will help you to realize the power and the bravery of this great man of God. We will learn more about his courage in a later chapter in Matthew.

In verses 13-17, Jesus comes "from Galilee to John at the Jordan to be baptized by him." John feels unworthy to baptize Jesus, but He tells him that "it is fitting for us to fulfill all righteousness" and John agrees to do so. After they both come up out of the water (that would be immersion, which is what the original term means), the heavens open up and the Spirit of God descends like a dove and lands on Jesus. A voice from heaven (it was God Himself speaking) declares Jesus to be "My beloved Son, in whom I am well pleased." God's Son is ready to begin His ministry.

## Matthew 4

Immediately following His baptism, we read about the temptation of Jesus by the devil (verses 1-11). It is often the case that right after someone devotes his or her life to the Lord and is baptized into Christ, that person will have things happen in his life that can only come from Satan. He has lost a soul and he is desperate to get it back. So he pulls out all the stops to make that person question the commitment that has been made to God. We can learn how to handle these temptations by looking at how Jesus defeated Satan.

Hebrews 4:15 tells us that Jesus was tempted in all the same ways we are tempted, yet without sin. But He wasn't tempted to look at internet pornography or to steal someone else's identity or to cyber-attack someone's bank account, or to swindle people out of their life savings with a pyramid scheme. So how can it be said He was tempted like we are? Well, in 1 John 2:16, the apostle John lists the three major areas of sin that all temptations fall into: the lust of the flesh, the lust of the eyes and the pride of life. Every temptation fits into one of those three areas. With Jesus, the temptation to turn stones into bread is the lust of the flesh (His flesh was hungry). The lust of the eyes describes the world and all its possessions. To jump off the pinnacle of the temple and be protected by God appeals to the pride of life. So He was indeed tempted just like we are, but did not yield to those appeals. When you have time, can you see those same three areas of temptation in the account of Eve and the serpent (Genesis 3:1-6)?

Three times Jesus was attacked by the devil. Each of the temptations was answered by Jesus as He reminded Satan of what is written in the Bible. He quoted three Old Testament passages, one for each temptation. We can do the same thing when we are tempted. We can say, in every situation, what God would want us to do. Honestly, if we will do that, won't we sin less? We might still give in to some temptations (Satan knows how to make bad things look really good to us, doesn't he?), but it will be a bad choice given what we know about what God expects of us. Remember those words: "It is written."

One interesting side point is that, in the second temptation (verses 5-7), the devil himself quotes and then misapplies Scripture to try to convince the Son of God to disobey His heavenly Father. Satan apparently knows the Bible and won't hesitate to misuse it in his efforts to get us to rebel against God. Don't ever allow someone to use the Bible in an attempt to justify sinning against God.

In verses 12-25, Jesus begins His earthly ministry in the region of the world He grew up in, Galilee. He moves from Nazareth, his hometown, to Capernaum, which will now be the base for His work. His initial message parallels that of John the Baptist, "Repent, for the kingdom of heaven is at hand" (verse 17).

He begins by calling the first four disciples, who will later become His apostles. Peter and Andrew, James and John (two sets of brothers) are fishermen who work on the Sea of Galilee and Jesus recruits them to begin their training as He will put them to work for God. "Follow Me, and I will make you fishers of men" (verse 19). Immediately, they leave everything behind and follow the Savior.

Do you see the connection between the message, "the kingdom of heaven is at hand," and the statement, "I will make you fishers of men?" Although most Jewish people were looking for an earthly King who would lead Israel in battle and overthrow the political domination of the evil Roman Empire, the emphasis of Jesus is a spiritual kingdom that calls people, not to war but to salvation from sin. He came to bring people into a right relationship with God, and to change the world spiritually.

Jesus went all about Galilee, teaching in the Jewish synagogues and preaching the good news about the kingdom of God. Great multitudes followed Him, from Galilee, Judea and beyond the Jordan. Everyone seemed eager to hear His message. His work of turning the world upside down has begun.

## Matthew 5

Chapters 5-7 are a single unit. They contain what has come to be called "The Sermon on the Mount" (verse 1). They contain powerful teaching from Jesus about the coming kingdom of God and what being a citizen of that spiritual kingdom would involve. The transition from the Old Testament to the New Testament is underway and Jesus, from the very beginning, makes it clear that He expects His followers to be totally and completely surrendered and committed to Him and His teaching. Many have referred to this as the greatest sermon ever preached.

The first section (verses 2-12) contains the Beatitudes. It is a series of verses, which pronounce God's happiness (to be blessed means to be happy) on that kingdom citizen who would possess the quality or characteristic of life that is spoken of. They are not so much actions to be taken, but first of all they describe attitudes that a faithful disciple of Jesus must have in his heart. (Actions will follow the proper attitudes, as in Matthew 12:34-37.) Jesus wants to change not merely our outward conduct, but the inward spirit that will result in proper deeds. And each one of the beatitudes also contains a blessing or reward for the one who would live out the inner quality in his behavior.

Verses 13-16 instruct us on the kind of godly example that the Savior wants us to live out in front of others. He uses two illustrations (word pictures) to describe the positive influence we should be on the unbelieving world around us, salt and light. Our example is meant to lift others up and bring them closer to God. Unbelievers should be able to see the impact of Christ in our lives and want to have that kind of good feeling about themselves that only comes from doing right. Verse 16 concludes the section with the thought that our faithful example should be such that people glorify our heavenly Father, not that they praise us. It's all about bringing glory to Him.

Verses 17-20 tell us about the relationship between Jesus and the Old Law. He came to institute the new covenant prophesied in the Old Testament (Jeremiah 31:31-34; quoted in Hebrews 8:8-13). He says that He did not come to destroy the Old Testament and He didn't, because we still have it today to study and learn from. But He did come to fulfill it, that is to be the living fulfillment of the Old Law in His life, death and resurrection. God's law for man is about to change from the old to the new.

Beginning in verse 21 and continuing through the end of the chapter, Jesus will show six contrasts between the old covenant and the new one. Several of these contrasts will begin with words, "You have heard that it was said to those of old...But I say to you." Not all six examples use those exact words, but that is the point of each of His illustrations. And, in each of these cases, Jesus again emphasizes the condition of a person's heart as being both greater than and the source of a person's actions. (He is not saying deeds are unimportant; He is stressing the greater importance of a person's heart condition.)

Verses 21-26 show us that we must not murder other people, but also that we must not harbor ill will toward them in our hearts. He goes behind the action of murder to the attitude of hatred that would bring about mistreatment, including murder, of others. (John makes that same point in 1 John 3:10-15.)

Verses 27-30 warn us about committing adultery in our hearts, not just with our bodies. Verses 31-32 prohibits divorcing a spouse, except for the sin of adultery. Verses 33-37 teach us to always be honest and trustworthy people, not only when we are sworn to tell the truth in a court of law. Verses 38-42 say that we should be willing to be mistreated by others, so that we might influence them for good. Verses 43-48 instruct us about the importance of loving both our friends and our enemies. He reminds us that God sends material blessings (sunshine and needed rain) on the just and on the unjust. If we want to be like God, we must be fair and gracious to those who might not return the favor. This is a sign of spiritual maturity ("be perfect, just as your Father in heaven is perfect"). It's not always easy.

## Matthew 6

Jesus' Sermon on the Mountain continues in Chapter 6. The first 18 verses emphasize the importance of doing the right thing for the purpose of serving and pleasing God, not to be seen by others. The three areas of life that He chooses as illustrations of this principle are helping others, praying and fasting. We will look at each of these actions in turn.

Verses 1-4 speak of helping others who are less fortunate than we are. Jesus refers to these acts of kindness as "charitable deeds." It is always appropriate and right to do what we can to remember the poor (Galatians 2:10) and to help people who may be struggling or having a rough time financially. Jesus makes the point that, if we do these things in a public manner to be praised by people, we already have our reward. But if we do them secretly, then God, who sees in secret, will reward us openly. Are we doing things for others to help them or to help our own reputation? Sometimes you cannot help it if other people find out about your kind deeds for people, but don't do things just to look good to others.

Verses 5-15 shift the conversation to the subject of prayer. Jesus again emphasizes that we should not lead prayers in front of others for the purpose of impressing people with our words. Prayer is intended to be a conversation between us and God. There are times when we lead others in prayer, like in a public worship service or even at a family meal. The Lord is not saying that we should never pray when others can hear us; He is saying that we should not be praying to be heard by others. There are several specific warnings about prayer that Jesus mentions. In verse 5, He says something about praying "standing in the synagogues and on the corners of the streets, that they may be seen by men." He is clearly saying, don't put on a show when you pray, just talk to the Father. That's why He suggests going to a private place (verse 6) where it is just you and Him.

In verse 7, He tells us not to use "vain repetitions," thinking we will be heard only if we pray a really long prayer. Sometimes prayer needs to be long, if we have much to talk to God about. But repeating the same things over and over again does not impress God. (A good friend of mine said in a sermon once that when his wife was dying of cancer that he spent a whole night praying that God would heal her. He didn't do that to impress anybody else, he was genuinely asking God for help.) Jesus simply says that the length of prayers is not the important factor. Rather it is the contents of our hearts that matters.

In verses 9-15, we read what is commonly called the Lord's prayer. It is an outline of some of the vital aspects of an acceptable prayer. I don't think His plan was for people to memorize those words and use that prayer in every situation in life. But there are powerful lessons about our relationship with God that we can learn from looking at those various aspects of prayer outlined by the Savior here.

Verses 16-18 talk about fasting and the application remains the same as the previous two areas of helping and praying. Don't fast just so people will be impressed with your dedication to God. There is value in fasting and probably most Christians do not even consider the worth of fasting as we should. But we should realize that Jesus says, "when you fast," not "if you fast." Any understanding of fasting that does away with the practice altogether is a mistake.

Verses 19-24 help us to have the proper attitude toward material possessions. It is all too easy for us to accumulate wealth and make that the priority of our lives, but Jesus tells us not to store up treasures on earth and miss the treasures of heaven.

Verses 25-34 teach us valuable lessons about worry and anxiety. If we put God and His kingdom first (verse 33), we will not become overly concerned with the trials and troubles in life. He says, "Don't worry." That's often a very difficult challenge, but Jesus will help us if we ask Him to.

## Matthew 7

Chapter 7 concludes Jesus' Sermon on the Mount with more powerful teaching from the Son of God. We would be wise to listen carefully and apply everything Jesus says here to our daily lives. He addresses several helpful subjects in this chapter.

Verses 1-6 warn us against hypocritical judgment of others. It does not teach us that judging is always wrong, but rather that we must first take care of sins and weaknesses in our own lives before we try to help other people overcome their struggles. Verse 1 is often misunderstood by people who know little about the Bible in general and less about the context of what Jesus meant when He said, "Judge not, that you be not judged." He specifically states that another individual has a speck of dust in his eye. But the one who judges him has a plank (a huge piece of wood) sticking out of his own eye. If he tries to help the person with the speck without dealing with the log in his own eye, Jesus calls him a hypocrite. But verse 5 says that, if he first removes the plank out of his eye, then he can "see clearly" to help the other fellow. Verse 6 teaches that it is unwise to "cast your pearls before swine." How can we decide who that applies to if we cannot make some judgments about other peoples' lives? But our top priority should be to straighten up our own lives before we begin to talk with others about their issues.

Verses 7-12 talk about the importance of persistence in prayer. He promises us that we will continue to ask, seek and knock that the Lord will be with us. If we ask, He will give. If we seek, we will find. If we knock, He will open a door for us. Jesus uses the example of an earthly father who tries his best to bless his son and to give him what the son needs. If we understand a father's love for his children, then we can rest assured that God loves us and will bless us also. Sometimes God answers those prayers of His children through the lives and actions of other believers who will do for them what they want and need (verse 12).

Verses 13-14 remind them and us that there are two pathways in life, right and wrong. Jesus says that many will choose the broad way with a wide gate that leads to destruction. Few will look for and find the difficult way with a narrow gate that leads to (eternal) life. Which does God want us to choose?

In verses 15-20, Jesus spends some time discussing "false prophets," those who appear to be righteous but are actually wolves in sheep's clothing, nothing more than disguised and deceitful hypocrites. Most of them will ultimately be revealed as false teachers, but it might take some time before that happens. Jesus said, "by their fruits you will know them." Keep your eyes open and stay alert.

Verses 21-23 are somewhat frightening. They warn us that many who believe they are in a right relationship with God are actually not. They have either been misled by others or they have allowed circumstances in their lives to color their thinking. They love to say, "Lord, Lord," but they are not doing "the will of My Father in heaven." How sad it will be in the final judgment for some who were led astray by the false prophets who teach the doctrines and commandments of men to realize, when it is too late, that they have been deceived. While believing themselves to be pleasing to God, Jesus will tell them to depart, "you who practice lawlessness." Lawlessness means to be without law. What that tells us is that they have not been doing what the Bible teaches, although they thought they were.

The sermon concludes with the parable of the two builders, a wise man who builds his house on a rock and a foolish man who build his house on the shifting sands. Jesus says they both heard His teaching; the wise man did what Jesus wanted and the foolish man did not. One will be saved; the other will be lost.

When the sermon ends, those who heard "were astonished at His teaching, for He taught them as one having authority, not as the scribes." Are you hearing and obeying the sayings of the Messiah?

## Matthew 8

As the Sermon on the Mount ends and Jesus descends from the mountain where it was delivered, the New Testament tells us that "great multitudes" continued to follow Him, hoping to receive more of His teachings (verse 1). The Bible doesn't normally use many comparative or superlative terms, preferring to simply tell the facts of every situation without embellishment. So when it uses a phrase like "great" multitudes, that tells us a lot. A multitude would be a large crowd, so great multitudes must have been huge numbers of people who want to hear more of what Jesus is giving them. "No man ever spoke like this Man" (John 7:46). That informs us about the power of His message and the authority with which He delivered it. We have all heard some great preachers in our time, but no one else can teach like Jesus.

In verses 2-4, Jesus touches and heals a leper. Notice that, as grateful as the man would have been, Christ reminds him to follow the teachings of the Law of Moses concerning such skin diseases (you might want to take the time to go back and read Leviticus 13 and 14; Chapter 13 describes the various skin conditions, including what was considered a form of leprosy back then and Chapter 14 gives the process to follow up when a healing occurred). Jesus always encouraged people to obey God's law (some today would call Him a "legalist").

In verses 5-13, Jesus, in Capernaum, is approached by a centurion, a Roman soldier in charge of 100 men, who asks Him to heal a beloved servant who is "paralyzed, dreadfully tormented." When Jesus offers to go to his home and help the troubled servant, the centurion, showing great humility, says that he is not worthy for Christ to enter his home. While he emphasizes that he is man of great authority in the Roman army, he impresses Jesus with his great faith. Jesus heals the servant "that same hour."

The next miracle in the chapter is found in verses 14-15 where the Savior heals Peter's mother in law of a fever. In verses 16-17, Jesus shows His power over Satan as He heals "many who were demon possessed" and others who were sick as well. Matthew points out that these healings are a fulfillment of Isaiah 53:4.

Jesus discusses the cost of being His disciple in verses 18-22. The reward is great for following Jesus and making Him the Lord of our lives. But so is the sacrifice that many will have to make to walk after Him. It has been said that grace is free, but it isn't cheap. We are taught in other passages that our bodies must be given as "a living sacrifice" (Romans 12:1-2; see also Galatians 2:20). If our hearts are full of love for the things in this world, we will have no room left in our lives for total surrender to Jesus.

In verses 23-27, the disciples and Jesus are in a boat (on the Sea of Galilee) and while Jesus is sleeping, "a great tempest" arises and the boat is being swamped by the waves. The disciples are convinced that they are going to die and so they wake Him up and ask Him to save them. He tells them they should not be fearful and says to them, "O you of little faith." He gets up, rebukes the winds and the sea and the storm instantly dissipates to a "great calm." His disciples are stunned by His power and ask among themselves, "Who can this be?"

Verses 28-34 bring the chapter to a conclusion with the account of Jesus, in "the country of the Gergesenes," casting demons out of two men who are possessed by the evil spirits. This story is repeated in Mark 5:1-20, with some details included here that are not in the Mark account and vice versa. In Mark, there is only one man who is mentioned (He was called Legion because he was possessed by many demons all at the same time). Both gospel writers tell us that the demons begged to be sent away into a nearby herd of swine and Jesus allows them to enter into the pigs. The animals immediately run down a steep incline into the water where they perish. The whole city comes out when they hear of the episode and, in fear, they ask Jesus "to depart from their region."

## Matthew 9

The first eight verses of this chapter record the account of Jesus healing a paralyzed man. A parallel description of this episode is found in Mark 2:1-12. Mark tells us that the sick man was brought on a mat to Jesus by four of his friends and that they were unable to get close to the Savior because of the crowd around Him. So they climbed up to the roof, tore a hole in it and let the man down through the roof to get him near the Healer. Of course, Jesus heals the man when He sees their faith.

There is an interesting exchange between Jesus and the scribes who were present on this occasion. When Jesus tells the man that his sins are forgiven, the scribes immediately (and incorrectly) conclude that He is guilty of blasphemy, since only God can truly forgive sins. Jesus uses this opportunity to prove to them that He is God in the flesh (Immanuel, remember Matthew 1:23?) and that He has the power on earth to forgive any sin any way He chooses to do so. He uses this miracle as evidence of His divine authority to forgive sins. When the previously paralyzed man gets up and walks to his home, all the crowd can do is glorify God "who had given such power to men."

In verses 9-13, we read of the calling of Matthew to follow Jesus. Matthew was a tax collector; he is called Levi the son of Alphaeus in Mark 2:14. Many Bible characters are given at least two different names, primarily because there were two major languages spoken in the Bible. One was Greek, the other was Hebrew (or sometimes a variation of Hebrew called Aramaic). Matthew is, of course, the author of this book and he chose to call himself Matthew here. That is the more well-known name for this future apostle.

He invites Jesus to his home for a meal and tells us that "many tax collectors and sinners came and sat down with Him and His disciples." The Pharisees, as usual, criticize Him for spending time with such characters, but Jesus puts them in their place quickly. "Those who are well have no need of a physician, but those who are sick." He quotes Hosea 6:6 and reminds them God is a merciful Father and that He came into the world to call sinners to repentance. Jesus never ignored or approved of a person's sin, but

He always gave them an opportunity to repent and do the right thing. We should be people who forgive others and, in mercy, give them another chance (see James 2:13).

Verses 14-17 deal with the subject of fasting (Jesus said some other things about fasting in the Sermon on the Mountain – Matthew 6:16-18, remember?). Jesus said His followers would fast.

Verses 18-26 contain two miracles. One was a woman with a bleeding disease whom Jesus healed after 12 years of suffering and the other was the daughter of a synagogue ruler (his name was Jairus, Mark 5:22) who was raised from the dead by Jesus. Verses 27-31 record the account of two blind men who are given their sight by the Lord. Verses 32-34 tell us about a demon possessed man who was mute. Jesus casts out the demon from the man and he is then able to speak. The Pharisees, rather than rejoicing that the man has been healed, are angry and accuse Jesus of casting out demons by the ruler of the demons (that's terrible logic).

Verses 35-38 list a number of other miraculous healings by Jesus, as He travels to various cities and villages, teaching in the synagogues and preaching the good news of the kingdom. When Jesus sees the multitudes of people following Him, He has compassion on them. He sees them as weary and scattered sheep with no shepherd to provide for them. Christ concludes the thoughts in the chapter with these words: "The harvest truly is plentiful, but the laborers are few. Therefore pray the Lord of the harvest to send out laborers into His harvest." We could do so much more for the lost with more workers. Are you praying for workers, like Jesus tells us to do? Are you willing to be a worker to help save lost souls?

## Matthew 10

Chapter 10 begins with the account of Jesus choosing and then sending out the 12 apostles. Out of the many hundreds (perhaps even thousands) of disciples that Jesus has at this time, He selects 12 of them to be His closest followers. It is no coincidence that the number of apostles parallels the number of tribes of Israel in the Old Testament. There is almost always a logical and connected reason to most of the "numbers" that are used in the Bible. Numerology in both testaments can be a fascinating study. The numbers mentioned in the word of God are rarely random.

You would probably find it helpful to compare the various lists of the apostles from the different places in the New Testament where they are found (here, Mark 3:13-19, Luke 6:12-16, Acts 1:13). Many people in the first century had more than one name, as we have mentioned in the last chapter notes, because of the multiple languages that people spoke then. Bartholomew is also called Nathanael. Lebbaeus is also called Thaddaeus and Judas the son of James. Simon the Canaanite is also called Simon the Zealot. We noticed in Chapter 9 that Matthew is also called Levi. Simon, of course, is also called Peter and Cephas. There are many more examples of this, as well.

Verse 1 tells us that the apostles were given supernatural powers from the start of their assignments. They were not only to preach the gospel, but were enabled by the Lord to perform various kinds of miracles in order that there might be proof behind their words. Mark 16:15-20 says that "these signs" would follow them as they taught the world (verses 17-18). Verse 20 tells us that the Lord was working with them and "confirming the word through the accompanying signs." Hebrews 2:2-4 emphasizes the importance of the confirming miracles, "God also bearing witness both with signs and wonders, with various miracles, and gifts of the Holy Spirit, according to His own will."

Taking the gospel to the world, "to the Jew first" (verses 5-6), but eventually to the Gentiles as well, they were to share the good news of salvation through the Messiah to the world of their day. Jesus, while He was still here with them, sent them out on several training missions and then used their successes and their failures as further teaching opportunities for them to learn and grow. It is a teaching method that will still be valuable for us today in leadership training. It goes beyond a classroom setting into real life. The word apostle means "one sent," not simply "one studied with."

In verses 16-26, Jesus acknowledges that He is sending them out like soldiers into enemy territory, "as sheep in the midst of wolves." They were to use wisdom in their work (that's always helpful), but in spite of their best efforts, some would oppose them and, in reality, they would face great hardships. He says, "And you will be hated by all for My name's sake. But he who endures to the end will be saved." The Holy Spirit would be with them and help them in many difficult circumstances (verses 18-20). The Master tells them not to be afraid (verse 26).

In verses 27-33, Jesus promises them that God will protect them from harm. (That doesn't mean that their lives won't be in very real danger, but that their souls will be protected.) God is the One who can destroy both soul and body in hell (verse 28). All other people can do is kill you; they can't cause you to lose your soul. Others, including the devil himself, can only hurt your body or take your life. You control the eternal destiny of your soul. Continue to confess Jesus as your Lord every day you live (this is not simply something you do one time when you are obeying the gospel). Confessing Him or denying Him is something you decide to live out in your daily life.

Verses 34-42 help us to realize the importance of the confession of God we make in our lives and warn us of some of the possible consequences of our choices. We are taught to help those who are serving God, even if it is with just a cup of cold water in His name.

## Matthew 11

Chapter 11 begins with an interesting exchange between Jesus and the disciples of John the Baptist. John is in prison for telling Herod Antipas that he has no right to be married to his brother's former wife (more in Chapter 14). We were initially told that John had been thrown into prison in Matthew 4:12, but we were not told why, nor are we informed in this account. But John sends some of his followers (who would ultimately become disciples of Jesus) to ask some important questions that were obviously very much troubling the Baptizer (verses 1-3). "Are You the Coming One, or do we look for another?" John had previously described Jesus as "the Lamb of God who takes away the sin of the world" (John 1:29). So why would he ask these questions now? It was not because he was looking for an earthly king and Jesus just wasn't working out. John was inspired by God in his teaching and so his concept of a spiritual kingdom would have been accurate, unlike many other followers of Christ who were looking for a warrior king who would free them from Roman rule.

John knew that he was likely going to die and it is possible that he wanted to be absolutely certain that Jesus was really the promised Messiah of Old Testament prophecy.

And John may well have had them ask those questions for the sake of his disciples and not for himself. Perhaps he wanted to convince them that Jesus truly was the Christ and so he sent them to ask Him.

Notice that Jesus did not answer the questions by simply saying, "Yes, I am the Messiah." Anyone could say those words, but instead He pointed them to His deeds (verses 4-6). His actions, especially the miraculous ones, authenticated His words (see Mark 16:20; Hebrews 2:4).

John the Baptist was not someone who was easily swayed by others; he was not tossed back and forth by the doctrines and teachings of human origin. He was not a self-indulgent person who met his own personal needs in a materialistic fashion (he ate locusts and wild honey, remember?). He was more than just a prophet. He was both the cousin of Jesus in the flesh and he was the spiritual forerunner sent to prepare the way for the Savior. Jesus said these positive and powerful things about John (verses 7-10). Christ also said that John was the prophesied "Elijah," who stood for what was right in a society that was going wrong (verses 14-19; see Luke 1:17 which explains why that comparison is made).

But did you notice the ironic statement Jesus made in verse 11? "Assuredly, I say to you, among those born of women there has not risen one greater than John the Baptist; but he who is least in the kingdom of heaven is greater than he." John was never a Christian. He was a believer in God and Jesus, but he lived in the period of time before the church was established. John never saw the cross and he did not experience the resurrection of the Savior. Every Christian, today, weak or strong, is more blessed (and therefore, "greater") than John was. That's you and me, my friend.

In verses 20-24, Jesus rebukes those who would ultimately reject Him as the Messiah. Many of them had personally witnessed His miracles and yet still would not repent and live right. He specifically mentions the first century inhabitants of Chorazin, Bethsaida, and Capernaum. They refused to accept His sacrifice on their behalf; they would not obey Him while they had the Savior of the world right in front of them.

We must realize though that many did accept Jesus and give their lives to Him. The chapter ends (verses 25-30) as Jesus offers eternal life to those who are burdened by their sins. He tells them that there can be relief for their hearts and rest for their souls. Jesus still offers that hope to the whole world.

# Matthew 12

Verses 1-14 contain two accounts of Jesus interacting with His enemies (they weren't His opponents because He didn't love them, but because they foolishly chose to oppose Him).

The first verses of the chapter, 1-8, deal with the Lord and the disciples passing through farm land as they journey from one place to another. It is the Sabbath Day and they are hungry, so they pick some of the grain to eat. This was not stealing, by the way, as the Law of Moses made provision for the poor to do this as a means of survival (see Deuteronomy 23:25).

The Pharisees consider this to be working and therefore, a violation of the Sabbath. Their default reaction is to criticize now and ask questions later, so they accuse them of "doing what is not lawful." Jesus knew that they were not sinning and reminds them of the Old Testament account of David, one of their greatest heroes, and his followers eating the showbread (that original account is found in 1 Samuel 21:1-6). What David did was illegal and yet, the Pharisees justified his action because of the prevailing circumstances at the time. The Lord is showing them their inconsistency here, not trying to rationalize away bad behavior. They were fine with David's action, which was indeed wrong, but felt the need to accuse Jesus and the disciples of sin, when they were not truly guilty. He used the example of the priests serving God in the temple on the Sabbath to show them that all activity on that day was not wrong (verse 5). Jesus quotes Hosea 6:6 to help them understand that this was a human compassion issue, not a matter of breaking the Sabbath. (He says the disciples were "guiltless" in verse 7). And He concludes the discussion by saying that He is the Lord of the Sabbath (verse 8). He knew right from wrong, in this and any other situation.

On the heels of that episode, a man with a "withered hand" is brought to the Master and He heals his infirmity, still on the Sabbath Day (verses 9-14). They again criticize the Savior and He again uses a couple of helpful illustrations to show their inconsistency. The Pharisees lose every time they challenge Jesus and their anger builds and grows. They are not concerned about right and wrong. Their only goal is to destroy Him.

As the popularity of Jesus grows stronger, great multitudes follow Him and He performs many miracles of healing (verses 15-21). Matthew points out to us that this is all a clear fulfillment of the prophetic description of the Messiah in Isaiah 42:1-4. Jesus didn't do anything to draw attention to Himself.

In verses 22-32, Jesus casts a demon out of a man who is blind and mute so that he can see and speak. When the Pharisees accuse the Lord of performing this miracle by the power of the devil, He points out the foolishness of their reasoning while telling them that "blasphemy against the Spirit" is an unforgivable sin.

Verses 33-37 remind us that good actions come from a good heart while bad actions come out of an evil heart. Judgment will be given against the ungodly.

In verses 38-42, when the scribes and Pharisees ask Jesus for a sign, He calls them "an evil and adulterous generation." He tells them to remember the account of Jonah, three days and nights in the belly of the great fish and He applies that Old Testament account to His own death and resurrection.

There are some words about filling our lives with good things after we get rid of the bad (verses 43-45). If we do not replace evil with good thoughts and actions, the evil can easily return. And in verses 46-50, Jesus refers to those who obey God as "My brother and sister and mother."

## Matthew 13

Parables are the prominent feature in Chapter 13. There are seven parables, two explanations, some discussion about the purpose of parables and some other really helpful material. This is a powerful chapter in a powerful gospel.
The chapter begins with Jesus teaching the "great multitudes" gathered by the sea. He tells a spiritual story, a parable, about a farmer who plants seed that falls on four different types of soil (verses 1-9). Some "by the wayside," (NKJV) or "on the path," (NIV) produces no fruit, some of the seeds (some on rocky ground, some on thorny soil) produce fruit that starts well but doesn't end well, and other seeds, those on the good soil, produce an abundant harvest. Like all parables, this earthly story has a heavenly meaning, a spiritual application. When Jesus explains the story to His curious followers, He tells them that the four types of soil represent conditions of the human heart (verses 18-23). Some people are not interested at all, some have a degree of interest and so they become disciples but then allow other things to get in the way of a deep and abiding relationship with the Lord and so they fall away. Still others have a real interest in the things of God and so their lives and their eternal destiny are completely given over to the Master.

After the parable, but before the explanation, the disciples ask their Teacher why He was speaking in parables (verses 10-17). He tells them that parables (literally, a laying alongside) teach spiritual truths. Those who are interested in "the things which are above" (Colossians 3:1-2) can immediately understand the story and apply its teachings to their lives. Those who have no spiritual interests just don't get it. In this sense, it has often been said that parables both reveal and conceal the truth. Those who love God will be touched by the parable; those who do not love Him will be further unaffected.

Jesus tells the parable of the tares (weeds, NIV) next in verses 24-30. A man plants seed in his field and an enemy comes at night and plants weeds that look a lot like the wheat. They grow together and are not separated until the harvest. In His explanation of this story (verses 36-43), Jesus points out that the enemy is the devil. We should never see Satan as a friend or an ally who wants to help us. He is trying to send as many people to hell as possible. Do not cooperate with him in any way. He hates you.

The parable of the mustard seed (verses 31-32) is a personal favorite, because it reminds us that small things (even small people) can accomplish great deeds for God. That encourages me. Verse 33, the parable of the leaven, is often interpreted as teaching the same message as the mustard seed and perhaps it is. But leaven is not used as a positive analogy anywhere else in the Bible and this may be a warning that like the tares, it can be difficult to tell the difference in the church between those who try to do right and those who are only pretending. We may not know the difference until the judgment.

Three more parables follow in rapid succession. The parable of the hidden treasure (verse 44) shows us that the kingdom of heaven is of great spiritual value. The parable of the pearl of great price (verses 45-46) helps us to see that any sacrifice we make for God will be rewarded. The parable of the dragnet (verses 47-50) again reminds us that the church may have both good and bad people in it (hypocrites are an example of the bad) and that, while we may not know how to distinguish the two, God will not be deceived and those who deserve to be lost will be cast out into the furnace of fire, with wailing and gnashing of teeth. God will not make any mistakes in the final separation of the godly and the ungodly.

In verses 53-58, Jesus returns to His hometown of Nazareth and teaches in the synagogue. The people are astonished at His teaching and wisdom and power, especially those who remember Him from His youth and were familiar with His family. Jesus makes the famous statement that a prophet is not without honor except in His own town and in his own home.

## Matthew 14

John the Baptist had been thrown in prison (Matthew 4:12) by Herod Antipas and was ultimately killed because of his message to the king that his marriage to Herodias, his brother Philip's former wife was not pleasing to God. Herod Antipas was "tetrarch of Galilee" (Luke 3:1). We have already noted, in Chapter 11, that John had sent some of his disciples to Jesus to reassure him and them that Jesus was indeed "the Coming One," in other words, the predicted Messiah of more than 300 Old Testament prophecies.

Because the fame of Jesus was spreading, Herod heard about some of His miraculous powers and was concerned that John the Baptist had come back to life. We are then told for the first time (verses 1-12) about the circumstances of John's death. Herod had been furious with John when he told the king that his marriage was wrong in the sight of God. He wanted to kill John then and there but "he feared the multitude, because they counted him as a prophet." Herod decides instead to throw John into prison.

On Herod's birthday, things changed. As part of the drunken celebration that accompanied such events, Herodias' daughter (history tells us her name was Salome) danced before the gathered dignitaries and her immoral gyrations "pleased Herod." He was so worked up sensually by all of this that he promised to give her anything she wanted (Mark 6:23 adds, "up to half my kingdom"). After consulting with her evil mother, she asks for the head of John the Baptist "on a platter." The king is sorry for this, but cannot go back on his promise and so, he sends an executioner who beheads John. His disciples come and bury the body and then inform Jesus about the death. The lessons from this account are many, but one of them is that God takes "one man and one woman" for life very seriously, much more so than our society today.

The second event recorded in this chapter is the feeding of the 5000 (verses 13-21). After John's death, Jesus wants to spend some time alone, but the multitudes follow Him and He performs a number of miracles of healing for them. When the time runs late, Jesus wants to feed the people, but the disciples tell Him they only have five loaves and two fish. Jesus takes this small amount of food, asks God's blessings and gives it to the disciples who then distribute it to all the people who are there. We call it the feeding of the 5000, but this was actually the number of men only, "besides women and children."

A third important episode in the life story of Christ is found in verses 22-33. After feeding the multitude in the preceding verses, Jesus sends them away and then instructs the disciples to get into a boat and cross the Sea of Galilee. He goes alone up on a nearby mountainside to pray. As the boat gets further away from the shore, a storm arises (the text mentions the wind blowing the ship around as the waves hit their vessel). It is "shortly before dawn" (NIV); the NKJV says, "in the fourth watch of the night," which would be somewhere between 3-6 am.

The tired and frightened disciples (several of them were former fishermen who were quite experienced in piloting boats, so if they were scared of this storm, it must have been pretty bad) are startled to see a solitary, dark figure coming toward them, walking on top of the water of the lake. Already exhausted from fighting the waves and wind, they are terrified and assume they are seeing some kind of spirit being, a ghost, because they realize no human can walk on water. When they cry out in fear, Jesus seeks to calm them down by saying, "Be of good cheer! It is I; do not be afraid." Peter asks to be allowed to come to Jesus and for a brief time, he walks on the water as well. He begins to sink, when he looks around at the raging wind and waves, and Jesus rescues Him and stills the storm. The disciples worship Him and say, "Truly You are the Son of God." That is the logical conclusion of His powerful signs.

The next day Jesus performs many more miracles in the land of Gennesaret to verify His identity as the Savior of the world for the disciples and others who witness His power and authority (verses 34-36).

## Matthew 15

The word, tradition, simply means something that is handed down. It might be a family recipe, or an old wives' tale or a method of decorating a house for the holidays. "Tradition" can apply to almost anything. The New Testament sometimes uses the word to refer to the inspired teachings of the apostles (see 1 Corinthians 11:2; 2 Thessalonians 2:15 and 3:6). At times, however, it refers to the traditions of men, not God (Colossians 2:8; 1 Peter 1:18). Even in those cases, the tradition itself is not automatically wrong; the problem comes with our attitude toward the tradition.

In the first 20 verses of this chapter (and paralleled in Mark 7:1-23), Jesus rebukes the Pharisees and the scribes for their traditions. They begin the discussion by asking Him why His disciples do not wash their hands before they eat. They actually might have washed their hands, but, if they did, they didn't do it in the Pharisee-approved way (Mark 7:3-4).

Verse 3 explains the problem with traditions. Jesus said, in response to their question, "Why do you also transgress the commandment of God because of your tradition?" They were more concerned about keeping their traditions than they were with obeying the commands of God. He gives the example, in verses 4-6 that they are using their own rules to do what they wanted and, as a result, are not doing what God wants, in this case, honoring their parents. They found a way around God's will (they thought) while still trying to appear to be doing God's will. He calls them hypocrites, as He quotes Isaiah 29:13, in verses 8-9. There are still many today who are more upset if you violate their man-made traditions than if you ignore clear Bible teaching.

Part of the problem you notice as you read these verses is that they put so much emphasis on the external. They wanted others to see them and to recognize their spirituality by what they saw them doing. Jesus, as usual, tries to get them to understand that the important thing is what is in your heart. He knew that, if their hearts were in the right place, the proper actions would follow. And, if their hearts were not right with God, then even if they did some of the right things, God would still not be pleased. He has never wanted a mere outward show from those whose hearts are far from Him. That's why He spends time discussing "what goes into the mouth" as it compares to what comes from the heart, beginning in verse 11 and continuing to verse 20. He concludes this teaching in verse 19 by listing several sins that come "out of the heart." They were upset that the disciples ate with unwashed hands (which Jesus says does not defile a person) while He shows them that they should be concerned with having the right kind of heart.

In verses 21-28, Jesus and the disciples travel to the region of Tyre and Sidon, to the northwest of Galilee. A woman of Canaan (meaning that she was a Gentile) comes to Him and asks Him to heal her "severely demon-possessed" daughter. Jesus ignores her initially, but as she continues to plead with Him, He relents and heals her child. Verse 24 should be understood in the context. It wasn't that God and Jesus didn't love Gentiles, but the scheme of redemption outlined in the whole Bible had both a plan to save all and a divine timetable in which that plan was to be carried out. Beginning in Acts 10, when Peter will preach to the Gentiles, the universal aspect of the kingdom of heaven will be realized.

More miracles are performed in verses 29-31 to the glory of "the God of Israel."

Verses 32-39 record for us another miraculous feeding of a great multitude, with only seven loaves and a few little fish. 4000 men were fed on this occasion and seven large baskets of fragments were taken up for later use. Jesus sends the multitude away and travels to the region of Magdala. (That would be the hometown of the first person to see Jesus after His resurrection, Mary Magdalene.)

## Matthew 16

As Chapter 16 begins, two groups that did not care at all for one another decide to join forces against a common enemy, Jesus of Nazareth (verses 1-4). The Pharisees and the Sadducees working together is a rare political alliance toward a mutual goal, the destruction of this so-called Messiah. (You have heard that the enemy of my enemy is my friend? They don't like each other, but they hate Jesus so much that they decide to put their enmity for one another aside and conspire together to try to bring Him down.) They ask Him to perform a miracle for them. Of course, He has already worked many miracles by this time, but they want Him to do something special, just for them. He refuses to perform any miraculous signs for them, calls them hypocrites and tells them that the only sign they need is the Old Testament story of Jonah. He has already told them this was a sign which foreshadowed His own death and resurrection in Matthew 12:38-41.

As the Savior and the followers travel to the other side of the Sea of Galilee, Jesus uses the knowledge that they had not brought any bread to teach them a spiritual lesson about the evil leaven (yeast, NIV) of the Pharisees and Sadducees (verses 5-12). Yeast is the ingredient that makes a lump of dough rise so as to be baked into a loaf of bread and this is a common analogy that Jesus uses to speak of the evil influence of the ungodly. (See Matthew 13:33 and 1 Corinthians 5:6-8.) The disciples are thinking about literal leaven in bread, while Jesus is trying to get them to realize that a small amount of bad influence can quickly spread to do a lot of damage to the faith of godly people. We should learn that lesson as well; that's why stories like this one are included in the New Testament.

In verses 13-20, Jesus and the disciples come "into the region of Caesarea Philippi," which is the area of Galilee where Herod's palace was located. They were likely in a location where they might have been able to see his residence as this dialogue between Christ and His disciples takes place. The discussion begins as Jesus asks them, "Who do men say that I, the Son of Man, am?" They report several thoughts that people have about Him, all of them name godly people, but all of them are wrong answers. Then He asks them, "But who do you say that I am?"

Simon Peter, who often answers too quickly before he has thought through his comments, in this case, responds with an astonishing claim, "You are the Christ, the Son of the living God." His answer was both powerful and completely accurate. It is easy at times to criticize Peter for his impetuous nature, but he was spot on here. Jesus affirms Peter's response and identifies him as "Simon, Bar-Jonah," the son of Jonah (or John). Then He makes the statement that Peter's confession, that He is the Messiah and the Son of God, will be the bedrock foundational truth for the establishment of His church, the community of believers that He is preparing during His teaching ministry.

Jesus states that the gates of Hades (some versions incorrectly translate that as "hell") will not prevent Him from His purpose of establishing His church, the kingdom of God manifested here on earth. It will be a spiritual kingdom, not a physical one like many Jews were looking for and like some today still think He intended to start. His death/blood would be the purchase price for this universal group of saved, redeemed souls, rather than an event that would keep Him from His purpose.

He continues on to speak of His death and resurrection (verses 21-23). Peter, who has just responded so well moments before, foolishly tells Jesus that He will not die. His Master sharply rebukes him. (He calls him "Satan.") The Savior tells Peter to focus on the "things of God," not on worldly concerns.

Jesus tells them that they will all have to deny themselves if they wish to belong to God (verses 24-27). He reminds them that their souls are their most valuable possession and promises them that the kingdom will be established in their own lifetime.

## Matthew 17

Verses 1-8 tell us one of the most exciting and fascinating stories from the life of Christ; it is the account of the transfiguration of Jesus.

The Savior takes three disciples, James and John and Peter, up on a mountain (lots of Bible things happen on mountains, don't they?). Suddenly, two miraculous things occur. First, the appearance of Jesus is dramatically altered (transfigured) so that His face and clothes begin to shine brightly, more than would be humanly possible. Secondly, two important Old Testament characters appear with Jesus, Moses and Elijah. Moses lived 1500 years before Jesus and Elijah lived approximately 850 years before the Messiah. Moses had died and was buried in a valley in the land of Moab (Deuteronomy 34:5-6) just before the children of Israel began to take control of their promised land. Elijah prophesied for God during the period of the Divided Kingdom and was taken directly into heaven in a chariot of fire sent from God (2 Kings 2:11). Yet here they appear with Jesus, to talk with Him about His death and perhaps to strengthen and encourage Him to face His approaching trials and difficulties (Luke 9:30-31).

The Old Testament is often summarized as "the Law and the Prophets" (Matthew 7:12; 22:40; Luke 16:16; Acts 28:23). These two great men represent the Old Covenant, also known as the Hebrew Bible. Moses was the great lawgiver of the Old Testament, so much so that it is often referred to as the Law of Moses. Although it is called that, it was the Law of God that was given through Moses. And, in many ways, Elijah is one of the greatest prophets of God. Many of these men (and some women also) played very significant roles in God's plan, but no one more so than Elijah.

Jesus came to fulfill the teachings and prophecies (along with the types and shadows) of the Old Testament and, having done that, to replace the Old with the New (and Last) Testament from God. The transition began with the work of John the Baptizer, continued with the teaching work of God's Son and then culminated with the death of Jesus (Hebrews 9:16-17), the resurrection, the preaching of Peter on Pentecost (the birthday of the church) and then finally, with the destruction of the temple and the city of Jerusalem in A.D. 70 by the Roman legions. Today we live under and follow the gospel of Christ.

Peter, in his immature zeal for God, wanted to erect three tabernacles, one in honor of each of these great men. But the Father Himself put an end to such talk when a voice came out of the cloud, saying, "This is My beloved Son, in whom I am well pleased. Hear Him!" As great as the other two men were, only Jesus is to be followed today. He is "the way, the truth and the life" as we can only get to God now by following Him (John 14:6).

The disciples wonder if this event is a fulfillment of Malachi 4:5-6, which says that Elijah would appear before the coming of the Messiah. Jesus makes it clear to them that this prophecy was speaking about John the Baptist, not a literal reincarnation of Elijah (verses 9-13; see also Matthew 11:14).

Verses 14-21 record the account of a father who approaches Jesus on the behalf of his son who suffers from epilepsy, in this case caused by demon possession. The disciples had earlier tried to heal the boy but were unable to do so. Jesus heals the epileptic and then turns His attention to teaching His followers that they needed to have more faith to perform this miracle (verses 17, 20-21). He promises them that with "faith as a mustard seed," they would be able to move mountains. They aren't at that point yet in their faith. (We are often critical of the disciples for their lack of growth, but how strong is our faith?)

Jesus then tells them again about His upcoming death and resurrection (verses 22-23). In Capernaum, there is a question about paying taxes (verses 24-27) and Jesus performs another miracle to get the money to pay "the temple tax." He will soon leave Galilee and travel to Jerusalem.

## Matthew 18

When the disciples of Jesus ask Him, who is the greatest in the kingdom of heaven, do you think they all thought they would be the one He named (verses 1-5)? Maybe Peter, James and John had talked about this (we do know that they discussed things like that at times; see Mark 9:33-37) and each one was convinced that he was Jesus' favorite disciple? At any rate, Jesus takes a little child from the surrounding group of people and tells them that humility is the key to greatness in the spiritual kingdom. Little children symbolize purity and innocence and trust. They often obey without question. That likely wasn't the response they expected, but Jesus often surprised His followers with His answers to their questions.

Verses 6-14 have more to say about the innocent ones. Jesus says we must never cause others to sin, by our teaching or influence or example. He emphasizes that it would be better to lose a physical part of our bodies than to be led to hell by the weaknesses of the flesh. And He tells us to not despise little ones, because heaven is watching over them and we must do all we can to protect them from evil. Just as a shepherd leaves the ninety-nine in the fold to go into the wilderness to search for the one that has gone astray, "Even so it is not the will of your Father who is in heaven that one of these little ones should perish." Every soul is important to God and if we want to be like Him, we must do all we can to help save those who are lost.

Verses 15-20 contain teaching exclusive to the gospel of Matthew. This section deals with healing problems between brothers in the Lord. Jesus describes a three stage process that should be followed when there are differences between believers. The first step, when one has sinned against another, is for the innocent brother to go to the offender and work things out. (Matthew 5:23-25 tells the guilty one to go to the innocent one; if both sides did what Jesus says, they would always meet each other on the way, wouldn't they?) Often a face to face discussion, one on one, resolves the conflict. But if it does not, step two is to take some witnesses, either witnesses of the original offense or at least those who can hear both sides of the disagreement and try to smooth things out between the two brothers. (Jesus quotes here Deuteronomy 19:15 which teaches us that "at the mouth of two or three witnesses every word may be established.") It often helps to discuss things in the presence of impartial brothers who just want to do what is right, with no personal feelings involved in the issue. If the guilty one will still not repent and do the right thing, then Jesus says that you are to have nothing to do with him. That seems harsh but, if people refuse to do right, there is nothing more that can be done.

In verses 18-20, Jesus assures us that, when we have done all we can to resolve such differences, then heaven itself will be pleased that we put forth the appropriate effort to resolve a conflict. We should, of course, pray throughout such a three step process that those guilty of actual sin will repent of their evil.

The remainder of Chapter 18, verses 21-35, continue to discuss the subject of forgiveness. Peter, after the teaching of Jesus about resolving conflict, asks how many times a Jesus follower must be willing to grant forgiveness to others. He suggests "up to seven times" and probably felt he was being quite generous. Jesus says, "I do not say to you, up to seven times, but up to seventy times seven." Many modern translations render the seventy times seven as up to seventy-seven times. Whether the number Jesus used is 77 or 490, His point is clear. We must be willing to forgive others many more times than most of us are usually ready to offer. Peter's suggestion of seven would be way too many for most of us.

The Savior then delivers a parable about forgiveness that should really make us examine ourselves. A king settles accounts with his servants and the first man owes the king "ten thousand talents." That is around 10 million dollars, an impossible amount for a man to pay. The king cancels the debt and the forgiven one turns around and sends a man to prison who cannot pay him a hundred denarii, about $18.00. The king hears and throws the original servant in prison because he showed no mercy.

## Matthew 19

The Pharisees were constantly trying to trap Jesus in His answers to their set-up questions. The early parts of this chapter are an example of that. In most of these situations, they were not really interested in learning truth or in finding out what God wanted. Their objective was to find a way to criticize Jesus. They desperately wanted to turn public sentiment against Him, but the harder they tried, the more everyone realized that the Jewish leaders were the real problem, not the carpenter from Nazareth.

In Chapter 19, they try to use the emotional subject of divorce and remarriage against the Savior. They begin by asking Him if God is pleased when men divorce their wives, "for just any reason." Jesus and the followers are in a territory of Judea, on the east side of the Jordan River, that is sometimes called Perea. (You may read commentaries and other study tools that refer to the Perean ministry of Jesus; this happens in that area.) Notice in verse 3 that the Bible says clearly that the Pharisees are "testing Him." It was a battle of wills between them and the Savior. Jesus doesn't directly answer the question. He goes back to the beginning and tells them God's plan for marriage, one man and one woman for life. He quotes several verses from Genesis 1 and 2, based on the original creation account about Adam and Eve. Husband and wife are to become one flesh and God intended for that relationship to be permanent. So His conclusion, verse 6, says, "Therefore what God has joined together, let not man separate."

They press Him further and ask why the Law of Moses allowed divorce then (likely a reference to Deuteronomy 24). He admits that is true, but that doesn't change what God really wants from marriage, a lifetime commitment. He then tells us that there is one exception that God will allow, which is adultery. If an innocent man divorces his adulterous wife (Mark 10 reverses that and states it that an innocent woman divorces a guilty husband), the innocent party is free to remarry, while the guilty party, if he or she remarries, will be guilty of further adultery in that marriage.

This all seems quite strict by current American standards. Divorce and remarriage (even multiple times) are just widely accepted by our culture. But notice that even in the first century, the disciples seemed surprised by these standards. They said to Jesus, "If such is the case of the man with his wife, it is better not to marry" (verse 10). Jesus wanted them to realize that this was intended by God as a safeguard of the marriage bond and was designed to make divorce a rare event, unlike the loose ideas of society today. (There is much more we could say about the subject; please recall that this is just a chapter summary and is not intended to answer every question on this or any other subject.)

There is some follow up discussion between the Teacher and the students about the ability of some to make themselves eunuchs (celibacy is the point here) for the kingdom of heaven's sake (verses 11-12).

In verses 13-15, Jesus pronounces His blessings upon children, "for of such is the kingdom of heaven."

Verses 16-22 tell us about the encounter between the Savior and the rich, young ruler, a godly man who asks Jesus about eternal life. When the Lord realizes that the man, while sincere and desirous of living forever with God, is still clinging to his wealth ("he had great possessions," verse 22), He tells him to sell everything, give it all to the poor, and "come, follow Me." The young man goes away sorrowful. "The love of money" is said to be a "root of all kinds of evil" (1 Timothy 6:10) and we would do well to understand that there are some choices and decisions in life that are far more important than what job to take so we can make the most money possible. Your soul is much more valuable than anything the world has to offer (remember Matthew 16:26).

In verses 23-30, the chapter concludes with Jesus reminding them that "with God all things are possible." We must put Him first above anything and anybody else.

# Matthew 20

"For the kingdom of heaven is like a landowner who went out early in the morning to hire laborers for his vineyard." This chapter starts (verses 1-16) with the story of this landowner and those who came to work for him. Of course, as with all of the parables, there is a spiritual application of these words. Jesus is going to be talking about the rewards of those who serve God in His spiritual kingdom, the church.

The landowner quickly finds workers who were willing to work for a denarius per day. This was an average day's wages in the first century and a denarius (the King James Version uses the word, penny, most of the time) was equivalent to about 16-18 cents. It was a fair salary and most people then were more than willing to work for a denarius per day. The Jewish day began at 6am and that's about the time the first group of workers started on the job.

This language of "working" in the kingdom is often used in the New Testament. Many of the Lord's parables condemn idleness or an attitude against doing what we can. The parables of the two sons (Matthew 21:28-32) and the talents (Matthew 25:14-30) are a couple of examples. We have already noticed, in Matthew 9:35-38, that Jesus tells us to pray for more workers in the spiritual kingdom.

The landowner goes out at the third hour (9am) and finding others who are "standing idle in the marketplace," he hires them and promises to pay them appropriately for their work. The same thing happens at the sixth hour (noon) and the ninth hour (3pm). When he goes out at the eleventh hour (5pm), with only one more hour remaining in the work day, he finds more workers and hires them as well. He promises to pay them "whatever is right."

As the work day ends, the owner of the vineyard calls his steward (the manager in charge of the work site) and tells him to pay the workers the appropriate amount. Starting with those who just worked one hour, he gives them a denarius. As they get to those who started at 6am, they assume they will receive more, but each one is given a denarius as well (remember that's what they had agreed to in verse 2). They complain and so the landowner reminds them of their previous discussion and they have to admit that they had agreed to work for that amount. He also tells them that he has the right to pay all of the laborers whatever he wants. Because he was a good man, he wanted to be generous with all of the workers.

This parable teaches us to work for God. There are advantages to serving God from our youth (Ecclesiastes 12:1), but God will reward those who only begin to obey and follow Him in their later years. He really doesn't want us to wait to serve Him, but He will reward those who do the right thing even if it is for a shorter time than others.

In verses 17-19, Jesus again tells the disciples that He will be put to death by crucifixion and will rise on the third day.

There is a discussion between James and John (along with their mother) and Jesus about greatness in the kingdom (verses 20-28). Jesus wants His followers then and now to realize that greatness is not determined by title or position or prominence, but rather by our willingness to serve others. He points them to a perfect example of this principle when He concludes this section. "Just as the Son of Man did not come to be served, but to serve, and to give His life a ransom for many." Jesus was a servant.

Verses 29-34 conclude the chapter by telling us of the healing of two blind men. Just outside of Jericho, a great multitude is walking with Jesus and these men hear that Jesus is nearby. They cry out to Him and He calls them to Himself and immediately has compassion for them and heals their blindness.

## Matthew 21

Chapter 21 begins as the Messiah and His followers come to Jerusalem. They have been headed there for some time and finally they arrive. The first 11 verses record for us what is often called "the triumphal entry." The people give Jesus an entrance fit for a king.

As the group draws near the city, the Savior sends two of His disciples into a nearby village (there were several of these around Jerusalem) to bring a donkey and her colt for Jesus to ride on as He enters the capital city of the Jewish faith. This fulfills a prophetic statement by the Lord originally found in Zechariah 9:9. This shows us the humble nature of our King Jesus. Humility is one of those admirable qualities of Jesus followers that the world doesn't really understand; many believe humility to be a sign of weakness when it is actually a sign of spiritual and internal strength.

The gathered multitudes line the city streets and spread both their clothes and leafy branches from trees on the road to make things smoother for His entrance. They cry out, "Hosanna to the Son of David! Blessed is He who comes in the name of the LORD! Hosanna in the highest!" Matthew tells us that "all the city was moved." This must have been quite impressive to see, large multitudes of people praising and glorifying the Son of God as He comes to Jerusalem, knowing that He will soon be put to death for the sins of the world.

They ask, "Who is this?" The crowds report, "This is Jesus, the prophet from Nazareth in Galilee." (Remember the statement in Matthew 2:23 that the Messiah "shall be called a Nazarene"?) Nathanael initially thought Jesus could not be the Christ because of His origin in Nazareth (John 1:46); he soon changed his mind, didn't he? Nathanael was likely in this throng of people praising God through Jesus. Many have now accepted Jesus as the Messiah.

In verses 12-17, Jesus quickly enters the temple of God and drives out the money changers and those who sold doves, claiming that they had turned the house of prayer into a den of thieves (this combines two Old Testament prophecies from Isaiah 56:7 and Jeremiah 7:11). This does not set well with the chief priests and the teachers of the law (scribes).

Verses 18-22 tell us about Jesus withering a fig tree, which was symbolic of God's rejection of the Jewish nation due to their disbelief in His Son.

The chief priests and elders of the people confront Jesus the next morning to ask Him by what authority He is doing these things, referring primarily to the cleansing of the temple. "By what authority are You doing these things? And who gave You this authority?" (verses 23-27). This provides us with a good definition of what is meant by authority; it is the right to act, granted by one who has the power to give it. He asks them, in return, "The baptism of John – where was it from? From heaven or from men?" If they will honestly answer His question, they would know His authority was from heaven. But they are not honest and refuse to answer. He, in turn, does not answer their demands.

Verses 28-32 contain a parable of two sons, one who obeys his father and one who does not. He uses this earthly story to teach them a spiritual lesson about repentance.

Many tax collectors and harlots were changing their lives because of Jesus' teachings, but the leaders of the Jewish people were unwilling to repent.

The chapter ends (verses 33-46) with a second parable, one about a landowner who leases his vineyard to vinedressers who prove to be unreliable and refuse to follow the owner's authority. Jesus compares this to the Jewish rejection of Himself (see Psalm 118:22-23). The Jews want to kill Him even more.

## Matthew 22

Jesus continues to use parables to teach God's truth as this chapter begins. Verses 1-14 contain the parable of the wedding feast. He compares the kingdom of heaven to a king who invites others to a marriage (or wedding feast) in honor of his son. Many of those who were invited were not willing to attend and so he continues to send out more servants to encourage those who are invited to come.

But verse 5 tells us that "they made light of it" and continued to live their normal lives, following their own routines. Doesn't that sound familiar? When we invite people today to come to a Bible study or regular worship services or just to learn about Jesus, many treat such invitations lightly and go about their normal lives without the Lord. They don't really see the need for having Jesus in their lives. Verse 6 refers to some who respond violently; they are so opposed to the king that they mistreat his servants and even kill some of them. (That does seem extreme to us in the United States, but in other parts of the world, just inviting someone to a service or telling them that you are a Christian can get you killed.)

The king is furious and sends out his armies and destroys the murderers. But the wedding feast is not canceled so he sends out more servants "into the highways" to invite others who might be interested in attending the dinner. Soon the wedding hall is "filled with guests." When the king comes into the hall, he sees a man who is not properly dressed for such an occasion. He casts the man into outer darkness where there is weeping and gnashing of teeth. This is not speaking about how we are supposed to dress up to "go to church," but it is teaching us that our lives are to be appropriate for those who claim to be following our King, Jesus Christ (see Titus 3:10; that's what Paul meant by adorning the doctrine of God our Savior in all things). There are certain standards of behavior that are appropriate for Jesus followers.

The parable ends with the statement, "For many are called, but few are chosen" (verse 14). This teaches us, once again, that everyone is invited to follow God through His Son, Jesus, but only a few make the proper decision to do so (remember the broad and narrow ways in Matthew 7:13-14?).

In verses 15-22, the Pharisees come to Jesus as they have plotted how to entangle Him in His teaching. They ask Him if it is lawful to pay taxes to Rome. Either way, they think they can use His words against Him. Either He will refuse to pay taxes and therefore, disobey Caesar. Or He will say yes and they can accuse Him of disloyalty to Moses or God. He separates the spiritual from the physical by saying, "Render therefore to Caesar the things that are Caesar's, and to God the things that are God's." Those are not mutually exclusive possibilities as they had thought and so He wisely points out the right way to think about this subject.

On "the same day," the Sadducees try to trap Him by creating a "what if" scenario that they think He cannot answer (verses 22-33). Referring to the Law of Moses requirement for a brother to help his deceased brother's widow have a family heir (Deuteronomy 25:5-10), they tell him about an imaginary family with seven brothers, who all take their turn being married to a single woman, but without any children being born to any of them. Because they did not believe in the resurrection (verse 23), they want to know whose wife she will be in the afterlife. He answers their question by saying that there will be no marriage in eternity. But He answers their real question about the resurrection also, by a "necessary inference," that there is such a thing as life after death (verse 32).

Verses 34-40 lists for us what are often referred to as "the greatest commands." He says the first is to love God with your whole being and the second is to love your neighbor as yourself. (The implications of those two commands are deep and serious.) In verses 41-46, He asks them how the Messiah could be known as "the Son of David." They decide not to argue with Him anymore. Every time they try to trap Jesus, He wins and they lose. Every time. Jesus is always right.

## Matthew 23

Chapter 23 contains some of the strongest words that Jesus delivered during His earthly ministry. He is speaking about "the scribes and the Pharisees" (verse 2). He has some remarkable things to say about their hypocrisy and self-righteousness. People often say that we should follow the example of Jesus (which is right) as we teach people. We should be loving and caring and gentle with people who are wrong in what they believe (that's right also). But sometimes the most loving thing you can do for someone is to help them see that they are wrong. It isn't loving to ignore their error and allow them to be lost eternally. They need to be kindly and lovingly told if they are wrong (that's what Ephesians 4:15 calls "speaking the truth in love"). That is what Jesus does in this chapter; He was more concerned with helping them spiritually than with making sure they liked Him. Be as kind as you can, but people have to learn the truth (John 8:32).

He starts out by explaining that the Pharisees often taught what was right, but they did not always live or do what was right (verse 3). That's a pretty good working definition of hypocrisy, saying one thing but doing something else. The scribes (the NIV calls them, "teachers of the law") would hold others to higher standards than they were willing to follow themselves (verse 4). They did lots of religious things to be seen by others as godly, they loved being honored by sitting in the most prominent seats in the synagogue and they loved for others to acknowledge that they were Rabbis, teachers of God's will. Jesus spoke against the popular idea of distinguishing some from others by giving them fancy titles (much like the false clergy/laity concept in many religions today). They loved anything that would elevate them in the eyes and thinking of others. Jesus emphasizes that God will exalt those who willingly humble themselves (verses 8-12).

A common phrase that Jesus uses here is, "Woe to you, scribes and Pharisees, hypocrites!" That had to really sting them as they heard Him say it over and over. He called them blind guides, fools, serpents, and brood of vipers. They want others to adore them and Jesus is telling them how they corrupt they really are spiritually. He tells them that they make long prayers to God, but it is all a pretense (verse 14).

Jesus accuses them of devouring widows' houses and not allowing others to enter "the kingdom of heaven" (a phrase the Savior uses a lot in the book of Matthew; the other gospel writers mostly refer to "the kingdom of God"). He accuses them of making proselytes (a Gentile who would become a Jew), but only make him "twice as much a son of hell as yourselves."

He tells them that they are not honest and so they swear by the temple, or by the altar or by heaven itself (verses 16-22). If they would just tell the truth, they wouldn't have to swear. Others would know they were trustworthy and their word could be believed. Verse 23 says that they were very strict in their observance of some Old Testament regulations (like tithing everything), but they were neglecting "the weightier matters of the law," like justice and mercy and faith. Their play acting didn't fool God.

Verses 24-30 tell us that the scribes and Pharisees were often one thing on the outside (when others could see them), but another thing entirely on the inside (where only God could know their hearts). He compared them to a beautiful white tomb that looks good but inside is full of death and corruption. They were guilty of grievous sins, including the murder of many who were righteous (that is a theme from the Old Testament, their fathers). He says their ancestors were guilty of this and so is "this generation."

In verses 37-39, Jesus weeps and laments over the sad spiritual condition of the Jews. It should bother us, as it did Jesus, when peoples' souls are not right with God.

## Matthew 24

As Chapter 24 begins, Jesus and the disciples are in the temple area and as they depart, Jesus tells them that the temple is going to be destroyed. "...Not one stone shall be left here upon another, that shall not be thrown down" (verse 2). The discussion that follows in the chapter is primarily, if not exclusively, about the A.D. 70 destruction of

Jerusalem by the Roman armies. Most people believe this chapter is completely about the second coming, but there are many verses which show us otherwise.

As they all sit together on the Mount of Olives, overlooking the site of the temple. the disciples ask Jesus three questions (in verse 3) that determine what is being discussed here.

- When will these things be? – This is dealt with in verses 4-14
- What will be the sign of Your coming? – This question is answered in verses 15-35
- (What will be the sign) of the end of the age? – This is discussed in verses 36-51

Jesus does not answer their first question with a direct answer of a date, which is probably what they were hoping for. "When will these things be?" He begins by warning them of false Messiahs who would arise and try to deceive others. There were people before Jesus who made such claims and there have been many since. He mentions things like wars, rumors of wars, nations rising against one another, famines, pestilences, earthquakes. He calls these things "the beginning of sorrows" (not the end of the world; do you see the difference?). He predicts that many of them will be subjected to persecution, tribulation, hatred and betrayal. He says that these hardships will cause "the love of many" to grow cold. He encourages their continued faithfulness, in spite of these trials. And He prophesies that the gospel of the kingdom will be preached "in all the world" before the end (verse 14). He is not talking about the end of the world, but rather the end of the Jewish system and the force of the Old Law. Judaism would essentially be wiped out as a world power; Israel has never been the same since A.D. 70. The transition from the Old Testament to the New Testament as God's law for man today would be complete, as the remnants of the old system are erased from the earth (see Hebrews 8:13). The change actually took place in Acts 2, after the crucifixion and resurrection, but it took a while for the effects of the transition to reach the whole world.

Verses 15-35 describe "the sign(s)" of Christ's coming. Again, this is His coming in judgment on Jerusalem, not the end of the world. He describes "the abomination of desolation" (verse 15) which is the Roman (Gentile) peoples inside the holy temple, prophesied in Daniel 11:31 and 12:11. He warns them to flee when they see these things. There will be no fleeing from the Day of Judgment at the return of Christ. It won't matter if people are pregnant, if they are working on their house, if they have extra clothes when the final judgment occurs. But these things would be important warnings to run for your life when you see the Roman armies (with their "eagle" insignia on their shields and banners). No one is going to be able to run away and hide from the judgment seat of Christ. Some believers could save their lives by running away from the city of Jerusalem before it is too late.

Jesus tells the parable of the fig tree in this context (verses 32-33). Just as the tree blossoms and leaves begin to regrow after the winter season, they could see some of the warning signs and protect themselves from the Roman devastation. Verse 34 assures them that it would happen in their own first century generation. That should prove to us that He is not talking about the end of time.

Verses 36-51 seem to shift direction slightly to talk about the end of time, again telling us that no one knows exactly when that will be, except the Father. Some Bible students believe these verses deal with the final judgment, while other excellent students think the whole chapter is about Jerusalem. You will have to read carefully and decide for yourself which one makes more sense to you.

## Matthew 25

There are three major sections in Chapter 25. They are the parable of the ten virgins (verses 1-13), the parable of the talents (verses 14-30) and the description of the final day of judgment (verses 31-46).

The parable of the ten virgins begins with similar language to many other parables of Jesus. "Then the kingdom of heaven shall be likened to..." (verse 1). He will follow those words with an everyday, easy-to-remember earthly story that teaches a deep spiritual lesson. (Not all parables start that way.)
In the parable, there are ten young women who are invited guests at a wedding feast. Their marriage customs were different from ours today. The bridegroom would go to the home of his fiancé (his betrothed) and there would follow something like a parade from her house to the hall where the wedding feast would take place. Some friends would join them in the very beginning while others who were invited would be waiting along the way and as the procession passed by them, they would join the company and escort the couple into the facility where a fine feast would take place. Once the procession was complete and the door was closed, no one else would be allowed to enter. Most marriages in the East would occur at night and so lamps to light the way to the feast were common. (They didn't have nice street lights like most of our modern neighborhoods to show them the way.)

In the parable, the marriage party was delayed and so while they waited, their lamps went out. Five of them had brought extra oil and five had not. The five with extra oil did not have enough to share with the others so as they went to buy more, the procession came by, they entered the wedding hall and the door was shut. When the five latecomers knocked on the door, they were not allowed in.

The main lesson of this parable is that we must always be prepared for the return of Christ because we don't know when it will be. We should be ready all the time, just in case.

In the parable of the talents, a wealthy businessman goes away on a business trip and leaves some of his money in the hands of his servants. A talent in Bible times was a valuable coin (most Bible students say one talent was worth about $1000). The most talented man was given five talents; the one in the middle was given two and the third man was given one talent. The five talent man used his money to earn another five talents and the two talent man earned two more talents. The one talent man hid the money in the ground and when the master returned, they presented him with their gifts. He told the 10 and 4 talent servants, "Well done, good and faithful servant." The one talent man was rebuked by the master and sent into outer darkness.

The main lesson here is that we should use our abilities and opportunities to serve the Lord and grow in our diligent efforts to please the Lord. If we do not, there will be negative consequences to our failures.

Some see the final section in the chapter as another parable, while others understand it as a literal description of what will take place when we all appear before the judgment seat of Christ to give an account of our lives (Romans 14:12; 2 Corinthians 5:10). The lessons are the same either way.

Jesus separates the obedient from the disobedient, as a shepherd divides his sheep from the goats. The godly are placed at His right hand, a position of honor and glory. The ungodly are placed on His left and are sent into everlasting punishment. There are other passages that speak of the standards of behavior that will judge our eternal destiny. This text tells us that one of those standards will be how we have treated the poor and needy among us. Those who have helped others will be saved; those who have selfishly done little or nothing for others will be lost. Which one best describes you?

## Matthew 26

These are some of the events of the final days in the life of Jesus before His crucifixion. Verses 1-5 date these events as beginning two days before the Passover (verse 2). The Jewish leaders are plotting for His arrest, but don't think it would be wise to arrest and kill Him during the Festival.

In verses 6-13, we read the account of Mary (see John 12:1-8) anointing the feet of Jesus in preparation for His burial. While the disciples are critical of her actions, Jesus expresses only gratitude and love in appreciation for the sacrifice she has made for Him.

Upset by what has just happened, Judas Iscariot approaches the chief priests with an offer to betray Jesus to them (verses 14-16). They agree on the price of 30 pieces of silver, the price of an adult slave in the Old Testament. This turn of events changes the whole timetable of the Jews and moves up His execution.

In verses 17-30, Jesus and the disciples eat the Passover meal together. He tells them all that one of their own number will betray Him; all of them are exceedingly sorrowful and one by one, they ask Him, "Lord, is it I?" He says that it would have been better for that one never to have been born than to do what he is about to do. When Judas asks Him the question, Jesus replies, "You have said it." Jesus then institutes the Lord's Supper as a memorial of His death.

Verses 31-35 contain some of the saddest words about this whole sordid affair. When Jesus says, "All of you will be made to stumble because of Me this night," He quotes Zechariah 13:7 as being fulfilled in these events. The Shepherd will be arrested and the sheep will be scattered. He also mentions that He will be raised, but they don't seem to understand that part. Peter insists that even if every other disciple deserts the Savior, he will not. Jesus assures him that "this night, before the rooster crows" the next morning, Peter will deny (some versions say, disown) Him three times. Peter promises that he would die before denying the Lord. All of the disciples say the same thing.

In verses 36-46, the apostolic group is led to the Garden of Gethsemane and Jesus has eight of them (Judas had left by now) sit and wait for Him in one spot. He takes Peter, James and John a bit further with Him. He tells them that He is "sorrowful and deeply distressed" and asks them to "watch with Me." He goes a little farther by Himself, falls on His face and prays fervently to God. (The Hebrew writer says, in 5:7, "in the days of His flesh, when He had offered up prayers and supplications, with vehement cries and tears to Him who was able to save Him from death, and was heard because of His godly fear.") Matthew tells us here that He prays for deliverance from the wrath of God as it is poured out on the sins of the world, but ultimately says, "Not as I will, but as You will."

The disciples fall asleep and the Lord reminds them, "Watch and pray, lest you enter into temptation. The spirit indeed is willing, but the flesh is weak." This happens three times and then Judas arrives with the soldiers. Judas leads them to Jesus and kisses Him in the ultimate act of betrayal (verses 47-57). When the soldiers arrest the Son of God, Peter tries to protect Him by cutting an ear off of one of the high priest's servants. Jesus surrenders to the soldiers and the disciples all run away.
The Jewish part of His trial is recorded in verses 57-68. After many false witnesses testified against Him, Christ is accused of blasphemy. Standing outside in the courtyard, Peter is asked three times if he is a follower of Jesus. Three times he denies even knowing who Jesus is. After the third denial, the rooster crows and Peter remembers the earlier conversation with Jesus. He goes out and weeps bitterly. Lest we think we would have done better, let us recall 1 Corinthians 10:12, "Therefore let him who thinks he stands take heed lest he fall."

## Matthew 27

Verses 1-26 deal mostly with the trial of Jesus before the Roman governor over Judea; his name is Pontius Pilate. It is now early Friday morning when the Jews, after their mock trial in Chapter 26, bring Him before the lawful Roman court. Some Bible students have estimated that, since the illegal Jewish trial took place overnight, this trial in front of the Roman governor occurred somewhere between 5:30 and 9:00am. (Jesus was nailed to the cross at approximately 9am (the third hour, Mark 15:25).

Shortly after telling us that Jesus has been delivered to the Roman courts, Matthew shifts his narrative to inform us about the sad fate of Judas Iscariot (verses 3-10). Judas, who probably never thought Jesus would die (he had personally seen Him escape many life threatening situations before), when he realizes that Jesus could be put to death, tries to return the money to the chief priests and elders, hoping that perhaps they will change their minds and cancel the whole deal. Their callous response is "What is that to us? You see to it!" He throws the thirty pieces of silver down in the temple, departs and hangs himself. The Jewish leaders debate what to do with the money because "the price of blood" cannot be given into the temple treasury. So they use the money to buy a plot of land that will be known as "the potter's field" or "The Field of Blood." This fulfills an Old Testament prophecy that is found in Zechariah 11:12-13, while attributing the quote to Jeremiah. This is likely a simple scribal error that has been transmitted down through the years. Many Bible footnotes attribute the quote to Jeremiah 32:6-9.

Returning to the trial, Pilate listens to numerous accusations from the Jews, while Jesus refuses to even acknowledge their charges. It is a fulfillment of Isaiah 53:7, "He was oppressed and afflicted, Yet He opened not His mouth; He was led as a lamb to the slaughter, And as a sheep before its shearers is silent, So He opened not His mouth." You will notice as you read the various trial accounts in the gospels, that the only time Jesus said anything was when His deity was questioned. He always told them who He really is. Pilate "marveled greatly" when Jesus would not speak in His own defense (vs. 11-14).

In verses 15-26, Pilate makes the decision to offer up Jesus and Barabbas as the two choices for a prisoner release that occurred annually at the Passover Festival, a gesture of kindness from Rome to the Jews. Of course, they selected Barabbas for freedom and Jesus for death.

Barabbas is a name which means the "son of Abbas." The prefix Bar- in front of a name means "son of."
A couple of Bible examples include Bartimaeus (Mark 10:46) whose name means son of Timaeus as the text indicates. Peter is called Simon Bar-Jonah in Matthew 16:17, meaning he was the son of Jonah (or some translations say John). And the name Abbas is a form of Abba, which is the Aramaic word for Father (see Mark 14:36 and Romans 8:15). So when you put all of that together, it is interesting that Barabbas means "son of the father," which is exactly what Jesus is, the Son of the heavenly Father. One son was released (the criminal) by the crucifixion of the other Son (the innocent Jesus). That's what the sacrifice of Jesus symbolizes for us, the innocent Child paying the price for the sins of the guilty sons.

Pilate, realizing Jesus' innocence, tries to release Him, but the Jews will not have it. Pilate's own wife tells him to free Jesus because of a dream she has (was it from God or a coincidence?). Pilate tries to soothe his conscience by literally "washing his hands" of the matter, but of course, he is not innocent in spite of his foolish claim.

The rest of the chapter, verses 27-66, tells us of Jesus' six hours on the cross, of the darkness that covered the land from noon to 3pm, of the onlookers at the crucifixion, of Joseph of Arimathea who buries the body in his own new tomb and of the attempt by the Jewish leaders to set a guard to prevent the followers of Jesus from removing His body from the tomb.

## Matthew 28

On the third day, which was the first day of the new week, early in the morning, just as the day is dawning, two women come to the tomb (verses 1-8). They are Mary Magdalene and the other Mary, whom most believe to be Jesus' mother. They have bought spices and have come to anoint the body of Jesus. As they approach, there is "a great earthquake" which was caused by an angel of the Lord coming from heaven and rolling back the large, heavy stone from the door of the tomb. The guards are terrified and become "like dead men." The angel speaks to the women (other accounts tell us there were two angels; Matthew only mentions the one who speaks) and tells them that Jesus, who was crucified, "is risen" from the dead. He then instructs them to go and tell His disciples that Jesus will meet them in Galilee. They quickly depart from the empty tomb "with fear and great joy" and run to inform the apostles of the good news.

As they are heading to the disciples, Jesus Himself meets them and tells them simply, "Rejoice!" In their excitement, they hold Jesus by the feet (they have bowed down before Him in worship) and honor Him now as the resurrected Savior of the world (verses 9-10). He tells them not to be afraid (how could they not be frightened?) and repeats the words of the angel that the apostles are to go to Galilee where He will present Himself to them. Remember that, as apostles, they were to be "witnesses" of His resurrection and they will preach every sermon in Acts with the reality before them that they had seen His death, His burial and His resurrection (Acts 1:8, 21-22). That's why the gospel means "good news." It assures us that the Son of God became man, lived a perfect (sinless) life and then was crucified to pay the price for the sins of man, but that He rose from the grave on the third day, victorious over death and Satan (1 Corinthians 15:1-4). That's not just good news; it's the best news in the history of the world.

In verses 11-15, the guards who had earlier passed out for fear, have revived and realize they could get in a lot of trouble for losing the body of Jesus which they had been asked to protect. They first report to the chief priests about what has happened. When the chief priest and the elders of the people realize the implications of the resurrection, they give "a large sum of money" to the soldiers and instruct them to tell anyone who asks about it that the disciples of Jesus came while the guards were sleeping and stole the body so they could claim He had risen from the dead. (If they were asleep, how would they know what had happened?) "So they took the money and did as they were instructed; and this saying is commonly reported among the Jews until this day" (verse 15). There are still many people today who believe that this is what happened, that the followers of Jesus removed the body from the tomb and simply claimed that He was resurrected.

Matthew skips most of the forty days Jesus spent with the eleven apostles between the resurrection and His ascension back to God. He gets right to the heart of the matter as Jesus gives the apostles their final assignment before He returns to His Father. We commonly call this "the Great Commission" and it is the basis for all the work that the early church accomplished in the continued story of Jesus and the Holy Spirit, which is recorded for us in the book called The Acts of the Apostles. It tells us how the first century disciples shared the message of salvation with their lost and dying world.

The foundation for the Great Commission is the authority of Jesus (verse 18). He has all authority and He commands His followers to tell everyone about what He has done and how they can be saved through Him. He wants the message to be told all over the world, in every tribe and nation of people, throughout every generation (verse 19) and promises that He, Jesus Himself, will be with those who seek to carry out this task as long as the earth is standing (verse 20). After people are converted to Christ by the power of the gospel, they are to be further taught and trained and sent out to tell others of the eternal difference that the Messiah can make in their lives and their spiritual home forever.

# The Gospel according to MARK

## Mark 1

The gospel according to Mark begins at a later point than the other three gospel accounts. Matthew and Luke begin with the genealogy of the Messiah (Matthew) and the appearances of Gabriel to Zacharias and Mary telling of the pending births of John the Baptist and Jesus (Luke). John goes all the way back into eternity to the pre-creation existence of One who is called "the Word."

Mark starts with John the Baptist and Jesus as adults, as they begin their earthly work for God. John is listed as fulfilling Old Testament prophecies from Malachi and Isaiah as the forerunner of the Savior. He quickly goes into the baptism of Jesus by John and then to His temptation in the wilderness. As with many of the events Mark will include in his inspired version of the life of Christ, we are given few details about each of these episodes, only a brief summary. By Mark 1:14, we are already into the beginning of the Galilean ministry of Jesus, when He was about 30 years of age according to Luke 3:23.

Jesus is preaching the gospel of the kingdom of God and saying, "The time is fulfilled, and the kingdom of God is at hand. Repent, and believe in the gospel" (Mark 1:15). This message is similar to the one preached by John the Baptist (compare with Matthew 3:2).

The early stages of choosing His apostles are also described in this part of Chapter 1. Walking by the Sea of Galilee (remember that He was reared in Nazareth, a small village bordering this huge lake in Galilee), Jesus sees two sets of brothers who are professional fisherman. The first are Simon (later called Peter) and Andrew. The others are James and John, sons of Zebedee. The other gospel accounts would show us that this was not their first encounter with the Savior, but, at this time, He calls them to follow Him and tells them they will become "fishers of men." Everyone seeks a higher purpose in life and Jesus offers His followers the opportunity to be a part of something bigger than anything else in the world. He calls us to change the world we live in through the power of the gospel. These four early disciples leave their nets to follow Jesus "immediately" (a key word in this gospel account).

They go to Capernaum where Jesus, on the Sabbath, enters the synagogue and teaches with authority. Capernaum will become a kind of home base for the Messiah from now on, as He teaches throughout Galilee and, at times, goes down into Judea, primarily in Jerusalem. People call easily tell a difference in the teaching of Jesus and that of their scribes. His message is powerful and obviously, from and for God.

In verses 23-28, a man with an unclean spirit is healed. The demon possessed man calls Him both "Jesus of Nazareth" and also "the Holy One of God." In the unseen realm, "the heavenly places" as they are called in Ephesians, even those who serve the evil one know and recognize the deity of Jesus. This miracle causes people to take notice of this carpenter who has special powers from God. Jesus then performs numerous additional miracles that will draw many others to His teaching (verses 29-34).

Verses 35-39 show us that Jesus believed in prayer. Early in the morning, "a long while before daylight," He rises and goes to a solitary place to talk to His Father. Jesus is a man of purpose, realizing that His time on this earth is limited, and He focuses on speaking to God and then for Him, to people who need the Lord (that's everyone). He performs miracles to confirm His message as truly being from God.

In the final section of Chapter 1, verses 40-45, a leper comes to Christ and asks Him to heal him. Jesus is moved with compassion for the man and reaches out, touching Him with God's power. A leper was not allowed to have personal contact with others and so it quite likely had been a long time since he has experienced human touch. Jesus touches him as no one else could and the fame of the Messiah spreads everywhere. People come to Him from every direction. The Savior has come into the world to redeem the lost.

## Mark 2

Jesus is at one of the highest points of His earthly teaching. Great crowds are following Him everywhere He goes. All the people want to hear His message and see His miracles. One such episode in His life is recorded for us in Mark 2:1-12. (This true story is also found in Matthew 9:1-8 and Luke 5:18-26.)

In this account, the emphasis is not on the man who is healed, but rather on the faith of his four friends who brought him to Jesus.

A paralyzed man is brought to Jesus for healing by four men. The crowd is so large that there is no way to get the helpless man near Jesus. Everyone wants to listen to Him and hopefully witness a miracle or two. But these men are determined to help their friend and so they go up on the roof and uncover a spot large enough to let the man down into the house where Jesus can heal him. Verse 5 makes certain we realize that Jesus "saw their faith." (James tells us that the only way to see faith is through actions.)

Jesus tells the paralyzed one, "Your sins are forgiven you" (verse 5). This triggers the grumbling and complaining about Christ that will intensify in the future until they put Him to death. The scribes and others there consider this to be blasphemy against God. Jesus will show them the connection between His words and His actions as He heals the man. He tells us why He did. "But that you may know that the Son of Man has power on earth to forgive sins..." (verse 10). Jesus, while on the earth, had power to forgive the sins of anyone He wanted and in any way He desired. Mostly He just said so. There are numerous examples of Jesus forgiving the sins of people and, therefore, saving them.

- This paralyzed man – Mark 2:1-8
- The "sinner" woman – Luke 7:36-50
- Zacchaeus – Luke 19:1-10
- The woman taken in adultery – John 8:1-12
- The thief on the cross – Luke 23:39-43

These are examples of some of the people who were saved by the Lord, during His earthly ministry. He could forgive people any time, any place, any way He wanted while He was here on the earth. And He often did. This passage tells us "that all were amazed and glorified God, saying, 'We never saw anything like this!'" (verse 12). When people trust God today, we should be amazed and give Him all the glory.

Mark 2:13-17 tells us about the calling of Levi to be a disciple of the Christ. We generally know him better as Matthew the tax collector. It was not uncommon for people in New Testament times to have more than one name, sometimes in more than one language. Matthew worked for the Roman Empire as a tax gatherer. That made him extremely unpopular with most of his fellow Jews. The leaders disliked tax collectors (the Old King James calls them publicans) so much that they often lumped together "tax collectors and sinners" in one phrase (verse 15; see also other passages like Luke 15:1-2). Jesus is eating in Matthew's house which also upsets the religious class. The Messiah reminds them that those who are well do not need a doctor, but those who are sick do. He came into the world because lost people need salvation, not to stay away from the very souls He came to redeem.

There are a couple more events in Chapter 2 which show Christ's conflict with the Pharisees. We read in verses 18-22 about questions surrounding fasting. In verses 23-28, there are issues about what is lawful to do on the Sabbath and what violates the Law of Moses. As the Creator of the Sabbath, no one knew better than Jesus what was lawful and what was not. He is "the Lord of the Sabbath" and of every other day for that matter. We should seek to walk in His footsteps.

## Mark 3

The third chapter of Mark finds Jesus in a Jewish synagogue (possibly in Capernaum; remember in Mark 1:21 that we made the comment that Capernaum was kind of like His headquarters for most of Jesus' ministry). There are a couple of reasons that we so often read of Jesus teaching in a synagogue. First, He was Jewish and Mary probably had taken the family to the synagogue regularly for instruction and prayer. Luke 4:16 tells us that going to the synagogue in Nazareth, "where He had been brought up," was a regular custom for Jesus. Secondly, that's where the religious people were. They would be familiar with the Old Testament, including the Messianic prophecies, and Jesus could use that foundation of knowledge as the basis for convincing them that He is the promised Savior they have read about for many years.

As usual, the Jewish leaders have their eyes on Jesus to find a source of accusation against Him. In this case, as in many others, they want to accuse Him of breaking the Sabbath. He meets a man with a withered hand and after asking them if it is lawful to do good on the Sabbath, He heals the man completely. The Pharisees leave to meet with the Herodians, another sect of the Jews with whom they have great differences, to plot together to destroy Jesus. Unholy alliances are often formed by the wicked to accomplish their evil purposes.

Jesus takes His disciples, as He often did, to the Sea of Galilee for a time of rest. He gets little respite from the crowds however as they find Him and bring to Him many people with various afflictions who need His healing hand. Some of those with unclean spirits acknowledge Him as "the Son of God" but He doesn't need confirmation from evil beings so He tells them not to "make Him known."

In verses 13-19, Jesus selects the twelve apostles, out of a much larger group of followers. After a night of prayer (Luke 6:12), He names the men whom He has chosen. They are appointed to do three things.

1) Be with Him (time with Jesus will change anyone into a more godly person).
2) Preach (we have to tell others what we know about Jesus).
3) Heal sicknesses and cast out demons (miracles gave confirmation to others about the truth of their message).

So many people hear about Jesus and the multitudes of people gathering to Him have grown so large that He and His disciples don't have enough time to eat on some occasions. Even some of His own family and close associates are not certain what to make of everything He is saying and doing.

In verses 22-30, there is a major conflict with "the scribes who came down from Jerusalem." They accuse Him of performing miracles and casting out demons by the power of Satan. Jesus reminds them that a city, house, army or nation that is divided against itself will be destroyed. If Satan is casting out Satan, he will come to a powerful "end" (verse 26). Jesus tells them that to accuse Him of performing miracles by the power of Satan, rather than God, is blasphemy and is an unforgivable sin. We cannot witness the miracles of Jesus personally as they did, so we cannot commit this same sin today. Anyone who did this in the first century "is subject to eternal condemnation."

Chapter 3 ends as the brothers and mother of Jesus come to Him. We are not told what they wanted to speak to Him about (Matthew 12:46-47); it would serve no real purpose for us to speculate about it. But what we do learn here is that, while earthly family is indeed important, our relationship to God is even more important and we must make the things of God of primary importance in our lives (Matthew 10:34-39).

## Mark 4

Chapter 4 contains several parables of Jesus. A parable has been defined as "an earthly story with a heavenly meaning." They are illustrations of spiritual truths. It is sometimes easier to understand and remember a story than a list of facts, but a parable is designed to help people comprehend the spiritual lessons that Jesus intended for them to learn.

Mark 4

The first parable found in Mark 4 is the parable of the sower. It is recorded in verses 1-20 with a brief side trip in verses 10-12. It is interesting to note that Jesus taught this parable while He was in boat on the sea and the "great multitude" was on the land facing Him. (This may be the most unusual pulpit that Jesus preached from.)

The parable itself is fairly short and to the point. A sower (NIV says farmer) goes out to broadcast his seeds. The seeds he plants fall on four different types of soil – wayside (some versions call it the path), stony ground, thorny ground, and good ground. Each of these types of soil represent different kinds of hearts that receive the word of God. (Some have preferred to call this the parable of the soils, but Jesus personally called it the parable of the sower in Matthew 13:18 so, with all due respect, I will side with the Master.)

Before He explains the parable to the disciples, they ask Jesus "Why do You speak to them in parables?" (Matthew 13:10). So He answers that question. Verse 11 seems to imply that there are two different kinds of people who hear the parables, genuine and insincere. For those who are genuinely searching for truth, a parable will help them to understand more clearly the spiritual truth intended by the Lord. For those who are not sincere, the parable will seem like a fairy tale to them, with no real meaningful purpose. He quotes Isaiah 6:9-10 to identify some who hear but are unaffected by the truth.

Then, in verses 13-20, Jesus outlines four basic responses to the gospel. Some (wayside, path people) are uninterested from the start. Some (the ground covered with stones) hear, are touched by the message, but do not continue when things get hard. Others (the thorny soil) hear and accept but are ultimately distracted with the cares of the world and quit. Then there are those who hear, believe, accept and obey. They bear much fruit for God in their lives.

In verses 21-25, Jesus speaks of those who hide their light under a basket rather than letting the truth shine out through their example for others to follow and imitate.

Another parable about growing seeds follows in verses 26-29. Jesus tells us we need to scatter as much seed as possible and then leave the growth to God (see also 1 Corinthians 3:5-9).

The parable of the mustard seed is next (verses 30-34). The kingdom of God would begin small, but grow until the whole earth had heard the message of salvation. Great things can come from small beginnings. The "small things we can do" may seem insignificant to us, but God can do marvelous things with our humble efforts to serve Him and glorify Him in our daily lives. Never underestimate the good that you can accomplish in your life. Bloom where you are planted; do what you can with what you have and then watch what God will do through your efforts.

Verses 35-41 conclude the teachings of Chapter 4 with a miracle that Jesus performs. He and the disciples are together in a boat on the sea and a great windstorm arises suddenly. The followers are fearful for their lives, but Jesus rebukes the wind and the sea and there is a great calm. They are quite amazed. Trust Jesus in all circumstances of life; He will carry you through.

# Mark 5

There are three major storylines in this chapter, all of them miraculous. Jesus casts multiple demons out a man who calls himself Legion, a twelve year old girl is raised from the dead and a woman with a long term bleeding disorder is cured simply by touching the hem of Christ's robe.

The first miracle is contained in verses 1-20. It takes place in "the country of the Gadarenes" (the NIV calls it "the region of the Gerasenes"). After stilling the storm at the end of Chapter 4, Jesus gets out of the boat and is immediately met by a wild man who was living among the tombs (like a cemetery today) because he is possessed by an impure spirit. The spirit has given him unusual human strength so that he cannot be captured or tamed. He has easily broken multiple chains and shackles and cannot be contained. There is a very sad description of the man telling us that he cried out day and night, living alone and isolated from other people, cutting himself with stones. He says when asked by Jesus that his name is Legion for, in reality, the poor man is possessed by many demons, not merely one (although to be possessed by a single demon would be terrifying enough).

Notice also that the demon knows Jesus by name and that he calls him "Son of the Most High God." James tells us that the demons believe in God and tremble (James 2:19), but they do not obey Him. They are an example of dead faith, without works of obedience.

There are two unusual things about this case of casting out unclean spirits. First, there were multiple demons in one man; usually only one demon was in a person. But the second thing is found in the rest of the story. The demons ask Jesus for a favor. Rather than being cast "out of the country," they ask if He would send them into a nearby herd of swine. Jesus grants their request, they enter the swine, and immediately the 2000 pigs run down a steep bank into the sea and all of them drown.

I am not certain what usually happened to a cast out spirit. I have a feeling that they (as spirit beings) went to a place called Tartarus (in the Greek language). It is translated "hell" in 2 Peter 2:4 and is the location of fallen angels (I don't know much about them either). It seems to be parallel to the place of torment that the rich man went to in the teaching of Jesus in Luke 16:23 and may also be the same place as the bottomless pit or the abyss mentioned in the book of Revelation. This may be completely wrong.

When the people from that area come to see what has happened, they are amazed to find the former demoniac, sitting, clothed and in his right mind. They are terrified and ask Jesus to leave the region. The man asks the Lord if he might go with Him but Jesus sends him back to his family and asks him to tell others "what great things the Lord has done for you, and how He has had compassion on you."

The remainder of Chapter 5, verses 21-43, tells us about 2 miracles that Jesus performs back to back. In verse 22, Jesus is approached by a synagogue ruler named Jairus who asks him to come and heal his critically sick daughter. As Jesus is going to his house, a "great multitude" follows Him, pressing Him on every side. In that crowd of people is a woman who has had a bleeding disorder for 12 years. She has spent all of her money on doctors who were unable to help her and she was continuing to get worse. She comes up behind Jesus and knows that if she can simply touch His garment, she will be healed. She does and she is healed instantly. Jesus realizes that power has gone out of Him and so He turns around to see the person who has done this. She confesses what she did and Jesus pronounces a blessing on her (verse 34). Just then someone comes from Jairus' house to tell him that his daughter has died and that he should no longer bother the Teacher. Jesus continues to the house where many are mourning. Jesus takes the parents and three disciples with Him into the room where He indeed raises her from the dead to the amazement of all. It is no coincidence that the girl is 12 years old, the same number of years the lady has suffered her bleeding disease. Jesus helps them both.

## Mark 6

This chapter opens with Jesus going back to "His own country," which is most likely a reference to Nazareth where He grew up. Again, He enters the synagogue and the people are simply amazed at His teaching. "Where did this Man get these things? And what wisdom is this which is given to Him, that such mighty works are performed by His hands?" They knew Jesus, His parents, His siblings. It just didn't make any sense to them how He could know and do so many marvelous things. He makes the famous statement about not being respected in your hometown by the people who knew you when you were younger. He performs only a few miracles there, but continues teaching in other villages around the area (verse 6).

In verses 7-13, Jesus sends out the twelve, two by two, to preach the truth that "the kingdom of heaven is at hand" (Matthew 10:7). The disciples are also given special miraculous powers to cast out demons and heal the sick. He issues strong warnings about those who would choose to reject their message ("more tolerable for Sodom and Gomorrah in the day of judgment").

Then we read the sad account of the death of John the Baptist at the hands of King Herod (verses 14-29). As the popularity of Jesus spreads, people are confused about who He really is. Some say He is Elijah, some the Prophet (a reference to Deuteronomy 18:15-19), or one of the other well-known Old Testament prophets risen from the dead. But Herod is convinced that this must be the resurrected John the Baptist whom he put to death earlier.

John got into trouble with Herod because he told the King that he had no right to be married to Herodias. She had been his brother Philip's wife, but this Herod (Antipas) had stolen her from his brother and married her. John told him, "It is not lawful for you to have your brother's wife." Neither Herod nor Herodias liked that very much, but Herod knew John to be "a just and holy man" and he enjoyed listening to him, so he protected John from his wife's wrath for a while.

On Herod's birthday, he threw a feast, a grand party, in his own honor and invited many important people from his realm. Herodias' daughter (history tells us her name is Salome) dances before these dignitaries and everyone is so pleased (and probably under the influence of alcohol). Herod rewards the girl by telling her that he will give her anything she asks for, up to half of his kingdom. She asks her mother what she should request, the mother tells her she wants the head of John the Baptist on a platter and the girl passes the news on to a horrified Herod. He cannot back out because so many people heard his offer to Salome, so he reluctantly sends an executioner who beheads John in prison. The disciples of John come and take his body away for burial.

Verses 30-44 record Mark's account of the feeding of the five thousand. A great multitude has come out to hear Jesus' teaching and when they grow hungry, the Savior is moved with compassion for them and asks His disciples to tell Him how much food they have available. The answer is five loaves of bread and two fish. The disciples have the crowd sit down in groups of fifties and hundreds, Jesus blesses the food and then gives it to the followers to distribute among the people. Everyone eats until they are full and the disciples gather up twelve baskets of fragments.

As soon as everyone has eaten, they disperse, Jesus goes up to a mountain to pray and the disciples set sail across the Sea of Galilee. Just before dawn the next morning, Jesus walks on the water near the boat which held the disciples. They are frightened, but Jesus tells them to "Be of good cheer!"

In verses 53-56, we read of even more miracles by Jesus, confirming His teaching and further assuring them of who He really is.

## Mark 7

The first section of Chapter 7 (verses 1-23) tells us about a discussion between Jesus and the Pharisees, along with some Jewish scribes. It begins by saying that these Jewish leaders observed some of Jesus' disciples eat food without washing their hands "in a special way," that is, according to a long-standing Jewish tradition. This leads to an important lesson from the Savior about human traditions and what we should learn about our attitude toward traditions in general.

In verses 3-4, Mark explains for us, by inspiration, how the Pharisees and other Jews felt about the importance of washing your hands in a very specific way, "holding the tradition of the elders." It is a good idea, of course, to wash your hands before you eat, but to please the Jews it had to be done their way. The problem is that the Law of Moses did not teach this, it was merely a human idea.

As Jesus deals with this matter (verses 6-13), He says four things about their view of traditions that should concern all of us. (We don't want to make the same mistakes they did about this, right?)

- verse 7 – they taught as doctrines the commandments of men
- verse 8 – they laid aside God's commandments to hold the tradition of men
- verse 9 – they rejected the commandment of God to keep their traditions
- verse 13 – they made the word of God of no effect through their traditions

As a result, the Lord makes it clear to them that they were hypocrites (verse 6), that their hearts were far from God (verse 6), that their worship was in vain (verse 7), that they were ignoring what God actually wanted in favor of what they wanted (verses 10-12), and that they were doing "many such things" (verse 13).

The most frightening thing about all this is that they really thought they were doing the right thing, when Jesus informs them that what they were doing was very, very wrong. It wasn't that it is sinful to wash your hands in a special way, but because they were binding that on everyone else, including Jesus, they were requiring people to do things that God did not require.

In other passages, the New Testament encourages us to hold to apostolic traditions (see 1 Corinthians 11:2; 2 Thessalonians 2:15 and 3:6). But we are taught to reject the traditions of men (Colossians 2:8; Galatians 1:14; 1 Peter 1:18). All traditions are not necessarily wrong, but we must be careful not to bind where God has loosed. God's way is always right; our way may not be the best way.

Jesus has much to say about the origin of sinful attitudes (verses 14-23). He tells us that evil attitudes begin in the heart and then are reflected in one's life choices. We must be careful.

Verses 24-30 tell us about Jesus in the region of Tyre and Sidon, meeting a Syro-Phonecian woman (a Gentile), whose young daughter was possessed by an unclean spirit (Satan hates everybody and often misuses even the young and innocent to accomplish his will). The mother asks Jesus to heal her child and Jesus, knowing He was sent "to the Jew first," tells her initially that He will not, but the mother shows her faith in her persistence and Jesus casts the demon out of the young girl.

In verses 31-37, Jesus is passing through Galilee again, "through the midst of the region of Decapolis," which means an area with ten prominent cities or villages. He is headed to the Sea of Galilee (lots of important Bible stories occurred around this body of water) and they bring to Him a man who is deaf and has a speech impediment. Jesus heals him (of course) and the multitude that sees the miracle is "astonished beyond measure." We would be too, if we were to witness the power of God in Christ.

## Mark 8

Often the New Testament refers to the group of people following and listening to Jesus as a "multitude." This chapter begins by Mark telling us that the multitude on this occasion was "very great." Most of the time we are left to imagine for ourselves how big the crowd might have been; here we are told that there were about 4000 people whose lives were deeply blessed by the miracle Jesus performs in verses 1-10. Many people were interested in what the Savior had to say. He spoke with authority and those who heard His message often left with their lives changed forever by the encounter with God's Son. On some occasions, Jesus not only taught (and that must have been amazing by itself), but He also multiplied food in this situation where the people had nothing to eat. Jesus took seven loaves and "a few small fish" and multiplied them so that

the whole group of 4000 souls ate until they were full and then the disciples gathered up seven large baskets of leftover fragments.
This account is recorded as just another episode in Christ's life, but it had to have been something that these people would never forget. Even those who did not end up following Jesus (and somehow not everyone did) had to think about that day from that point on.

Verses 11-12 say that the Pharisees began to argue with Jesus, while at the same time asking Him to perform a "sign from heaven." Apparently feeding 4000 people with a small amount of food didn't count? The Messiah sighs deeply in His spirit and tells them there will be no more signs today.

Jesus and the 12 get into a boat and cross to the other side of the Sea of Galilee. They have a discussion about the leaven (yeast; negative influence) of the Pharisees and Herod. We must always remain alert.

In verses 22-26, Jesus comes to Bethsaida where a blind man is brought to Him. Jesus restores His sight (in two steps, which is highly unusual) and tells him not to tell others about what He has done. Sometimes Jesus performed miracles just to help those who needed it, not only to convince multitudes.

Verses 27-30 take place at Caesarea Philippi as Christ asks the disciples who people were saying He is. All of the answers describe Jesus as a righteous person, John the Baptist, Elijah or one of the prophets. But those answers were all wrong. So He asks them who they think He is. Peter answers for the entire group when he says, "You are the Messiah" (NIV). Again, He tells them not to tell others. This is pointing out Jesus was working a plan according to a divine timetable. If too many people came to believe in Him too soon, He would probably die before He was able to accomplish all that the Father wanted Him to do. That's what He meant on those occasions when He said, "My hour has not yet come." It wasn't that He didn't want people to acknowledge Him as the Son of God, the Savior of the world. He would eventually tell His followers to tell that good news to the whole world. But He would not die prematurely. Near the end of His ministry, He would say, "I have glorified You on the earth. I have finished the work which You have given Me to do" (John 17:4). But it was not that time yet. (A longer account of these verses is recorded for us in Matthew 16:13-20 if you are interested in reading more.)

Once again, Jesus predicts His death and resurrection. For those who believe that the death of Jesus at the hand of the Jewish people was unexpected, they need to explain why the Son of God/Son of Man so often told His followers that it was going to happen. It was not a surprise to the Father or the Son. He rebukes Peter for saying that he would not allow Him to die. His death was an integral part of God's plan (verses 31-33).

The chapter ends (verses 34-38) with Jesus declaring again the terms of true discipleship. One must deny himself, take up his cross and follow Jesus. Nothing is more important than saving your soul. Nothing.

# Mark 9

Chapter 8 ends with a reminder that our most valuable and precious possession is our soul. We must be a part of the kingdom of God and do our best to live a pure and godly life in His sight. Chapter 9 opens with Jesus assuring His listeners that some of them would not die until the kingdom had come. It was not something 2000 years in the future. Many of them would be a part of God's kingdom in the first century. (Some Bible students believe that verse 1 should be the final verse of Chapter 8.)

In verses 2-13, we are told about the event commonly called the transfiguration. It is a time when Jesus takes Peter, James and John onto a mountain where His physical appearance is altered. His face and His clothes begin to shine "exceedingly white, like snow." Suddenly, Elijah and Moses appear and these three Bible giants begin to talk with one another. (According to Luke 9:31, they spoke primarily about His coming death.) Peter, afraid and uncertain what to say, suggests that they build a tabernacle (shelter, NIV) in honor of each of these great men. Just then, a cloud overshadows them and a voice from the cloud says, "This is My beloved Son. Hear Him!" This event was picturing for the disciples the transition from the Old Testament (the Law and the prophets represented by Moses and Elijah) to the New Testament (the gospel as seen in Jesus, the Son of God).

Next, we find a number of verses dedicated to a miracle of Jesus in which He casts out an unclean spirit from a man's son. He has been possessed by this "mute spirit" since childhood and the father has brought him to Jesus' disciples and asked them to cast out the demon. The disciples were unable to do so and the father, in his desperation, has turned to Jesus. Christ heals the young man.

There is an interesting phrase in verse 24. Jesus has told the father that "all things are possible to him who believes." The father immediately cries out, with tears, "Lord, I believe; help my unbelief!" The two parts of that sentence seem to contradict each other. What did the man mean? Perhaps he knew he had some faith in Jesus, but realized that he might not have a strong enough faith. He might be asking the Lord to accept his weak faith and heal his son. Or maybe he was acknowledging that while he may be strong in faith in some areas of his life, he is weak in others. We all have weaknesses that we must strive to overcome. Maybe the father did not want his weak faith to be the reason that Jesus might not heal his troubled child?

One more time, Jesus mentions His coming death and resurrection to the disciples (verses 30-32) and once again, they still didn't understand what He was telling them.

In verses 33-37, there was some discussion between Jesus and the disciples about greatness in the kingdom. The followers thought they (each one of them about himself) would be the greatest of all. Jesus reminds them that true greatness comes being a servant to others. It is a lesson that is as challenging for us to put into practice as it was for the original twelve.

Verses 38-41 contain teaching from Jesus about accepting followers of Christ who may not be well known to us. These people had worked miracles in the name of the Savior; they were true believers.

And finally, the chapter draws to a conclusion (verses 42-50) with important teaching from Christ about not being a stumbling block or cause of offense to others. (It is vital to realize that He is not talking about doing something that another doesn't like, but rather that, by our example, we would cause others to sin.) There are references to hell in this text, a place where Jesus said, "their worm does not die, and the fire is not quenched." Hell is real, Jesus had much to say about it, and we all need to obey what the Lord says to avoid eternity in this place of outer darkness with weeping and gnashing of teeth.

## Mark 10

Chapter 10 informs us that Jesus is now teaching in "the region of Judea by the other side of the Jordan." A large group of people have come together to hear Him. Have you noticed how often the New Testament tells us that "multitudes" have gathered around the Savior to listen to His teaching? Can you try to imagine in your mind what it might have been like to be a part of that audience?

The Pharisees (who are usually up to no good in such situations) ask Him a question. "Is it lawful for a man to divorce his wife?" The passage also tells us that they ask the question to test Him. Questions about divorce and remarriage are always good for starting conflict. (Sincere and honest questions about divorce are fine and appropriate, of course.) His answer should guide our response to similar questions, "What did Moses command you." Or we would say today, "Let's see what the Bible says about that." God's word is always the right answer even if the question is a hard one.

Jesus reminds them that marriage was started by God "from the beginning of the creation." God made man and woman and brought them together as husband and wife. "Therefore what God has joined together, let not man separate." Although Matthew 19:1-9 lists an exception that is not found here, what Mark includes about the response of Jesus is God's basic marriage law, one man and one woman for life. Anything outside of that violates what God intended marriage to be. He further explains that a spouse who puts away a mate and marries another commits adultery. Again, Matthew includes the exception of adultery, but that is an exception, not the basic law. Jesus was never afraid to tell the total and unvarnished truth on this or any other matter.

Verses 13-16 show us the tender side of Jesus when some parents bring little children to Him. The impatient disciples rebuke the parents for taking up Jesus' time, but He says, "Let the little children come to Me, and do not forbid them; for of such is the kingdom of God" (verse 14). He holds them in His arms, lays His hands on them, and blesses them. That would be something they would never forget, no matter how old they might get to be.

Verses 17-31 are a prominent part of Chapter 10. The one we call "the rich young ruler" comes to Jesus to discuss eternal life with the source of all life. The young man seems sincere, has been living a commendable life in many ways and certainly, he came to the right person to ask this question, "What shall I do to inherit eternal life?" But when Jesus perceives that the young man has the wrong priorities in his personal life, He tells him to sell everything he has and give the proceeds away and then come to follow Him. It was a test of his loyalty. What was most important to him, his money or his soul? He shows the answer as he goes away sorrowful. (We can only hope he changed his mind later.)

Jesus then makes application of this encounter to everyone else by warning us that there are far more important things in life than money and the stuff that money can buy. Those who are willing to put God first in their lives, even at great personal sacrifice, will be rewarded both in this life and in the age to come. But, of course, that doesn't mean that it is easy and that is why so few do the right thing. While speaking of sacrifice, Jesus again predicts His death and resurrection (verses 32-34).

In verses 35-45, James and John, the sons of Zebedee (along with their mother, according to Matthew 20:20-28) come to Jesus to ask for the privilege to sit at the right and left hands of Jesus in His kingdom and glory. They thought they deserved those places of honor; the rest of the disciples thought they were the ones who did and a discussion follows about greatness and service in the kingdom. It is such a hard lesson to learn.

The chapter concludes with Jesus healing blind Bartimaeus outside of the city of Jericho (verses 46-52).

## Mark 11

The first several verses of Chapter 11 record for us the entrance that Jesus made into the city of Jerusalem. The events that follow will lead to His death, burial and resurrection.

The first part of the chapter (verses 1-11) is often referred to as the triumphal entry.

As Jesus and His followers come near Jerusalem, Jesus sends two of the disciples into the city and tells them to bring Him a donkey and its colt (Matthew 21:1-7). Only the colt is mentioned by Mark and it has never been ridden by anyone before. (This was done to fulfill the prophecy found in Zechariah 9:9.) Although one might expect the Savior to ride a white stallion into Jerusalem (as in Revelation 19:11-13), and many other kings have done similar things (Alexander the Great was well known for his fiery black stallion, Bucephalus), King Jesus chose to ride in on a donkey's colt, a perfect combination of both royalty and humility.

As Jesus comes into Jerusalem, "many spread their clothes on the road, and others cut down leafy branches from the trees and spread them on the road." Many of them, going before and following after their King, cry out saying, "Hosanna! Blessed is He who comes in the name of the LORD!" (quoting Psalm 118:26). Others say, "Blessed is the kingdom of our father David that comes in the name of the Lord! Hosanna in the highest!" With these words, they are praising both God the Father and Jesus the Messiah, the Savior of the world. "Hosanna" means O Lord, save us.

After these events, Jesus and the twelve go to Bethany for the night. Bethany was the home of Lazarus and his sisters, Mary and Martha, who often cared for Jesus when He was in the area.

Verses 12-14 and verses 20-24 tell us about an interaction between Jesus and a fig tree. Jesus is hungry and sees a fig tree "having leaves." This indicates that there is possibly some fruit on the tree and so Jesus checks, but finds none. He makes a statement, "Let no one eat fruit from you ever again." The next morning, as they again pass that tree, it is dried up from the roots, completely withered away. Jesus uses this opportunity to teach His followers about the need for fruitfulness and the punishment of the disobedient. The lesson has to do with the Jews rejecting Him as the Christ and the subsequent judgment they would bring on themselves. It is a warning for everyone who would rebel against God.

We read in verses 15-19 about Jesus cleansing the temple, as He drives out the moneychangers and those who were selling animals for sacrifice. This is likely the second time He has done this. The similar episode recorded in John 2:13-22 seems to have been earlier in His ministry (although it is possible that they describe the same event). It does contain a strong warning for those who would turn "a house of prayer" into a "den of thieves." (These are Old Testament references to Isaiah 56:7 and Jeremiah 7:11 that would be profitable for further study).

Verses 22-26 tie together the ideas of faith in God, fervent prayer and our forgiveness of those who have sinned against us. Our trust in God must not be simply words we say, but indicative of the life we live. People should be able to see the difference that being a believer in Christ has made in our lives. We must be a forgiving people who do not hold grudges and hide bitterness toward others in our hearts.

The chapter concludes with an interesting exchange between Jesus and the Jewish religious leaders, "the chief priests, the scribes and the elders." They challenge Him with the question of where He got the authority to "do these things," including the cleansing of the temple. He summarizes the truth in the simple question, "was it from heaven or from men?" That should always be our question as well.

## Mark 12

The first twelve verses of Chapter 12 are a parable of Jesus, the parable of the wicked vinedressers (the NIV simply calls them farmers). Its message is clear.

A man has a vineyard and hires workers to work in it for him, similar to tenant farmers who do not own the land but raise various crops on it and the profits are shared between the owner and the workers. When the harvest comes, in the parable, the owner sends someone to collect his share, but the greedy vinedressers rebel against him and decide not to give his portion to him. So he sends others and they likewise are rebuffed, treated poorly and a few are killed. Finally he sends his son and they mistakenly believe that, if they kill the son, the land and all its produce will be theirs. The owner of the vineyard then returns in force, destroys the wicked farmers and allows others to work the land and enjoy its benefits.

Jesus reminds His listeners of the passage in Psalm 118:22-23 where the rejection of the Messiah by the Jewish people had been prophesied. Jesus is called "the stone which the builders rejected." After that rejection, which in their own lifetime would happen soon, others (Gentiles) would be given the chance to obey God. That's what is meant in Romans 1:16 where it says the gospel is the power of God for salvation "to the Jew first and also to the Greek." People are never forced to accept the truth of God, but once they reject it, others will be given the opportunity to hear and obey. We must continue to look for open and honest hearts.

In verses 12-17, the Pharisees and Herodians (another Jewish sect) join together to try to catch Jesus by His words. They ask Him if it is lawful for Jews to pay taxes to Rome. They believe that, if He says yes, they can accuse Him of not being loyal to the Law of Moses. But if He says no, they can accuse Him of being rebellious to the Roman Empire. They think they have found a no win scenario for Jesus. He responds with the (now) famous statement, "Render to Caesar the things that are Caesar's, and to God the things that are God's." Once again, He wisely escapes their trap.

Next the Sadducees try to trick Him (verses 18-27). Their dilemma for Jesus has to do with the afterlife, which the Sadducees did not believe in (that's why they were sad, you see). The Old Testament taught that the wife of a man who died without an heir must then marry his brother. This is often called Levirate marriage and is part of the Law of Moses; see Deuteronomy 25:5-10. Seven brothers all marry the same woman with no children under their made up example. Whose wife will she be in eternity? Jesus answers their question by saying that there will be no marriages in heaven. Then He answers their real issue, the afterlife. He quotes Exodus 3:6 as He quotes, "I am the God of Abraham, the God of Isaac, and the God of Jacob." By saying, "I am" and not "I was" (after their deaths), Jesus shows that these three patriarchs were still alive, not dead forever like the Sadducees thought they were.

Verses 28-34 record the encounter with a scribe who asks Jesus which commandment of God is the most important. Jesus says the most important one is to love God and the second is to love others.

In verses 35-37, Jesus explains how it is possible for the Messiah to be a descendant of King David and also to be David's Lord.

Jesus warns them of the evil influence of the scribes, in verses 38-40. They were one thing on the outside, but something else on the inside. The chapter ends (verses 41-44) with a story about a poor widow who gave her whole livelihood to the temple. She may well be an example of sacrificial giving (as preachers often use her), but it is more likely that He is pointing to her as a real life example of a widow whose house was being devoured by the evil scribes He has just warned them about.

## Mark 13

This chapter begins while Jesus and the 12 are in the area of the temple courts. As they are going out of the temple, one of the disciples comments to the Messiah about the beauty of the physical structure where God had placed His name in the Old Testament.

The response of Jesus is that this building will one day be destroyed. Not one stone will be left on another; all will be thrown down. This exchange sets the stage for the teaching in the remainder of Chapter 13. (By the way, the teaching of this chapter is paralleled in Matthew 24 and Luke 21.)

Many sincere Bible students mistakenly interpret the events of this chapter as things that will happen at the end of time, when Christ returns for the final Day of Judgment. Some have heard these verses used incorrectly for so long that it is hard for them to imagine them speaking of anything else.

But contextually, it appears obvious that what Jesus is telling them is that, in connection with His rejection by the Jews and the subsequent crucifixion that the Son of God will endure, there is going to be a time of judgment upon the Jewish nation.

God has already made it clear in the Bible, in both Old and New Testament references, that the Old Covenant (the Law of Moses) is going to be replaced with a New Law, the gospel of salvation (Romans 1:16). Because of the connection between this change in God's Law and the widespread rejection of Jesus by His fellow Jews (John 1:11), the city of Jerusalem is going to be destroyed. This plundering of the capital city of Judaism has already happened on several occasions in the Old Testament, with the Babylonian destruction of the city being the most widescale and pervasive. In those incidents, God allowed Jerusalem to be punished because of her sins, not because the rival nations were so powerful. It was a teaching lesson for them about obedience to God. They failed after most of those events to learn what God wanted them to know. The Babylonian desolation of Jerusalem in 586 B.C. most closely mirrored the event that would occur in A.D. 70, primarily because both included the demolition of the temple. After the Babylonian conquest, the city and the temple were rebuilt. After A.D. 70, the temple would not be reconstructed.

The disciples and their Rabbi (Teacher) go to the Mount of Olives, from which they can still physically see the temple as Jesus describes the events that would occur, along with some warning signs to help them realize the destruction was soon to come. (We know this day of vengeance occurred in A.D. 70 but they were not told exactly when it would happen.)

So, in verse 4, some of the followers of Christ ask Him for more details. "Tell us, when will these things be? And what will be the sign when all these things will be fulfilled?" In verses 4-27, some of the specific signs are laid out. They include false Messiahs, wars and rumors of wars, earthquakes, famines, troubles, sorrows, persecution of His disciples for their faith in Him, public arrests and trials, the spreading of the gospel to all the nations, family members betraying one another to the authorities. He describes many of these events as "tribulation, such as has not been since the beginning of creation which God created until this time, nor ever shall be." In figurative language, He tells them of dark days of persecution and governments falling around the world. All of these things literally happened in the first century world.

In verses 28-31, Jesus tells a parable about a growing fig tree and the signs that its fruit is near. He compares that to these warning signs He has given them. And He says, in verse 30, "Assuredly, I say to you, this generation will by no means pass away till all these things take place." He is not talking about the end of time, but the final end of the Jewish faith, due to their rebellion against God. In verses 32-37, they are told to "watch" for these events; they would happen in their first century lifetime.

## Mark 14

Numerous events led up to the death of Jesus on the cross. Some of them were the fulfillment of Old Testament prophecies; all of them are filled with important lessons for us to learn. Many of these events are found in this chapter, which is the longest of this gospel account.

The first nine verses of the chapter tell us that the Passover Festival of the Jews is quickly approaching and that the chief priests and scribes, the Jewish religious leaders, want to find a way to put Jesus to death. They express some concern about how "the people" will react when this happens.

In the village of Bethany, just outside of Jerusalem, Jesus and the disciples have gathered together in the house of Simon the leper. While there, a woman brings some very expensive perfume (oil of spikenard) and uses this to anoint the feet and head of the Savior in preparation for His death and burial. Although the disciples criticize her for this action, Jesus is pleased and says of her, "...wherever this gospel is preached in the whole world, what this woman has done will also be told as a memorial to her."

Then, we read in verses 10-11 that Judas Iscariot, one of the twelve, goes to the chief priests and agrees to betray Jesus to them for money. Matthew 27:3 tells us that He betrayed the Messiah for thirty pieces of silver.

In Mark 14:12-26, Jesus observes the Passover Festival with His 12 disciples, including Judas. Although the chronology is a bit uncertain because no single account gives all of the details, it seems that Judas probably left the group after this Passover meal to go to the Jews to betray Christ.

It is at this time that He tells them about the Lord's Supper which they will later partake of in their worship in the church as a memorial to His death.

In Mark 14:27-31, the Savior tells Peter that he will deny that he even knows Jesus, not once, not twice, but three times, before the rooster crows in the morning.

After that, they leave the upper room where they have eaten the Passover meal and they go to the Garden of Gethsemane. This was a familiar place where Jesus had often taken His followers, for both teaching and rest. He takes Peter, James and John apart from the others and asks them to watch carefully as He goes a little further alone. Then Jesus prays fervently to God as the weary disciples sleep (Mark 14:32-42). The most touching part of the prayer is recorded in verse 36: "Abba, Father, all things are possible for You. Take this cup away from Me; nevertheless, not what I will, but what You will."

Next, Judas appears with a mob of people armed with swords and clubs. Judas kisses Jesus on the cheek as a signal to the soldiers of which man they are to arrest. When they see that Jesus has been arrested, the disciples all run away in fear (Mark 14:43-52). Mark 14:53-65 gives us some details about the Jewish trial before the Sanhedrin Council. This trial was illegal as they were not supposed to meet at night, but in the daylight hours. After hearing from false witnesses, they come up with a charge of blasphemy based on Christ's claim to be the Son of God. They spit on Jesus, blindfold Him, strike Him with their fists and beat on Him, as they mock and ridicule Him.

In verses 66-72 (still in Mark 14), we read about Peter, who despite his claim that he would die for Christ, indeed denies Him three times. After the resurrection, Jesus makes Peter state three times that he loves Him (John 21:15-17).

## Mark 15

Chapter 15 opens with the Jews taking Jesus to Pontius Pilate, the Roman governor who will decide His fate. Because the Jews are under the rule of the Roman Empire at this time, they do not have the legal authority to put anyone to death. They need Pilate to condemn Him to die.

The typical Jewish method of capital punishment, in the Old Testament, is stoning. On at least a couple of occasions, the Jews got so angry with the teaching of Jesus that they decided to take matters into their own hands and defying Roman authority, they tried to stone the Savior (John 8:59; John 10:31-39). Each time, the Lord escaped their evil intentions. (Acts 7 tells us of the death of Stephen by stoning. Apparently, their anger became so intense that they lost control of their emotions and violated Roman law by killing him.)

But the Romans used their favorite method of execution, which was crucifixion. It had been prophesied that the Messiah would be "lifted up" during His death and that was a reference to His crucifixion (John 12:32-34).

In verses 1-15, Pilate wants to release Jesus because he can clearly see His innocence. However, Pilate is a politician and desires to pacify this large contingent of Jewish citizens and so, against his better judgment, he allows the Jewish leaders to have their way.

In keeping with a long standing custom and agreement between Rome and the Jews, the Jewish mob asks Pilate to release a notable prisoner named Barabbas. Barabbas was an insurrectionist, who, along with his fellow rebels, had committed murder during the rebellion. Interestingly, some translations of the New Testament list the criminal's name as Jesus Barabbas. Pilate asks them which "Jesus" he should release, Jesus Barabbas or Jesus the Christ? They choose the real criminal for release and the innocent Savior for death.

In verse 15, before Jesus is crucified, Pilate has the Roman soldiers to scourge Christ. This means that they beat Him severely with whips until His back is bloody and throbbing with pain. Some people died simply because this scourging was so violent and cruel. But Jesus does not die yet.

During this time (verses 16-20), the soldiers clothe the Messiah in purple robes (a mocking, but accurate picture of His royalty), they twist a crown of thorns to place on His head and they salute Him as "the King of the Jews" (again, not sincerely, but correctly). They strike Him repeatedly on the head with a reed, spit on Him and, in mockery, bow before Him in worship.

Then they nail Him to the cross. The nails had to be large enough to hold His body on the cross once it is raised to its upright position. It is hard for us to fathom the amount of pain that these nails would cause.

Mark 15:21-39 records the account of His crucifixion. It began at about 9:00 in the morning and He dies shortly after 3:00 in the afternoon. The Son of God has died for the sins of the world to make salvation possible for all of us. In verse 39, a Roman centurion who witnesses these events says, "Truly this Man was the Son of God!"

The final verses of Mark 15 (verses 40-47) tell us about Jesus being buried in a nearby tomb, which belongs to Joseph of Arimathea, a wealthy and important member of the Sanhedrin Council. Jesus' mother and Mary Magdalene follow to see where He is buried.

## Mark 16

The crucifixion of Jesus took place on Friday. The Last Supper meeting with the apostles was on a Thursday; He was arrested later that evening. After His all night long trial before the Jewish rulers, He was taken early Friday morning to Pilate and, by about 9am, Jesus was crucified, dying at approximately 3:00 in the afternoon.

Prophecies (both Old and New Testament ones) had stated that Jesus would remain in the grave for 3 days and then He would rise from the dead. He had told His followers on many occasions that His body would not see decay, but that He would arise on the third day. Friday, Saturday and part of Sunday fulfilled these prophecies.

That Friday was the Preparation Day for the Jewish Passover meal, which would occur on Saturday (or, as it is called in the Bible, the Sabbath). So, after His death on Friday and the Passover meal on Saturday, some of the women who traveled with Jesus came to the tomb early on Sunday morning to anoint His body with spices.

These spices were a first century form of embalming, preparing a body for burial. They would serve two purposes. One would be to slow down the decaying process and the other was to provide some pleasant scents (or smells) for when the body did start to turn into dust.

So, the women approach the tomb, early on the first day of week (Sunday), just after the sun rises, and are concerned about how they will roll away the heavy stone in front of the tomb. As they arrive, they are surprised to see that the stone has already been moved.

Entering the tomb, they are startled to see a young man in a long white robe. He is sitting on the right side of the now empty tomb. Matthew 28:2-6 records that this young man was actually an angel, a messenger from God. He tells them not to be afraid (most people in the Bible are quite frightened when they meet an angel). But the angel gives them some wonderful news. Jesus is not here; He has risen, just as He has been telling you. He instructs them to go and tell His disciples about this and to meet Him in Galilee, a region north of Jerusalem, where Jesus had grown up, in the ancient city of Nazareth.

Mary Magdalene is the first person to see Jesus (Mark 16:9; more details are found in John 20:11-18). Others see the resurrected Savior also (verses 12-13).

The rest of Mark 16 has some important lessons for us, as well. In many ways, they are similar to the teachings found in Matthew 28 and Luke 24.

We read, in Mark 16:14-18, that all of the apostles (except Judas who has died by this time) are allowed to see Jesus alive again with their own eyes and they are given an important assignment to take the good news (the word, gospel, means "good news") to the whole world. Jesus tells them: "He who believes and is baptized will be saved; but he who does not believe will be condemned" (verse 16). This is often referred to as the Great Commission. In total, they spent about 40 days with Christ after He arose from the dead.

Mark 16:19-20 records the ascension of Jesus back to heaven, where He reigns over His spiritual kingdom at the right hand of God. His followers then continue to obey Him and preach the good news of salvation. Colossians 1:23 tells us that the early disciples were successful in taking the gospel to the known world of the first century.

# The Gospel according to LUKE

## Luke 1

Unlike the other gospel accounts, Luke (the only known Gentile author in the New Testament) starts off by telling us why he wrote his inspired version of the life story of Jesus. (By the way, the only other possible book that might have been written by a Gentile, along with the book of Acts which Luke also wrote, would be Hebrews, since we don't know the author of that book for sure. Of course, it is unlikely that the message of Hebrews would have been well received by the Jews if a Gentile wrote it.)

Verses 1-4 state clearly his purpose in compiling this gospel record. Two things stand out in these verses. The first is that Luke tells us he had "perfect understanding" of the things he wrote, either from personal investigation of the facts or from the things he received from his Jewish friends who were the witnesses he mentions in verse 2. And we must remember that this book is inspired by the Holy Spirit just like the rest of the New Testament. The second point to emphasize here is that he refers to this as "an orderly account" and it is probably the most chronologically accurate gospel.

Verses 5-25 tell us about the interaction between Zacharias and the angel Gabriel. Zacharias (some versions say Zechariah) and his wife, Elizabeth, were "both well advanced in years" (verse 7), but they had no children. They had been praying for a child (verse 13), perhaps for a long, long time. So far, God's answer had been, no. But one day, while Zacharias was working in the temple (he was a priest of the division of Abijah), Gabriel (verse 19) appeared to him and told him that they would have a son, whom they were to name, John. This son would "turn many of the children of Israel to the Lord their God" as the one who would go before the Messiah. He would be best known as John the Baptist.

Verses 26-38 record the appearance of Gabriel to Mary. He tells her about the upcoming birth of God's Son. When the angel appears to Mary, the mother of Jesus, and tells her about the upcoming birth of her own Son, she is stunned by this news. He convinces her of God's power to perform this virgin birth through her by telling her what God had done for Zacharias and Elizabeth, giving them a son in their old age. For many years, God was telling them, not right now, so that at just the right time in human history, He could use the birth of their child to assure Mary that her own Son would be the Savior of the world. The virgin birth of Jesus makes Him different from any other baby ever born. God was bringing His "only begotten Son" (John 3:16) into the world as the Savior of mankind (see Galatians 4:4-5).

In verses 39-56, Mary travels to the hill country of Judea and visits with Elizabeth. Notice that, as Elizabeth is filled with the Holy Spirit, she refers to Mary as "the mother of my Lord." That was exactly right. Verses 46-55 are often referred to as "the song of Mary," although it is basically a poem which magnifies the Lord. It refers to God's mercy, His strength, His provision for the helpless and His love for His people, Israel, as seen in the fulfillment of His promise to Abraham (Genesis 12:1-3) that, through one of his descendants, all nations of the earth would be blessed.

Verses 57-66 tell some of the details of the birth of John and his subsequent naming as John, as predicted by Gabriel. (The "the Baptist" part of his name came later, as he took on the actual work that God planned for him as the forerunner of the Messiah.)

Verses 67-79 show that the Holy Spirit came on Zacharias and he delivered this short prophecy. The first part of the prophecy speaks of God's faithfulness and the redemption He provided for mankind in Jesus (verses 68-75). The second part tells of the important work that Zacharias' son, John, would fulfill in preparing the hearts of the Israelites for the coming of their Savior.

Verse 80 mentions the upbringing of John in the deserts. Many believe he was reared by the Essene sect of the Jews, the people who copied the Dead Sea Scrolls, which were discovered in 1947 and which give us some of the oldest and most complete manuscripts of the Old Testament.

## Luke 2

As prophesied in Micah 5:2, Jesus the Messiah was born in Bethlehem, in the region of the world known as Judea (verses 1-7). Although Joseph and Mary lived many kilometers away in Nazareth of Galilee, God, who is control of everything, caused Caesar Augustus, the leader of the Roman Empire, to decree that a census should be conducted to both register and tax the citizens of the Empire. Each family was required to travel to their "own city," the place of their birth and family inheritance. Mary is pregnant with the Son of God and this census occurs at the end of her pregnancy. Quirinius was the Roman governor over the region of Syria at the time. Travel, of course, would have been quite difficult for her.

The Son of God, born of a virgin (Isaiah 7:14), was born into humble surroundings (verse 7). The most glorious birth the world has ever known was not achieved with pomp and glorious circumstance, but with humility and grace. It was a humble birth, with crude surroundings and no complaining by the mother of the Savior. We are not told that Jesus was born in a barn, although the text does say that, after the birth, the Son of God and Mary is laid in a manger, which is an animal trough. We also read that there was no room for them in the inn.

In verses 8-15, an angel appears to shepherds who are protecting their flocks at night. When they appear terrified, he calms their fears by telling them, "Do not be afraid, for behold, I bring you good tidings of great joy which will be to all people. For there is born to you this day in the city of David a Savior, who is Christ the Lord." He then tells them where they can find the Christ Child. A heavenly chorus appears, praising God and saying: "Glory to God in the highest, And on earth peace, goodwill toward men!" With haste, they make their way in Bethlehem and they find the baby and His parents. When they tell them what had happened to them out in the fields, Mary ponders their words. How much did she know? She obviously knows some things and yet, other facts remain a mystery to her. She goes ahead to rear God's Son. Try to imagine the weight of that responsibility.

When Jesus is eight days old, his circumcision occurs (verse 21). As the days of Mary's purification are completed, they bring Jesus to Jerusalem "to present Him to the Lord" (verses 22-24). Two Law of Moses passages are quoted in connection with this ceremony (Exodus 13:2 and Leviticus 12:8).

We are told about two faithful Jews, who have both been waiting in anticipation of the Messiah's birth (verses 25-38). The first is a man named Simeon, a godly man who had been promised by the Holy Spirit that he would not die until he had the blessing of personally seeing the Savior. When the Joseph family arrives at the temple for their sacrifice to God, the Spirit directs Simeon to go there as well. He realizes that the baby Jesus is the Messiah and the fulfillment of the salvation promises by God. Joseph and Mary are astonished at his words about their Son.

The second elderly person to be waiting for the Christ to appear is a righteous widow named Anna. Note that she is from the tribe of Asher, one of the Northern ten tribes of Israel, which were mostly destroyed in the Assyrian captivity. She rejoices in the blessing of seeing Jesus as well.

After these events, the family returns to Nazareth (verse 39). There Jesus grows up. Basically, from day 8 to year 12, there is little that we know about the life of Jesus (verse 40). We are told that Mary and Joseph had other children in the following years (Matthew 12:46-50; Matthew 13:53-56). We also know from Matthew 2:13-15 that the family spent some time in Egypt to protect Jesus from Herod the Great.

Verses 41-52 tell us about a single event in the childhood of Jesus when He was twelve years of age. Verse 52 informs us that He grew in four areas: wisdom (mental growth), stature (physical growth), favor with God (spiritual growth), and in favor with men (social growth).

## Luke 3

We now jump ahead approximately 30 years. Chapter 3, verses 1-6, tell us about the beginning of the work of John the Baptist. John the Baptist is the forerunner of Jesus, that is, he is the one who came before the Messiah to prepare His way.

In ancient times, a traveling king would be preceded by a team that would make certain things were ready for the monarch's arrival. That might include clearing away a path or a road for the king and his entourage to travel on and, at times, might even require many slaves who would be asked to remove a path through a mountain for the traveling party to pass through. This might involve removing anything unsightly that would discourage or anger the king. It might include arresting criminals or vagrants who could pose a threat to the king. And a forerunner's job was also to excite people and prepare them emotionally for the arrival of their king. Over a period of 400 silent years, the people of Judah (or Judea as it came to be called in New Testament times), had slowly moved away from God. John's responsibility was to begin to bring them back closer to where they ought to be. That's why he practiced a baptism of repentance for the remission of sins. He was to make people begin thinking again about the importance of serving God. Verses 4-6 quote from Isaiah 40:3-5 and give us an inspired explanation of John's responsibilities before God. (Malachi 3 and 4 also contain some prophecies about John and his work.)

Some of the teaching that John did is recorded for us in verses 7-20. We don't really have a lot of his specific words; we have more details about the powerful effect of the things that he taught than we do the actual things he said. This section is an exception to that. When he saw multitudes coming out to listen to him, he called them a brood of vipers and taught them to bear fruits of repentance. He warned them that the ax of God was at the root of the Jewish trees and that they needed to get right with the Lord before it was too late. When they ask him some specific questions about what that meant, he told them what they needed to do (verses 11-14). And there was the perpetual question about whether John was actually the Messiah himself and, with his typical humility, he makes it abundantly clear that he did not want anyone to believe that. He says that Jesus is "mightier than I" and that he was not even worthy to untie Jesus' sandals. He warns them about coming judgment and emphasizes that there are only two groups of people in the world, the saved and the lost. He wants to encourage everyone to be in the saved group. Herod the tetrarch (this is Herod Antipas) doesn't like what he tells him and so John is thrown into prison. He will not get out alive.

An account of Christ's baptism is recorded in verses 21-22. Two other accounts are found in Matthew 3:13-17 and Mark 1:9-11. Jesus was baptized by John the Baptist. John was reluctant to baptize the Lord and said that Jesus should be baptizing him. Jesus did not need to be baptized for the remission of His sins (Acts 2:38; 22:16) because He had committed no sins (John 8:46; 1 Peter 2:22). His baptism was not for His salvation (1 Peter 3:21). He didn't need to be saved, because He was never lost. Christ was baptized "to fulfill all righteousness." He wanted to obey God in every way. And, do not forget, that He is our perfect example in all things. He has never asked us to do something that He Himself was unwilling to do. So the Savior of the world was baptized to show us the way to God.

After telling us that Jesus was "about thirty years of age" when He begins His ministry (not exactly 30, just about 30, maybe a little older or maybe a little younger), Luke lists the genealogy of Jesus. Two major differences from Matthew's list should be noted. First, Luke lists the lineage through Nathan, David's son, while Matthew goes through Solomon. Second, Matthew starts with Abraham and goes forward to Jesus. Luke starts with Jesus and goes in the opposite direction all the way back to God. In verse 23, by the way, Heli is actually Mary's father, not Joseph's father (see Matthew 1:16 which tells us that Joseph's father was named Jacob). Both sides of Jesus' family can be traced back to Abraham.

# Luke 4

Jesus is led by the Spirit into the wilderness to be tempted by the Devil (verses 1-13). Why would He do that? In Hebrews 4:15, we find the answer. "For we do not have a High Priest who cannot sympathize with our weaknesses, but was in all points tempted as we are, yet without sin." As our High Priest, Jesus had to experience temptation so He could sympathize with our own experiences in facing such spiritual trials. It is not easy to overcome the Devil. Jesus could successfully overcome all temptation. We are not so fortunate (Romans 3:23). But with the Savior on our side, we can be victorious as He was. The next verse (Hebrews 4:16) reminds us: "Let us therefore come boldly to the throne of grace, that we may obtain mercy and find grace to help in time of need." Jesus lives to make intercession for us (Hebrews 7:25). When you are tempted, don't forget to pray for the Lord's help; that will make victory easier.

Notice as you read the account of Jesus' temptation, that He went into the battle prepared for victory. He knew God's will, as indicated by His use of the phrase, "It is written." He understood what God would want Him to do in response to the temptations of the devil. He was prepared to do the right thing, because He had previously decided that He would not give in to the evil actions that Satan wanted Him to do. He knew right from wrong and was determined to do the right thing. If you wait until the heat of the moment to decide if you will be strong or give in, you will probably do the wrong thing. And He resisted the temptation to do Satan's will. He did not second guess His choice; He knew the right thing and He did it. He had to deny Himself things that He might have enjoyed (for example, He was really hungry and would have loved to eat some bread). It is not easy to say no to the lust of the flesh, the lust of the eyes or the pride of life. But Jesus always obeyed God.

In verses 14-15, the next major section of Jesus' work begins. It is commonly referred to as His Galilean ministry, as this was the geographical area where most of this part of His life occurred. He did make occasional journeys into Judea, including Jerusalem. But much of His teaching started in His hometown around Nazareth and Capernaum.

An instance of the kind of teaching He did is described in verses 16-30. Jesus goes into the Jewish synagogue in Nazareth and stands up to read. They hand Him a scroll of the prophecies of Isaiah and He opens it to the section we know as Isaiah 61:1-2. After reading it, He sits down and everyone waits in anticipation as He says, "Today this Scripture is fulfilled in your hearing." He explains further, in the following verses, that God's love and salvation are going to be extended to everyone, including Gentiles (that's the point of His examples in verses 25-27). The Jews respond with great wrath and anger at His words, so much so that they decide to throw Him off a nearby cliff to His death. But He miraculously passes through the crowd and goes on His way. (I remember reading this Bible story as a little child and thinking that was the coolest thing! As an adult, I continue to be amazed by the power of Jesus.)

Next, Jesus goes to Capernaum and again teaches the Jews on the Sabbath in their own synagogues (verses 31-37). The text emphasizes that "His word was with authority." What it must have been like to sit at the feet of Jesus and listen to Him teach! A man with "a spirit of an unclean demon" enters and Jesus casts out the demon from the man. Jesus not only has authority, but power from God as well.

In verses 38-41, Jesus performs many miracles. He heals Simon Peter's mother-in-law of a high fever (notice that Peter was a married man). Others with various diseases are touched and healed by the power of Jesus and many more demons (unclean spirits) are cast out of people. The demons realize that Jesus is the Messiah, the Son of God. James 2:19 tells us that they had a dead faith, which does not obey God. In verses 42-44, the chapter ends by telling us that Jesus continues to travel around, preaching everywhere He goes, "because for this purpose I have been sent."

## Luke 5

The first section of this chapter takes place on the shoreline of Lake Gennesaret, better known as the Sea of Galilee (verses 1-11). The heading of this section in most Bibles is titled, Four Fishermen called as Disciples. Two sets of boats indicate two separate fishing parties, two sets of partners, Simon and Andrew his brother (who is not named here, but both Matthew and Mark tell us he was there) and also James and John, the sons of Zebedee. The text tells us that they have fished all night long with no success and had begun to wash their nets for the next night's work. Notice that Jesus gets into one of the boats, goes into the sea a short distance and teaches a multitude of people who have been following Him (verse 3). After the Bible lesson is over, He tells Simon to launch out into the Lake and to let his nets down into the water. Simon doesn't expect any results from the effort, but agrees to do what Jesus has told him, "At Your word, I will let down the net." When he does so, they catch a great number of fish, so many that their net begins to break under the weight of the many fish. The other fishermen come to help them, they fill both boats completely with fish and the ships begin to sink. They realize that this is no ordinary Rabbi and He challenges them to leave their nets behind and follow Him. They do.

In verses 12-16, Jesus heals a man with leprosy. This usually fatal disease was one of the greatest tragedies of the Bible. It was essentially a death sentence for the individual and yet, Jesus not only healed a number of people with this terrible skin disorder, but often, as in this case, actually touched the person, adding a more human element to the healing. Verse 14 mentions that there were certain offerings that those few lepers who recovered from their disease were expected to sacrifice to God in appreciation for their cleansing (these are found in Leviticus 14). The other noteworthy point here is that a miracle of this magnitude obviously created an aura of the divine around Jesus that helps to explain both His popularity among the people and the jealousy created in the hearts of the religious leaders of the Jews. Verse 16 emphasizes to us the importance that Jesus placed on His prayer relationship with God. Even though He was divine Himself, He still felt the need to discuss things with His heavenly Father. If He felt that need acutely, shouldn't we?

The next section, verses 17-26, tells us about Jesus both forgiving and healing a paralyzed man. Parallel accounts are found and discussed in Matthew 9:1-8 and Mark 2:1-12. Great multitudes of people have gathered to listen to the teaching of the Galilean and He has gone to a house to continue His teaching. Again, a large crowd has gathered and four men (Mark tells us there were four of them) have carried a paralyzed friend on a bed with the hope that Jesus will heal him. Due to the size of the audience, the men go up onto the roof of the home, tear a hole in the roof (that would be easier to fix then than it would now), and let their friend down, still on his bed, into the room where Jesus is teaching. The Savior forgives the man's sins, which causes the scribes and Pharisees to accuse Him of blasphemy. Jesus proves His authority to forgive sin by healing the man of his paralysis. Jesus could forgive anyone of sins in any manner He wanted while He was on the earth. These cases do not invalidate the need for baptism for the remission of sins after His death, burial and resurrection (Mark 16:16; Acts 2:38; Acts 22:16). The Law of Moses was in effect during His lifetime, whereas the gospel (His last will and testament) took effect after His death (Hebrews 9:16-17; 10:9-10).

Verses 27-31 record for us the call of Matthew/Levi to follow Jesus. A tax collector, Levi (as he is called here; although he calls himself Matthew in his own gospel record; Matthew 9:9-13) begins his journey with Jesus and never looks back.

There is a short discussion about fasting (verses 32-39) in the closing section of Chapter 5. Jesus tells them that His followers will indeed fast after He has departed back to heaven. He refers to His teaching as "new wine" that must be put into new wineskins, while many prefer the old wine of the Old Law.

## Luke 6

Chapter 6 begins with the account of Jesus and His disciples traveling (they did that a lot back then; they obviously walked everywhere they went). They pass through a grainfield and they pick some of the heads of grain and eat them (verses 1-5). Notice that it is the Sabbath. The ever critical Pharisees accuse them of engaging in illegal activity and Jesus reminds them of their Old Testament hero, David, who traveled with some of his soldiers and, on their journey, ate the showbread from the temple. There are times when we must make choices between obeying what the Bible says and helping people in need. If we are on our way to Sunday worship services and we come upon a serious vehicle accident, should we stop to help those who are injured or should we go on to church services because God tells us not to forsake the assembling of ourselves together? Sometimes those are not easy decisions; other times it is clear that we need to serve others in need. Jesus reminds them that He is the Lord of the Sabbath; He knew what was right to do in every situation.

Another Sabbath situation arose in verses 6-11 where Jesus is teaching in the synagogue on the Sabbath and a man with a withered hand is brought to Him. The hypocritical Jewish leaders watch Him closely so they can criticize Him for working on the Sabbath. Jesus heals the man's hand and the Jews are filled with rage at His actions.

Verses 12-16 tell us that Jesus spends an entire night in prayer and then the following day, chooses His twelve apostles from the larger group of disciples. "Jesus called them one by one..." So sing our children about the apostles of Christ. As a group they are called "the twelve" numerous times in the New Testament (Matthew 10:1-5; 26:14; 1

Corinthians 15:5). Actually, there were fourteen of them. The song continues, "Matthias then took Judas' place, to preach to men of every race; Paul, three preaching trips did make and went to Rome for Jesus' sake." The word, apostle, literally means "one sent forth" (W.E. Vine, *Expository Dictionary of New Testament Words*, page 65).

There are others who are called apostles in the New Testament. Sometimes the word is translated as "messenger." These would include Titus and "our brethren" (2 Corinthians 8:23), Barnabas (Acts 14:14), Epaphroditus (Philippians 2:25), Andronicus and Junia (Romans 16:7) and James, the Lord's brother (Galatians 1:19). Also, 1 Thessalonians 2:6 uses the plural term to include not only Paul, but also Silas and Timothy. These others were not "official apostles," but they were sent out by churches on various missions. The "official" apostles had to meet certain qualifications (see Acts 1:21-22) and, because no one today can match these requirements, there are no apostles in the church today.

Verses 17-49 are another example of the public teaching of the Savior. It has been said that this is Luke's account of the sermon on the mount. Verse 17 says that He was "on a level place" when preaching this lesson. It could have been a level section of the mountain slope. Or it could have been a different occasion with a different crowd of people where Jesus repeated many of the lessons that He also taught to a different group on another occasion (Matthew 5-7). There are enough differences in the messages to believe that they are not the same sermon. But He does include many things here that are dealt with in Matthew's sermon on the mount.

The section begins with some Beatitude like points; then He pronounces some woes on those who do not obey and serve God. He speaks about loving your enemies, about being careful when you judge others to do so with righteous judgment and reminds them (and us) that good deeds come from a good heart and evil deeds from a wicked one. He concludes with the parable about building our lives on a solid foundation of God's will and not the shifting sands of human wisdom. "But why do you call Me 'Lord, Lord,' and not do the things which I say?" We should ask ourselves that question every day.

## Luke 7

Jesus next goes to Capernaum where He is approached by "the elders of the Jews" on behalf of a Roman centurion whose servant is sick and about to die. The Jewish men ask Jesus to help the centurion because he was loyal to the Jewish people and had actually built a synagogue for them there. As Jesus is heading to the soldier's home, the centurion sends friends to the Savior; he states through them that he is a man of authority over others, but that he does not deserve to have Jesus in his house. Jesus marvels at the man's faith and, when the servants return to the house, they find that the servant has completely recovered (verses 1-10).

The next day Jesus travels to the nearby village of Nain and there He performs the miracle of raising a young man from the dead. He did so because He had compassion on this widow and wanted to comfort her. This miracle causes many to glorify God and acknowledge Jesus as "a great prophet."

John the Baptist is in prison and sends two of his disciples to Jesus to ask the simple question, "Are you the Coming One, or do we look for another?" (verses 18-23). Remember that John had baptized Jesus by this time and had seen the Spirit of God descending like a dove upon Him and had heard the voice of God saying, "This is My beloved Son, in whom I am well pleased." John had also declared in the presence of many witnesses that Jesus of Nazareth was "the Lamb of God who takes away the sin of the world!" John had learned that Jesus was the Messiah and had told others of that important truth.

But now, in prison, he wants to make sure and so he sends these disciples to plainly ask Jesus, Are You the Coming One? Jesus performs many miracles in response to their question and, by those mighty works, answers John's final doubts.

It is not wrong to doubt or to question our faith. But we must go to the right source to find the right answer. We will not find the answer to our doubts in human philosophy or man-made creeds or higher education in the liberal arts. We will find the answer to all our doubts in the inspired word of God (Acts 17:11). God in His word will remove all our questions and relieve all our fears.

After the disciples of John had left to return and report back to him, Jesus spoke to the multitudes about the importance of John in God's plan (verses 24-30). He asks a series of questions about what the people thought about John. Did they consider him a "reed shaken by the wind?" Were they looking for "a man clothed in soft garments?" Was John just another prophet?

Christ says that John was "more than a prophet." He was a prophet, of course. But he was also the prophetic forerunner of the Savior, as we recently noticed. The Lord quotes Malachi 3:1, another Old Testament prophecy which had foretold John's commission. That's why the Master says that "among those born of women there is not a greater prophet than John the Baptist." What a powerful and gracious commendation from the Lord. But then notice that Jesus says, "he who is least in the kingdom of God is greater than he." Do you realize who that is? You and me and every Christian who has ever lived and ever will. We hold a more important place in God's plan than even the great prophet, John. Do you realize how important you are to God? Shouldn't that cause us to live better?

Verses 36-50 contain the account of Jesus in the home of a prominent Pharisee. While eating there with this man, "a woman in the city who was a sinner" comes in and anoints the feet of Jesus with an alabaster flask of fragrant oil. The Pharisees are upset that He allows a "sinner" to touch Him. Jesus responds with a short parable about two men who owe differing amounts of money to a creditor. He shows that the one who owes the greater amount will appreciate being forgiven of the debt. He points out that this woman will be more grateful to God for her forgiveness than the others who had less sin.

# Luke 8

Chapter 8 begins by introducing us to several women who helped Jesus (verses 1-3). There is nothing remarkable about any of these women, to be honest. Mary Magdalene is the most well known of the group and we are told that she had formerly been possessed by seven demons. That must have been an unbelievably terrifying experience for her. She showed her gratitude to Jesus by following Him and helping to provide for him, likely with obtaining and preparing food for the Master and His followers as they traveled through cities and villages, preaching the good news of the kingdom. Two other ladies are named, Joanna whose husband was a steward for King Herod and a woman named Susanna, about whom we know nothing else. It also says "many others" helped Christ as well. They will be rewarded for their service in eternity. Women are often honored in the Bible (both testaments) because of the prominent place they held in the heart of the Savior.

Verses 4-15 contain the parable of the sower and its explanation by Jesus. It is one of the more famous parables of the Lord and it shows us that everyone who hears the good news of the kingdom responds in one of four ways. Only one group receives the blessings of obedience however. They are described as soil. representing human hearts that are "noble and good." They bear fruit for God in a way that glorifies Him and brings Him honor. We all need to examine ourselves, through the eyes of Jesus and His explanation of these soils. Are we those who reject the gospel? Are we those who start on the path to heaven and then give in to sin and temptation and fall away? Are we those whose hearts and lives are too cluttered with the activities and issues of life and leave no room for God? Are we those who love His will, do it and continue to grow in our faith and our relationship with the Savior? It is important for us to think about personal applications of teachings like this as we read and study the Bible.

In verses 16-21, Jesus' physical family (mother and brothers) come to see Him. He makes an application of this visit by referring to "those who hear the word of God and do it" as His spiritual family.

Verses 22-25 are the story of Jesus calming a storm. There were several of his miracles that involved His power over nature. It is not uncommon for Him to be on the Sea of Galilee during a windstorm that frightens the disciples. They thought their lives were in grave danger, but Jesus, who had such inner peace that He was sleeping, simply speaks to the wind and the waves and they immediately calm down. The disciples ask one another, "Who can this be?"

In verses 26-39, Jesus casts out demons from a man who is called "Legion" because many evil spirits had possessed him. He was terrorizing the people of that region with his superhuman strength and ferocity. The demons, who immediately recognize Jesus (verse 28), ask to be sent into a nearby herd of many swine. When Jesus permits them to enter the pigs, they run violently down a nearby hillside and drown in a lake. Jesus asks the healed man to tell others "what great things God has done for you."

The final section of this chapter (verses 40-56) tells the story of two powerful miracles of healing by the Savior, one of an older woman with a serious bleeding disorder and the other, an account of Jesus raising a young girl from the dead. The girl's father, a Jewish synagogue leader named Jairus, comes to Christ and begs Him to help his dying daughter. Jesus follows Him and, as they are traveling with a "multitude" of people (verse 40), a woman "having a flow of blood for twelve years" simply touches the edge of His robe and "immediately her flow of blood stopped." Jesus knows someone had been healed and looks around to see who it is. The woman tells Him in front of the crowd what she has done and Jesus instructs her to go in peace. A friend comes from Jairus' house to tell him that his daughter has died, but Jesus continues on to the residence. He then raises her from the dead. She is twelve years old which is the same length of time the older lady has been sick.

## Luke 9

This chapter (verses 1-9) opens with Jesus sending the twelve apostles (sent ones) out on what is probably their first preaching assignment. He tells them to "preach the kingdom of God" and gives them power and authority over all demons and to cure diseases. They are also told to take very little in the way of money and extra clothes (they probably didn't have many physical possessions anyway). They were to look for those who were interested in their message and to "shake off the very dust from your feet" against those who were uninterested. There are so many lost people in the world today and we often spend too much time on those who will never want to follow the Lord and too little time trying to find those who have open and honest hearts. Herod the tetrarch (his name is Antipas) hears about Christ and wonders exactly who He is. There is some concern that John the Baptist (whom Herod had beheaded) has risen from the dead. Others think Jesus might be a reincarnation of Elijah or another of the Old Testament prophets.

Verses 10-17 are Luke's account of the feeding of the 5000. This miracle is recorded in all four gospel accounts. There were actually many more people fed than that, the text simply says there were 5000 men. When you add the women and children, it could have been more like 20,000 people. Jesus takes five loaves of bread and two fish and miraculously multiplies the food to feed the large crowd following Him and listening to His teaching.

In verses 18-27, Peter makes the great confession that Jesus is the Messiah. The Savior warns them that He is going to suffer many things, be rejected by the Jewish elite and be killed, but also predicts that He will rise from the dead on the third day. In view of this event, He then tells them that they must be willing to take up their own cross (figuratively, although most of them were also killed physically in due time) and follow after Him. He reminds them that their soul is their most valuable possession and that they should not be willing to trade it for anything in the whole world.

The event called "the transfiguration" occurs in verses 28-36. Jesus takes three of the disciples onto a mountain to pray and His appearance is altered dramatically. Suddenly Moses and Elijah appear with the Messiah. The disciples suggest building a tabernacle in honor of each of these three great men and a cloud overshadows them. A voice comes from heaven and God declares Jesus to be His beloved Son and the only One they should listen to. This shows us that the Law (symbolized by Moses) and the Prophets (represented by Elijah) are being replaced by the gospel of Jesus. It is a transition from the Old Testament to the New Testament as God's law for man today.

Jesus heals a demon possessed boy in verses 37-43. The disciples had tried to heal the boy but they could not. Jesus easily rebukes the unclean spirit and the young boy is healed.

Jesus predicts His death again, the disciples argue about which of them is the greatest and there is a discussion about a Jesus follower who was not one of the twelve (verses 44-50). Christ tells them that "he who is not against us is on our side."

Some interaction with a Samaritan village is the focus of verses 51-56. There was great animosity between the Jews and the Samaritans and the apostles were included in the number of Jews who had no use whatsoever for any Samaritan (that hatred was mutual, by the way). Jesus reminds them that He came to save souls, not to destroy lives. God loves the whole world, every soul (John 3:16).

In verses 57-62, Jesus discusses the importance of putting Him first, above anything or anyone else. Three men come to Him and He shows them the level of commitment that He requires from His followers. Many Bibles call this section, The Cost of Discipleship (or the cost of following Jesus).

## Luke 10

This chapter contains perhaps the most well-known of the parables of Jesus, the Good Samaritan. There are hospitals, food pantries, free clothing centers, and other benevolent societies named after the character in this parable who cares for the man who was in need. It is found near the end of the chapter.

But first (verses 1-24), Jesus sends out seventy disciples, two by two, to prepare the way for His gospel. (Many versions say 72, rather than 70.) He reminds them that the harvest is great, but that there are not enough workers in the field. That is still the case today. We could be saving many more souls than we are today, but we just need more laborers to get busy. How long has it been since you invited someone to have a Bible study with you or the preacher or someone else who could help to save their soul? We need to pray for more and more workers to be busy about the Father's business in the harvest.

Jesus pronounces a woe upon those who will not hear the truth and repent of their sins (verses 13-16). When the workers return with joy, Jesus compares the results to Satan falling like lightning out of heaven (verses 17-20). He says that, in God's wisdom, they are experiencing what prophets and kings have desired for centuries to see, thousands of souls being won for God.

Only Luke records this story of Jesus, the parable of the Good Samaritan (verses 25-37). Even those who may not be aware that this parable is in the New Testament will refer to someone who helps another person as a good Samaritan. Among those who know the parable, many are probably not knowledgeable of the interaction between Jesus and "a certain lawyer" that preceded the telling of the story. This lawyer was testing Him, which was a common occurrence in the Lord's ministry. People were constantly trying to catch Him in some inconsistency that they could then use against Him.

The lawyer begins with a good question, "Teacher, what shall I do to inherit eternal life?" (verse 25). Christ asks him, in essence, "What does your Bible say?" The man then responds with what Jesus called in another place, the two greatest commands. Love God with all your being and love your fellow man.

But the man wanted to "justify himself." And so, he asked one more question, about who should be considered his neighbor. That's when the Savior told the parable. The interesting thing about the parable is that the one person you would least expect to help someone in need is the one person who did help. This twist in the teaching is possible because of the tremendous hatred the Jews had for anyone who was not a fellow Jew.

The Gentiles were unclean, uncircumcised and the Jews despised them. They called them dogs and other such derogatory terms. And Samaritans, if possible, were even worse than the average Gentile. They were looked upon as unclean, part Jew and part Gentile. Useless and unworthy of any spiritual consideration was the Jewish opinion of Samaritans. Yet, the Samaritan was the one who helped the man in need (by the way, he is never actually called "the Good Samaritan"). This parable is a powerful rebuke of the scribes and Pharisees, in their self-righteousness. They are represented in the parable by the priest and the Levite who do nothing to help the wounded traveler.

The Bible also praises a Samaritan in the account in Luke 17:11-19, where ten lepers are healed and only one, a Samaritan, returns to thank Jesus. Maybe the Lord is trying to teach us that every person has a soul and is important to God and needs salvation and that we should not pre-judge people based on their racial or cultural background. What do you think?

The account of Jesus in the home of Mary and Martha in Bethany (verses 38-42) teaches us about the importance of having the proper spiritual priorities. Is Jesus the most important part of your life?

## Luke 11

Chapter 11 starts with Jesus delivering the model prayer (often referred to as the Lord's Prayer) to His disciples (verses 1-4). He does so in response to their request, "Lord, teach us to pray, as John also taught his disciples." Have you ever asked a more mature Jesus follower to help you in your prayer life? This model prayer covers four important areas of life, God's will being done on earth, our daily bread (and other physical provisions from God, James 1:17), the forgiveness of our sins as believers, and help in overcoming the temptations of life.

The theme of prayer continues in verses 5-13 as Jesus tells the disciples to be persistent in their prayers and not to doubt that the heavenly Father will answer those prayers in the best way.

In verses 14-23, some people accuse Jesus of casting out demons by Beelzebub (Beelzebul, in some versions), the ruler of the demons. He points out to them that a house divided against itself cannot stand. (You thought Abraham Lincoln said that first, didn't you? Nope, it was Jesus.) He assures them that He casts out demons by "the finger of God" and not by any power from the devil.

There is an interesting lesson in verses 24-26 about those who get rid of evil in their lives needing to fill up that empty space with good things so that the sinful things cannot make their way back into the disciple's heart. Evil spirits do not possess people today as they did in New Testament times, but the spiritual principles of good and evil still apply to us.

As crowds gather around the Savior to hear His teaching, a woman (no doubt a mother, from the context) pronounces a blessing upon Mary, the mother of Jesus. Christ says that those who are truly blessed are those who hear the word of God and observe it in their lives.

When they ask Jesus for a sign that He is truly from God, He tells them to think back to the Old Testament account of Jonah and the big fish. (Jonah was three days and three nights in the belly of the great fish just as He will be three days and nights in the grave until His resurrection; Matthew 12:40.) He also refers to the Queen of Sheba who came to observe the wisdom and wealth of Solomon. He says that He is greater than Solomon and the people of Nineveh and that they should listen to Him if they wish to please God.

Verses 33-36 use the illustration of physical eyes seeing the light and it is comparing that to the wisdom of seeing the truth that He is preaching, so that they will not walk in darkness, but in the light of God's truth.

In verses 37-54, the Messiah is invited into the home of a Pharisee to eat a meal. Jesus uses this opportunity to condemn the general attitude of the Pharisees and lawyers (experts in the law, NIV). Some of the strongest teaching of Jesus is found in this section of Luke's gospel. He criticizes their hypocrisy and their external self-righteousness compared with their internal greed and wickedness. He pronounces a series of six woes upon them (the very opposite of the blessings they were looking for). He compares their wickedness and sin to the vile crimes committed by their forefathers during the time of the Old Testament; they were guilty of persecuting and murdering the prophets who had been sent to help them get closer to God (verses 47-51). In verse 52, He accuses them of taking away the key of knowledge from the people who wanted to learn God's will and obey it in their lives.

The chapter ends with great strife between Jesus and the religious leaders of the day (verses 53-54). They are determined to find something to use against Jesus, in order that they might justify themselves and to be able to have Jesus put to death.

# Luke 12

Verses 1-12 seem to be a typical day with Jesus teaching large groups of people who were constantly finding Him, waiting for an opportunity to hear Him. He deals with a number of subjects in these verses, from warning them about the false teaching (leaven) of the Pharisees, which He calls hypocrisy, to the reality that God knows everything that goes on in peoples' lives, even if others do not, to telling them that they should fear (respect) God more than worrying about what other people might think about them. He encourages them to confess Him in their daily lives and not to deny Him by the choices they make. He makes a promise (verses 11-12) that, if they are arrested for their faith in Him, the Holy Spirit will help them in such situations to say the best and right thing. Other contexts indicate that this was a specific promise to His future apostles, not a general assurance for everyone.

The Parable of the Rich Fool is found only in the gospel of Luke, here in verses 13-21. The context (or setting) of this parable is interesting. Jesus has been teaching, as usual, the message of God. The first twelve verses of this chapter were delivered to "an innumerable multitude of people" who were gathering around Him to hear His teaching. As a matter of perspective, when Jesus fed the 5000 men with the loaves and fishes, that was a lot of people, but not an innumerable crowd. This was obviously even more than that, maybe many more. Imagine if you had been in that company of people, having the opportunity to listen to the Messiah as He was teaching words from God.

Right in the midst of His comments, a man from the crowd interrupts the spiritual feast to ask Jesus to mediate a financial dispute between him and his brother (verse 13). Christ quickly points out to him that He didn't come into the world to handle such matters and then states clearly that they all needed to beware of covetousness, "for one's life does not consist of the abundance of the things he possesses" (verse 15).

Jesus then delivers a parable about a successful farmer, from an earthly perspective, whose value system is out of touch with one who wanted to serve God. His crops are plentiful, so much so that he will have to build bigger facilities just to store them. He is essentially set for life. But he dies that very night, leaving all of his material possessions to others. The farmer indicates nothing to tell us he has a relationship with God, the one from whom all blessings flow (James 1:17). There is nothing that would lead us to believe he planned to use any of his money or possessions to bless others. Someone has said that the man obviously had "I" disease, for he only spoke of himself and what he had accomplished and what he would do for himself. He uses the words "I" and "my" ten times in his short speech.

He was prepared to live a long time and to "eat, drink and be merry" for many years. But he wasn't prepared to die. Which preparation is more important, really? And do we realize that is true in our own lives as clearly as we can see it about this man? Christ calls this one a fool for failing to think beyond the material things he owns. Materialism can be a deadly, captivating sin. Jesus concludes the parable by saying this: "So is he who lays up treasure for himself, and is not rich toward God." That was said for the man who was mad at his brother and for the others who were there in that "innumerable multitude." And it has been preserved in the Bible for us today to learn from, as well. As Jesus often says, on many similar occasions, "He who has an ear, let him hear."

Verses 22-34 emphasize the priority of the spiritual over the physical and that they should trust God in all things. Verses 35-53 distinguish between faithful and evil servants, the former doing the will of the Father and the latter failing to do right. The final verses, 54-59 speak of the importance of discernment in all that they do. God expects us to use wisdom as we represent Him and the gospel in our daily lives. It is important for us to honor and glorify God in all that we do.

## Luke 13

Verses 1-5 deal with the subject of repentance. Jesus is teaching us that all those who sin (and that's all of us; Romans 3:23) need to repent. What is repentance? It is a turning away from something, a change of mind. From a biblical point of view, it refers to turning away from sin and turning toward God.

What is the result of repentance? What happens when people repent? They then must show their repentance by their changed lives. What would be some examples of this? If you use bad language, stop. If you steal, stop. If you lie, stop. If you are materialistic, start being generous with others. Some people have referred to repentance as the most difficult of all commands. Do you agree with that?

Jesus followed up this teaching with a parable in verses 6-9. It is short, but powerful. Its lessons should serve as a warning to each of us. The purpose of a fig tree is to bear figs. That may seem like a foolish statement, but it is important for us to realize that the Lord was not really talking about trees, but people. The primary application of this parable was for the Jewish people of the first century. The Messiah was living in their midst and they did not accept Him. "He came to His own, and His own did not receive Him (John 1:11). When Christ first delivered the parable, it was not too late for them to change. But if they did not repent, they would be "cut down." Unfortunately, they did not repent and the nation was destroyed in A.D. 70.

Notice that the fig tree in the parable was given a second chance to bear fruit, one more year to do better. If not, it would be cut down. Do you need to do better? How many "second chances" do you need? If you need to repent of sin in your life, maybe this lesson of the fruitless fig tree will help.

As Jesus taught in a Jewish synagogue (verses 10-17), a woman with "a spirit of infirmity" is brought to Him; she was "bent over," could not stand up straight, and had been in that condition for 18 years. Jesus healed her but was immediately criticized for "working" on the Sabbath. No human compassion is seen from the ruler of the synagogue and his friends.

The parable of the mustard seed is found in verses 18-19. The emphasis in this parable is that the kingdom of the Lord (His church) would begin small and grow until it had covered the whole earth. If only a few Christians live in a community, if they will band together in love and unity and faithfulness to God and His word, great things can happen. It also shows us that when we do seemingly small and insignificant things for God, He can accomplish much through our efforts. All too often, we are hesitant to do the little things, perhaps because we are looking to do bigger things. We should learn that the small things we do in the kingdom can make a big difference in peoples' lives and in their eternal destiny.

Verses 20-21 contains the parable of the leaven. Many people believe this is teaching the same lesson as the mustard seed, that something small can grow and become bigger. And perhaps that is true. But it is also possible that He is warning us about the malevolent influence of seemingly small and insignificant wrong deeds we may do. They too can grow and become worse and worse as time goes on. In the church and in our personal lives, sin may start small but it grows and the consequences can be very serious indeed.

Verses 22-33 detail some of Jesus' travels toward Jerusalem as He taught in various cities and villages. He emphasized the narrow gate that leads to life and called those who opposed Him "you workers of iniquity." When warned that Herod (Antipas) was looking for Him, Jesus fearlessly says that He will continue to do God's will. In verses 34-35, the Redeemer laments over the lost condition of the city of Jerusalem.

## Luke 14

As we study Luke 14:1-14, it is important to remember that two groups of people in the New Testament watched Jesus closely. One group was searching for truth and thought that He might be the promised Messiah of Old Testament history. The other group was searching for something to use against Him to justify their decision to reject Him as the Messiah (or Christ).

One group allowed the miracles of Jesus, such as healing the man with dropsy, to convince them that Jesus was truly a man from God. The other group became outraged because He healed the man on the Sabbath. Today, some people read the New Testament and become convinced that Jesus is the Savior, while others read the same accounts and turn away from Him. 1 Corinthians 2:14-15 describe these two types of hearts as "the natural man" and "he who is spiritual." It has been said that the same sun that hardens bricks (a hard heart) also melts butter (a soft and tender heart).

When Jesus pointed out the inconsistency of the lawyers and the Pharisees, they had nothing further to say (verses 3-6). The Savior told this parable (verses 7-14) in response to those who "chose the best places," apparently the seats closest to the most powerful and influential people. There have always been, and always will be, those who want to be close to the rich and powerful, not because of true friendship, but because of the advantages those people can offer.

Christ told His hearers not to sit in the places of prominence, when invited to a formal occasion. He described a situation where someone takes the best seat and then is replaced by the host for "one more honorable than you." His advice was to take the lowest place and then when the host asks you to move to a higher position, "you will have glory in the presence of those who sit at the table with you." Then Jesus gave some specific instructions to His host, one of the rulers of the Pharisees. He told him not to invite people to a meal who could repay him by inviting him in return to their homes.

This is a word of encouragement for people to invite the disadvantaged. He specifies "the poor, the maimed, the lame, the blind." The Lord is reminding all of us that we need to care for those who have a difficult time in life. Many don't even have the basic necessities for survival. Helping others is more important than helping ourselves by including only those who can repay us.

The parable of the great banquet is recorded in verses 15-24. This parable was told in response to a man who was dining with Jesus and who heard the Master discuss the need for humility. This man stated, "Blessed is he who shall eat bread in the kingdom of God!"

Jesus tells the story of a man who gave a great feast and invited many people to attend. But most of the people who were invited, rather than to appreciate the great honor of being a guest of this man, began to make excuses for why they would not attend the banquet.

The primary teaching of the parable had to do with the Jews' rejection of Jesus as Messiah. Although given the first opportunity to obey the Lord under the new covenant, the Bible tells us that "He came to His own, and His own did not receive Him" (John 1:11). The gospel is said to be the power of God for salvation, "to the Jew first" (Romans 1:16).

There is an important application of this parable to all people, however, and not just to disobedient Jews. The Savior has invited everyone to His great banquet (Matthew 11:28-30). But, of course, both in the first century and now, many souls continue to rebel against God.

Verses 25-35 are an important conclusion to this chapter and remind us that it is important for new believers to count the cost of following Jesus and be willing to give their all in His service.

## Luke 15

"Then all the tax collectors and the sinners drew near to Him to hear Him. And the Pharisees and scribes complained, saying, 'This Man receives sinners and eats with them'" (Luke 15:1-2). With these words, one of the most beautiful chapters in the Bible begins. Verse 3 continues on and says, "So He spoke this parable to them, saying:" Although the text says, this parable, Jesus actually delivers three parables, the lost sheep (verses 4-7), the lost coin (verses 8-10), and the lost sons (verses 11-32). While the illustration is different in each, the main lesson is the same. God loves the souls of the lost and wants all people to be saved (1 Timothy 2:3-4).

First is the parable of the lost sheep. In the story, a shepherd watching over 100 sheep realizes that one of them has wandered away. He leaves the 99 "safe" sheep and goes to search for the one which is lost. He continues to look for it until he locates it and then brings it back triumphantly and adds it back into the fold. Verses 6-7 give us a "behind the scenes" look at heaven's response when a lost soul returns to God. The parable is reminding us how much the Lord loves us and how much "joy" there is in heaven when "one sinner" repents.

His second example is a woman who owns ten coins and loses one of them. Some have suggested this might refer to a piece of jewelry that had ten coins in it as decoration (much like diamonds or other jewels) and that the loss of one piece makes the entire thing worthless. Or it might simply be speaking of her personal worth of ten coins. Either way, the lesson is that the lost coin meant a great deal to her and so she turned on the light, swept the house and searched carefully until she recovered the coin. And again, Jesus lets us know that this lost coin, now found, represents "one sinner who repents." We should never underestimate the value of one soul. The Savior taught us, in another setting, that one soul is worth more than the whole world (Matthew 16:26).

That should cause us all to make certain that our own soul is in a right relationship with God. If it isn't, not much else matters. It should also help us, as Christians, to remember once again the value of the souls around us who do not know our Lord. Will we be like the scribes and Pharisees who hated the lost or like the Lord who loves all souls and wants them to be saved?

In verses 11-32, the parable of the prodigal son is one of the most famous of all the parables. Luke 15 has been referred to as "the gospel in the gospel," since it tells us of the love of our Heavenly Father for lost souls. A man has two sons and the younger one decides he didn't want to live at home and follow his father's rules. He asks for his part of the inheritance, which was unusual, of course. Normally, one does not inherit something from another until that person had died. But the Father grants his request (perhaps this is symbolic of our free will and God's willingness to allow us to make wrong, really foolish decisions). The young man heads off to a far country (any place away from his father). This, in itself, is a parabolic picture of sin. The consequences of his choice are significant and severe. He soon wastes all of his inheritance with wild and ungodly behavior. His friends, no doubt abundant when he had plenty of money, quickly desert him. Unable to survive for long, he gets a job feeding pigs.

Brought to his senses by his memory of the things he had learned from his father, he repents ("when he came to himself"), and walks home in shame and disgrace. His loving father sees him coming from afar and runs to meet him (something quite undignified for Jewish father). He welcomes him home and throws him a party. The older brother, who has stayed at home and served and obeyed their Father, is not at all happy to see his younger sibling. He is jealous of the love the Father still has for his foolish and rebellious child. Jesus is driving the lesson home to the envious tax collectors and sinners (verses 1-2) who didn't understand why Christ spent time with sinners. He just wanted to save them. He still does.

## Luke 16

Found in verses 1-13, the Parable of the Unjust Steward is widely regarded as the most difficult of the parables of Christ. But in spite of the challenges in interpreting this parable, there are some important principles found here that teach valuable lessons.

The main character in the story is the steward himself. A steward is a manager or overseer of another person's property. The master is the actual owner. Verse 1 says that the steward was accused by others of dishonesty. In the parable, the owner believes the accusations and fires the steward. Jesus does describe him as "the unjust steward" (verse 8), so apparently the charges are true.

There were two debtors. When the steward realized he was losing his job, he forgave both of a portion of their debt, one by 50% and one by 20%. The other primary character is the master, called "a certain rich man" (verse 1).

There are several things we are not supposed to learn from this parable. It is not recommending dishonesty. The master commended the steward for acting shrewdly (or wisely, KJV). But he did not reward him by giving him his job back. The Bible never condones dishonesty. The parable also does not suggest that we bribe people to get them to do what we want. And it does not tell us that if we are good managers of our money that this will secure us a home in heaven.

What it does teach us is that being wise (or shrewd) is always more beneficial to us than being foolish or dishonest. The word translated as "shrewdly" (Greek – PHRONIMOS) means prudently, sensibly or practically wise. It is the same word used to describe the man who builds his house on the rock and the five virgins who made the appropriate preparation for the wedding. Jesus makes the point that at times "the sons of light" can learn some lessons from "the sons of this world" (verse 8). Non-Christians often behave more prudently and sensibly than some disciples of Jesus. Christ wants us to be faithful in all areas of our lives (verses 10-11). If we are going to be loyal to the Lord, we must be wise, faithful and dependable in all things. The Savior does not say it is hard to serve God and mammon (money). He says it "cannot" be done.

Verses 14-18 teach us spiritual lessons about several subjects, including men's hearts, the law and the prophets, the kingdom of God and divorce and remarriage. It is quite an eclectic set of issues that the Savior deals with here. There doesn't seem (to me anyway) to be a single thread that connects all of these matters, but that's probably because Jesus has a depth of understanding that we can only dream about.

Verses 19-31 are the account of the rich man and Lazarus. Some people believe this to be a parable; others understand it to be a literal story about the life and death of two real people. It doesn't change the meaning of the passage either way you think about it.

This text teaches us about Hades, the realm of the dead. It is an unseen spirit world, where all souls go when physical death occurs. Death is not annihilation, but rather a separation of the human spirit from the physical body (Ecclesiastes 12:7). Hades consists of two "sections," both described here. Those who are saved go to "Abraham's bosom" or "side" (NIV), elsewhere described as Paradise (as in Luke 23:43). Those who are lost go to a place of torment (compare to 2 Peter 2:4, translated as hell from the Greek word, TARTARUS). There is "a great gulf" fixed between the two, so that no one can pass from one to the other. After the final judgment, those in Paradise will go to heaven. Those in torment will live forever in hell, a place of great darkness, sorrow, weeping and gnashing of teeth (see Matthew 25:46).

# Luke 17

Verses 1-10 deal primarily with the subject of forgiving others. The New Testament has much to say about forgiveness. Because we are all sinful, fallible people, we make mistakes and do wrong things. Sometimes these sins are against God and sometimes we do wrong things to other people. When we are the ones sinned against, it falls to us to forgive others. That is often not easy. But when we think about those times when we are the ones who have done wrong, we know we would like to be forgiven. We need to offer that same degree of mercy and grace toward those who have done wrong things to us.

There are many examples in the Bible of human beings forgiving their fellow man. Esau forgave Jacob (Genesis 33), Joseph forgave his brothers (Genesis 45), Moses forgave the Israelites (Exodus 32), David forgave King Saul (1 Samuel 24 and 26), David forgave Absalom (2 Samuel 15), Solomon forgave Adonijah (1 Kings 1). In the New Testament, Stephen asked God to forgive those who were stoning him to death (Acts 7), Paul was willing to be lost if it meant his fellow Jews who persecuted him could be saved (Romans 9) and Jesus pleaded for the forgiveness of those who were crucifying Him (Luke 23:34). And, as Christians we must never forget that we are not perfect; we are all forgiven sinners (Romans 3:23). If we had not received God's mercy in forgiveness, we would all be lost. That's what we deserve.

How slow we are at times to forgive others. Jesus is emphasizing in this text that we need to practice the forgiveness we desire and preach. If you do not forgive others, your heart will be filled with bitterness, animosity and anger. I have never met a bitter person who had any joy (which is a fruit of the Spirit, Galatians 5:22-23). When we are unwilling to forgive others, God warns us that He will withhold forgiveness from us. That's the whole point of the parable of the two servants in Matthew 18:21-35. And, in the model prayer found in Matthew 6, Jesus concluded by saying, "For if you forgive men their trespasses, your heavenly Father will also forgive you. But if you do not forgive men their trespasses, neither will your Father forgive your trespasses" (verses 14-15). We need forgiveness, so we must forgive others.

In verses 11-19, we read about Jesus healing ten lepers. In Bible times, leprosy was an incurable disease that ultimately led to death. The power of the Savior is on full display here, as He miraculously heals ten lepers at the same time. He tells them to go and show themselves to the priest (according to the Law of Moses in Leviticus 13 and 14). When they realize they have been cleansed, one leper, a Samaritan, returns to thank Jesus for this gift. His power proves to us that He is from God (John 3:2; 20:30-31). It also confirms His claims to be the Son of God. There is an important lesson here for us about gratitude. We should be thankful for all of the blessings God gives us, both physical and spiritual (Colossians 3:15; Hebrews 13:15). It is hard to imagine, as you read this story, that the other nine men did not have it in their hearts to thank the Lord for their healing. Perhaps they thanked God the Father in prayer, but they should have returned with the Samaritan to thank God the Son as well. He was disappointed that they did not. Let's be careful not to be ungrateful for all God has done for us.

Verses 20-37 record some information about the coming of the kingdom and God's judgment. When the Pharisees ask Him about the kingdom, He responds by telling them it was not going to be a single event like the Super Bowl or the World Series. It would occur one person at a time as people give their lives to Jesus and make Him the Lord of their lives. It would happen in the hearts and minds of people as long as the world stands, beginning on the first Pentecost after His resurrection and would continue to exist as long as people put Him first in their lives. He warns them that, "first" (verse 25), He would be rejected by His own people (John 1:11) and they would disobey God, in a similar way to the days of Noah and the disobedience of Sodom and Gomorrah, and this would result in the destruction of the Jewish nation at the hands of the Roman Empire. He tells them to obey God and never look back (verse 32).

## Luke 18

The first parable in this chapter is found in verses 1-8. There are two characters in the parable. The first is an unjust judge who does not fear God and who does not respect other men, that is, he does not care what others think about him. The second is a widow who comes pleading for justice. She is helpless on her own and could never have received what was fair and right without help from another. She asks him, "Give me legal protection from my opponent" (NASB, 1995).

The reason the judge is called "unjust" is that the widow deserves this legal protection and he has failed to provide it for her. He refuses to do the right thing initially and is lazy, corrupt, and indifferent to the sufferings of others. Of course, we serve a just God. Christ is not pointing out a similarity between the two, but rather a difference. Everything this judge is (unjust, reluctant to help, selfish), God is not. God will always do the right thing. He will respond to our patient, persistent and heartfelt prayers.

Sometimes God says no or not right now or He answers our prayers differently than we wanted. But in His wisdom, God knows what is best and when is best. Why did the woman keep asking? What if she had quit asking? Do we quit asking Him too soon sometimes? Those are some important questions we need to ask ourselves. Notice how the Holy Spirit began this chapter: "Then He spoke a parable to them, that men always ought to pray, and not lose heart" (Luke 18:1). Don't grow discouraged; keep praying in faith (verse 8).

The parable of the Pharisee and the Tax Collector is recorded in verses 9-14. According to verse 9, Jesus spoke this parable to the self-righteous (that's always someone else, but not me, right?). And while both men went into the temple to pray, this is really not about prayer. The primary lesson of this parable is pride versus humility. Prayer is simply the example Jesus uses to teach us that important lesson.

The Pharisee was well respected in society and probably considered to be a religious leader. The tax collector would have been hated by almost everyone (everybody, that is, except Christ). The Pharisee's prayer is found in verses 11-12. It is not really a prayer. It is a list of accomplishments reminding God of how good he is, especially when compared with others. He wants to make certain God knows how fortunate He is to have this Pharisee on His side. The tax collector's prayer (verse 13) is a humble plea for divine forgiveness. He acknowledges his guilt before God and simply asks for pardon. He even "stood afar off," symbolizing his separation from God because of his own disobedience. He knows he is a sinner. The tax collector went home forgiven, because that was what he had asked for. The Pharisee did not, because he had not asked for forgiveness and, in reality, didn't think he needed forgiveness.

We see Jesus interacting with little children and infants in verses 15-17 and He tells His disciples who are displeased with the parents for bringing them to Him that "of such is the kingdom of God." We must all humble ourselves "as a little child" to be pleasing to God. Doesn't that show us that the doctrine of total hereditary depravity is wrong? Children are innocent and pure in the sight of God until they reach an age where they know right from wrong and choose to sin. Sin isn't something you inherit from your parents or from Adam, but rather something an accountable person before God commits by personal choice.

Verses 18-34 tell us about Jesus meeting one whom we have come to call the rich, young ruler who asks the Savior about eternal life. Christ sees that he is in love with his riches and so He calls the young man to give all that up and follow Him. As He takes the twelve aside, He tells them again about His death and resurrection. This is the third time He has told them He will be put to death (9:21-22; 9:43-45; 18:31-34).

The final section of the chapter (verses 35-43) informs us about the healing of a blind man, which causes "all the people," to praise God.

## Luke 19

The account of Jesus meeting with Zacchaeus is recorded in verses 1-10. The setting is the city of Jericho. Zacchaeus is a wealthy, chief tax collector who literally climbs up in a sycamore tree to catch a glimpse of the Messiah. Jesus calls him down from the tree, goes to his home to eat with the man and, when Zacchaeus repents of cheating people, Jesus announces his salvation. That is why the Savior came to the earth in the first place, to seek and save those who are lost (verse 10).

Found in Luke 19:11-27, this parable of the minas is similar to the parable of the talents from Matthew 25:14-30. In the parable, a "certain nobleman" is the lead character. He is obviously a man of means and authority. He goes to a far country "to receive for himself a kingdom." This would indicate to us that he was a person of royalty, as a king he would be the most powerful man in that kingdom.

He is also a man of wealth, as we see that he has many servants. It doesn't say that he called every one of his servants, although that would be a lot of servants anyway. But rather, the text says that he called ten of his servants, which would indicate that he actually had many more than that, but just used ten of them in this business venture.

He gave them each a mina. Like the parable of the talents, this refers to an amount of money that he distributed. Unlike the parable of the talents, where three men were given money, "each according to his ability," in this story, ten men receive one mina each. A mina was approximately three months' wages, so its value was considerable. They were expected to invest the money after he left.

As with the talents, these servants were expected to invest this money wisely and to increase its value. That's what people who work for others are expected to do. They are to take what they are given and to make more money for their employer.

Why would some of the servants (at least one is specifically stated, only three of the ten are addressed) not do what they should have with their master's money? The answer he gave was that he was afraid of doing something wrong with the mina, so he didn't do anything with it. Was that a reason or an excuse? The nobleman was not pleased, leading us to conclude that it was a poor and rejected excuse.

The question for us is, what are we doing with what the Lord has given us? Are we serving Him faithfully with our time and abilities or are we trying to make excuses for not doing so? Is Jesus really the Lord of your life or are you just taking up space and wasting your life? Read Luke 19:27 again for the chilling conclusion to this parable.

What has come to be called Jesus' triumphal entry into Jerusalem is recorded in verses 28-40. He rides humbly on a donkey as the people spread their clothes on the road, rejoice greatly and praise God with a loud voice for all the mighty deeds He has done. This fulfills the Messianic prophecy found in Psalm 118:26. The Pharisees call on Him to rebuke the disciples, but Jesus says that, if they kept silent, "the stones would immediately cry out." Isn't that fascinating? What would the Pharisees have done then?

In verses 41-44, Jesus weeps over the spiritual condition of the city of Jerusalem because of their rejection of Him as the Messiah. It saddened Him that many would not accept Him as their Savior.

In verses 45-48, the Lord cleanses the temple and accuses them of turning God's house of prayer into a den of thieves (Isaiah 56:7 and Jeremiah 7:11). As He teaches daily in the temple, the chief priests, scribes and leaders of the people want to destroy Him, but the people in general are "very attentive to hear Him." It must have been something really special to hear Him speak as He did.

## Luke 20

The first section of Chapter 20 (verses 1-8) describes a confrontation between the Son of God and the scribes and chief priests. This follows the cleansing of the temple at the end of Chapter 19. This was likely a pretty good money making enterprise for the religious leaders and they didn't appreciate what Jesus did. They ask Him pointedly, "Tell us by what authority are You doing these things? Or who is he who gave You this authority?" In response Jesus says He has a question for them. "The baptism of John – was it from heaven or from men?" If they had answered His question correctly, that it came from heaven, then they would have had the answer to their questions. But they could not admit that because they had not accepted John's baptism. They also could not claim it was from men because "all the people" knew John was a prophet. They refused to answer Him and Jesus did not answer them either.

The parable of the wicked vinedressers is found in verses 9-18 and also in Matthew 21:33-46 and Mark 12:1-12. The story is simple, as most of the parables are. A wealthy landowner buys a vineyard, builds a guard tower in it and goes away, leasing the vineyard to vinedressers. When he sends servants to collect his share at the harvest time (after the vinedressers have been paid their fair wages), the vinedressers mistreat and kill various messengers. The landowner then sends his son whom they also kill, so he destroys the vinedressers and leases the property to others. In verse 19, the chief priests and Pharisees realized that Jesus was referring to them and wanted to kill Christ, but could not because "the people" considered Him to be a prophet.

In the midst of this parable, the Lord quotes from Psalm 118:22-23. "The stone which the builders rejected has become the chief cornerstone. This was the Lord's doing and it is marvelous in our eyes." This Messianic psalm is quoted numerous times in the New Testament and, in each case, refers to those who did not accept Jesus to be the prophesied and rejected Messiah of Old Testament scripture. In Acts 4:11, it is used to refer to those rulers and elders of Israel who were condemning Peter and John, as well as the rest of the apostles, for healing a lame man in the name of Jesus (the healing itself took place in Acts 3:1-11). The apostles were using this miracle to confirm their message of resurrection from the dead (4:1-2). The Jewish leaders could not deny that a powerful miracle had occurred (4:16) but they did not want the news of the healing to spread any further. In 1 Peter 2:7, this Old Testament passage is quoted also, along with two others that taught the same lesson, Isaiah 28:16 and Isaiah 8:14. Peter mentions those who rejected Jesus of Nazareth as the Messiah and refers to them as being "disobedient to the word." Anyone with an open mind and an open heart should have easily recognized that Jesus was exactly who and what had been foretold in the old covenant.

This passage from Psalm 118 and the others mentioned above, as well as many others we have not listed, should convince us that the doctrine of premillennialism is false. That theory is based on the view that Jesus came to establish an earthly kingdom, but was unable to do so because He was unexpectedly rejected by His own people (John 1:11). God knew all along that most of the Israelite people would not accept and obey the Christ when He came into the world. God also foreknew that Jesus would not only be rejected, but also killed by those unbelievers. As a matter of fact, Psalm 118 goes so far as to say, "This was the Lord's doing." He did not make them reject Jesus, but He knew they would and He used their disbelief and rebellion to fulfill His plan of human redemption.

In verses 20-26, the Jews try to trick Jesus with a question about whether Jews should pay taxes to Rome. When Jesus easily handles that issue, the Sadducees invent an imaginary story about seven brothers who all marry the same poor woman without any of them having children (verses 27-40). Whose wife will she be in the resurrection? Again, He quickly dispatches their question. In verses 41-47 there is more conflict with the Jewish leaders. They keep trying but they cannot get an edge on Jesus.

## Luke 21

The events of verses 1-4 actually belong contextually to the things in the previous chapter. We are told about a poor widow who comes to the temple and puts her entire livelihood (two mites) into the treasury. She is often used as a godly example of one who loves the Lord so much that she gives Him everything she has. Churches and preachers often tell this story in an attempt to encourage sacrificial giving to God. Those principles about sacrificial giving are biblical and important. Many verses in the New Testament tell us to be willing to sacrifice physical possessions in order to lay up treasures in heaven. But nowhere does the Bible ask us to give everything to God so that we have absolutely nothing left to eat or wear or dwell in. God blesses us materially so we might survive in this world and He does want us to return some of that to Him. But He does not expect us to give the whole of our material blessings in His service. However, that's what the scribes and Pharisees demanded (go back and re-read Luke 20:45-47). Remember that the chapter and verse divisions were added later and realize that there is a direct connection between the end of Chapter 20 and the beginning of Chapter 21. One of the accusations Jesus made against the scribes was that they "devour widows' houses." That's what this poor widow is an example of, not sacrificial giving. Now we don't know her heart, of course. She may have graciously and lovingly given everything to God because she wanted to. Or she might have been forced to do so by the money hungry, greedy scribes and Pharisees who cared more for their own comfort and satisfaction than they ever cared about really serving God from the heart.

The rest of this chapter (verses 5-38) talks about the destruction of Jerusalem. This event happened in A.D. 70. Jesus told about it in A.D. 33, 37 years before it happened. In A.D. 66, the Jews, who were ruled by the Romans, rebelled against their authority. Two Roman generals, Vespasian and Titus, led their armies against Jerusalem to dismantle this uprising. Vespasian began this conquest, but was called back to Rome to become the emperor. Titus, Vespasian's son, was the one in charge when the desolation was completed. They destroyed the city, killing many people and also demolishing the temple.

As they are standing in front of the elaborately beautiful Jewish temple, Jesus comments that "the days will come in which not one stone shall be left upon another that shall not be thrown down" (verse 6). That provides the context (setting) for the rest of the teaching in this chapter.

The Jews in the first century were convinced that they would never be defeated, because they believed that God would always protect them, due to the presence of the temple. To them, it was proof that God was on their side. It is interesting to note, in Jeremiah 7, that the Old Testament Jews thought the same thing. However God allowed Babylon to destroy the original temple of Solomon, because of the peoples' sin and used that destruction to emphasize that even God's people will be punished for rebellion. The whole 70 year captivity in Babylon should have been evidence to the first century Israelites that the presence of God's temple (at this time, the one built by Zerubbabel) did not mean they could do anything they wanted and still be safe from God's judgment.

Many people today use passages like this one (along with Matthew 24 and Mark 13) to talk about the second coming of Christ at the end of time. But clearly, Jesus is speaking of something that was going to occur in their lifetime. "Assuredly, I say to you, this generation will by no means pass away till all things take place" (verse 32). False teachers will try to convince people that Jesus simply means these events will occur in a single generation, whenever that might be. But the Lord didn't say, in a single generation, He said "this generation." It included the people to whom He was teaching, and even the apostles. The judgment He describes would occur in their generation, in their lifetime.

In verses 34-37, He tells them to "take heed" and "watch" so that these events, the destruction of Jerusalem, would not come upon them unexpectedly. They were forewarned and should be prepared.

## Luke 22

The events of this chapter are often referred to as the Last Supper because the text tells us about the final meal that Jesus and the apostles ate together before His betrayal, arrest and crucifixion. They will eat more meals together after His resurrection, of course.

At this gathering, the Lord takes the opportunity to teach the apostles some final important lessons. They will also talk with Jesus after the resurrection, in those final forty days before His ascension. But this event, immediately before His betrayal, contains their last instructions before His death.

It is a close, personal encounter between the Master and His servants and Jesus takes advantage of the opportunity to try to strengthen their resolve to be faithful and carry out the tasks He has assigned to them. It is also on this occasion that Jesus institutes the Lord's Supper, the touching memorial to His death that Christians today observe every Lord's Day. Many more details are found in John 13-17.

Immediately after the Last Supper, Jesus takes the eleven disciples to the Garden of Gethsemane. Jesus, along with Peter, James and John, goes apart from the main group to pray. But the three apostles are sleepy and so they fall asleep, leaving Jesus to pray alone.

The Lord knows what is about to happen. Although He has warned the apostles during the Last Supper about His impending arrest, they either didn't understand what He was saying or didn't realize that His betrayal and subsequent arrest are imminent.

In the Garden, Jesus faces one of the most heartbreaking of human experiences, the betrayal of a close friend. Judas Iscariot, who has been paid thirty pieces of silver to lead the soldiers to Christ, shows up and turns Jesus over to the guards with a betrayal kiss.

We see in this account the agony that the Savior endured (sweating drops of blood), His determination to obey God the Father no matter what ("Not My will, but Yours be done"), and his humanity (which gives us a perfect example to follow). Perhaps the most striking lesson from the Garden is the contrast between the ever-obedient Christ and the unprepared, spiritually immature disciples, who all flee when Jesus is apprehended.

When Jesus is taken into custody in the Garden of Gethsemane, the Bible tells us that all of the disciples flee. They are concerned for their own safety and thought perhaps that some of them might be arrested as well.

We learn that Peter follows Jesus, but at a distance. When he gets to the judgment hall, he is let into the courtyard by John, who knew the high priest. As he warms himself by the fire, against the chilly night air, he is asked three times if he is a disciple of Jesus. Each time, he claims that he does not even know who Jesus is.

Of course, just earlier that evening, Christ had warned Peter that this would happen. Peter adamantly claimed that he would rather die than to deny His Lord. But deny Him he did.

Luke tells us (verses 59-62) that after the third denial, the rooster crows, just as Jesus had predicted. But then it adds, "And the Lord turned and looked at Peter." Peter leaves and weeps bitterly. It is almost impossible for us to imagine how he must have felt at that moment.

We must be careful that we do not deny Jesus today, by our words, our actions, or our decisions. It is easier than we think to let Him down.

## Luke 23

After the Jewish trial of Jesus in Chapter 22, the first 25 verses of Chapter 23 describe Luke's version of His trial before Pontius Pilate, the Roman governor who had the authority to order Jesus' death. Pilate announces that he finds no fault with Jesus and the Jews accuse Christ of "perverting the nation... beginning from Galilee to this place" (Jerusalem). Pilate sends Jesus to Herod (Antipas) who really only wants to see a miracle and when Jesus refuses to entertain him, Herod sends Him back to Pilate. The soldiers mock Jesus, Pilate tries desperately to free him, but the Jews will not have it, so he condemns the Son of God to death.

Jesus has been condemned to die, by both the Jewish authorities and the Roman governor. He has been scourged (and many strong men died from the scourging alone). As Jesus is being led away to His crucifixion, the Romans compel (force into service) a man from Cyrene, named Simon (verse 26). He is a Jew, in Jerusalem to observe the Passover feast, with his two sons (see Mark 15:21). And Simon is given the great honor of carrying the cross of Jesus for the Savior of the world.

There is a sense, of course, in which this is a distasteful job. After all, an innocent man is being put to death unjustly, for crimes He did not commit. He has broken no laws, either of man or of God. He is not guilty of blasphemy as the Jews have accused Him of, because He really is the Son of God. He is sinless, yet became sin for all of mankind. There is also a sense in which this is one of the greatest honors ever bestowed upon an individual. To be able to help ease the pain and discomfort of God's Son as He walked that Via Dolorosa, the way of sorrows, toward Golgotha, to die for the sins of the world.

We are given many details about the crucifixion itself (verses 27-46). The innocent Savior, the Son of God, was crucified on a cross between two thieves. The only sinless human being who ever lived was bearing, in His body, all the sins of all other human beings. And He did it all so that we might be saved. "For He made Him who knew no sin to be sin for us, that we might become the righteousness of God in Him" (2 Corinthians 5:21). "And as it is appointed for men to die once, but after this the judgment, so Christ was offered once to bear the sins of many. To those who eagerly wait for Him He will appear a second time, apart from sin, for salvation" (Hebrews 9:27-28). "But this Man, after He had offered one sacrifice for sins forever, sat down at the right hand of God" (Hebrews 10:12). "(Christ)...who Himself bore our sins in His own body on the tree, that we, having died to sins, might live for righteousness – by whose stripes you were healed" (1 Peter 2:23). How ungrateful we often are when we ignore what Jesus did for us and go our merry way, sinning and rebelling against God by doing what we know to be wrong, what we know will cause us to be lost and what we know put Jesus on the cross. We can do better.

One interesting aspect of the crucifixion account is the story of the two thieves. Both of them began by reviling Jesus (Matthew 27:44). One of them continued his blasphemy (Luke 23:39), but something happened in the heart of the other thief. Perhaps he was touched by how Jesus responded to the mocking and insults; perhaps he was amazed by the grace of Jesus when He said, "Father, forgive them, for they do not know what they do" (verse 34). For whatever reason, he changed (repented) and Jesus told him that they would be together in Paradise after they had both died. This example is often used by those who deny the importance of baptism for salvation, but don't forget that the Law of Moses was still in effect at this time. It was not until the day of Pentecost (Acts 2) that baptism for the remission of sins became effective under the gospel of Christ (Romans 1:16). Jesus could and did forgive people in many different ways while He was on the earth (Mark 2:5; Luke 7:48; John 8:11 are a few examples).

The gospel (the good news) says, "He who believes and is baptized will be saved; but he who does not believe will be condemned" (Mark 16:16). Believe it and obey the Father's will (Matthew 7:21).

## Luke 24

Jesus died and was buried in a tomb which belonged to Joseph of Arimathea (Luke 23:50-56). He was sealed in a cave-like sepulcher with a large rock rolled in front of the tomb. Soldiers were placed there to stand guard and protect the body from grave robbers (and from His disciples, because the Jews were afraid that Christ's followers might steal the body and then claim He was resurrected). Three days later, the tomb was empty (verses 1-12). "...knowing that Christ, having been raised from the dead, dies no more. Death no longer has dominion over Him" (Romans 6:9). It is the most spectacular of all of Christ's miracles.

The empty tomb means:

- that Jesus is God's Son (Romans 1:4).
- that salvation is available to all men (Hebrews 2:9)
- that we will all be raised from the dead (1 Corinthians 6:14)
- that we will all be judged (Acts 17:31)

Verses 13-35 give us the story of two despondent disciples who are journeying from Jerusalem to the village called Emmaus (about seven miles away). As they are talking about the events surrounding the crucifixion and the report of some of the witnesses who have now seen Him alive, Jesus appears to them and walks along the road with them. When they tell Him about why they are confused (they don't know it is Jesus), He begins with the Law of Moses and the Prophets and explains many Scriptures about Himself. As they eat a meal together and Jesus prays and then breaks the bread to give them, their eyes are opened and they realize it is their risen Savior, who promptly disappears from their sight. They rush back to Jerusalem to join the other followers and tell them they have seen the Messiah alive. They say, "Did not our heart burn within us while He talked with us on the road, and while He opened the Scriptures to us?" (verse 32). As they are telling the others, Jesus appears in their midst and shows them all that He is alive and well.

In verses 44-49, the Savior assures them that "all things must be fulfilled which were written in the Law of Moses and the Prophets and the Psalms concerning Me. And He opened their understanding that they might comprehend the Scriptures."

The final instructions of Jesus to His apostles, right before His ascension to the right hand of God the Father, have come to be called "the Great Commission." They contain the greatest mission ever given to any group of people. The three gospel accounts which record it for us each render it just a little differently.

"Go therefore and make disciples of all the nations, baptizing them in the name of the Father and of the Son and of the Holy Spirit, teaching them to observe all things that I have commanded you, and lo, I am with you always, even to the end of the age. Amen" (Matthew 28:19-20).

"And He said to them, 'Go into all the world and preach the gospel to every creature. He who believes and is baptized will be saved; but he who does not believe will be condemned'" (Mark 16:15-16).

"Then He said to them, 'Thus it is written, and thus it was necessary for the Christ to suffer and to rise from the dead the third day, and that repentance and remission of sins should be preached in His name to all nations, beginning at Jerusalem'" (Luke 24:46-47).

In verses 50-53, the gospel of Luke concludes with the ascension of Christ to heaven where He sits at the right hand of God. The followers return to Jerusalem as He instructs them. His work continues.

# The Gospel according to JOHN

## John 1

"In the beginning was the Word, and the Word was with God, and the Word was God. He was in the beginning with God. All things were made through Him, and without Him nothing was made that was made" (John 1:1-3). The gospel according to John begins with these statements about Jesus the Messiah, here called "the Word" (the Greek word is LOGOS, referring to both reason and speech). This teaches us of His eternal existence, and points to the fact that He is indeed divine (God) and to His role in the creation of the universe as we know it. Jesus is the very revelation of the being, character, and nature of God.

Later, near the end of the book, John will affirm the deity of Jesus again and state that his overarching purpose in writing the things he included in his account of the life of Christ were given "that you may believe that Jesus is the Christ, the Son of God, and that believing you may have life in His name" (John 20:31). There are many things about Jesus that were not included (John 20:30), because it would be literally impossible to tell us everything (the whole world could not contain the books that would be written, John says in John 21:25). But that means those things that are revealed about Jesus are very important, that they lead us to faith in Him and, therefore, to salvation through Him. We will notice many of those important lessons as we journey through this fourth gospel.

After verses 1-5 introduce us to Jesus, verses 6-13 introduce us to His forerunner, John the Baptist. Sent by God to be a witness to the true Light (Jesus Himself), John prepared the hearts and minds of the Jewish people to accept and obey their Savior. Many, perhaps most of them, did not ("He came to His own and His own (the Jewish people) did not receive Him," John 1:11).

Verses 14-18 tell us that the Word became flesh and dwelt among us (among people). This means that the Son of God (deity) became flesh (a human being). Through Him we receive grace and truth.

In verses 19-34, we read of John's testimony (remember he came to "bear witness") about Jesus. His teaching sounded Messianic (as he spoke of the coming of the kingdom, etc.), but he assured them that he was not the Christ. He spoke of Jesus as "the Lamb of God" who came to take away sin. A voice from heaven assured John that Jesus was the promised Messiah of Old Testament prophecy.

Verses 35-51 tell us of some of the early disciples of Jesus. They had initially followed and learned the teaching of John but he quickly pointed them to the one true Light who could save them from their sins. Andrew, Simon Peter, Philip and Nathanael (he will be called Bartholomew in other New Testament passages) were the earliest disciples mentioned in this chapter.

There are several titles or descriptions of Jesus in Chapter 1 that will be repeated and expanded in the rest of the book. Notice these terms used to refer to Jesus and watch for them again and again as you read through the gospel of John.

- verse 1 – the Word
- verse 1 – God
- verses 7-9 – the Light
- verse 18 – only begotten Son
- verses 29, 36 – the Lamb of God
- verse 38 – Rabbi
- verse 41 – Messiah/Christ
- verse 49 – Son of God (also verse 34)
- verse 49 – King of Israel
- verse 51 – Son of Man

## John 2

John is going to record seven miracles of Jesus, plus a bonus eighth miracle, His resurrection. Remember that John 20:30-31 will tell us that He performed many miracles which are not recorded in this book. But John was certain (and don't forget that he wrote under the influence of divine inspiration) that he included enough examples of Jesus' signs to convince a reader with an honest heart that Jesus is God's Son and that we must believe this truth in order to trust Him and be saved from our sins. Each of the miracles in John will show His power over a different realm of creation. We will mention this again as we look at the individual miracles in the gospel. Although we cannot witness the miracles in the same way that the first century disciples did, we have the recorded evidence of four eyewitnesses (Matthew, Mark, Luke, and John) along with others (Peter, Paul, etc.) who saw many of them personally and have recorded them for us by the inspiration of the Holy Spirit (2 Timothy 3:16-17; 2 Peter 1:20-21).

Most of us were not eyewitnesses to the assassination of President John Kennedy, but we know it really happened because we have read or heard about the testimony of many who were there on that tragic occasion. The same thing is true of many historical events that are commonly accepted by society at large as being true. We know about them because of the writings of historians who have documented those historical occurrences and we believe them to be true due to the testimony of those who actually saw them happen. We believe them to be literal historical events. The death of Julius Caesar, the defeat of Napoleon at Waterloo, the assassination of Abraham Lincoln, the fall of the Berlin Wall are all examples of important events of human history that we could not be there to experience personally, but we believe that they really did happen. This same principle applies to the miracles of the Bible.

The first recorded miracle of Jesus is found in verses 1-12 of John 2. It is the account of Jesus at a wedding in Cana of Galilee (remember that Christ grew up in Galilee, to the north of Judea and Samaria) where He turned water into wine.

Jesus was there; his mother Mary was there; some of the disciples were there; the brothers of Jesus were there (verse 14); others were there as well; they all witnessed what happened. As time went on, they ran out of wine. Mary tells Jesus about the situation (verse 2) and then tells the servants at the wedding to do whatever Jesus tells them to do (verse 5). She is demonstrating her faith in her Son.

Jesus replies to her that "My hour has not yet come." This shows us that Christ is following a divine timetable in His ministry and He has much to accomplish before His plan is completed. But He, perhaps out of love and respect for Mary, tells the servants to fill six waterpots (20 or 30 gallons each) with water. They do so and when the master of the feast tastes the transformed water, he declares it to be the best wine at the feast. This first miracle of Jesus shows His power over quality. He made better wine than the wine provided by the bridegroom. (It can be helpful and informative to discuss the question of alcohol content in the wine, but that is beyond the scope of these chapter summaries. If you wish to do so, take the time to study and discuss what the Bible says about wine and strong drink in many, many passages.) This miracle causes some to believe in Jesus, which is the primary purpose of all the miracles.

Verses 13-22 record for us the incident of Jesus cleansing the temple of the ungodly influence of those who sold sheep and oxen and those who exchanged foreign money for Judean currency. Jesus and the disciples have traveled to Jerusalem for the Jewish Passover (verse 13). Jesus reacted strongly and swiftly to their disrespect for God (verse 17 quotes Psalm 69:9 as an example of Messianic fulfillment of Old Testament prophecy). We learn in verses 23-25 that Jesus continues to perform other "signs," some of them miracles which are not recorded in detail. We are also told that Jesus knows "what was in man," referring to peoples' thoughts, their desires, their faith and their unbelief.

## John 3

This chapter begins by introducing us to a man named Nicodemus, a Pharisee who is described as a "ruler of the Jews." This means he was a member of the Sanhedrin, a council of Jewish leaders, made up of men from each of the various sects of Judaism. They were like the Supreme Court in the United States of America, in that they interpreted the various laws for the Hebrew nation, commonly known as Israel. (Rome allowed the countries which they controlled to exercise some degree of autonomy in passing laws and enforcing them, as long as those laws did not conflict with Roman laws.)

Nicodemus came to Jesus by night. Perhaps he worked during the day, perhaps he didn't want to be seen by his fellow Jews as interested in talking with Jesus, maybe that was the last item on his "to do " list for the day, perhaps that's the only time Jesus was available to him; we are not really told why. Nicodemus is mentioned three times (John 3; John 7:50-52; John 19:39-42) and only in the gospel of John (Matthew, Mark and Luke do not include him in their narratives about Jesus).

He is interested in Jesus because he sees Him as "a teacher come from God" as he realizes that "no one can do these signs that You do unless God is with him" (verse 2). The word, sign, here refers to the miracles that Jesus has been performing (the same word is found in 2:11, 2:23 and 20:30-31). That was exactly the response that miracles were designed to bring about.

Jesus and Nicodemus engage in a discussion (a Bible study?) about the subject of the new birth and what it means to be born again. Nicodemus was thinking of earthly things (verses 8-12) while Jesus was speaking about spiritual, or heavenly, things. This was often the challenge to the listeners of Jesus, to understand the spiritual meaning behind His teachings. Jesus mentions His upcoming death when He compares Himself to the bronze serpent lifted up in Numbers 21:1-9 as the means of salvation of the Israelites who were bitten by real snakes as a punishment from God. Jesus says that He would be lifted up in a similar way to save people from their sins (He will again refer to this in John 12:32-33). Verses 16-17 tell us that God sent "His only begotten Son" into the world because God loves the whole world and wants everyone to be saved.

Being born again means that, when we obey the gospel of Christ, we become a new creation (compare to Romans 6:3-4; 2 Corinthians 5:17). It is how a lost sinner is converted into a disciple of Jesus, as we are given a new start, a second chance to serve God when we have previously chosen to disobey Him. To be born "of water" is talking about baptism for the forgiveness of sin (Acts 2:38; 22:16). To be born "of the Spirit" means according to what the Holy Spirit teaches us to do, which is revealed in the Bible.
Jesus concludes His discussion with Nicodemus by a discussion of light and darkness, comparing these two physical conditions to faith and unbelief, to being saved or lost. My personal favorite verse in the chapter is verse 17 where Jesus states, "For God did not send His Son into the world to condemn the world, but that the world through Him might be saved." How grateful we ought to be that God loves us and was willing to sacrifice His Son so that our rebellious, disobedient, often ungrateful souls can be redeemed from our iniquities. What a wonderful blessing is the grace of God, not giving us what we deserve (punishment), but what we should desperately seek after (eternal salvation).

Verses 22-36 show us a little bit about the dynamics of the relationship between Jesus and John the Baptist. Many people thought that John might be the promised Messiah, although John not only never claimed to be the Christ, when asked, he stated unequivocally that He was not the Savior. He was the forerunner for the true Messiah and John clearly states that Jesus was going to continue to "increase," while he (John) would decrease in prominence. Faithful people always point others to Jesus.

## John 4

After a brief discussion about Jesus baptizing more people than John the Baptist, Jesus leaves Judea and returns to Galilee. He decides to pass through Samaria. Many Jews refused to even travel through Samaria because of the enmity between the Jews and Samaritans. So some would travel east of the Jordan to take the "long way" between

Judea and Galilee. This made it a 7 day walk rather than a 3 day journey if you took the more direct route through Samaria.

Jesus comes to the Samaritan city of Sychar, modern day Nablus, where "Jacob's well" was located. His disciples have gone into the city itself to buy food and the Savior is sitting near the well, resting and awaiting their return. It is about noon and a Samaritan woman comes to the well to draw water from the well. Jesus simply says to her, "Give Me a drink."

This was unusual for a couple of reasons. First, Jews and Samaritans normally did not speak to one another. (I have wondered how they knew which person was which nationality?) Secondly, men did not speak in public to women even of their own nation, unless they were personal acquaintances. She is naturally surprised to have a Jewish man ask her for water. It would have made Jesus unclean, according to Jewish tradition, if He drank from her bucket or cup. If you want to learn more about the beginning of the Samaritan people, read 2 Kings 17, especially verses 24-41.

The Lord, as He often did, quickly turns the conversation from the physical to the spiritual and begins to talk with her about "living water." Jesus didn't have a bucket to get water from the well and so she mentions that to Him. He says, "Whoever drinks of this water will thirst again, but whoever drinks of the water that I shall give him will never thirst. But the water that I shall give him will become in him a fountain of water springing up into everlasting life." She is interested and asks for some of His living water.

Jesus tells her to go and get her husband and He will explain more to them together. She admits that she has no husband. Jesus, knowing the truth, says that she has had five husbands and is now living with a man who is not her husband. She guesses that He is a prophet and asks Him about the best place to worship. The Jews would answer Mount Zion, but the Samaritans would say it is Mount Gerizim. Jesus speaks to her about true worship, in spirit and truth, and says that God is looking for such worshipers. She knows that the Messiah is coming to the world and she realizes He will know the answer to her question. Jesus says, "I who speak to you am He." She believes that He is telling her the truth and she goes back into the city and tells her fellow Samaritans that she thinks (although she is not yet totally certain) that Jesus is the Messiah and He is at Jacob's well. The men of the city go out to meet Jesus. At their request, He spends two days teaching them and they are convinced that Jesus is the Messiah, the Savior of the whole world (not just of the Jews).

After two days, He travels the rest of the way to Galilee.

In verses 46-54, a nobleman from Capernaum comes to meet Jesus and he asks Him to come to his home and heal his son, who is at the point of death. The nobleman expresses his trust in Jesus and His healing power and Jesus, impressed with his faith, tells him, "Go your way; your son lives." The man leaves immediately, confident that his son will live. As he enters the town, his servants meet him with the good news that the fever has left his son and he will be alright. When he asks about the time his son recovered, it was at the "same hour" when Jesus had told him his son would be healed. This is called "the second sign Jesus did" in Galilee. It shows His power over time and place, or over distance. Jesus didn't even have to be in the house with the sick boy to heal him; He was miles away from the object of His healing power. More people believe in Jesus (verse 53) as a result of this sign.

## John 5

In Jerusalem in the first century, there were several gates in the city wall, where certain activities would take place. One of those gates was called the Sheep Gate, a literal gate in the wall around the city where sheep would be taken in and out of the confines of the city itself. Near the Sheep Gate was a pool called Bethesda, which consisted of five porches. Near this pool, one could often find "a great multitude of sick people, blind, lame, and paralyzed." It was perhaps a type of healing mineral springs that gave people some relief from physical aches and pains, much like a jacuzzi or hot tub would be used today. In the past in America, such springs of water with high mineral content would be sought out by those who were suffering from physical ailments for relief. (Hot Springs, Arkansas is an example of a place named for these healing springs; they used to be located all over our country.)

In verses 1-15, Jesus and His disciples find themselves in Jerusalem for a Jewish Festival (many, but not all, Bible students believe it was most likely Passover) and they meet a man who has been lame for 38 years, lying on a mat near the water. He was hoping to get some pain relief by getting into the pool, but he has been unable to do so. Jesus asks him what seems like an unusual question when He says to him, "Do you want to be made well?" Of course, the man answers in the affirmative and Jesus tells him, "Rise, take up your bed and walk." The Bible informs us that "immediately" the man was healed.

The Jews jump on the situation and let the man know, "It is the Sabbath; it is not lawful for you to carry your bed." You don't see much human compassion from the Pharisees, do you? Rather than rejoice that the man was healed after almost four decades of suffering, they are critical of him for "working" on the Jewish day of rest. (Don't forget that the Creator of the Sabbath laws is the One who had told him to pick up his mat and He knew better than anyone what the Law of Moses allowed or prohibited. What Jesus told the man to do did not violate the Sabbath regulations, but it did go against Jewish traditions about what a person could or couldn't do.)

The man was unsure about the identity of Jesus when asked by the Jews, but the Savior found him in the temple later and told him, "See, you have been made well. Sin no more, lest a worse thing come upon you." Spiritually, to be lost is worse than being physically limited or lame, as this man was. This was John's miracle #3, showing Jesus' power over disease.

In verses 16-23, Christ refers to God as "My Father." This further infuriates the Jews who recognize that this is a claim to Deity, making Jesus equal with God. Jesus equates honoring Him with honoring God and shows that you really can't honor One while dishonoring the Other.

Verses 24-30 consist of Jesus' teaching about life, judgment and resurrection.

In verses 31-47, Jesus states that He is not simply making claims about Himself; if He were the only witness to His Deity, it would not be reliable (verse 32). But then He refers to five other witnesses to His claims of being God's Son.

- John the Baptist (verses 32-35) – the forerunner to the Messiah
- "The works" (verse 36) – His miracles showed His words to be true
- The Father (verses 37-38) – the voice of God from heaven (at His baptism and transfiguration)
- The Old Testament Scriptures (verses 39-44) – more than 300 Messianic prophecies
- Moses (verses 45-47) – their great Lawgiver had foretold "a prophet like me" – Deut 18:15-19

We can have great confidence that Jesus is the only begotten Son of God, as we read His teachings about God and also learn of the miracles He performed to confirm His words.

## John 6

The events of Chapter 6 take place almost a year after the things we have been reading about from Chapter 5. If the Jewish feast of 5:1 is Passover, the one mentioned in John 6:4 is one year later. John's gospel covers very little of what is commonly called Christ's Galilean ministry. We can go to the synoptic gospels to learn about what happened in Galilee (see Matthew 4:12-15:20, Mark 1:14-7:23 and Luke 4:15-9:62). John focuses most of his writings on the Judean ministry of Jesus (in and around Jerusalem) and only briefly mentions a few events in Galilee. The feeding of the 5000 (John 6:1-14) is one of them.

The feeding of the 5000 takes place near the city of Bethsaida (Luke 9:10-17). Jesus is teaching the people, including His disciples (the word means learner, so it is a generic word to refer to all of those who were following Him to learn from Him). He sees "a great multitude" coming to Him and asks Philip, one of His closest followers, where they could buy enough bread to feed them all. Jesus knew all along how He was going to feed them; He was testing their faith with the question. Andrew, who is known for bringing people to Jesus, takes a young boy to Jesus who has brought with him five barley loaves and two small fish.

Christ has the multitude sit down on the grassy area (in groups of 50 and 100, according to Mark 6:40) and He gives thanks to God for the food, distributes it to the disciples and then they divide it out to the crowd, with each person eating "as much as they wanted." They gather up twelve baskets of leftovers. The 5000 men (there were doubtless women and children there as well) conclude "This is truly the Prophet who is to come into the world."

In verse 15, the people, concluding that Jesus must be the promised Messiah of Old Testament prophecy, decide to take Jesus by force and make Him their King. He is exactly what they have been looking for, a leader who can meet their every physical need and lead Israel into rebellion against the Roman Empire and deliver them from that foreign oppression to true freedom. Their concept of the Messianic King, while common, was completely wrong. Jesus departs to a mountain to pray. Miracle #4 shows Jesus' power over food (or over quantity).

In verses 16-21, later that same evening, the disciples get into a boat and cross the Sea of Galilee headed toward Capernaum. The Sea of Galilee lies about 700 feet below sea level and sudden, violent storms were common on this huge lake, approximately 8 miles across and 12 miles from top to bottom. Sure enough, a storm arises, with powerful winds and crashing waves. In the midst of the storm, they see a figure coming toward them, walking on the water and they are greatly afraid. Jesus identifies Himself and tells them not to be afraid. He gets into their boat and immediately they find themselves at the land. Miracle #5 (in some ways, there are two miracles here, walking on water and arriving at the shore immediately) shows Christ's power over nature itself. "And they (the twelve disciples) were greatly amazed in themselves beyond measure, and marveled" (Mark 6:51).

In the remainder of Chapter 6, verses 22-71, Jesus preaches another of His powerful sermons, this one on the subject of the Bread of Life, which is appropriate given the miracle He performed in the early verses of the chapter. He tells them that He is the Bread of Life from heaven, which confuses them, much like the discussion of Living Water confused the Samaritan woman in Chapter 4. In each case, Jesus was teaching a spiritual lesson, but they were trying to interpret it in a physical way. Many of His followers stated, "This is a hard saying; who can understand it?" A large number of disciples leave Him at this time (verse 66). Turning to the twelve, He asks, "Do you also want to go away?" Peter answers for all of them (and hopefully, for us as well), "Lord, to whom shall we go? You have the words of eternal life. Also we have come to believe and know that you are the Christ, the Son of the living God."

## John 7

Jesus is in danger. The Jewish leaders (often referred to as the scribes and the Pharisees) want to kill Him. They are threatened by His popularity, by His success, by His influence over the masses. Large numbers have begun to follow Him, listen to Him, learn from Him. The Jews don't know how to react to His widespread authority over people, so they decide the best thing to do is to get rid of Him. This sense of antagonism will eventually result in His death. To relieve some of this tension, Jesus, while not ignoring Judea (much of His ministry takes place in and around Jerusalem), also spends a lot of time in His boyhood home of Nazareth and the nearby cities of Capernaum and Bethsaida, parts of the region known as Galilee. For special times and specific reasons, He will sometimes teach in the area of Bethany and Jerusalem.

The Festival of Tabernacles was one of three annual Jewish feasts that required all Jewish males to travel to Jerusalem (Passover and Pentecost were the other two; read Leviticus 23 for more information about these festivals). His brothers (at this point, all unbelievers – verse 5) taunt Him, encouraging Him to go to Judea so He can expand

His influence. He tells them He won't go there, but after they leave for the Feast, He indeed goes to Jerusalem also, not openly, but in secret.

There are many discussions about Jesus at the Feast this year; some people believe in Him, while others oppose what He is teaching and doing. Many people are uncertain what to believe. Everyone wonders if He will show up or not.

In the middle of the week long celebration, Jesus goes to the temple and begins to teach. He starts His lesson by telling the Jews, "My doctrine is not Mine, but His who sent Me. If anyone wills to do His will, he shall know concerning the doctrine, whether it is from God or whether I speak on My own authority." He challenges them to state why they are trying to kill Him and the Jews deny that they are trying to do that (verse 20). Jesus knows that they are still upset with Him for healing the lame man on the Sabbath Day (verses 21-23; John 5:16).

This is followed by more discussion among the people about who Jesus really is. Is He the Messiah? Is He good or bad? Is He telling the truth or is He a deceiver? Can the Messiah come from Nazareth?

When the Pharisees hear all of this debate about Jesus, they send officers to arrest Him so that they might question Him about these things. There is more teaching from Jesus. He tells them, in figurative language, that He will soon return to the Father. He says they will not be able to find Him. On the last day of the feast, Jesus returns to the theme from Chapter 4 about living water, an analogy for eternal life and invites all who are interested to come to Him and drink. Verse 39 applies this analogy to the sending of the Holy Spirit which would take place after Christ was glorified at God's side.

Some think He is the Prophet; others are certain He is the Messiah (Christ). There is division among the Jews. Jesus often divides the faithful from the unfaithful, the obedient from the disobedient, the wheat from the chaff.

The officers return to the chief priests and Pharisees empty handed. When asked why they haven't brought Him, their only response is "No man ever spoke like this Man!"

In his second appearance in John's gospel, Nicodemus speaks up to ask, "Does our law judge a man before it hears him and knows what he is doing?" He is reviled by his fellow council members who remind him that "no prophet has arisen out of Galilee."

## John 8

John 7:53-8:11 contains the story of Jesus and the woman caught in adultery. There has been much discussion over the years about whether these verses are part of the original text and some have concluded that they should not be in our Bibles. I am no expert on manuscripts and that question is beyond the purpose of these summaries. I will say that while it is true that a few manuscripts do not contain this passage, these verses are found in more than 900 ancient manuscripts. That should say something about its veracity.

Jesus is teaching in the temple when the scribes ("teachers of the law," NIV) and Pharisees approach Him, bringing with them a woman whom they claim was caught in the very act of adultery. They remind Him of the passages in the Law of Moses that say such a person should be stoned to death (Leviticus 20:10; Deuteronomy 22:22) and ask Him what they should do. I would point out that, if they really did catch her in adultery, where is the man? The Old Testament says that both should be stoned. They were not interested in God's will here; they were simply trying to trap Jesus and get Him in trouble with the Romans. If Jesus said to let her go, He would be approving of her immorality and breaking Moses' law. If He said to stone her, He would violate Rome's prohibition and would be breaking Roman law. They thought they had Him either way.

Jesus ignores them for a while, but then tells them that the one who is without sin should cast the first stone at her. As dishonest as they were, their consciences began to bother them and then, one by one, they walk away. Jesus looks up and tells the woman, "Neither do I condemn you. Go and sin no more." He does not condone or ignore her sin, but He does show grace and mercy by forgiving her. He encourages her to do better.

This episode is followed by the statement of Jesus, "I am the light of the world" (verse 12). This is the second "I am" claim of Jesus in this gospel (the first one in Chapter 6 was "I am the bread of life"). There will be several more of these phrases in John and each one is a claim to deity by Jesus. You will recall that "I am" is the name God told Moses to use at the burning bush when answering the question of who sent him to Pharaoh to demand that the Israelites be freed. "I am" is a translation of the Hebrew word, EL, which refers to God's eternal nature, based on the meaning "to be." Old Testament words like Israel and Bethel contain that root word EL and say something about God in relation to their meaning.

In verses 13-20, Jesus defends Himself against their criticism. In verses 21-30, He speaks of His approaching death. In verses 31-36, Jesus offers true freedom from sin for those who continue in His teaching and who seek to live by His truth.

In verses 37-47, there is a discussion between the Jews and Jesus about whether they were Abraham's descendants (of course, that was physically true). But as they have wandered so far away from God, Jesus tells them that they have become children of their father, the devil. In this section, Jesus refers to Satan as the father of all lies (verse 44), including religious error and moral depravity.

In verse 46, Jesus issues a challenge that only He could make. He asks them to name one sin He has committed. Don't you know that they would have done that, if they could? But the truth is that He is sinless and they can not tell Him even one thing He has ever done wrong.

In verses 48-59, they give it their best shot. They accuse Him of two things. First, of being a Samaritan (one of the worst insults you could give a Jew) and second, of having a demon. He tells them that, in spite of their religious zeal, they do not even know God. And He again uses the phrase about Himself, "I am" (verse 58).

# John 9

This entire chapter centers around a single event, the healing of a man who had been born blind.

The disciples ask Jesus if the blindness was due to the man's own sins or those of his parents. The common thinking of the day was that all problems are the consequence of sin. Many of them are, but clearly some are not. (Job's debate with his friends is another example of that kind of thinking.) Jesus says that God would bring good out of this situation and be glorified by the man's healing.

Verse 4 teaches us an important principle about time management. We always seem to think we will have lots of time to do whatever we want. We need to use what time we do have wisely (Ephesians 5:15-16). Time flies whether you are having fun or not, so don't waste your life by wasting your time.

Jesus heals the blind man (after the man shows his faith by washing in the pool of Siloam). This is miracle #6 in the gospel of John and shows His power over darkness. There is a spiritual lesson to learn here about the power of light over darkness that is illustrated in the physical healing of the poor man. We might well feel sad for the man who had been blind all his life, but we should realize that there is something worse than physical blindness. We are surrounded by spiritually blind people who need someone to tell them about Jesus. Maybe we should be helping some of them see the light of truth.

This healing took place on the Sabbath (verse 14). Soon the Pharisees get involved; they ask the former blind man about what happened and when he tells them, some of them say that Jesus cannot be from God because He violated the Sabbath. Others ask how He could be a sinner and do such signs. They ask him more details but are still disturbed by his answers. They call for his parents to confirm his identity. They say plainly, "We know that this is our son, and that he was born blind; but by what means he now sees we do not know, or who opened his eyes we do not know. He is of age; ask him. He will speak for himself." This shows the tremendous fear that people had of the religious rulers of the day. They had made it clear that anyone who believed Jesus was the Messiah would be "put out of the synagogue." That would be a great disgrace for a Jewish family.

The Jews take another approach as they tell the man to give the glory to God because Jesus is a sinner. (Remember in the last chapter when He challenged them to name one sin He had committed. They could not do so, of course, but they keep referring to Jesus in that way.) I love how the man responds to their accusation. "Whether He is a sinner or not I do not know. One thing I know; that though I was blind, now I see." As much as they might try, that logic is hard to argue against, isn't it?

They ask him again how it all happened. He says, "I told you already, and you did not listen. Why do you want to hear it again? Do you also want to become His disciples?" (verse 27). Well, that really got them going and they reviled him and said of Jesus, "we do not know where He is from." His response again centers on the reality that Jesus healed his life long blindness and that only someone who was from God could do such a thing. That is his main point in verse 31, not whether God ever answers a sinner's prayers but whether God would allow a sinner to perform miracles. "If this Man were not from God, He could do nothing" (verse 33). They again accuse the man of being completely born in sins and then they excommunicate him from the synagogue (remember John 7:13; see also John 12:42-43).

Jesus finds him and asks him, "Do you believe in the Son of God?" He makes it clear that he really does not know Christ's true identity and so the Lord tells him, "You have both seen Him and it is He who is talking with you." The man responds with, "Lord, I believe!" and worships Jesus. The chapter ends as Jesus tells the Pharisees that they remain in sin until they will confess Him as God's Son. Their blindness continues.

## John 10

Jesus uses two beautiful illustrations in the first 16 verses of Chapter 10, in referring to His followers as sheep. This is a common analogy found in the Bible. We are said to be "like sheep going astray" (1 Peter 2:25, a reference to Isaiah 53:6). In Luke 15, Jesus told a parable of a shepherd with one hundred sheep, having one sheep to become lost, leaving the 99 safe in the wilderness and going to search for "the one which is lost until he finds it" (verse 4). In Matthew 9:36, Jesus saw the people in a multitude around Him as "weary and scattered, like sheep having no shepherd." Even the apostles were described in this way, in Mark 14:27, when Jesus tells them that, on the night of His betrayal, they would all abandon Him and He says of them, "the sheep will be scattered" (a quote from Zechariah 13:7).

The first analogy speaks of the followers of Jesus as sheep in a sheepfold (or a pen where they would often be gathered at night for protection). Jesus says, "I am the door of the sheep" (verses 7, 9). He is the way into a right relationship with God. In Him, we have safety from the world and the devil. He protects us and keeps us safe.

In the second illustration, He refers to Himself as "the good shepherd" (verses 11, 14). Remember the beautiful language of Psalm 23 which tells us, "The LORD is my shepherd; I shall not want." It might be helpful for you to take the time to read that psalm, if you haven't done so recently. It also reminds us of the safety and protection and provision that a good shepherd provides for his sheep.

The Savior tells us that His sheep know His voice. They listen to Him and obey His words. They follow His leadership (and enjoy the benefits of His loving, watchful care). They will not follow a stranger. The "thieves and robbers" He mentions are those who would lead people away from God, not toward Him. An example of these ungodly leaders are the Pharisees He confronts in the final verses of Chapter 9.

Verse 10 provides a stark contrast between Satan and Jesus. Satan is "the thief" who comes to steal and kill and destroy peoples' souls. Jesus came "that they may have life, and that they may have it more abundantly." A hireling (one who would serve the devil rather than God) runs away when confronted with the troubles of life. It is easier to run from problems than to solve them. Jesus says He would lay down His life for the sheep (which, of course, He did).

The "other sheep I have which are not of this fold" (verse 16) refers to the Gentiles, as the salvation Jesus came to provide is available to all people, both Jew and Gentile alike.

It is important for us to see that the death of Jesus was voluntary (verses 17-18).No one could have killed Him against His will. He laid down His life so He could take it again (a reference to both His death and His resurrection).

Verse 22 dates the events of the remainder of the chapter as occurring at the time of Feast of Dedication (sometimes called the Feast of Rededication) in the winter season. This was a civil, not a religious festival, commemorating the recapture, cleansing and rededication of the temple from Antiochus Epiphanes. Judas Maccabees started this feast in 164 B.C. Today, this Jewish holiday is known as Hanukkah. At times it is referred to as the Festival of Lights.

There is more conflict between Jesus and the Jews. He reminds them of His miracles which should have convinced them that He truly is the Son of God. They try to stone Him because they believe Him to be guilty of blasphemy, but He once again escapes. The chapter ends with these words, "And many believed in Him there." While there are those who reject Him, there are also many who trust Him.

## John 11

In a similar way to Chapter 9, John 11 deals with a single event. In this case, it is the raising of Lazarus from the dead. This is John's miracle #7 and it shows Christ's power to raise the dead. The only remaining miracle that will be detailed in the gospel of John is the resurrection of Jesus Himself from the dead.

This miracle takes place in Bethany, a suburb of Jerusalem (about two miles away), which was the home of two sisters and a brother, Mary, Martha, and Lazarus. The brother, Lazarus, is extremely sick as the chapter begins. When the news reaches Jesus, He is probably in Perea, the region to the east of Judea, on the other side of the Jordan River (that's where He was in John 10:40). He decides to go back to Judea, but His disciples remind Him (as though He ever needed to be reminded of anything) that the Jews there recently wanted to stone Him (John 10:31). But He came to earth to give His life for the sins of the world and now one of His closest friends is dying and Jesus, knowing it will result in His own death, wants to go there and raise Him, "for the glory of God, that the Son of God may be glorified through it" (verse 4).

An interesting detail is mentioned in verse 16. It was Thomas who insists, "Let us also go, that we may die with Him." We almost always refer to this apostle as "Doubting Thomas" because of His initial reluctance to believe that Jesus had been raised from the dead (John 20:24-29), but here he is the one who is willing to die for the Lord. Maybe we should start referring to him as "Courageous Thomas." (Thomas is an Aramaic/

Hebrew word and Didymus is the Greek word for the same name. Both of them mean "Twin." When we get to heaven, we can find out who his twin was and learn whether it was someone we already know without realizing he/she was the twin or if it is someone not mentioned in the New Testament.)

So Jesus and the disciples (apostles) arrive in Bethany after Lazarus has been buried for four days (verse 17). Many Jewish friends have gathered around Mary and Martha to support and comfort them in their loss. Martha first hears of the arrival of Jesus (verse 20) and comes out to greet Him. She says to Him, "Lord, if You had been here, my brother would not have died." Jesus talks with her about resurrection and eternal life and Martha makes a powerful confession, "Yes, Lord. I believe that You are the Christ, the Son of God, who is to come into the world."

Then Mary is told that Jesus is here and she comes out to meet Him and greets Him with the same words that Martha had said. When they all go to the tomb together, we are told, "Jesus wept." As with anyone who has lost a loved one, tears are an appropriate response and Jesus is touched by the sadness that the sisters of Lazarus are feeling.

Then Jesus tells them to remove the stone from the front of the tomb. Martha is concerned about the smell of his decaying body. Jesus tells her, as He told the twelve earlier, that she is about to witness "the glory of God" (verse 40). They move the stone away, Jesus prays so that all can hear and then cries out with a loud voice, "Lazarus, come forth!" And the dead man walks out of the grave alive.

Verses 45-57 reveal that the intensity of the anger of the Jewish leaders grows to a fever pitch and they decide that they have only one option: Jesus has to die. Caiaphas, the high priest, makes a prophecy concerning Jesus, stating that it is more expedient for one man to die "for the people," than for the whole nation of Israel to perish. The Son of God is much closer to death than He has ever been before. The Jewish Passover is drawing near (verse 55) and the Jewish leaders spread the word that anyone who knows where Jesus can be found must report it so they can arrest Him with the goal of killing Him. Jesus must die "for the people." He would indeed be dying for the sins of all men (Hebrews 2:9; 5:8-9).

## John 12

Chapter 12 opens with the story of Mary anointing the feet of Jesus (verses 1-11). This means she cleaned them by pouring oil or perfume on His feet and then wiping the oil away with her own hair. These events most likely took place at the home of Mary and Martha in Bethany. This was Mary's way of showing the great love she felt for the Son of God, Jesus of Nazareth. She knew He had predicted His death and she was preparing His body for burial.

There was quite a gathering of people on this occasion. Jesus and the disciples were there; Mary, Martha and Lazarus were there; other Jews had also come together to see Lazarus (his reputation was growing as the news about Jesus restoring his life was spreading).

The disciples criticize Mary for wasting this expensive perfume on Jesus (it was valued at an entire year's salary, approximately 300 denarii). Jesus very clearly expresses His appreciation for the kind gift of love that Mary had given Him. Anytime we try to do good things for God, there will always be those who will find fault.

You might notice it was Judas who complained the loudest about Mary's sacrifice. The text tells us that Judas did not really care about poor people, but that he was a thief and often took for himself some of the money given to help Jesus and His disciples. There are no indications in Scripture that any of the other disciples realized Judas' true character, but they were all surprised when he betrayed Jesus. That shows us that hypocrites can be very good at deceiving others.

The scene shifts in verses 12-19, as the next day Jesus leaves Bethany and goes to Jerusalem. This is often referred to as "the triumphal entry" into the very city where He will be put to death. A great crowd of people gather to watch as the Lord rides a young donkey into the city amidst cries of praise from the multitudes. They say, "Hosanna" (Lord, save us), "the King of Israel" (spiritually true, not literally), "Blessed is He who comes in the name of the Lord!" (a quote from Psalm 118:26). His disciples were amazed at all of these things and did not fully understand it all until after the resurrection. Even the Pharisees admit that they are frightened and intimidated by the support of the people for Jesus.

In verses 20-34, Jesus predicts His death. He compares it to a seed that is planted and then dies in order to bring forth new life (the harvest). His death would bring newness of life for all of the obedient (Romans 6:3-6).

Christ asks the Father to glorify His name. A voice from heaven says, "I have both glorified it and will glorify it again." He had previously glorified Jesus at His baptism as well as at the transfiguration event. In both cases, God affirmed the deity of Jesus by saying, "This is My beloved Son, in whom I am well pleased."

Jesus also makes reference here to the manner of His death by crucifixion when He says, "And I, if I am lifted up, will draw all peoples to Myself." Verse 33 tells us that this is speaking about His death through being hung on a cross.

In the final section of the chapter, verses 35-50, the Savior refers to light (that is an ongoing theme of His teaching) that shines in a world of darkness. Jesus reminds them that He has come to be a light to the world (verse 46) and to save the world (verse 47). The standard of our judgment in the last day will be the words that Christ taught while He was here on the earth (verse 48). They are to be found in the entire New Testament, not just the ones printed in red ink.

## John 13

We now enter a section of the gospel of John in which we read some of the most personal and intimate teachings of Jesus. Chapters 13-17 are part of the event commonly called "The Last Supper," where Jesus and the twelve are alone in an upper room in

Jerusalem. They eat the Passover Festival meal together and, during that time, Jesus teaches them many important lessons that will serve them well as they seek to obey His will, after He returns to His Father. John gives us many details in these chapters that are not contained in Matthew, Mark or Luke.

In verses 1-17, Jesus washes the feet of the twelve apostles. Just imagine what that scene must have looked like. The sinless, glorious, perfect Son of God who has come down from heaven to save the world from sin, stoops down with a towel and a basin of soapy water and washes the dirty feet of twelve sinful, unworthy men. The King of the universe humbles Himself and performs a job usually reserved for the lowliest of household servants. What was this all about?

You will remember that the twelve often discussed among themselves who would become the greatest. Which one of the twelve would be the most famous, the most important, the most powerful? Who would save the most souls? Who would be the favorite preacher of the multitudes? When they were all gone, who would be remembered with the fondest memories? Maybe they even wondered which one of them was the personal favorite of Jesus? Who did He prefer above all the rest?

On one such occasion, Jesus taught them, "...whoever of you desires to be first shall be slave of all. For even the Son of Man did not come to be served, but to serve, and to give His life a ransom for many" (Mark 10:44-45). He washed their feet to show them, in the flesh, what serving others looked like and soon He would die on the cross to show them how far He was willing to go to serve them and their spiritual needs. He would give His life for them.

The lessons He wanted to teach them included humility, service, love, devotion, selflessness, patience, kindness, self-control, gentleness, faithfulness, joy. If the Son of God could serve them, they could serve others also. There are literally thousands of ways to love and humbly serve others; He was not binding the specific method of foot washing. He was emphasizing that we need to think of others and their needs, not merely our own interests and desires. If what they need is a good foot washing, then do that. But find out how you can serve others and then do that for them, whatever it might be.

In verses 18-30, Jesus tells the twelve that one of them will betray Him. All of them are surprised (eleven of them really are; one of them knows the truth already). Even after Jesus dips a piece of bread and gives it to Judas Iscariot, the son of Simon, and tells him, "What you do, do quickly," the rest of the disciples still don't realize that Judas is going to be the betrayer.

Verse 27 says that after the piece of bread was given to Judas, Satan entered him. It is important for us to realize that the devil's power is limited by God (the book of Job shows us that) and he can only enter the hearts of the willing. If we resist him, he will flee from us (James 4:7). Our sins are by our own choice, not because we are unable to help ourselves. We sin because we decide to.

Jesus then has some things to say about glorifying God by loving Him and loving "one another" (verses 31-35). He reminds us that the world will know we are truly disciples of Jesus when they see how much we love and serve each other.

In the final verses (36-38), the Savior warns Simon Peter that he will deny Him three times before the rooster crows the next morning. Peter thinks he will die for Jesus before he would deny Him.

## John 14

Jesus has just told the disciples that He is going to be killed ("where I go, you cannot follow Me now"). But then He quickly tells them, "Let not your heart be troubled." Just trust God. That sounds easy enough, but the reality is somewhat more difficult.

There are two ways to interpret the first six verses. The most common view is that He is speaking of heaven, with many places to live there. Various translations refer to these places as mansions, rooms, or dwelling places. He assures them that He is going to die in order to prepare a dwelling place for them. Heaven is often described as a prepared place for a prepared people. The second explanation is that He is referring to the church (called "the house of God" in 1 Timothy 3:15 and Galatians 6:10, for example.) He died to prepare ("build," Matthew 16:18) the church, a place they can live and serve God in unity. Thomas speaks up to inform the Lord that they really do not understand what He is saying to them. Jesus responds with a powerful statement. "I am the way, the truth, and the life. No one comes to the Father except through Me." Jesus makes a very exclusive claim, that He is the only way to God.

In verses 7-14, we read about the relationship between Jesus and the Father. He says that those who have seen Him have seen the Father (verse 9). He is not telling us that they are the same being, as some misunderstand His words. He is telling us that they are one in character and nature. They are both deity. He promises them that, if they will do the Father's will, whatever they ask will be done for them.

In verses 15-26, Jesus tells them (and us) about His relationship to the Holy Spirit. The Holy Spirit is a member of the Godhead (popular religious culture today uses the term, Trinity, a contraction of the idea of tri-unity. That concept is biblical, but the word, Trinity, is not found in God's word). The Godhead is composed of God the Father, God the Son and God the Holy Spirit. Manifested in three separate beings, they are referred to repeatedly as "One." An illustration that has helped some to understand this concept is the idea of water. The chemical formula for water is H2O (two molecules of hydrogen and one molecule of oxygen). But H2O can exist in three forms, liquid (water), solid (ice) and gas (steam). All three have the same chemical formula; all are really the same; yet all three have differences. Another illustration that may help is an egg. An egg (one egg) has three different parts, a shell, the egg white and the yolk. Yet they all fit together and make one egg. While not exactly parallel, maybe these ideas will help you to understand the One God, composed of three divine beings, Father, Son and Holy Spirit.

Jesus promises the apostles (and remember that these 5 chapters, 13-17, are private teaching to prepare the apostles to continue on with the Lord's work after His ascension) that He will send the Holy Spirit to help and guide the apostles when He returns to the Father's right hand in heaven. He calls the Holy Spirit, the Helper (other versions use different words, like Comforter, Advocate, or Counselor). The Greek word is PARAK-

LETOS, a word which means someone who stands beside another to assist him. It is like a lawyer in a legal setting who helps to defend his client's innocence. He is also called "the Spirit of truth" in verse 17.

In verse 26, Jesus tells the apostles that the Helper (Holy Spirit) will do two things for them. First, He will teach them "all things." There were many things that Jesus had not taught the apostles up to this point because they were not ready for them. The Holy Spirit would reveal to them these new things. Second, He could help them to remember what Jesus had taught them during the three and a half years of His earthly ministry. This is not a general promise for all believers, although this verse and others like it are often misused in that way. This was for the apostles, not for "the world" (verse 17) in general.

In verses 25-31, Jesus tells them that, in spite of the trials and difficulties they would face in serving Him, they could be blessed with peace (verse 27).

## John 15

The first section of Chapter 15 (verses 1-11) deal with the apostles' relationship to Christ. In verse 1, the idea is introduced that Jesus is the vine and God is the vinedresser (the NIV uses the word, gardener). That makes the disciples the branches of the vine that He goes on to talk about. (The branches are not all of the various man-made denominations that the Bible says nothing about. But many people are taught the false concept that all the denominations added together make up the one church of the Bible.) The church is made up of all of the disciples in the world. Here Jesus is focusing on His relationship to the apostles. There are certain aspects of this relationship that can be applied to all those who follow Jesus.

Jesus (the vine) makes it clear that He expects the branches (His followers) to do what literal branches in a grape vine do: they are to bear fruit. Christians can bear fruit in three ways:

- Saving souls – Colossians 1:6
- Developing the fruit of the Spirit – Galatians 5:22-23
- Doing good works in general – Colossians 1:10

Any branch that does not bear fruit will be cut down, taken away and burned (that doesn't sound good, does it?). Apparently Jesus takes this bearing fruit stuff very seriously. It should be really important to us because it is obviously really important to our Messiah.

Branches that do bear fruit will be pruned so that they will be even more fruitful. Jesus would like for us to bear as much fruit for Him as possible. He uses several phrases to describe this – more fruit (verse 2), much fruit (verses 5, 8), and fruit that will "remain" (verse 16).

There are three things in verses 1-11 that really seem to stand out. The first is that He tells us, in verse 8, that this is one of the important ways in which "My Father is glorified." That makes God happy.

The second idea is that this is one way Jesus says, "your joy may be full" (verse 11). There may be other things that give us great joy also, but Jesus here is emphasizing that it is a very special feeling when we help to bear fruit for God. There is nothing like helping to convert a lost soul.

The third thing to remember from these verses is that Jesus stated clearly, in verse 5, "for without Me you can do nothing." The Lord says, in several places in the gospels, "with God all things are possible" (Matthew 19:26 is one example). And, don't forget that, in the Great Commission, Jesus promised, "I am with you always, even to the end of the age" (Matthew 28:20). He will be with us; He will help us; we will be victorious with His help. We are not on our own.

Verses 12-17 deal with the apostles' relationship to one another. They were not twelve separate, independent workers. They were a team, a unit, a group of people who would work together with the Lord, but also with each other to accomplish the huge task of world evangelism. After Judas died, Jesus told eleven of them to "Go into all the world and preach the gospel to every creature" (Mark 16:15). Imagine how they must have felt when Jesus gave them that assignment. Matthias took the place of Judas (Acts 1) and later, Saul (Paul) was brought in to help with the job of reaching the whole world. We read in Colossians 1:23 that they completed the task well before the end of the first century. If they could do it without the many advantages we have in our world today, why can't we? We can. Will we?

Verses 18-27 speak of their relationship to the world in which they lived. They were opposed at every turn. This will always be true of God's people; we cannot allow persecution to slow the progress of truth.

## John 16

On the Thursday evening of the night in which He will be betrayed and arrested, Jesus spends several hours teaching His apostles and preparing them for the work that lies ahead of them, after His death, burial, resurrection and ascension to heaven. In Chapter 13, He teaches them about humility and serving others. In Chapter 14, He comforts them ahead of their loss. In Chapter 15, He emphasizes the concept of bearing fruit for God in every aspect of their lives. Chapter 16 focuses on some future predictions about the struggles they would face in serving God. Throughout all of this time together with them, Jesus is encouraging and strengthening them to remain faithful to their God no matter what.

In verses 1-4, Jesus tells them that they will often be rejected by those in the world. That's the way it has always been, of course. He goes so far as to warn them that some of them will be killed for their faith (that was actually true of all of them, with the exceptions of Judas and John) and that those who do such horrible things to them will think they are serving God. In truth, their actions show that they do not even know God (verse 3).

Verses 5-15 tell them Jesus had to go away for their own good. "It is to your advantage that I go away." Jesus would send the Helper to them after He left the earth. The Holy

Spirit would guide them and direct them and convict the world of sin, righteousness and judgment through their faithful preaching.

There is an important principle taught in verse 12. Jesus says that He did not reveal everything to the apostles during their time together because they were not ready for the whole truth yet. That shows us that we should not rush to teach all of God's word to everyone too quickly. Some people are not ready yet to receive certain truths that they will grow into later. Hebrews 5:12-14 says the same thing; some can only handle the milk of the word, while others are ready for solid food.

Verse 13 says that the Spirit of truth would guide the apostles into all truth. He would not speak on His own authority but He would reveal those things that He heard from the Father. There are two important conclusions from this verse.

First, once the Holy Spirit finished the work of revelation with the final book of the New Testament, there would be no more truth to deliver. We don't need additional written revelations from God. Many have claimed to be delivering new truth, including the Koran and the Book of Mormon, along with many other writings that claim to be divine, Also, no verbal messages from God are being delivered today (although many people refer to "God told me" this or that). No such thing is happening today. God speaks to us through His Son (Hebrews 1:1-2) and that message is contained solely within the New Testament.

Second, if God hasn't revealed it in the New Testament, He doesn't want us to do it (2 Timothy 3:16-17). This concept, along with passages like 1 Peter 4:11, is the basis for the phrase that "we speak where the Bible speaks and we are silent where the Bible is silent." If God doesn't tell us to do something, it should be evident that it is not something He approves of.

Chapter 16 concludes with Jesus warning the apostles (verses 16-33) that there would be sorrow in their near future. The most immediate sadness would be His death, which caused great heartache for His followers. But their sorrow would be turned to joy on the third day when He was raised from the grave, never to die again. They would abandon Him when He was arrested, but He would never leave them or forsake them. They would face trouble and tribulation, but they could rejoice because, even through trials and hardships, the Lord would always be with them.

## John 17

After all of the teaching found in Chapters 13-16, Jesus concludes this section of the gospel of John with a prayer to the Father. There are many references to Christ and His prayer life in the gospels; this chapter contains the longest recorded prayer of Jesus. It divides into three sections:

- verses 1-5 – For Himself
- verses 6-19 – For His disciples (apostles)
- verses 20-26 – For all Christians

John 17

Jesus first prays for Himself (verses 1-5). Notice that Jesus is not simply talking to Himself; He and God are two separate beings. God is the Father and Jesus is the Son. Christ is talking to His heavenly Father, God and asking for His blessing on the remainder of His earthly life.

Do you remember all the times before when Jesus had said, "My hour has not yet come?" Now it has. His earthly ministry is drawing to a close; He has accomplished those things that God sent Him to do (except His death and resurrection, which will follow very shortly). God would glorify Jesus in both His death and His resurrection. He is given authority over all flesh in that He has the power to command people to obey Him. He offers eternal life in heaven to His followers. He states that the way to eternal life is through knowing the Father, having a real relationship with Him. Everything that Jesus did glorified God; He did everything that God wanted Him to do.

In verses 6-19, the Savior prays for His disciples, especially the apostles. God gave these men to Jesus. Jesus taught them God's word and they kept it. It's that simple. God's people are those who keep His word. In this prayer, Jesus states that He is not praying for the world (verse 9). He does pray for the world to be saved and come to a knowledge of God in other places, but here He is focusing on His own followers. Jesus makes several important comments about those disciples.

First, He says that they are "not of this world" (verses 14-16). It is often stated, and correctly so, that true believers are in the world but not of the world. We live in the world, but we are not to partake of the sinful pleasures of the world. We should not pray to be taken out of the world, because the lost people need the saved people to tell them how to live forever with God. But Jesus does pray for His own, "that You should keep them from the evil one" (verse 15). Clearly, Jesus knows about Satan and his influence on so many in the world and He asks the Father to protect His people from the wicked one.

Second, He asks God to "sanctify" His followers. This word has often been defined as "set apart." We have been transferred out of the realm of darkness and into the kingdom of God's dear Son (Colossians 1:13). We are to be different, not conformed to the world, but to live holy and acceptable and righteous lives (Romans 12:1-2). Jesus says that this sanctification (our separateness from the ungodliness in the world) is achieved through the truth of God's Word (verse 17). That's why we read and study and learn to apply the word of God to our lives, so it can make us better and more like God.

Third, Jesus was going to send them into the world with His truth to save as many as possible (verse 18). The word, apostle, means one who is sent. We are not "official" apostles like the twelve, but God also wants us to take the gospel message to the lost world (Matthew 28:18-20; Mark 16:15-16).

In the final section, verses 20-26, Jesus prays for those who will accept and obey the teaching of the apostles (that's us). He especially prays (verses 21-23) for us to be united in love and harmony with one another and says that this is how "the world may know" that we belong to Him. This glorifies God and we must seek to draw others to Christ by the things we teach and the life we live together.

# John 18

After the prayer in John 17, Jesus and the apostles (except Judas who has already left) go to the Garden of Gethsemane (Matthew 26:36), a place where Jesus often took them for rest, relaxation and teaching. It was in this place that Judas shows up with a cohort of soldiers to arrest Jesus (verses 1-14).

Notice that the soldiers are carrying lanterns, torches, and weapons. They need the lights because it is most likely around midnight when this episode begins and about 1:00 am when Judas betrays Jesus. They need the weapons in case anyone tries to protect Jesus and prevent His arrest.

When Jesus sees the mob arriving, He steps forward and asks them, "Whom are you seeking?" They respond with "Jesus of Nazareth" and He immediately states, "I am He." John tells us that the whole group drew back and fell to the ground. He asks again and when He tells them once more that He is Jesus, He asks them to release the disciples. Simon Peter, impulsive as usual, draws a sword and cuts off the right ear of the high priest's servant, a man named Malchus. Jesus tells him to put away the sword (he probably would have been killed very quickly if he did not) and then, according to Luke 22:51, Jesus touches the man's ear and heals it. (It is interesting that it is the doctor among the gospel writers who notes the healing.)

Jesus is arrested and He is taken first to Annas, the father in law of Caiaphas, the official high priest at the time. In the Law of Moses, the high priest served until his death. But Annas had been removed from the office in A.D. 15 by the Romans. He was a clever politician, however, so that when the Romans were appointing someone to take his place, Annas was able to position his son in law, Caiaphas, to be the legal high priest, in the eyes of the Roman Empire. That way, Annas could still be in charge behind the scenes through his family connections.

Verses 15-27 give us some of the details about the Jewish part of the trial of Jesus (Matthew, Mark and Luke include other facts as well; when they are all put together we have a complete picture of what took place). While only the high priest's questions are recorded in John's account, this trial took place in front of the entire Sanhedrin Council, the Supreme Court of the Jews.

We have two major storylines unfolding at the same time here. One of them involves the mock trial before the Jewish leaders, complete with false witnesses who contradict each other because they have no legitimate charges to bring against Christ. The other part of the account tells us about the denial by Peter that he even knew who Jesus was. Jesus had told him at the Last Supper that he would deny Him and Peter had claimed that he would not. The three denials are listed in verses 17, 25 and 26-27. John records: "And immediately a rooster crowed."

When the Sanhedrin asks Jesus some questions about His disciples and His teaching, the Savior makes it plain that He has done nothing in secret. His teaching took place in the synagogues and in the temple. Many of them had heard His teaching; they just didn't want to believe it was truth from God. They finally decide to charge Him with blasphemy for saying He was God's Son (see Matthew 26:63-66).

John 19

Verses 28-40 shift the scene as the Jews take Jesus to Pontius Pilate, the Roman governor over Judea. He soon realizes that Jesus is innocent, but also that the Jews are determined to see Him put to death. In verse 31, they state no charges against Christ, but simply admit that they want Him to die. They realize they do not have the legal authority to kill Him. Jesus tells Pilate that His kingdom is not of this world and He and His disciples will not fight for His freedom. Jesus makes a powerful statement when He tells Pilate, "Everyone who is of the truth hears My voice." That is still true today.

Pilate insists that He finds no fault in Jesus and tries to convince the Jews to allow him to release Jesus as a gift from Rome in observance of the Jewish Passover. Instead they ask for Barabbas.

## John 19

Chapter 19 continues with the trial of Jesus before the Roman governor, Pontius Pilate. The first 16 verses give us more details about what happens during the final stages of this trial.

Verse 1 tells us that Pilate's next decision is to have Jesus scourged (flogged, NIV). This was an extremely painful and severe whipping across the bare back of the victim that was so cruel and destructive to the flesh that the person often died. Scourging was often done on a criminal so that he would be already weakened severely and the crucifixion death would come sooner. The physical pain caused by the flogging would likely be why Jesus was too weak to carry His cross all the way to Calvary without help. Because he was convinced that Jesus was innocent, it is possible that Pilate was hoping the Jews would be satisfied with simply scourging Jesus without having to kill Him.

After the soldiers dress Christ in a purple robe and place a crown of thorns on His head in derision, Pilate brings Jesus before the multitude. The governor again states that he believes Jesus is not guilty of any capital crime, but they tell him that Jesus has violated Jewish law by claiming to be the Son of God. This frightens Pilate and he returns to the Praetorium to ask Jesus, "Where are You from?" When Jesus won't answer, Pilate reminds Him of the power he has to crucify or release Him. Jesus then reminds Pilate that he only has whatever authority God has given him.

The Jews convince Pilate that Jesus has said He is a King and this would anger Caesar if he heard about it, so the Roman politician realizes he cannot let that happen. (They have threatened his job security now and he can't lose that.) Realizing he is running out of options, Pilate brings Jesus out before them one final time and they cry out, "Away with Him, away with Him! Crucify Him!" So the weak ruler gives in to what he knows is wrong and delivers Jesus to be crucified.

In verses 17-30, we are given John's account of the crucifixion of the Savior. Jesus is taken to a place called Golgotha, which means "the place of a skull" (no one is exactly sure what that means). He is nailed to a cross and hung up to die between two thieves (Luke 23:32-33). A sign is placed over Him which reads, "Jesus of Nazareth, the King of the Jews." It was written in Hebrew (some versions say Aramaic which is a form of

Hebrew), Greek and Latin. "Jesus of Nazareth" emphasizes His humanity; "the King of the Jews" emphasizes His deity. Hebrew is a religious language, Greek is the language of the common people and Latin is a legal or political language.

Four women are mentioned as being present, Mary (His mother), her sister (Salome, compare Mark 15:40 and Matthew 27:56), Mary (the wife of Clopas) and Mary Magdelene. John, the disciple whom Jesus loved, is also there and Jesus asks him to care for His mother after His death.

When Jesus states that He is thirsty, they provide Him with "sour wine," which would have been commonly used to help dull the pain of the crucified victim. Jesus then simply says, "It is finished" and passes away.

In verses 31-42, we read of some of the events immediately following His death, including His burial. The soldiers come to break the legs of the three men. This affected their ability to breathe and often resulted in a quicker death. They do so to the other two, but when they realize Jesus has already died, they do not break His legs. This had been prophesied in the Old Testament. A soldier pierces His side with a spear. Joseph of Arimathea and Nicodemus, previously secret followers, gain newfound courage and come to claim the body and bury it in a new tomb which Joseph owned and had prepared in a nearby garden. It's Friday, but Sunday is coming.

## John 20

On numerous occasions Jesus has told His followers that He was going to be killed and that He would rise on the third day. An example is found in Mark 9. "For He taught His disciples and said to them, 'The Son of Man is being betrayed into the hands of men, and they will kill Him. And after He is killed, He will rise the third day.' But they did not understand this saying, and were afraid to ask Him" (verses 31-32). In spite of the frequent statements about His impending death and resurrection, the disciples still did not realize that His death was not the end of everything for Him and them. In many ways, His death, burial and resurrection were simply the beginning of a whole new life for His followers.

This new chapter in their lives is recorded for us in John 20. They are discouraged, probably to the point of despair. Their leader has been brutally murdered, an innocent man who didn't deserve to die. Although He had told them several times, they didn't realize how the whole plan of God was working out and they thought they would never see Him again. One by one (or sometimes in groups), they are told about His resurrection from the dead and they don't believe until they physically see Him alive.

Chapter 20 begins in a similar way to the other gospel accounts of this first day of the week. Several women go early in the morning to the tomb of Jesus (verses 1-18). They apparently begin their journey while it is still dark and arrive just as the sun is rising. John only records about Mary Magdalene doing this, while the other writers tell us that Mary (Jesus' mother), Salome and Joanna and perhaps other women are also present. They have bought spices with which to anoint His body (Mark 16:1; Luke 23:55-24:1).

They want to show one final act of love for their Teacher. But as they arrive, they realize that the large sealed stone in front of the tomb has already been rolled away (Mark 16:4).

Mary Magdalene runs quickly to the disciples and, finding Simon Peter and John (who calls himself "the other disciple, whom Jesus loved"), she quickly tells them that the body of Jesus is missing "and we (notice the plural) do not know where they have laid Him." She and the other ladies assume that either the Romans or the Jews have moved the body of Jesus to another location. She doesn't yet realize what has really happened.

Peter and John run to the grave. When they look inside, they see the linen cloths from His body and the handkerchief from His head lying there, folded up. They leave the tomb, uncertain and confused.

Mary, who has also returned to the empty tomb, is standing outside, weeping. When she looks inside again, this time she sees two angels sitting where the body of Jesus had previously been. When she turns around, she sees a man, whom she thinks is the gardener and tells Him, "Sir, if You have carried Him away, tell me where You have laid Him, and I will take Him away." Jesus calls her by name and she immediately realizes that this Man is Jesus Himself. She calls Him by the affectionate term, Rabboni, and then goes to tell the other disciples that she has seen and talked with the resurrected Messiah.

In verses 19-23, Jesus appears later that same day (still the first day of the week) to ten of His apostles and allows them to see and touch His wounds. He tells them He is going to send them forth just as the Father has sent Him into the world. Remember that the word, apostle, literally means "one sent." Thomas is not present at this time and when told about it, he does not believe the good news.

Verses 24-31 tell us that one week later (eight days, Sunday to Sunday), Jesus appears again to all of them (Judas is gone by this time) and Thomas declares Jesus to be "My Lord and my God." The eighth miracle of John has shown Him to have power over Satan, Hades, and death itself. Truly Jesus is the Messiah and, through faith in Him, we can have eternal life in His name.

## John 21

The events of Chapter 21 are exclusive to the gospel according to John. We would know nothing of any of these post-resurrection deeds and words of Jesus if we only had Matthew, Mark and Luke. In all four accounts, God has given us the full revelation of information about Jesus that we need. We might wish for more details about certain things, but we will have to wait until we get to heaven to find them out.

The events of the first 14 verses of this chapter take place by the Sea of Tiberias. This body of water is usually referred to as the Sea of Galilee (as in Matthew 15:29) and also as the Lake of Gennesaret (Luke 5:1). This is where the fishermen who became apostles of Jesus had worked for most of their adult lives, until the Lord called them to follow

Him. Some of the disciples, Peter, Thomas, Nathanael, James, John and two unnamed followers go out for a fishing adventure. They fish all night but don't even catch a single fish.

The next morning, they see a lone figure on the shore. It is Jesus but they do not recognize Him at first. When they tell Him that they don't have any food, He tells them to cast their net on the right side of the boat. They do and immediately catch so many fish that they have difficulty dragging the net back into the boat. Peter realizes instantly that this is Jesus and dives out of the boat to swim to shore to meet Him; they are about 200 cubits (about a hundred yards, the length of a football field) from land.

They caught 153 large fish. There were two prominent types of fish in the Sea of Galilee. One is referred to as a large fish and most likely is what we would call Tilapia. I have heard that restaurants in the area still serve this today and refer to it as St. Peter's fish. The smaller fish would be what we call sardines (that's what the little boy brought in his lunch in John 6:9 that Jesus used to serve 5000 men). Jesus and these men all eat breakfast together.

After they have eaten, Jesus turns His attention to Simon Peter (verses 15-23). There remains to be resolved the issue of Peter denying Jesus three times during His arrest and trial.

Jesus asks Peter three times, "Do you love Me?" Each time, Peter responds with, "Yes, Lord. You know that I love You." And Jesus instructs Him, three times, "Feed My sheep."

It seems clear that He asks the same question three times because that is the same number of times that Peter denied Jesus, one affirmation for each denial. Jesus instructs Peter that one of his obligations as an apostle will be to take care of His people. Everyone needs leaders who will love them, protect them, provide for them, and watch over them. The writer of Hebrews 13:17 refers to some of these same shepherding concepts in speaking about the work of elders in the church and our responsibility to follow their godly example.

One of the greatest blessings of serving Christ is His forgiveness for our sins (Hebrews 8:12). We all make mistakes (we commit sins, Romans 3:23), but God is a God of second (or more) chances. Peter had sinned grievously against Jesus and yet, when he repented and acknowledged his faith in Christ, he was lovingly and graciously accepted back and served the Lord faithfully from that day on (not sinlessly, but faithfully). Verse 18 prophesies that Peter will ultimately give his life in his service to the Messiah. There is a great contrast between Peter and his restoration and forgiveness and the sin of Judas who did not repent, but rather died out of a right relationship with the Lord.

The final two verses of the chapter identify John as the disciple who wrote these things and tell us that the whole world could not contain the stories of all that Jesus has done. To God be the glory, great things He has done.

# ACTS of the Apostles

## Acts 1

The final assignment Jesus gave His eleven apostles was the command we have called "The Great Commission." He told them, "Go into all the world and preach the gospel to every creature. He who believes and is baptized will be saved; but he who does not believe will be condemned" (Mark 16:15-16). The book of Acts is the inspired record of the early church fulfilling that mission.

Some people have referred to this book as Some of the Acts of Some of the Apostles. God has given us enough information, all we need in fact, to see how faithfully the apostles carried out the assignment that the Lord gave them. Some have also called the book of Acts, The Ongoing Work of Jesus and the Holy Spirit in the Early Church. That is also an accurate description of the contents of this exciting book in the New Testament.

This first chapter gives us a few details about the preparation that is made for accomplishing this mission of telling the whole world about Jesus and the salvation that is available through Him (verses 1-11). The plan that Jesus outlines for them is simplicity itself. They are told by the Savior to "be witnesses to Me in Jerusalem, and in all Judea and Samaria, and to the end of the earth" (verse 8). Although we are obviously not eyewitnesses as they were to His resurrection, the outline He gives them helps us to see how we might carry out world evangelism as well. We can preach the same gospel they preached, starting in our own town, city or village, then reach out to the surrounding area (in our case, like the state where we live), and then take the word of God to the rest of the world, as more and more people are converted to Christ. The number of disciples can grow exponentially in this manner and the church can grow as new local churches are planted and the number of Christians multiplies.

That they are successful in fulfilling the Great Commission and taking the gospel to the whole world is revealed to us later (see Romans 10:18 and Colossians 1:23, for example).

After the resurrection of Jesus from the dead, He spends forty days with the apostles, "speaking of the things pertaining to the kingdom of God" (Acts 1:3). These have been referred to as the "forty days that changed the world."

It is during this period of time that the disciples are transformed from fearful sheep into powerful shepherds. No longer are they reluctant followers, but fearless servants. They have seen the resurrected Lord and have received their final, personal instructions from the Master. The death, burial and resurrection of Christ will be the primary message that they take everywhere and share with everyone.

And then, Jesus ascends to heaven to sit at God's right hand with a promise from the angels that He would return some day.

During the next ten days, the apostles and other disciples spend time together, encouraging and helping one another to prepare for the work that is ahead (verses 12-14). They pray, they study and they build each other up. It is noteworthy that there are some women in their number and especially touching is the fact that Mary, the mother of Jesus is there, along with His formerly skeptical, but now believing brothers (remember John 7:3-5?).

Then they take one more important step. In order that they might fulfill Old Testament prophecy (Psalm 69:25 and Psalm 109:8), they choose a replacement for their fallen companion, Judas Iscariot (verses 15-26). Two men are proposed, Joseph and Matthias. Matthias is selected in God's providence and the apostolic group is complete once more and ready to reach their lost world for Christ.

## Acts 2

Acts 2 has been referred to as "the birthday" of the church.

It was the first day of the week, the day Jesus rose from the grave. The apostle John would later call the first day of the week, "the Lord's Day" (Revelation 1:10). It was a special day in the New Testament system as it became the day that God's people around the world would assemble to remember their Savior's death on the cross of Calvary.

It was also Pentecost, the Jewish celebration of the harvest. Pentecost was one of three annual feasts of the Old Testament which required all Jewish males to travel to Jerusalem for its observance. You can read about the three festivals in Leviticus 23, if you would like to learn more about them. Pentecost occurred after seven Sabbaths, plus one day from the Passover Sabbath. That meant that Pentecost always took place on Sunday. Due to the difficult travel conditions of the day, many, perhaps most, of them would simply remain in Jerusalem for the fifty day interval between Passover and Pentecost.

The first few verses (verses 1-4) describe the fulfillment of the prophecy of the apostles' baptism in the Holy Spirit (Matthew 3:11; Luke 3:16). This is what Jesus meant when He told the apostles that they would receive power from God (Acts 1:8) that would confirm them as spokesmen for the Father (Hebrews 2:4). A rushing, mighty wind from heaven overwhelms them ("it filled the whole house where they were sitting"). Baptism is an immersion and they are all completely immersed in the Holy Spirit on this occasion. Divided tongues, as of fire, sits upon each of them and they are filled with the Holy Spirit, which gives them the ability to speak in languages they have never known before.

Devout Jewish people, from every nation under heaven, are present and this ability to speak in new languages, all at the same time, is a miraculous supernatural evidence that their message is true, and that it comes from God (verses 5-13). They are amazed and perplexed by this event, since nothing like it has ever happened before. Their critics mock them and claim that they are "full of new wine." It seems unlikely that getting drunk would have helped them speak foreign languages they didn't know. Usually a drunk person can't even speak his own language clearly.

In verses 14-36, Peter preaches the first gospel sermon and includes the death, burial and resurrection of Christ. After quoting three Old Testament passages (Joel 2:28-32; Psalm 16:6-11; Psalm 110:1), he shows Jesus to be the fulfillment of all the Messianic prophecies. Declaring Jesus to be both Lord and Christ, he then accuses them of the sin of having crucified the Son of God. Cut to the heart, they ask what to do to be forgiven and he tells them to repent and be baptized in the name of Jesus (verses 37-39). Three thousand souls respond in obedience and are added to the new church by the Lord (verses 40-41).

Verses 42-47 tell us that these new disciples of Jesus devote themselves to God and to one another. They spend time worshiping Him (some of their worship is detailed in verse 42). They feel a new common bond between themselves; their relationship with Christ gives them a new spiritual family to be a part of, as they spend time together and help each other to begin the growing process of a new Christian. They share with each other in the material blessings that some had, while others did not have them. They come together daily in the temple courts as the Holy Spirit inspired apostles continue to teach them God's will for their lives and they spend time together in the homes of those who are from Jerusalem. They have committed their whole lives to the Lord and the church continues to grow daily.

Acts 2 has also been called "the hub of the Bible." Everything prior to Acts 2 points to the establishment of the church/kingdom. Everything after Acts 2 points back to this chapter as "the beginning."

## Acts 3

As Chapter 3 opens, two apostles, Peter and John, are headed to the temple to pray and to preach about Jesus Christ. It is the hour of prayer, the ninth hour, which was 3pm. Historically, there were three hours of prayer for a typical Jewish devotee, the third hour (9am), the sixth hour (noon) and the ninth hour (3pm). As the Jewish day ended at 6pm, the ninth hour was considered the time of the evening sacrifice and burning of incense. Remember from Luke 1:10 that it was a custom of many Jews to assemble outside the temple while the priest was burning the incense. With this gathering of devout people at the temple at this time, it would have been a good time for those who needed financial help to ask from those who were committed to serving God.

As they are going to tell people about the Messiah, they meet a man lame from his mother's womb and perform their first miracle of healing in the name of Jesus. This miracle draws a multitude to Solomon's porch where Peter preaches the second gospel sermon. The Beautiful Gate (verse 10) was likely located on the eastern side of the temple courts, near what was referred to as the court of women and also nearby to Solomon's Porch (verse 11).

Expecting to receive some money (the word "alms" means financial help, either as money or goods; Jesus called this "charitable deeds" in Matthew 6:1-4) from the apostles, they inform the lame man that they have no money to share with him, but they will give him something much more valuable than gold or silver, the ability to walk. So in the name of Jesus Christ of Nazareth, they tell him to "rise up and walk." Realize that he had never walked before and that he had been in this physical condition for more than forty years (Acts 4:22). It is a miracle in itself that he not only was given strength in his legs, but also the ability to walk, run and jump (verses 7-8). All the people knew this man well and recognized that he was the same man they had seen as lame for most of their lifetimes. They were "filled with wonder and amazement" at this miracle.

Like the first sermon in Acts 2, this sermon is centered on the death, burial and resurrection of Christ (verses 13-15). The gospel is good news because of its message about the death, burial and resurrection (1 Corinthians 15:1-4). Because of the death of Jesus on the cross, we can have the forgiveness of our sins. And because of the resurrection, we can have hope of eternal life in heaven with God.

In a similar way as in the first sermon, Peter tells his listeners that they are guilty of crucifying God's Son, whom he calls "the Prince of life." There must always be conviction of sin in the process of conversion.

Peter's charge to them is to "repent and be converted." This is a parallel thought to Acts 2:38 – "repent and be baptized for the remission of sins." Baptism is the point at which one's relationship to God is changed from unsaved to saved. Here the forgiveness of sins is referred to as "times of refreshing" from the Lord. Salvation is a gift from God that is poured out on those who will be obedient to the gospel, the good news that Jesus died and rose again so that we might live with God forever in the glories of heaven.

Finally, Peter reminds them of an Old Testament prophecy by Moses, originally found in Deuteronomy 18:15-19. In that prophecy, Moses, one of the greatest heroes of the Old Testament, predicted the coming forth of another Lawgiver. He spoke, of course, of Jesus the Messiah, but when He came into the world, His own people, the Jews, did not accept Him as their Savior. He is making the point that would impact these Jewish listeners to remind them that to reject Jesus as the Messiah is to reject Moses.

Those who reject Him will be "utterly destroyed." Those who listen, trust and obey Him will be blessed.

# Acts 4

Acts Chapter 4 finds the apostles in trouble for their miracle in Chapter 3. All of them are taken into custody (verses 1-3). The Jewish leaders, including priests, the captain of the "temple guard" (NIV), and the Sadducees arrest them. The Sadducees held the majority of positions on the Sanhedrin Council, due primarily to their wealth and social position. The High Priest was almost always from the sect of the Sadducees. (The Pharisees were the political and religious conservatives, while the Sadducees were the liberals. The Sadducees did not believe in angels, spirits or the afterlife; Matthew 22:23-33; Acts 23:8). The Sanhedrin was comprised of 70 members, plus the High Priest.

Notice, from verse 4, that the church continues to grow, in spite of the opposition of the Jews. The number of men has grown to about 5000. (I always think it is amusing when some people today say that a church of 200-250 is just "too big.") Bible scholars have therefore estimated that the church in Jerusalem numbered somewhere between 15,000-25,000 members at this time.

Verses 5-12 describe for us the "trial" of the apostles. Annas is referred to as the High Priest. He was the High Priest according to the Law of Moses. But in A.D. 15, the Roman authorities had removed him from office and he was eventually replaced by his son-in-law, Caiaphas. So there were technically two High Priests at the same time (see Luke 3:2; John 18:13-14, 19, 22-24).

When the Jews ask them "by what power" they had healed the lame man, Peter, once again the spokesman, makes it clear that this miracle was performed in the name of (by the authority of) Jesus Christ. Notice that the apostles did not take any personal glory for themselves; they gave all the honor and glory to God. (Preachers should especially remember that.) He continues by identifying Jesus as the rejected cornerstone of Old Testament prophecy (Psalm 118:22). And he makes the powerful statement that the name of Jesus is the only name in which anyone will be saved (verse 12).

Several important lessons stand out in the remainder of Chapter 4 (verses 13-37).

What empowered the apostles and filled them with courage was the time "they had been with Jesus" (verse 13). This changed them from "uneducated and untrained men" (they were uneducated, but Jesus had trained them) into courageous and unstoppable defenders of truth. Only if we spend much time with Jesus will we have such courage today. Bible study, prayer and time enjoyed with strong, positive, encouraging Christians will help us to be more like Jesus also.

The enemies could not deny the reality of their miracle (verse 16). Everyone knew this man to have been lame for his entire life. This points up an important difference between Bible miracles and the so-called miracles of faith healing imposters today. The apostles were severely threatened to stop preaching and teaching in the name of Jesus, but they boldly proclaimed that they could only "speak the things which we have seen and heard" (verses 17-22)

Their response to persecution is group prayer (verses 23-31). This emphasizes their dependence on God and teaches us the same lesson. Jesus said, "...without Me you can do nothing" (John 15:5). In that prayer, they quote Psalm 2:1-2, the first of many Messianic psalms in that Old Testament hymnal. The Lord had predicted the rejection of His Son by the Jewish and Roman authorities, but their rebellion did not cancel out the plan of God for human salvation.

The early Christians took care of each other (verses 32-37). Even when it required selling of possessions, they shared what they had with their fellow disciples. We are introduced to Barnabas, a key figure later. They were motivated by love and devotion for one another. We should be also (see 1 John 3:16-23).

## Acts 5

Acts 4 ends with the positive example of disciples who sell property and give the money to the apostles to help their needy brothers and sisters. Not to be confused with forced, godless communism, this is a living model of willing, selfless sacrifice to benefit the less fortunate in the church.

Chapter 5 begins by showing us that there have always been those whose primary desire is to impress others (verses 1-11). Ananias and Sapphira (husband and wife) also sold some land, gave part of the proceeds, but claimed to have given it all. God's discipline was swift and severe, reminding us that lying is a serious sin. Verse 3 makes the point of telling us that Satan entered Ananias' heart, but we need to realize that he still had the ability to tell the truth. He chose to lie and God held him accountable for his disobedience. Verse 3 states that Ananias lied to the Holy Spirit and verse 4 says that he lied to God. This is a passage that shows us that the Holy Spirit is deity. He is a person/being who can be lied to, not simply a power or force that God uses to accomplish His purposes.

In verses 5-10, Ananias' wife, Sapphira, comes into the assembly and is asked the same question as her husband, tells the same lie he did and suffers the same immediate death.

Verse 11 (as in verse 5) tells us that "great fear" came upon all those who heard about these events. Church discipline is intended to cause fear in the hearts of those who are disobeying God; it helps to maintain purity in the church when people realize that sin is not to be tolerated among God's people.

Although others hear of this episode and are frightened by it, the church continues to grow (verses 11-14). Verse 14 is the first time that women are specified as obeying the gospel and being added to the church. It is certain that women have obeyed earlier, but this is the first specific mention of women becoming Christians. No doubt many of the 3000 on Pentecost were women also.

Verses 14-16 tell us about some of the miracles that the apostles were performing in Jerusalem at this time. Even the shadow of the apostle Peter was healing many who were sick. Multitudes are bringing "sick people and those who were tormented by unclean spirits" to them and Luke says that "they were all healed." Miracles were proof that their message was true (Mark 16:20; Hebrews 2:3-4).

In response to the growth of the church, the apostles are arrested by the very Sanhedrin Council that had crucified Christ (verses 17-32). An angel frees them from prison and tells them to continue speaking "all the words of this life." The Council brings them in again and acknowledges that they have filled all of Jerusalem with the message of salvation. It says much about the faith of the early disciples that they are eagerly spreading the gospel of salvation among their friends and family and many are being added to the Lord's church as a result of their zeal. When Peter again points out that they were guilty of the sin of murdering Jesus (verses 29-31), the Council becomes so enraged that they determine to put the apostles to death.

We are then introduced to Gamaliel, a Jewish rabbi of great influence, who convinces them that other men had arisen, gained a following, and then quickly fallen. He tells them to allow the apostles to continue their work so that it will either fail on its own or else the Council "even be found to fight against God." (Remember that Gamaliel was the teacher of a young Pharisee named Saul of Tarsus – Acts 22:3 – who will later figure prominently in the gospel story.)

Finally, they decide to release the apostles with a severe beating and a threat to stop speaking of Jesus (verses 40-42). The apostles leave rejoicing in the honor of suffering for Christ and continue their work of sharing the gospel with the lost. Nothing was going to stop them.

## Acts 6

The second major church problem arises in the church in this chapter (the first one was the Ananias and Sapphira issue). This one deals with a difference between the Hebrews (NIV says Hebraic Jews) and the Hellenists (NIV says Hellenistic Jews and the footnote reads, "that is, Jews who had adopted the Greek language and culture"). The gospel has not gone to the Gentiles yet, so only Jews have become Jesus followers, but remember there were political differences within Judaism, like the Pharisees, Sadducees, Zealots, Essenes, and the other Jewish sects. There were also cultural and language differences since the Jewish people had been scattered around the world by their various captivities. These differences are the basis for this church trouble that is dealt with in Chapter 6.

Do you remember in Chapter 4 (verses 32-37) that there were many needy Christians among the saints in Jerusalem? Have you thought about the reason for that?

First, there were no government programs designed to take care of the poor. If Christians didn't provide for each other, no one else would either.

Second, there were so many needs because of the situation they found themselves in. Think again about the circumstances surrounding the beginning of the church. The Jews had come to Jerusalem for Passover (about the time of the crucifixion) and had remained there for the next fifty days until Pentecost (Acts 2). When many of them were converted to Christ (3000 on the first day alone and then daily additions after that), they wanted to stay even longer in Jerusalem than they had originally planned.

No doubt, some of them went home sooner than others, but many of these new Christians didn't want to leave so quickly.

Naturally, they had brought enough provisions for almost two months, but have now been there for a much longer period of time. Their food was long gone. Many of them needed help. As a matter of fact, some of them needed daily help ("the daily distribution").

For the most part, everyone's needs seemed to be met. But there was a group within the church that was being overlooked. This neglect was probably unintentional. But unintentional or not, these Hellenistic widows were not being helped and it caused a serious problem that had the potential to derail the early church from its mission.

The apostles propose (by inspiration?) that the church members look among themselves, choose seven men, who met certain qualifications and who could be trusted to do the job faithfully. This solves the potentially divisive problem.

As important as that need was, there was one thing even more important. The apostles had to continue preaching the word, accompanied by prayer. While the seven cared for the physical needs of the widows, the apostles continued to meet the spiritual needs of both the disciples and the lost. Two of these men will be referred to in more detail, Stephen and Philip, in the following chapters.

There has always been debate and discussion in the church about whether these seven men who were chosen here for this important work were what will later be called deacons. The word, serve, in verse 2 is from the Greek word, DIAKONEO, in which you can see the root of the English word, deacon. However, all Christians are to serve others and this word sometimes refers to official deacons and other times, only to regular disciples. The full list of deacon qualifications is not given until 1 Timothy 3:8-13.

At the end of the chapter, Stephen is arrested, setting up the events of Chapter Seven.

## Acts 7

Stephen is one of the seven servants chosen in Chapter Six to care for the Hellenistic (Grecian) widows. The qualifications listed in Acts 6:3 describe Stephen as a man "of good reputation, full of the Holy Spirit and wisdom." He is trustworthy, dependable and always faithful. His description lists the kind of qualities that all Christians, male and female, of all time ought to try to possess. He is courageous and loyal, knowledgeable and reliable. In addition, the apostles have laid hands on the seven, imparting to them miraculous, spiritual gifts which enabled Stephen and the others to confirm their words with signs and wonders.

The false charges against Stephen (6:11-14) are that he spoke "blasphemous words" against Moses, God, this holy place (the temple?) and the law (of Moses). When evil people have no legitimate criticisms of the godly, they will simply make something up. It is up to the righteous, not to retaliate, but to seek to overcome evil with good by living a holy life that cannot be faulted. Chapter Seven is Stephen's response to these untrue charges.

Stephen's defense is basically a historical review of Israel's past. By mentioning some of the highlights of Hebrew history, Stephen emphasizes God's faithfulness to His people throughout the centuries. He draws the sermon to a conclusion in verse 52, by comparing their forefathers' persecution of the prophets and their own betrayal and murder of Christ.

Filled with anger, the Jews rush at Stephen and stone him to death. Before he draws his final breath, Stephen asks Jesus not to charge them with this sin. Can you imagine the agony of having the life crushed out of you with the intense pain of having your body hit repeatedly with large stones (or even small ones)? Do you think perhaps that Stephen's last thought was of His crucified Savior, who, in His own anguish on the cross, asked of God, "Father, forgive them, for they do not know what they do?"

Stephen is often referred to as "the first Christian martyr." Did he die in vain? Did his death count for nothing? Would it have been better if he had lived on and had many more opportunities to preach the gospel? Maybe that would be so, from our human point of view. But God always knows what is best. There are at least two positive things that resulted from Stephen's death.

First, from this point on, the gospel spread to the whole world. Stephen's martyrdom sent these evangelists all over their known world. What could have paralyzed them instead mobilized them.

Second, Stephen serves as a positive example of one who put the Lord above all else. It is easy to say that God is first in our lives, but Stephen showed that He really was first in his life. In that sense, he is like the godly men and women in Hebrews 11, who, though they were not perfect, trusted God and did what He wanted them to do. Stephen can be a real hero of faith for all of us. I despair at times when I hear of young Christians idolizing people from the entertainment world or the professional sports world or even the political realm. Our heroes need to be people of faith, both from the Bible and from our own life experiences. They should be your own parents, godly elders and deacons and their wives, faithful Bible class teachers who work so hard to instill faith in young lives. Or maybe our heroes should be the average Christians who are devoted to the Lord, year after year who never get much public attention, but who show us in so many ways what conviction and commitment are really all about.

The people we ought to want to be like are not the rich and famous, the powerful and popular. Our role models should be those who love the Lord with all their heart, soul, mind and strength, who love their neighbor as themselves and who try to make this world a better place by teaching the gospel of Christ.

## Acts 8

In Chapter 8, the persecution intensifies. With the opposition led by a young man named Saul (first mentioned in Acts 7:58), the whole church, except the apostles, is scattered throughout Judea and Samaria. Everywhere the disciples go, they preach the gospel. We noted at Acts 4:4 that Bible students estimate that the church then was around 20,000 members and most scholars believe the church by this time was probably made up of approximately 50-100,000 Christians. This scattering of the believers is one of the methods used by God to further the work of world evangelism.

We are next introduced to another of the seven, Philip. He has two major events in the rest of this chapter. First, he preaches to the entire city of Samaria and then to an individual, a government official from Ethiopia.

When he is forced out of Jerusalem, Philip initially goes to Samaria. The Samaritans were a despised group of people, half Jew and half Gentile, never fully accepted by either side.

Here are a few basic facts about Samaria:

- it was the capital of the Northern Kingdom, Israel
- captured by the Assyrians in 722 B.C. (you can read about this in 2 Kings 17)
- took away the ones who could help them – the smartest and strongest (as slaves)
- left the weak, the sick, the criminals, the lame and lots of women
- then they brought in similar people from other countries they had conquered
- so you had Hebrews marrying Gentiles from all the nations of the world
- that's why Samaritans were looked on as unclean by both Jew and Gentile alike

After the 70 year captivity was over, some Jews were allowed to return to Jerusalem. The Samaritans wanted to help rebuild the temple, the Jews said, no and the rift between the two became even greater. The Samaritans built their own temple on Mt. Gerizim (it was destroyed in 128 B.C.).

In the New Testament, there was total (and mutual) contempt between the two groups, the Samaritans and Jews. In Luke 9:51-56, James and John wanted to burn up a Samaritan village with fire from heaven.

Samaria figured prominently in the life and ministry of Jesus, including the woman at the well (John 4) and the time when 10 lepers were healed and only one came back to thank Jesus, a Samaritan (Luke 17:11-19). One of Jesus' most famous parables is the parable of the Good Samaritan (Luke 10:25-37; the Jews thought there was no such thing as a good Samaritan).

Philip has one message for these lost souls, salvation in Jesus Christ. Again, the miracles that he is able to perform convince many that Philip's message is the truth. Those who believe are baptized, and as Jesus promised in Mark 16:15-16, they are saved by the grace of Almighty God.

One of the Samaritan converts was a sorcerer named Simon, who immediately recognized the difference between his magical tricks and the genuine miracles of Philip.

After he becomes a Christian, he wants to buy some of this miraculous power from the apostles and is told to repent and pray to God for forgiveness.

Right in the middle of this city-wide revival, God calls Philip away to a deserted place for a providential meeting with the treasurer of the nation of Ethiopia. Returning to his home from a spiritual journey to Jerusalem, the official is reading from the book of Isaiah, but does not understand what he is reading. Philip preaches Jesus to him, he is baptized and the officer goes on his way rejoicing. Philip moves on to Caesarea.

## Acts 9

Acts 9 gives us an up-close look at a character we have only briefly met so far. Saul, a Jew from Tarsus in Cilicia, is a strict Pharisee who is completely convinced that Jesus was a false Messiah. He is extremely zealous for what he believes to be right and is determined to wipe out any traces of faith in Jesus. He doesn't realize yet is that Jesus really is the Christ, the Son of the living God, but he is soon to find out.

Here are a few basic facts about him:

- His birth name was Saul; later called Paul
- He was born in Tarsus of Cilicia (this made him a Roman citizen) – Acts 22:28
- He was raised in Jerusalem and educated by Gamaliel, a well-known Jewish Rabbi (Acts 5:34)
- All of this is mentioned in Acts 22:1-5; Paul was intelligent and well educated and this probably indicates that he came from a wealthy family
- In Philippians 3:5-6, he calls himself "a Hebrew of the Hebrews" – top notch, one of the best
- From the tribe of Benjamin – by birth
- A Pharisee—by choice (or conviction)—he believed in the afterlife, angels, etc.

Saul decides that he needs to extend his persecution against Christians beyond the walls of Jerusalem. So he receives authority ("letters" from the high priest) to go to Damascus and arrest those who are of the Way to return them to Jerusalem for trial. We haven't read of any Christians in Damascus yet. There are at least three possibilities for where they might have come from. First, they might have been in Jerusalem on Pentecost in Acts 2 and converted as part of the original 3000 or shortly after that. Second, they might have been some of the Christians who were scattered from Jerusalem in Acts 8:1. Or, thirdly, those scattered disciples might have preached in Damascus and converted some. Saul must have had reason to believe there were enough Christians there to justify going there to persecute them.

And then the miracles come. As Saul approaches Damascus, a bright light shines around him and he sees and hears the resurrected Lord, Jesus Christ. The Savior instructs him to go into the city and wait. A disciple named Ananias (the only Christian there whose name we know) comes to Saul, preaches the gospel to him and baptizes him into Christ for the remission of his sins.

Saul immediately begins preaching in the synagogue that Jesus is the Son of God. When he is opposed by the Jews, he escapes and ultimately makes his way back to Jerusalem where Barnabas, the Son of Encouragement, convinces the others that Saul's conversion was legitimate and that he should be welcomed into the church. "Then the churches throughout all Judea, Galilee, and Samaria had peace and were edified. And walking in the fear of the Lord and in the comfort of the Holy Spirit, they were multiplied" (Acts 9:31).

In 1 Timothy 1:12-16, the apostle Paul uses himself as an example of God's unlimited forgiveness. He was ashamed of what he had done (and some have suggested this was the reason he worked so hard for the Lord – to try to "make up" for some of his past mistakes). He was willing to be reminded of that if it meant more souls could understand that God can forgive anybody. If Saul of Tarsus could be forgiven, so can I. So can anyone you know, no matter how far away they are from God right now.

We all make mistakes; most of them are small things; some are huge. But they are all sins in the sight of God (Romans 3:23; 6:23). We all have things in our past that we are ashamed of and wish we could undo. But we can't. What we can do is to be forgiven of those sins by God and then go and sin no more.

Two miracles of healing conclude the events of Chapter 9; one of them is a resurrection of a dead soul (verses 32-43).

## Acts 10

One of the common threads of Old Testament prophecy about the coming kingdom deals with its universal nature. It was to be a kingdom of all nations, all races, all languages, all people.

That's why the Great Commission was to "preach the gospel to every creature" (Mark 16:15b). It was God's plan that the good news of salvation should be taken from Jerusalem, to all Judea and Samaria and then "to the end of the earth" (remember Acts 1:8?).

In God's plan, the gospel was first preached to the Jews and only when they rejected the Messiah, to Gentiles (Matthew 21:33-43, for example). Romans 1:16 points out that the gospel of Christ is "the power of God to salvation for everyone who believes, for the Jew first and also for the Greek."

Acts 10 is a significant turning point in the spread of the gospel as it records for us the first occasion on which the message is taken to the Gentiles. Finally "the promise" has reached those "who are far off" (Acts 2:39; see also Ephesians 2:14-16). These events occurred in approximately A.D. 41.

Peter is the preacher, as he was in Acts 2, and the household of Cornelius provides the audience. Miraculous circumstances on both sides ultimately bring them together. He has already used the "keys" to the kingdom of heaven for the Jews; now he is extending the reach of the gospel to include Gentiles.

Acts 11

An angel of God speaks to Cornelius to tell him to call for Simon Peter, in the city of Joppa, staying with a tanner whose name was also Simon. Verse 4 tells us that Cornelius' prayers and alms (gifts to the poor, NIV) have been heard by God. Cornelius, a Roman centurion, sends two of his household servants and a devout soldier under his supervision to bring Peter to Caesarea.

The apostle Peter, at the sixth hour (noon) on the same day, has gone up on the housetop to pray and sees a vision from God of unclean animals, according to the Law of Moses, being let down from heaven on a sheet. The voice of God tells him to kill and eat them as He has made them clean. This symbolizes the breaking down of the dividing wall between Jew and Gentile (Ephesians 2:14-16). Only at the culmination of these events does Peter realize that God is teaching him that the Lord truly shows no partiality.

As Peter preaches to Cornelius and those of his household (family, servants, etc.), they are baptized in the Holy Spirit, the second and final case of such in the Bible. Peter then commands them to be baptized in water for the remission of sins (compare verse 43 with Acts 2:38).

It took Holy Spirit baptism, plus the visions of Peter and Cornelius, to convince Peter to preach the gospel to Gentiles (Acts 11:15-18 and Acts 15:7-9). This is only the second example of Holy Spirit baptism in the New Testament; it is also the last example of it. As we study passages like this one, we need to make sure that we do not exclude any groups (nationalities, skin colors, languages, etc.); everyone needs the gospel (see Revelation 5:9).

The same message saved Cornelius that saves everyone else (see Acts 11:13-14). Part of Peter's defense of his action will be that he preached the same gospel to Cornelius that converted the Jews. There is not one gospel for the Jews and different one for the Gentiles. He taught them about Jesus Christ and Him crucified (Acts 10:36-43; Romans 1:16). Cornelius became a Christian the same way everyone else has (or ever will); he was not saved by his own morality, not by prayer or good works, not by being a good parent or a good boss. not by being a good worker or a good neighbor. Cornelius was and did all these good things, but he still had to obey the gospel to be saved (Acts 10:47-48).

## Acts 11

As Chapter 11 begins, Jewish brethren are upset with Peter for what has happened. When they hear that the Gentiles have had the gospel preached to them, "those of the circumcision contended with him saying, 'You went in to uncircumcised men and ate with them!'" (verses 2-3).

It is difficult for those of us who live two thousand years after these events to realize how deeply engrained in the Jewish people was their hatred for Gentiles. They have been persecuted, mistreated, taken into captivity, killed and tortured by Gentiles for centuries. The animosity between Jew and Gentile will not be easily forgiven by either side. The Jews simply could not believe that God would ever accept these uncircumcised heathens.

Faced with this intense opposition, Peter recounts for his fellow Jews the events that had occurred and tells them about the Gentiles' Holy Spirit baptism (Acts 11:15-17). And what was their response? "When they heard these things they became silent; and they glorified God, saying, 'Then God has also granted to the Gentiles repentance to life'" (Acts 11:18).

In Acts 8:4, we were told that the church in Jerusalem was scattered due to severe persecution. The text continues with details about four men, Philip, Stephen, Saul and Peter. During this period of time, Jews, Samaritans and Gentiles have had the gospel preached to them.

As Luke continues in Acts 11:19, we are told of disciples who went to Phoenicia, Cyprus and Antioch (in Syria). Antioch will now be a focus of the inspired record.

This account shows us that persecution doesn't stop the church from growing. Verse 19 refers back to Acts 8:1-4. That persecution could have caused them to stop following Jesus or stop teaching the gospel, but instead it only increased their determination to share the message of salvation.

That's what is sometimes referred to as Total Commitment, giving every thing you have, including your life, if necessary, to accomplish a mission. The fact of the matter is that "comfortable Christianity" is not conducive to growth; people easily become complacent and indifferent to sharing their faith.

A church sign I saw once said – The problem with Christians today is that nobody is trying to kill them. Now don't misunderstand me; I am grateful we are not constantly under the threat of losing our lives because we are Christians. But I am saying that if we reach the point where that is true, we need to remain faithful and still try to convert others to the Lord. When people are being killed for their faith, not a lot of people "play church." And there are plenty of Christians around the world, our brothers and sisters in Christ, who are under constant danger of being killed every day.

Men from Cyprus and Cyrene preached the Lord Jesus in Antioch. "And the hand of the Lord was with them, and a great number believed and turned to the Lord" (Acts 11:21). When the church in Jerusalem (mostly the apostles, perhaps) hears of these many conversions, they send Barnabas to encourage and strengthen the new followers. Barnabas goes to Tarsus to find Saul and brings him to Antioch where they work together for a full year. "And the disciples were first called Christians in Antioch" (Acts 11:26).

A famine arises in Judea and the relatively young church in Antioch sends relief to help these needy saints. Claudius ruled the Roman Empire from A.D. 41-57. This famine happened in A.D. 43-44. There were several churches in the region of Judea, not merely the congregation in Jerusalem. These gifts were sent to the elders of the churches for relief during a time of true need and the help was delivered directly to those leaders in each local church for distribution to the disciples who really needed help.

# Acts 12

In Chapter 12, Herod the king turns up the persecution (verses 1-4). The events of this chapter take place in approximately A.D. 44. The Herod referred to, in this chapter, is Agrippa I. He kills James, the brother of John, making him the first apostle to die for his faith. When he realizes that the Jews are pleased with this action, Herod also arrests Peter. The "Days of Unleavened Bread" referred to here are a part of the Passover Festival of the Jews. It was an annual feast. The days of unleavened bread were seven days long, followed by the Passover meal itself.

The church prays for Peter and God sends an angel in response to those fervent, righteous prayers to free him from prison. This should remind us that prayer is a powerful tool in the battle against sin and unrighteousness. We should always pray when times are difficult and the challenges to our faith are great. Prayer must never be looked at as a last resort, only when all else fails. It is interesting that, although the disciples were praying for Peter's release, when he is set free, some of them don't believe it at first.

The church (not assembled in this case, but dispersed, going about their every day lives) is praying for the apostle's safety. Some of them are gathering together in the homes of other Christians to pray, while many of them were living their lives as they normally did, but all the while, they were "praying without ceasing" (1 Thessalonians 5:17). As Luke describes it, "constant prayer was offered to God for him by the church." Do you think we do that today, as much as we should? Do you ever have some circumstance or some individual on your mind so much that you offer up "constant prayer" to God? Do we really expect an answer from God to those prayers? Or, like them, are we sometimes surprised when God answers us? The details of Peter's release from prison ought to assure us of God's power (vs. 7-11).

As an interesting side note, in verses 18-19, the New Testament tells us that "there was no small stir among the soldiers about what had become of Peter." Herod gets personally involved in the case and, after searching for him in vain, orders that the guards who let him escape be executed.

Chapter 12 concludes with the account of Herod's death (verses 20-23). While he is giving a speech, the people of Tyre and Sidon refer to Herod as a god. When he fails to give the proper glory to the one, true God, he is "eaten by worms" and dies. (Herod Agrippa I is a grandson of Herod the Great and the father of King Agrippa II, who will tell the apostle Paul in Chapter 26, "You almost persuade me to become a Christian"). Josephus, the Jewish historian, tells us that it took Herod five days to die; it must have been a painful, horrific way to die. One lesson for preachers here should be not to take the glory that belongs to God.

To me, the most interesting and exciting verse in the chapter is verse 24 which tells us, "But the word of God grew and multiplied." In spite of the troubles and difficulties and persecution, including the death of the first apostolic martyr, the word of God continues to spread and exert its saving power on the hearts of many of those who hear it. The first century Christians did not have it easier than we do; their lives were much harder than ours in many respects. People were not easier to convert then than they are now. The people of the world were just as caught up in sin as people are today. The early disciples saw everyone as a prospect for the truth, as a lost soul in need of salvation. It has been said that to a hammer everything looks like a nail. To a saved person, every lost soul should look like someone we love and we should try our best to tell them about Jesus and the salvation He came into the world to bring.

Barnabas and Saul return to Antioch from delivering the assistance to the region of Judea, bringing with them, John Mark (verse 25). The work of taking the gospel to the whole world continues. Things are really going to start getting exciting in Chapter 13.

## Acts 13

God's plan is for the gospel to be taken "to the end of the earth" (Acts 1:8). The church in Antioch of Syria is going to be the launching pad for this worldwide evangelization of all the nations.

The church at Antioch is spiritually strong. They have five primary Bible teachers – Barnabas, Simeon, Lucius, Manaen and Saul. Out of this group, the Holy Spirit chooses Barnabas and Saul to lead God's assault on the gates of hell. After the church has fasted, prayed and laid hands on them, they are sent on their way, taking John Mark with them.

They first go to Seleucia, then to the island of Cyprus, where they visit Salamis and then Paphos. Beginning in verse 9, Saul will be called Paul. Maybe this completed his break with his past.

When you decide to do something for God, Satan will attack you. In one of their earliest stops on this missionary journey, they are confronted and opposed by a false teacher, a sorcerer named Bar-Jesus (or Elymas). He is described as an enemy of righteousness and one who sought to pervert the ways of the Lord. Paul quickly and decisively utilized his supernatural powers (spiritual gifts they are sometimes called) and struck this man blind. This confrontation could easily have derailed this entire journey. Men of weaker faith than Paul might have said, well, this just isn't going to work out, is it? But Paul didn't slow down at all. He just kept on doing the Lord's work.

Have you noticed how often, right after someone is baptized into Christ, they have a life crisis that challenges their faith? It might be:

- family problems – children rebel and cause problems in the family (or maybe a spouse)
- health issues
- financial difficulties
- a family member who hasn't gone anywhere to church for years, decides to start going back to their "old church" and they want the new Christian to go with them (and that's always hard for a babe in Christ to resist)
- this could be anything that might discourage or dissuade you away from serving the Lord; but you need to see it as an attack from the Adversary

As they leave Paphos, they sail to Perga in Pamphylia. It is here that John Mark leaves them and returns to Jerusalem. We are not told why, but we do find out later that it displeased Paul (see Acts 15:38).

Next Barnabas and Paul come to Antioch in Pisidia and go into the synagogue on the Sabbath Day. They were not "keeping the Sabbath" as they had under the Mosaic Law, but they went where the people were, when they were there, to have opportunity to teach them the gospel. Given a chance to speak publicly, Paul reviews much Old Testament history with them. Notice how this breaks down.

- 13:17 – Genesis and Exodus
- 13:18 – Leviticus, Numbers and Deuteronomy
- 13:19 – Joshua
- 13:20 – Judges and Ruth
- 13:21-22 – 1 and 2 Samuel, 1 and 2 Kings, 1 and 2 Chronicles

In six verses of the text, Paul covers the first fourteen books of the Old Testament. He then begins to tell them about Jesus who was the fulfillment of these and other Old Testament passages (verses 23-41). A week later (verses 44ff), he continues teaching them, both Jews and Gentiles, about the Messiah. The Jews become jealous and expel them from the region. Their next stop will be Iconium.

## Acts 14

Chapters 13 and 14 relate the details of Paul's first preaching journey.

In Iconium, Paul and Barnabas speak in the Jewish synagogue and convert "a great multitude" of both Jews and Gentiles. They stay "a long time" until some local unbelievers want to stone them, so they flee to Lystra and Derbe, preaching the gospel in both places (verses 1-7). In a later chapter, we will be introduced to a young disciple named Timothy, who lived in this area and was probably converted to Christ on this part of Paul's journey. Paul will refer to him as his "son in the faith."

Verses 8-20 focus on Paul's work in Lystra. We are told that Paul performs a miracle of healing on a lame man who had never walked. This causes the people of Lystra to believe that Paul and Barnabas are gods, Zeus (Barnabas) and Hermes (Paul). When the Lystrans try to offer sacrifice to them, they are barely able to convince them to stop (verse 18).

One verse later (verse 19), Jews from Antioch and Iconium come and persuade the Lystrans to stone Paul to the point of death. He mentions this stoning in 2 Corinthians 11:25. Paul immediately arises and goes with Barnabas back to Derbe. Notice how quickly this situation deteriorated. At first they looked on Paul and Barnabas as gods and then, when the Jews persuaded them otherwise, they stone Paul. This shows us how fast the hearts of some people can be changed. This has always been an account that has amazed me; they thought Paul was dead and he just gets up and gets right back to work preaching. (I might have taken a week off.)

In Derbe, they make many disciples. Verses 20-21 tell us the simple plan by which they convert large numbers of people. "And when they had preached the gospel to that city and made many disciples..." Did you see it? Are you looking for the best plan for how to reach the most people? What should be our strategy for church growth? God's word says they made many disciples by preaching the gospel to them. Do you think that would work today? Teaching the gospel to as many people as possible is the only way to make disciples. Other things (social activities, Christmas and Easter plays, sports teams, free food, entertainment, giving away free clothes or paying someone's electric bill, etc.) will draw huge crowds and a place may even get the reputation of being "the fastest growing church in town." But only preaching the gospel, convicting people of sin and showing them how to obey God in faith, repentance and baptism will save their souls.

As the next phase in their ongoing mission, Paul and Barnabas revisit many of the cities where they have been before and strengthen the Christians to encourage them to remain faithful to the Lord even through difficult times. And they take the amazing step of appointing elders in every church they have planted.

After visiting a few more cities, Paul and Barnabas sail back to Antioch of Syria, where this first preaching journey began.

"Now when they had come and gathered the church together, they reported all that God had done with them, and that He had opened the door of faith to the Gentiles. So they stayed there a long time with the disciples."

"His truth is marching on." Whenever the people of God take the word of God to the lost people of the world, disciples are made. Souls are saved. Eternity is changed for many. Let's not grow discouraged when everyone we try to work with is not converted. Let's just keep on looking for lost souls who are interested in the gospel.

## Acts 15

Jesus came to break down barriers that had long existed, including male and female, rich and poor and, especially, between Jews and Gentiles (Galatians 3:28). He broke down "the middle wall of separation," made "one new man from the two," and reconciled them "both to God in one body through the cross." The purpose was to make "peace" and welcome everyone from every possible background into His universal kingdom (Ephesians 2:14-17).

That was not easily accomplished. There were centuries, at least 15 or more, of hatred between the Jews and everyone else. Long engrained enmity dies hard. To sit beside a Gentile Christian in a worship service was a very difficult concept for a Jewish Christian to contemplate. There was one issue that was especially contentious, the question of circumcision. For many generations, the Jews had considered circumcision to be a symbol of acceptance before God. A circumcised male was pleasing to the Lord; an uncircumcised person never would be acceptable.

While many Jews were willing to accept the idea that Gentiles could become Christians, this problem of circumcision remained. The solution that some came up with was simple. Gentiles who became Christians had to be circumcised. The only problem with that was that it was a "human wisdom" answer, not one that came from God. So when these "Judaizing teachers," as they are often called, began to insist, "Unless you are circumcised according to the custom of Moses, you cannot be saved" (Acts 15:1), the unity of the body of Christ was in danger.

It was left to the inspired apostles to sort through this matter. This chapter shows us how they solved the dilemma, by appealing to command, apostolic example and inescapable conclusion (often called necessary inference). Using these standards of authority, it was determined that circumcision was not essential for salvation after all. Please notice that they did not take a vote of the attending parties to determine God's will. Consider these thoughts.

Verses 7-11 teach us that apostolic examples are binding as God's authority for our actions. Directed by the inspiration of the Holy Spirit, the apostles showed us how they served God in a way that pleased Him. God chose the apostles to preach to the Gentiles (remember Acts 10 when He sent Peter to preach to Cornelius and his household?).

Verse 12 is a case of inescapable conclusion or as many prefer to describe it, necessary inference. The conclusion of Peter (and the others here) is that Paul and Barnabas could not be having success teaching Gentiles if God was not pleased with them.

Verses 13-21 show us James, the brother of Jesus, reminding them of statements from the Old Testament about the universal nature of the church, including Gentiles. Some refer to this as direct command (or direct statement).

At the end of Chapter 15, Paul and Barnabas decide to go on another preaching tour. A personal rift develops between Paul and Barnabas over who should go with them on this trip. Barnabas wants to take John Mark, but Paul does not (verses 36-41). Sometimes problems arise between brothers (and sisters). This was not a "truth" issue where one was right and the other was wrong. On matters of judgment or opinion (and that's what this was), both could be right. So they each set out to do what they thought was best. They did not disfellowship each other; they just went in different directions to preach the same gospel. It might be helpful to remember that later, Paul praises Mark (2 Timothy 4:11) and don't forget that God had Mark write the second gospel. That's a pretty good endorsement. The inspired record follows the progress of Paul as he begins his second preaching journey.

## Acts 16

After Paul and Silas have gone through Syria and Cilicia, strengthening the churches, they come to Derbe and Lystra. Here they add a young disciple named Timothy to their evangelistic team (verses 1-5).

The relationship between Paul and Timothy was strong, and it would continue to grow and develop through the years. Paul would later say that he knew no one else so "like-minded" and commended him for his "proven character" (Philippians 2:20, 22). Timothy has the distinction of receiving two personal letters from Paul that became part of the New Testament, including the final letter Paul wrote shortly before his own death.

The name, Timothy means "honoring God." Timothy was from a mixed family religiously (mother was a Jew; father was a Gentile). This is often a dangerous situation. If the Christian isn't really strong spiritually, the children often go the wrong way.

Timothy's mother (and grandmother) had taught him well (2 Timothy 1:5; 3:14-15). It is possible to raise a Timothy without help from a spouse. Timothy was well-reported of (v. 2); that's quite a statement to make about a young Christian. So Paul takes him on this journey (and on the third preaching journey as well). This says a lot about Timothy's character.

Verse 5 is quite encouraging as it tells us that the churches were strengthened in the faith and increased in number daily.

Not allowed by the Spirit to go to Asia or Bithynia, the team comes to Troas where Paul receives what has been referred to as "the Macedonian Call" and so they travel to a Roman colony called Philippi. This is the first time the gospel has gone to Europe. Note: they came to Troas (verse 8); but we sought to go to Macedonia (verse 10). That means Luke was already in Troas, met up with the apostle Paul and the others and joined them. God wants the gospel to spread to the whole world. That's what the Great Commission is all about. "Make disciples of every nation." And we see that plan unfolding here in the book of Acts.

There are three major events in Philippi—the conversion of Lydia (verses 13-15), the arrest of Paul and Silas for casting a demon out of a young girl (verses 16-24), and the conversion of the Philippian jailer and his household (verses 25-34). Each of these accounts teaches us some important lessons.

In verses 13-15, we find that the church in Philippi begins with the conversion of some devout women, including Lydia. There is no Jewish synagogue there, which means there are not ten faithful Jewish males in the area. Paul preaches to a group of women who had gathered at the river side to pray, the gospel touches and opens their hearts and Lydia and her household are converted. Later, the church at Philippi had both elders and deacons (Philippians 1:1; all men – see 1 Timothy 3:1-13), but they started with women.

In verses 16-24, Paul casts a demon out of a young fortune teller who was making a lot of money for her owners. Incensed by this loss of income, they have Paul and Silas imprisoned. This shows us that God can use difficult circumstances to accomplish His will, as is seen in the next section of the text.

In verses 25-34, through a providential earthquake, Paul and Silas have the opportunity to teach the jailer and his household. They are baptized "the same hour of the night" and the Philippian church continues to grow.

The next morning, Paul and Silas are released. They spend a little time encouraging the new Christians and then move on with the gospel. Luke remains behind to further strengthen the church.

## Acts 17

Paul's second preaching journey continues in Acts 17 as he and his companions travel to Thessalonica, Berea and Athens, establishing new churches in each of these metropolitan areas.

Their first stop in this chapter is Thessalonica, where they spend three weeks teaching about the Christ in the Jewish synagogue (verses 1-9). They convert "a great multitude," mostly Gentiles along with a few Jews. (Wouldn't it be interesting to know exactly how many were baptized into Christ there? We will have to wait until we make it to heaven to ask.)

Verse 2 says, "as his custom was," the first place Paul often went was the Jewish synagogue, because that's where religious people were, people who loved God and wanted to do what was right. Seventh Day Adventists try to use this passage as proof that Paul kept the Sabbath as a Christian. But he was not there to observe Jewish ritual or customs, nor did the first century church worship on the Sabbath (Saturday), but he went where he could find receptive people to teach the gospel to. I have attended Seventh Day Adventist services before, when studying with people from that group, so it could open up further doors of communication and study. I was not observing the Sabbath.

Verse 2 also says he "reasoned with them from the Scriptures." That's really all we have to bring to the table is God's word – the sword of the Spirit, which is the word of God. Notice in verse 3, that he taught them two things. First, that the Messiah had to suffer and rise from the dead – that didn't fit the Jewish preconceived notion about the Messiah. They expected a powerful, earthly Ruler who would deliver Israel from Roman rule. Instead, the Lord came to establish a spiritual kingdom, called the church. He didn't come to save them from Rome, but to save them from their sins.

And secondly, Paul explained and demonstrated that Jesus is that Messiah. There were more than 300 Messianic prophecies in the Old Testament about the coming Savior. Jesus fulfilled all of those prophecies, every single one.

Notice what is said in verse 6: "These who have turned the world upside down have come here too." That is a thrilling statement and hopefully we all want to have that kind of impact on our world.

Soon, a group of jealous Jews gather some evil men from the marketplace and they run Paul out of town. His next stop is Berea. The Jews at Berea are described as being "more fair-minded than those in Thessalonica, in that they received the word with all readiness, and searched the Scriptures daily to find out whether these things were so." Again, we are told that "many of them believed," both Jews and Gentiles alike. Jews from Thessalonica hear about Paul's success and send more troublemakers to force Paul to leave Berea also. He leaves Silas and Timothy there to help the new disciples and moves on to Athens.

Athens was the center of Greek philosophy, culture and learning. Paul speaks to the Jews in the synagogue and to the Greek philosophers in the Areopagus, also known as Mars' Hill. He tells them about "the unknown God" whom they were worshiping in their ignorance. He calls them to repentance and a few are converted.

Thessalonica is the local church that will receive two letters from Paul. They are perhaps the earliest epistles he wrote (Galatians may or may not have been first?). Paul wanted to spend more time with them but could not so he wrote them to try to strengthen them spiritually. Nothing further is revealed about the churches in Berea and Athens.

## Acts 18

Paul's journey takes him next to Corinth, an ancient city of immorality and depravity. If the first century had a place that could be called "Sin City," it would have been Corinth. It seems like an unlikely harvest field for the gospel and yet, the Lord makes it clear to Paul that "I am with you" and "I have many people in this city."

One of the most encouraging things that happens in Corinth is Paul's providential encounter with Aquila and Priscilla. They work together as tentmakers and will continue to be a constant source of encouragement throughout Paul's life. Everyone should have such faithful companions in the gospel as Aquila and Priscilla. And everyone needs to be that kind of friend for others.

It is verses 2-4 that mention Paul's friendship and working relationship with Aquila and Priscilla. They had been forced out of Rome by persecution; What would that be like? How would that make you feel? They were persecuted for no crime other than being a Christian. But notice that persecution didn't stop the church from growing. They "made tents" together; that phrase often describes one who works to support himself so he can preach without any financial obligation from others.

Paul preaches in Corinth for a year and six months. "And many of the Corinthians, hearing, believed and were baptized" (verse 8). That is exactly a description of the Great Commission from Mark 16:15-16, "Go into all the world and preach the gospel to every creature. He who believes and is baptized will be saved; but he who does not believe will be condemned." They heard the gospel, believed and were baptized; therefore they were saved. The unbelievers would be condemned.

Verses 9-10 tell us that the Lord appeared to Paul in a night vision and it was then that He told him, "I have many people in this city." This seems to refer to potential or prospective Christians, those who haven't obeyed the gospel yet but who need to be taught so they can make that decision. Do you think that is true of your city? Do you believe there are many people out there who are searching and just need someone to point them in the right direction? Do you know lost people who just need a bit of help to understand what they need to do? My guess is that we all know some people like that.

How did they find such people in the first century? They didn't have a red X on their foreheads. They had to search for them and find them and then bring them to Christ. And everyone they taught would not obey, just like today.

But once again, a group of Jews arrests Paul and they take him this time to Gallio, the proconsul of Achaia. He refuses to hear the case and Paul eventually leaves Corinth. He travels to Syria, then to Ephesus and Caesarea, finally returning to Antioch, where this second journey had started.

Acts 18:23 marks the beginning of Paul's third preaching journey. He begins by revisiting the regions of Galatia and Phrygia, strengthening the disciples everywhere.

A side note involves Aquila and Priscilla, whom Paul had left in Ephesus. An eloquent preacher named Apollos comes to Ephesus and begins preaching, although he is only familiar with the baptism of John. Aquila and Priscilla take him aside and teach him the full truth he does not know. When Apollos goes into Achaia, specifically Corinth, he powerfully preaches that Jesus is the Christ, using the Scriptures as proof.

We must always use the Bible when we teach others. The gospel is God's power of salvation.

## Acts 19

Chapter 19 finds Paul in ancient Ephesus. He had been there previously and had promised to return when he could (Acts 18:21). In New Testament times, Ephesus was a Roman city in Asia Minor. It is now part of modern day Turkey.

As Paul converts people to the Lord in Ephesus, another new congregation is established. The church in Ephesus will be a powerful influence for good. Paul will later write a letter to the church in Ephesus that becomes a part of the New Testament. Also, in Revelation 2 and 3, when seven churches in Asia Minor receive letters from the Lord, Ephesus is one of those congregations (Revelation 2:1-7).

This chapter begins (verses 1-7) as Paul finds twelve men who had been baptized with John's baptism. Upon further teaching, they are baptized in the name of the Lord. This passage does not teach that everyone should be baptized at least twice. But it does show us that some people do not understand fully everything they need to know when they are baptized and need to obey the Lord with that deeper knowledge.

In verse 6, the apostle lays hands on the new disciples and imparts spiritual gifts to them. This is seen in their ability to speak in tongues and to prophesy. There are five passages in the New Testament that show us how people in the first century received these miraculous powers; in each case it was through the laying on of an apostle's hands. See Acts 6:6; 8:18; 19:6; Romans 1:11 and 2 Timothy 1:6. These spiritual gifts were needed during the time before the written word of God was completed (see 1 Corinthians 13:8-10). The gifts enabled unbelievers to hear the truth and then see it confirmed (backed up) by miraculous, otherwise impossible powers. When the New Testament was delivered in its completed form, verified by miracles and signs, these spiritual gifts were no longer needed.

Paul preaches for three months in the synagogue of Ephesus and then sets up a teaching situation in a local school for two years. This allows the whole province of Asia to hear the gospel (verses 8-10). It was likely during this period of time that the church in Colosse began. Paul had never been there personally (Colossians 2:1), but as he taught and converted and grounded others during this two year period in Ephesus, it is probable that Epaphras took the gospel he learned from Paul in Ephesus, preached the same message in Colosse (Colossians 1:7) and that local church started up. That's how new churches can be planted today; someone must be willing to take the gospel to an area where Christ is not known. When the gospel is preached, souls will be brought to salvation and a local church is formed.

After performing many kinds of miracles (the Bible calls them "unusual miracles"), Paul casts out a demon which some "itinerant Jewish exorcists" had failed to remove (verses 11-20). These miracles have their intended effect (John 20:30-31) and many people come to faith. Their repentance is shown by their willingness to burn many expensive books of magic. The Bible makes this powerful statement: "So the word of the Lord grew mightily and prevailed."

One more incident concludes Chapter 19 (verses 21-41). A man named Demetrius, along with others of his fellow silversmiths, recognizes the danger to his trade caused by former idol worshipers converting to Christianity. So they put together a protest against Paul and his companions. For a long time, they cry out "Great is Diana of the Ephesians." (Some Bible translations call her "Artemis of the Ephesians." Diana was her Roman name and Artemis was her Greek name.) The whole city is in an uproar and chaos is reigning with some citizens not even knowing what is happening. Finally, the city clerk resolves the crisis by telling the silversmiths to pursue legal action against Paul and his friends or else to simply drop the matter.

## Acts 20

Paul spends more time in Macedonia/Greece as Chapter 20 begins. In verse 4, we are introduced to those who were traveling with Paul on this third preaching journey. He was accompanied, at this time, by Aristarchus and Secundus from Thessalonica. (By the way, Secundus probably is not a proper name as much as it informs us that he was a slave, or former slave, who was the "second" child born in his family. "Tertius" [Romans 16:22], who was Paul's scribe in writing the book of Romans, was probably the third child born into his master's group of slaves.) Gaius of Derbe and Timothy are also on the journey with Paul as are Tychicus and Trophimus of Asia. Luke is also present, although he does not mention himself by name. (Did you remember that Luke wrote the book of Acts?) But he does include himself throughout the book with pronouns like "us" (verse 5) and "we" (verse 6).

As these spiritual soldiers move on, we find them next at Troas. The disciples come together on the first day of the week to remember their Savior's death for their sins. Paul preaches to them and, as he prolongs his message, a young man named Eutychus falls asleep, slips from the third story window where he was seated and falls to his death. Paul brings him back to life and then continues his message until daybreak the next morning. (That's quite a long sermon, don't you think?)

Do you remember that approved apostolic example is one way of understanding what God wants His church to do today? (We talked about this in Acts 15:7-11.) We can know, from this passage, that God approves of His people gathering on the first day of the week to observe the Lord's Supper, referred to here as coming together "to break bread." We can be certain, therefore, that taking the Lord's Supper on the first day of the week is acceptable to God. This is the only day that is mentioned anywhere in the New Testament as being a time when the church partook of this memorial feast after the church began in Acts 2. There are other references to the Lord's Supper but none of them tell us when the early church observed this practice. If we can know for certain that God approves of Sunday observance, but we cannot know for sure about any other day, why would we want to risk displeasing Him?

Also, notice that they remained in Troas for seven days, a full week. They did so, in order that they might observe the Lord's Supper with the other disciples there before they moved on. If they wanted to take the Supper with these Christians, they had to wait until the day when the early church did this, the first day of the week. And, by necessary inference, this passage also teaches us that the early church ate the Lord's Supper every first day of the week. God never mentions details by accident in the Bible; there is always a purpose for such records. The message here is that first day of the week (Sunday) worship is to include the Lord's Supper. If He had wanted us to observe it annually, He would have told us the day of the year. If monthly, He would have revealed the day of the month. If He tells us the day of the week, there is a reason for that; He wants us to remember His Son's sacrifice on a weekly basis.

Paul and his companions set out on a ship and sail to Miletus. From there, he calls for the elders of the church at Ephesus to come to him. The rest of the chapter contains his discussion with these elders, Paul's only recorded sermon to believers. All the others were to convert sinners.

There are many lessons for churches, elders and preachers in this discourse of Paul's. We should serve the Lord with humility. We must teach people privately and from house to house to repent. He tells us to be certain to declare "the whole counsel of God." We must be on the alert for false teachers, inside and outside the church. We must rely on the word of God to build us up spiritually. He encourages us to help those who are weak.

They pray together, weep together and then the elders accompany Paul to the ship which will take him on to his next destination.

# Acts 21

Paul and his companions, after leaving the city of Miletus, sail to Cos, Rhodes, Patara, Cyprus and Syria before landing at Tyre. Finding disciples there, they stay for seven days. (Notice that the church at Tyre had men, women and children, verse 5.) Do you remember our study in Acts 20:6-7? Paul also stayed in Troas for seven days so he could assemble with the church for the Lord's Supper on the first day of the week. Maybe it's a coincidence? Or maybe he stayed here seven days for the same reason?

Next, they travel to Ptolemais where they spend one day with the church and then continue on to Caesarea. At Caesarea, they stay with the godly family of "Philip the evangelist." Do you remember the great things we learned about Philip? Our last discussion of Philip goes all the way back to Acts 8 and his work in Samaria and with the Ethiopian eunuch. Twenty years later, he is still serving God faithfully.

We learn that Philip has reared his family well. He has four daughters and we are told that they all have the gift of prophecy, so obviously they are faithful disciples. The NKJV says that they are virgins, while other translations say that they are unmarried. In God's plan, that is how it's supposed to be. Both men and women are to keep themselves morally pure and save that special physical relationship for marriage. Moral purity should be the standard for those who are unmarried. The physical relationship is reserved in God's will for those who are married to one another. (Philip's wife is never mentioned in the New Testament, but she must have been faithful to the Lord as well. It has been said that behind every good man, there is a great woman.)

It is also interesting to think about the fact that Philip and his family are now showing hospitality to the man whose relentless persecution had earlier forced him to leave his home and everything important to him behind. Remember that Saul of Tarsus (now known as Paul the apostle) was the one who led the charge against the Christians in Jerusalem that had resulted in the disciples being run out of Jerusalem and Judea as they fled for their lives (see Acts 7:58; 8:1-3; 9:1-2). When they left Jerusalem however, they all continued to faithfully teach the gospel (Acts 8:4) and this resulted in the gospel being known to the whole world. Now Philip welcomes him, along with several other men, into his home.

A prophet from Judea, named Agabus, comes to Caesarea and predicts that, if Paul goes to Jerusalem, he will be arrested and delivered to the Gentiles (Romans). Paul insists that he is willing not only to be arrested, but to die for the Lord. That is total commitment, a complete surrender of his life to God. The Lord expects and deserves nothing less from every disciple, including you and me! See Mark 12:28-30.

When the group (including Luke; remember the "we") comes to Jerusalem, Paul meets with the elders of the church and gives them many details about his work among the Gentiles. While they "glorified the Lord" for the good news, they are also concerned about the perception that Paul was teaching Jews "to forsake Moses," including circumcision and other Jewish customs. Paul helps to pay the expenses of four men who have taken a vow (verses 23-26) as proof that he still respects Moses and Jewish tradition.

Some Jews from Asia stir up the multitude with an accusation that Paul had taken a Gentile, Trophimus the Ephesian, into the temple. The charge is false, but many people believe that Paul is guilty. (We should learn from that to always hear all the facts before we make a decision about a person's guilt or innocence.)

Paul is about to be beaten to death, when a Roman commander, Claudius Lysias (Acts 23:26), hears the uproar and comes in to rescue him. The apostle asks for permission to speak to the assembled multitude and begins to do so, in the Hebrew language, as Chapter 22 begins.

## Acts 22

Paul begins his defense in the Hebrew language by referring to the Jews as "brethren and fathers." He is showing his respect for them and he captures their attention as "they kept all the more silent." He continues on to describe his own Jewish heritage.

Paul tells them of his early rabbinical training as he sat under the teaching of the highly respected Gamaliel. (Do you remember him from Acts 5:34-40?) He describes his attitude of persecution against the early Christians and then his trip to Damascus to continue his efforts to make havoc of the church.

This is the second of three accounts of Saul's conversion. After being introduced to Saul in Acts 7:57-59 and Acts 8:1-3, the original account of his conversion from Judaism to Christianity is found in Acts 9:1-19. It is repeated here in Chapter 22 and also is retold in Chapter 26.

In each of the repeats of his conversion story, Paul recounts the major change in his thinking that resulted in his conversion to Jesus. He came to realize that, while he thought he was doing God's will in opposing Jesus and His followers, he was actually fighting against the will of God. He was going to Damascus to persecute Christians because he truly believed that Jesus was not the Messiah.

And then a truly life changing event happens. The resurrected Lord appears to Paul personally. Remember that he was called, Saul, at that time. (It was necessary for an apostle to see the Christ after His resurrection – Acts 1:22. That's one of the reasons there are no apostles today.)

This is what changed Saul of Tarsus, Christian hater and persecutor into the apostle Paul, gospel preacher and defender of the faith of Jesus Christ. He knew that Jesus had been put to death on that Roman cross. He had no doubt in his mind, whatsoever, that Jesus had died on Golgotha. And now that he has seen Him alive, Paul realizes that Jesus of Nazareth is truly the Messiah.

Paul relates how the Lord brought him together with Ananias who teaches him the gospel and baptizes him into Christ to wash away his sins. There continue to be those in the religious world today who deny the proper place of baptism in God's plan of salvation. They refer to it as a "work" and deny that it is essential for salvation. But God says that it is the step in the plan, preceded by faith, that cleanses us of our sins. Acts

2:38 says to repent and be baptized for the remission of sins. Romans 6:3-4 tells us that we are to die to sins (in repentance), be buried with Him in baptism and be raised to live in newness of life. 1 Peter 3:21 says that baptism saves us (not by itself and not apart from the blood of Jesus). But it is an act of submission to the will of God. He is the One who works in baptism, not us (Colossians 2:12).

He tells them that he returned to Jerusalem, was praying and while in a trance, Christ commissioned him as an apostle ("one sent") and sent him to preach to the Gentiles. He concludes his retelling of his conversion story (some people call it his salvation experience) by stating clearly that God had told him, "Depart, for I will send you far from here to the Gentiles." This is, again, describing God's plan for the salvation of all people, including non-Jews.

The idea of God showing mercy to the Gentiles is just too much for these zealous Jews. They begin shouting their protest and the Roman commander retreats with Paul into the barracks and decides to scourge him to get to the real truth. As they are binding him with leather thongs, stretching him out so he might be beaten, Paul asks them "Is it lawful for you to scourge a man who is a Roman, and uncondemned?" Told that Paul is a Roman citizen, the commander comes to him and asks if this is true? When Paul confirms his Roman citizenship, the officer backs away and instructs Paul to appear the next day before the Jewish Sanhedrin Council.

## Acts 23

Chapter 23 continues with Paul's explanation of his change from Judaism to Christianity as he tells the Sanhedrin Council that he has acted with a completely clear conscience at all times. This should show us that an untrained conscience is not a safe guide. There are people in the world who can commit murder without even a twinge of guilty conscience. Paul had previously persecuted, arrested and given his approval for the murder of Jesus followers and it had not violated his conscience, at the time. After he was taught, he always felt a sense of guilt for his past mistakes, even though he knew God had forgiven him (see 1 Timothy 1:13-15).

There is an interesting exchange between Paul and the High Priest Ananias on this occasion. After Paul makes his opening statement about his clear conscience, the high priest commands that he be slapped on the mouth. Paul knows this is a violation of the Law of Moses (to strike an innocent man) and he calls the high priest to task about his order. The people around them rebuke Paul for "reviling" God's high priest. Either Paul did not realize who the man was (and he was therefore apologizing to him) or he denied that he was really God's choice for high priest, but rather the Roman Empire's selection.

Paul defends his own Jewish background as the son of a Pharisee (verses 6-8). Realizing that some of his listeners are Sadducees and some are Pharisees, Paul mentions "hope and resurrection of the dead" as the basis for their criticism of him. This has the immediate effect of dividing the Jews with the Pharisees not wanting to "fight against God."

Verses 8-9 provide a brief explanation of one of the major differences between the Pharisees and the Sadducees. The Sadducees did not believe in an afterlife, including resurrection, angels and spirits. They believed that this life was all there is. The Pharisees, on the other hand, were convinced that there is an entire spiritual realm, another level of existence beyond the physical, that includes our immortal souls, the part of man created in the image of God, that will live forever.

The Pharisees' belief in the spiritual realm (what the book of Ephesians calls, "the heavenly places") and the Sadducees' disbelief is what causes "a loud outcry" and a "great dissension."

The commander is afraid that Paul might be literally pulled to pieces by the two groups and so he takes him back into the barracks again for his protection (verse 10).

The Lord assures Paul that he will bear witness of Him at Rome, just as he has in Jerusalem (verse 11). We then learn of a conspiracy against Paul by more than forty Jews who agree together not to eat or drink until Paul is dead (verses 12-24). When Paul's nephew hears about the plot, he informs the commander who subsequently has Paul safely transported to Caesarea. This is the only reference to Paul's physical family and tells us specifically that he had a sister and that she had a son. This is another example of how God can use unknown, otherwise insignificant people to accomplish His will. Maybe that means that He can use you and maybe even me.

The letter that Claudius Lysias writes to the governor Felix (verses 26-30) is a good example of political rhetoric as his explanation contains some truth but twists many of the other details of the situation to make himself look better. His account is not the way it happened at all. But it is close enough for the commander to make himself look good in the eyes of a political superior.

The soldiers (there were 470 of them at first) escort Paul to Antipatris (about halfway between Jerusalem and Caesarea, approximately 38 miles from Jerusalem). They present him to Felix and the trial is set for a few days in the future, when his accusers will arrive to present their case against Paul.

## Acts 24

This chapter begins a series of trials before Roman officials, two governors (Felix and Festus) and a king (Agrippa II). Chapter 24 focuses on Paul's defense before Felix.

At this trial, the Jews are represented by a professional orator named Tertullus who tries to flatter Felix into condemning Paul. He refers to Paul as a plague, a creator of dissension among Jews around the world, a ringleader of the sect of the Nazarenes. He accuses him of only one crime, profaning the temple.

The apostle begins his defense to Governor Felix by denying that they can prove the charge against him, because it is not true. He confesses his allegiance to "the Way" and his hope of resurrection from the dead. When Felix hears of the resurrection, he has some knowledge of the matter and desires to hear more from Paul privately.

Soon, Felix and his Jewish wife, Drusilla, have a private Bible study with the inspired apostle. Paul speaks of the faith in Christ and reasons with them about righteousness, self-control (temperance, KJV) and the judgment to come. As Paul is preaching to the Roman governor, Felix is frightened when he realizes his unsaved condition and says to the apostle, "Go away for now; when I have a convenient time I will call for you" (Acts 24:25). There is no record that he ever obeyed the gospel.

I wonder how many people have died without obeying the Lord, fully intending to do so some day, but never taking the defining step. There should be a sense of urgency about doing what the Lord wants us to do. Jesus understood this principle. He stated in John 9:4, "I must work the works of Him who sent Me while it is day; the night is coming when no one can work." We have a saying, "There's no time like the present." As a matter of fact, that's all the time we have. The past is gone; the future is not promised to anyone. Only today do we have time to make our souls right with God.

Often, people know what to do, but they put it off. Ephesians 5:16 encourages us to redeem the time, because the days are evil. Several versions of the New Testament render that phrase as "buying up every opportunity." It is said that opportunity only knocks once. That may not always be true, but it is true that eventually opportunities to obey the Lord will be gone.

In the New Testament, many of the people who became Christians did so after hearing only one gospel lesson. Those on Pentecost (Acts 2), the Samaritans (Acts 8), the Ethiopian eunuch (also Acts 8), Saul (Acts 9), Cornelius and his household (Acts 10), Lydia (Acts 16), the jailor and his family (also Acts 16) and the Corinthians (Acts 18) heard the gospel one time and became disciples of the Lord. They believed and were baptized (Mark 16:16) and therefore, were saved. If they knew they were lost without Jesus and He was inviting them to come to Him, why would they wait?

There are two things that can rob us of another opportunity to obey God. One is death (James 4:14) and the other is the second coming of Christ (2 Peter 3:10-12). Now is the only time we have been promised. If there is anything about your life that isn't what it ought to be, don't put off doing something about it. You have a chance every day to become what the Lord wants you to be. Every day, what could be more convenient than that? Thousands of people have died waiting for an easier time to put off sin and obey the gospel. Please do not be one of them.

Felix spends the next two years hoping for a bribe to release Paul. He is ultimately succeeded by Porcius Festus. Paul will answer to the new Roman governor in the next chapter.

# Acts 25

It has been more than two years and the Jews still want to kill Paul. (Do you remember the 40 men who had taken a vow not to eat or drink until they had killed him? They must have been quite hungry by this time, don't you think?) Another plot to kill him fails here. You can see God's providence in His protection of the apostle.

As Acts 25 begins, Festus has succeeded Felix as Roman governor. In the first 8 verses, Paul and Festus talk back and forth and it becomes clear to Paul that Festus is not going to give him a fair trial because he wants to satisfy the Jews who want Paul dead. So Paul ends up appealing to Caesar for a decision on his case (verses 9-12).

Festus declares that Paul should be kept at Caesarea as he will soon journey there. He promises to examine Paul then.

When the Jews come down to Caesarea from Jerusalem, they accuse Paul of many things, none of which they can prove. As a favor to the Jews, Festus suggests that the whole group travel to Jerusalem for trial. Paul realizes the danger this puts him in and appeals to Caesar's judgment seat.

In Acts 25:13, we are introduced to King Agrippa. He is actually the second Herod named Agrippa. His father was Herod Agrippa I. We read of him in Acts 12 where he killed James the apostle, arrested Peter and planned to kill him also until God foiled that plan and at the end of Chapter 12, he was eaten by worms and died. This Herod is also the great grandson of Herod the Great who tried to kill the baby Jesus in Matthew 2. Bernice is his sister, not his wife (although history tells us that they were involved in an incestuous relationship). They also had another sister, named Drusilla who was married to the Roman governor Felix, about whom we studied in Chapter 24. Agrippa II was the last king of the Herod dynasty.

It had been prophesied about Paul that he would speak of Jesus to "Gentiles, kings and the children of Israel" (Acts 9:15). Acts 26 records one such opportunity for the aging apostle.

King Agrippa II comes to Caesarea and after he has been there for a few days, Festus tells the king about Paul. He expresses his dilemma to Agrippa by explaining that, even after listening to both sides, he doesn't know what the charges against Paul really are.

You will notice that one thing came out clearly from the testimony, however. Paul spoke of the Savior, "a certain Jesus," who had been put to death, "whom Paul affirmed to be alive." Everything the Bible teaches about salvation depends on the truth of the resurrection. The New Testament refers to Christ as "the firstfruits" (1 Corinthians 15:20-23) of resurrection. That means simply that everyone is going to be raised. Passages that speak of Jesus as "the firstborn" make this same point. Our souls are immortal; they cannot cease to exist. Every soul is going to live forever either in heaven or in hell. The resurrection makes all the difference and we must be certain to emphasize it in our teaching, as Paul did.

Many people believe that most of the world's major religions are basically all the same. They were started by a charismatic leader who convinced many others to follow his teaching. In most cases, that religious group survived beyond the founder's death. But the difference is that the Savior of Christianity was raised from the dead on the third day after His death. All the others died and remain dead.

King Agrippa's interest is raised and he says he would like to hear from Paul personally. The next day, the stage is set for the apostle to appear before a king to preach the gospel, just as it had been foretold that he would. Chapter 26 contains his powerful sermon.

## Acts 26

This chapter begins with Paul once again relating the events surrounding his past life in Judaism and his subsequent conversion to Christ. The original event is recorded in Acts 9 and he retells the story in Acts 22 and here.

Paul first tells Agrippa that he had been a faithful Jew his entire life. His zeal for God had led him to "do many things contrary to the name of Jesus of Nazareth." On his way to Damascus to persecute even more Christians, however, Jesus had personally appeared to him. The Lord told Paul that he would be sent to preach the gospel to the lost, "to open their eyes, in order to turn them from darkness to light, and from the power of Satan to God, that they may receive forgiveness of sins and an inheritance among those who are sanctified by faith in Me," that is, faith in Jesus. And that is what Paul has been doing ever since, preaching the good news of the resurrected Christ.

Do you realize how important the resurrection is to the gospel story? It is the crucifixion death of Jesus that gives us the remission of our sins. But it is the Lord's resurrection from the dead, never to die again, that gives us hope beyond the grave. If the resurrection is true, then all of Christianity is true – sin, grace, mercy, forgiveness, heaven, hell. If the resurrection is false, nothing else really matters. But because Jesus is the Son of God and not only died for our sins, but was raised from death, we have every reason to believe in Him and obey the gospel. He is the Lord, Jesus Christ our Savior.

Both Festus and Agrippa understand the point. Festus accuses Paul of being mad (insane). Paul focuses on Agrippa and challenges him to trust and obey. Agrippa refuses to submit to God's will. It is so sad to see a believer who will not obey the Lord. As the song says, "Almost, but lost."

Almost persuaded? What that means is that he was not persuaded; he did not obey; he was lost. We can think of many similar examples.

- You almost got a 4.0 gpa
- You almost scored the last second shot to win the basketball game
- You almost got that job
- You almost bought that house
- You almost married the girl (or guy) of your dreams

To be almost persuaded to become a Christian is to remain separated from God. Almost a Christian is not a Christian; to be almost a Christian is to be lost.

In Mark 12:28-34, a Jewish scribe is talking with Christ and Jesus tells him, "You are not far from the kingdom of God." Maybe he eventually became a follower of the Lord; we don't know. But what we do know is that he was not far from the kingdom and that means he was not yet in the kingdom. He was still lost. It doesn't matter how close you are to being a Christian. Until you obey the Lord fully and completely, you are still lost.

Through his Jewish heritage, Agrippa had a knowledge of the Old Testament prophecies about a coming Savior (verse 27). When Paul told him, "I know that you do believe," he wasn't trying to play mind games with the king; he really did believe.

Paul knew that Agrippa knew and believed – but it was not a saving faith (more like that of the demons who believe and tremble, but are not saved; see James 2:19). Saving faith, true faith, in the Bible sense of that word, means faith that trusts and reaches out to obey what the Lord says.

## Acts 27

Paul could have been set free because he was innocent of any crime. Why then did he appeal to Caesar? Wouldn't it have been better for him to be free? Couldn't he have reached more people for the Lord living free rather than being a prisoner?

Perhaps so, but now Paul has the opportunity to preach the gospel to the most powerful man in the world, the Roman Caesar. His name is Nero and as the leader of the Roman Empire, he is well known for his disdain for Christians. The great persecutor is about to meet the great apostle to hear about the Great Savior.

Just imagine how much good could have resulted from Nero's conversion. Everyone would know about it. Everyone could have the chance to hear about salvation in Christ, in many cases, sooner rather than later.

Is he likely to be converted? Probably not, and of course, history tells us he was not. He is more likely to order Paul to be executed immediately. Nero could easily reject the gospel message and we now know that he did.

But to Paul, it is a chance worth taking. He understands that the Great Commission says: "Go into all the world and preach the gospel to every creature. He who believes and is baptized will be saved; but he who does not believe will be condemned." Paul's job is not to pre-judge anyone's response to the gospel, even Caesar's. His mission is to preach the truth to everyone and to let each soul make the personal decision to accept or to reject the gospel. That was his point in 1 Corinthians 1:17-18.

We can learn from his example that we should just teach the message of the cross every chance we get and then allow the Holy Spirit to work through those efforts to convert the lost. We plant the seed and water it. God gives the increase, or not (1

Corinthians 3:6-8). We must simply be faithful to meet our responsibility. And we must not pre-judge someone's interest and decide not to give him the chance to accept or reject the message.

Acts 27 chronicles Paul's treacherous voyage by ship toward the headquarters of the Empire. There are many dangers and problems but the Lord's providence sees Paul and the other 275 passengers through. Verse 37 tells us that Luke is accompanying the apostle on this hazardous trip. This account describes one of three shipwrecks that Paul suffered in his life (2 Corinthians 11:25).

One of my favorite passages in this book is Acts 27:23-24a, "For there stood by me this night an angel of the God to whom I belong and whom I serve, saying, 'Do not be afraid.'" God is comforting Paul.

"To whom I belong." Christians belong to God. We have been purchased by the blood of Christ. Some are unwilling to belong to the Lord. They belong to their jobs, their spouse, their children, their hobbies, etc. Most simply belong to themselves. They do what they want, not what GOD wants. Many are controlled by sin.

"And whom I serve." Never forget that, because children of God belong to Him, we have a duty to do all that He asks us to do. Paul served God because he belonged to Him. When we understand that we have given control of our lives to God, we will obey and serve Him in all things.

Slowly, but surely the apostle Paul is making his way toward Rome.

## Acts 28

Matthew's record of the Great Commission reads like this: "Go therefore and make disciples of all the nations, baptizing them in the name of the Father and of the Son and of the Holy Spirit, teaching them to observe all things that I have commanded you; and lo, I am with you always, even to the end of the age" (Matthew 28:19-20).

The book of Acts is the inspired account of how the early church carried out that great mission. It also contains the pattern for how God's people can evangelize the world in every generation (Colossians 1:23).

Paul's dream of going to Rome with the gospel is finally being realized, but clearly not in the way he had planned. In verse 16, the apostle Paul arrives in the major city of the first century world, Rome. He meets with Jewish leaders to explain his relationship with God (verses 17-22). They desire to learn more and so they choose a day when "many" come to Him and he shows them that Jesus is the Messiah, "persuading them concerning Jesus from both the Law of Moses and the Prophets" (verses 23-28). One of the Old Testament passages that he uses to teach them is specified (verses 25-27). It is Isaiah 6:9-10 and is a strong warning to those who hear the truth and will not obey it. Jesus had personally used this prophecy to teach the Jews earlier (see Matthew 13:14-15 and John 12:37-41).

Acts 28

The book of Acts ends with the information that Paul spent two years under house arrest, with the freedom to teach everyone who came to him.

It was during this time frame (from when Paul was first arrested in Acts 21:33 through this two year house arrest – approximately A.D. 60-63) that Paul wrote four letters, commonly called his prison epistles. They are Ephesians, Philippians, Colossians, and Philemon.

After the events of Acts 28, Paul is released for a period of time. It was then that he wrote 1 Timothy and Titus and Hebrews (if he wrote Hebrews).

Paul was later arrested again and, during this imprisonment, he wrote his final letter, the book of 2 Timothy. Shortly after he wrote that last epistle, Paul was put to death, in approximately A.D. 68. History (or perhaps, legend) tells us that Paul was beheaded.

One more spiritual lesson. When Paul preached to these listeners in Acts 28, there were two responses. "And some were persuaded by the things which were spoken, and some disbelieved" (verse 24). There are only two responses to the gospel, obedience and disobedience. There are two groups of people, saved and lost. There are two eternal destinies, heaven and hell.

Jesus did not convert every person He taught and He was the best teacher of all time. The apostle Paul taught multitudes and converted many of them. But we have noticed as we have studied his preaching journeys in Acts that there were lots of times when Paul preached and few, or in some cases none, of the listeners became disciples of Jesus. We should not grow discouraged when some people we try to touch with the gospel do not become Christians. The Great Commission itself reflected the truth that some would "disbelieve" (Mark 16:16) and be lost. It is discouraging to us at times, but we must never "grow weary" of sharing our faith as we try to find those who have an open heart and will be interested in obeying the gospel of Christ. We have the blessed privilege of taking the gospel to the whole world and, as co-workers with God, helping to seek and save the lost. Don't give up.

World evangelism is accomplished one soul at a time.

# The Letter to the ROMANS

## Romans 1

The major theme of the book of Romans is "obedience to the faith." Paul states this theme at both the beginning of Romans (1:5) and the end of the letter (16:26). In this epistle, the apostle explains what it means to be "justified by faith" (Romans 5:1).

The letter begins by reminding these first century Christians that Jesus Christ was "declared to be the Son of God with power according to the Spirit of holiness, by the resurrection from the dead" (verse 4). Everything we are, everything we believe and any hope that we have comes from the reality that Jesus is God's Son and that He was crucified for our sins and was raised from the dead on the third day.

Christians are called to be saints (verses 6-7). This simply means that we have been set apart for service to God; it is a description of a lifestyle. It does not refer to perfection in this life, but to spiritual maturity that seeks to be holy and separated from the sin of the world.

In verses 8-10, Paul makes some personal comments to the Christians in Rome. He points out that disciples all over the world knew about the faith of the brothers and sisters in Rome. Imagine how difficult it would have been to live right in the headquarters of the ungodly Roman Empire. Just as it is a challenge to live a godly life in our day and time, it would have been very hard to serve Christ in the first century, especially in Rome. Paul hopes to visit them soon and has been praying for that to happen. God will answer that prayer, but probably not in the way Paul had thought. He will go there as a prisoner (the last chapter of Acts gives us some details about how that all happens).

The apostle wants to encourage and strengthen these disciples and to be encouraged by their faith (verses 11-15). He would preach to them (verse 15). He would impart spiritual gifts to them (verse 11). Notice the touching phrase he uses in verse 12 that speaks of their "mutual faith." (Peter calls it "a like precious faith," 2 Peter 1:1). We today have like-minded Christians all over the world. That should be a source of encouragement, especially when we feel alone. There are others trying to please God in every part of the world.

The message of salvation in Christ is found in the gospel. This "good news" is described in Romans 1:16 as "the power of God to salvation for everyone who believes." And in it (that is, in the gospel) the righteousness of God is revealed (verse 17). How God makes a person righteous, through obedience to the Lord's will, is revealed to us in this new covenant between God and man, otherwise known as the New Testament. This New Testament is also referred to as "the faith."

And don't forget that this salvation is available to both Jews and Greeks (or Gentiles). This phrase speaks of the universal nature of the church/kingdom of Christ. No one is unimportant to God. Jesus died to make salvation possible for every tongue, tribe, nation and people. God's plan for world evangelism (Acts 1:8) took the gospel to Jerusalem, all Judea, Samaria and to the ends of the earth. We must all do what we can, where we are, with everyone we have an opportunity to share the gospel with. There are people you know who are outside of Christ. You may be the only New Testament Christian they know. If you don't try to save them, who will?

The existence of God may be known by looking at the universe around us (verse 20; Psalms 19:1-6). But how God expects us to live and serve Him is revealed in His written word (see also Psalms 19:7-11). Those who are disobedient to God will be punished (verses 18-32). Many specific sins are listed here, representative of all sin against God. The sins found here are primarily referring to the transgressions of the Gentiles. Their idolatrous practices included many of these sinful things. Those who "practice such things are deserving of death" (verse 32; Romans 6:23). Only those who obey "the faith" will be saved.

## Romans 2

The end of Romans 1 was primarily a condemnation of the Gentiles, who had abandoned God as Creator and who began to worship and serve the creation instead. This led them to all sorts of immorality and, God had, therefore, given them up to their own uncleanness.

Chapter Two focuses on the reality that the Jews had also rebelled against God and His righteousness and were, therefore, just as guilty of sin before God as the Gentiles.

The chapter contains a warning to practice the truth, not just to preach it to others. It is one thing to know and teach the truth and another thing entirely to practice it in our own lives. The Jews were good at moralizing for others, but in their own lives, they were falling far short of God's standard. We need to believe, teach and practice the standards that the Lord sets forth in His word. We must also be careful that we do not hold others to higher standards than we are willing to live by ourselves (verses 1-3).

Paul expands on this point later in this chapter in verses 17-24. In those verses, he specifies stealing, adultery and idolatry as examples of things the Jews criticized the Gentiles for committing, all the while being guilty of those very same sins. This principle is not limited to those specific sins, but would include other forms of rebellion against God also.

In verse 4, the apostle reminds them that God, who forgives sins, is always good. The goodness of God (some translations call it His kindness) should lead souls to repentance. His grace offers us a second chance to please Him (or another chance, if we have already used our second or third or fourth chance) and should never be looked on as an excuse to sin more. When we realize there are only two options for eternity, God's reward or His punishment, we should be motivated to serve Him faithfully and in personal purity. God's grace, while amazing indeed, is not license to sin (see Romans 6:1-2 and Jude 4).

Verses 5-11 deal with the subject of future judgment. The Bible uses several terms here to describe the future reward of the righteous; glory, honor, immortality (verse 7) as well as glory, honor and peace (verse 10). He also describes eternal punishment in several different ways; wrath and indignation (verse 8) and tribulation and anguish (verse 8).

Verse 6 makes it clear that the Lord will deliver reward or punishment "to each one according to his deeds." In that sense, we will decide our own eternity. We choose the path of our lives. If we sin, it is because we decided to do so. If we do the right thing, it is a personal choice. He will judge without favoritism in the last day.

Verses 12-16 remind us that those who do the will of God will be rewarded. The Jews who had the Law and sinned were guilty before God. The Gentiles who did not have the Law of Moses, but also sinned before God were guilty. "Doers" of God's will are justified (verse 13). The Bible teaches us God's will and it will be the standard of judgment in the final day (see John 12:48; James 1:22; Matthew 7:21). We must practice what the will of God teaches.

Verses 25-29 emphasizes to these first century Jews that judgment will not be based on physical circumcision, but rather on "circumcision of the heart," a heart surrendered to the will of God. Salvation has nothing to do with a person's national heritage, but with the condition of his or her heart. Chapter Two ends with a reminder that external actions are important as we obey the Lord, but that our hearts, what we are on the inside, will determine whether we are acceptable to God or not. It is possible to appear to others to be serving God when we really are not. The Jews needed to learn that and so do we.

## Romans 3

Chapter One said the Gentiles were guilty of sin. Chapter Two said the Jews were guilty of sin. Chapter Three, therefore, says that everyone is guilty of sin. The first 18 verses of Romans 3 conclude that everyone falls under the condemnation of sin.

Paul first defends God's righteous judgment of the world (verses 1-8). After pointing out that the Old Testament scriptures were primarily written to and for the Jewish people, Paul reminds them that God is not unjust when He punishes the disobedient. His righteousness is seen in sharp contrast to man's rebellion and wickedness. Anyone who is punished eternally will be receiving what he has deserved.

There is an interesting point made in verse 8. Some were accusing Paul and others (he uses "us; we") of claiming that evil is justified if good comes from it. They stated that

Paul had said, "Let us do evil that good may come." This is the old "the end justifies the means" argument. Paul strongly states that he does not believe that and those who report that he does will receive a just condemnation (from God).

Then he quotes numerous verses from the Old Testament (verses 9-18) to show that all people who reach a point of accountability before God rebel against His will and commit sin. Most of these verses come from the book of Psalms and so the Jews would have been familiar with these concepts because the songs they sang every Sabbath in the synagogue are quoted here. Songs have a powerful way of getting into our minds and helping us to remember Biblical passages and principles. That's one way we teach and admonish "one another in psalms, hymns and spiritual songs" (Colossians 3:16) even today.

Next the apostle Paul reminds them that obedience to the Old Law will not justify one before the Lord. The chapter concludes with a discussion of salvation through faith in Christ apart from the deeds of the Law of Moses (verses 19-31). Two verses stand out in this section of the chapter.

Verse 23 states, in terms that cannot be misunderstood, that "all have sinned and fall short of the glory of God." Jesus is the only perfect, sinless person who has ever lived on the earth.

Verse 26 speaks of God's righteousness and says that He is both "just" (in that all sin is punished in the plan of God) and "the justifier" (the one who developed and delivered this saving plan to mankind).

The song, Nothing But The Blood (*Hymns for Worship, Revised*, #269), summarizes much of the teaching of this chapter.

- Verse 1 – What can wash away my sins? Nothing but the blood of Jesus; What can make me whole again? Nothing but the blood of Jesus.
- Verse 2 – For my pardon this I see, Nothing but the blood of Jesus; For my cleansing, this my plea, Nothing but the blood of Jesus.
- Verse 3 – Nothing can for sin atone, Nothing but the blood of Jesus; Naught of good that I have done, Nothing but the blood of Jesus.
- Chorus: Oh! precious is the flow that makes me white as snow; No other fount I know, Nothing but the blood of Jesus.

Verse 25 refers to the blood of Jesus as "a propitiation" for our sins. This word means that He died as an atoning sacrifice for the sins of the world. He paid the price for our sins, so that we would not have to (which would mean we would all be lost). This word is also found in Hebrews 2:14; 1 John 2:2 and 4:10.

We do not earn salvation through obedience; it is still a gift of God's grace. Salvation is never a matter of perfect deeds, but of mature and devoted faith.

# Romans 4

There are three principles we have learned so far in Romans.

- No one can be saved by perfect law keeping, because all have sinned.
- We must obey the Lord by faith.
- God's grace then saves us.

Romans 4 provides an illustration of these principles as set forth in Romans 1-3. Both Paul (Romans 4) and James (James 2) use Abraham as their example of the relationship between faith and deeds and many conclude that they contradict one another. Such is not the case at all. They were simply answering two different questions and so they approached the subject from opposite directions. Paul was fighting Judaizers who sought justification by the Law of Moses and so he emphasizes the importance of faith in Christ for salvation, not obedience to the Old Testament. James deals with those who claim faith in God but it is not demonstrated in their lives. He reminds them that faith without works is dead.

The Bible describes different kinds of faith.

- Little – Matthew 6:30
- Weak – Romans 14:1
- Dead – James 2
- Great – Luke 7:9
- Unfeigned – 1 Timothy 1:5
- Saving – Ephesians 2:8

The New Testament also speaks of different kinds of works (some versions say deeds).

- Of the flesh – Galatians 5:19-21
- Of the Law of Moses – Galatians 2:16; 3:11
- Of righteousness – Titus 3:4-8; Ephesians 2:8-10
- Of obedience – Hebrews 5:8-9

The works of righteousness that do not save us include things like reading the Bible, attending services, and praying and they do not make up for our sins. We should do those things because God tells us to in the Bible, but no matter how many of them we do, they will not save us.

Works of obedience do not save us apart from God either. They do not mean we earn or merit salvation; it is still a matter of God's grace. Even when we obey God, we do not deserve heaven. But works of obedience are the way we show God (and others) about the commitment of our faith. (James 2:19 uses the example of the demons, who believe, but do not obey God and therefore, their faith will not save them.)

When we teach baptism for the remission of sins (Acts 2:38; 22:16), we are often accused of believing in "works salvation." There are likely some who do believe that, but I don't know of anyone who does. What we believe is that we are saved by faith, through God's grace, but there are human conditions of obedience to show Him the commitment we are making to Christ as the Lord of our lives. We are baptized not as a human work that earns us heaven, but as a show of our willingness to obey whatever the Lord tells us to do (Matthew 7:21; Philippians 2:12; James 1:22). We are saved by faith that works.

Romans 4 shows us that faith in God has always been essential for salvation, by reminding us that Abraham was justified by faith, before the law of circumcision was given and before the Law of Moses had been revealed. Therefore, neither circumcision nor the Law of Moses is the basis of salvation. Rather, it is our faith and the grace of God that brings about salvation.

## Romans 5

Having been justified before God through our faith in Jesus Christ, we can have peace and hope (verses 1-11). Even through trials and difficulties, we develop endurance and strength of character, which give us hope. Verses 3-5 here sound very much like James 1:2-5. Both writers remind us that persecution and troubles can produce a strong spiritual character for one who is determined to trust God throughout every circumstance of life (Galatians 6:9).

Hope is more than just wishful thinking. It is desire, plus confident expectation. And it is hope that is described elsewhere as an anchor for our soul (Hebrews 6:19). A life lived without hope is mere existence. All life is not lived well and the Savior came that we might have abundant life (John 10:10). Peace with God is available through Jesus, as well as hope. Jesus (the Prince of Peace, Isaiah 9:6) came into the world to provide us with spiritual peace.

He offers us peace and hope because He loves us. That is the message of verses 5-11. Jesus didn't die on the cross because we were good or lovable or deserving. We were the exact opposite of what we should have been. Paul makes the point here that there are people in this world that any of us would die for, including our spouses, our children, our parents, our loved ones. But we would never die for criminals, thieves, or murderers. And yet, Jesus died for us when we were ungodly (verse 6) and sinners (verses 8).

Verses 6 and 8 emphasize two important truths. First, we could not save ourselves ("not of works lest anyone should boast," Ephesians 2:9). No one could ever invent a plan to forgive his own sins; only God could do that. But why would He do that? The second truth we learn is that He did it because He loves us. We (all human beings) are made in His image, after His likeness. That empowers His love for us in such a way that Jesus died for all people (Hebrews 2:9).

Through the blood of Jesus (we remember that each time we drink the fruit of the vine in the Lord's Supper), we can be justified in the sight of God and saved from His wrath (verse 9).

Verses 10-11 use the word, reconcile, twice and reconciliation, once. These terms essentially mean having an important but broken friendship restored or renewed. We begin life in a right relationship with God (contrary to what Calvinism teaches); we are not born totally depraved. But we reach a point of accountability (maturity) where we understand right from wrong, but we choose the wrong way. That is sin and this leaves us in a lost condition; our friendship with God is broken – by us; we become His enemies (verse 10). Through Jesus and His sacrifice, we can be reconciled to God. Because He loves us, He paid a very high price that we were unable to pay ourselves. As the song says, "What a friend we have in Jesus."

Could the sacrifice of one Man, Jesus Christ, really provide hope for all mankind? Could millions of souls be saved through the death of one individual? Paul reminds us here that it was through one man, Adam, that sin entered the world. Verses 12-21 remind us that just as one man brought sin and death into the world for everyone, so one man, Jesus, brought righteousness and life into the world also.

Many have misinterpreted verses 12-21 to teach the false doctrine of inherited sin. (Sometimes it is referred as "original sin.") This passage does not teach that. It is true that we suffer the physical consequences of Adam's sin, in that all people will die physically. It is not true that we suffer the guilt of Adam's sin. We suffer the guilt of our own sin and the spiritual consequence of an eternity separated from God. But God provided salvation for us through the death of His Son. Both spiritual death (due to sin) and spiritual life (through the righteous act of Christ) are conditional. We choose to sin and we can choose to obey God and live forever.

## Romans 6

A proper understanding of God's grace and mercy will lead people away from sin. There were, in the first century, and there are now, people who conclude that God's grace is permission to sin. Romans 6 was written to early disciples to show them the error of that kind of logic.

You should know that it wasn't only in Rome that some people had this mistaken idea about sin and grace. Jude 4 also speaks about those who wanted to "turn the grace of our God into lewdness" (he also says that they end up denying God and Jesus). God's grace should cause us to live better, not worse. It should make us forsake sin, not embrace it.

Paul reminds them (and us) that, when we were baptized into the death of Christ, we were raised to walk "in newness of life" (verses 3-4). It is in baptism that we contact the blood of the Savior. Just as He died, was buried and rose again, so too we die to our sins in repentance, are buried with Him in baptism and are raised as new creatures.

A key word in verse 4 is "buried." Verse 5 describes this as being "united together" with Christ. The word, baptism, literally means immersion. That is the original meaning of the Greek word used here and in every New Testament passage referring to baptism. Sprinkling and pouring are not alternative methods of baptism. They are not baptism at all. These ideas come "from men," not from heaven. Why do some people think they can change what God says?

In baptism, our old man of sin was crucified with Him, "that the body of sin might be done away with, that we should no longer be slaves of sin" (verse 6).

Verse 8 tells us that, when we are baptized into Christ, we have died to sin, that is, we no longer live for the sinful pleasures of this life, but rather, we live with and for Christ. Just as Jesus died and then rose, never to die again (verses 9-10), we are to live in "newness of life." We must not return to the deadness of sinful pleasure, that life is to have been crucified (Galatians 2:20).

We are, therefore, as followers of Christ, "dead indeed to sin, but alive to God" (verse 11).

His conclusion, then, beginning in verse 12 and continuing through the remainder of Chapter Six, is that sin must not reign in our bodies. We must not present our bodies as slaves of sin, but as instruments of God for righteousness (verse 13).

We were formerly slaves of sin, but now we have obeyed God from our innermost being (our hearts) and have become His slaves, bondservants of righteousness (verse 17).

And, finally, he tells us that sin will result in eternal condemnation ("death," verse 23), but that, through God's free gift, we can enjoy "eternal life in Christ Jesus our Lord."

Let's consider two applications of this chapter for our lives.

Chapter 6 was written as a reminder to Christians of the huge change in their lives that took place when they were baptized into the death of Jesus. It was written to encourage disciples to stop sinning and live better. It reminds them and us that the old man of sin is dead and gone (2 Corinthians 5:17).

These verses do teach non-Christians that God will give them a second chance at serving Him. God's grace is a wonderful gift that we could never deserve or earn but that we should appreciate very much. Without God's grace, we would all be lost.

## Romans 7

One of the major points of Romans, chapters 3-8, is that we are no longer under the Law of Moses.

His illustration to make that point in Romans 7 is marriage. Two people are bound by God's law to one another "till death do us part." If one puts away his or her spouse and remarries while the first spouse is still living, that person is in a state of adultery. Obviously, if a person dies, Paul says that the surviving spouse is free to remarry without sinning.

(He doesn't deal in this passage with the exception of sexual immorality. That exception was mentioned by Jesus in Matthew 5:31-32 and Matthew 19:1-9. His point here is the marriage law itself, one man and one woman for life, not the exception. The exception doesn't have to be mentioned every time the basic marriage law is given for the exception to be valid.)

But because the Old Law (of Moses) died or was nailed to the cross (Colossians 2:14), we are now under the Law of Christ, the gospel, or the New Testament. At one point, Jesus (as deity) was "married" to the Law of Moses. But it died on the cross, along with the Savior Himself, and Jesus is now "married" to the gospel. That's why, all the way back in Romans 1:16, the gospel is said to be "the power of God to salvation for everyone who believes."

Verse 6 emphasizes that "we have been delivered from the law, having died to what we were held by, so that we should serve in the newness of the Spirit and not in the oldness of the letter." Paul uses similar language in 2 Corinthians 3:6 – "(God) who also made us sufficient as ministers of the new covenant, not of the letter but of the Spirit; for the letter (the Old Testament, rh) kills, but the Spirit (the New Testament, rh) gives life."

The Law of Moses revealed to us what sin is and gives us many examples, as in the Ten Commandments (verses 7-14). He specifically mentions covetousness, the tenth commandment. We learn that violating any part of God's revealed will is sin. Obedience is compared to life; disobedience is referred to as death. His conclusion (verses 12) is that God's law is holy and just and good as it points us to God, if we are spiritually minded, not carnally minded (verse 14). Although the two covenants differ from one another, nothing that was immoral under the Old Testament became moral in the New.

But Paul, though no longer under the Old Law, still struggled with the weaknesses of the flesh. The final part of Romans 7, verses 15-25, describes his daily battles between what he wants to do and what he actually does. He wants (or wills) to do good, but his flesh is weak and so he often finds himself sinning.

Some people believe Paul is describing his battle against sin previously under the Law of Moses. Some believe he is describing, not himself personally, but the general struggle against lust and sin that all people (both Christians and non-Christians) have. I see no reason to believe, although Paul was a faithful and devoted Christian, that he had no current challenges in overcoming the devil in his own personal life. He may well have been more successful than average (I know he was more successful than I am), but that doesn't mean he had achieved a spiritual status that made him immune from all temptation.

We all face that battle, day by day. It is never easy to do only the right thing, because of the lure and power of temptation. Most of the time, when we sin, don't we realize that it was wrong? It is usually not a knowledge problem, but an obedience failure, a heart problem. But with the help of Jesus (verse 25), we can be victorious in this spiritual warfare, with its eternal consequences.

# Romans 8

Our daily battle, even for Christians, is between the spirit and the flesh. The theme of Chapter 8 is that, as God's people, we can be "more than conquerors" (verse 37).

Each person has a dual nature, the inward part (called the spirit or the soul) and the outer part (called the flesh or the body). Paul reminds us that, as Christians, we are to walk according to the spirit and not according to the flesh. This is a never ending struggle.

There is some debate about whether the word, spirit, in Romans 8 should be capitalized or not. Some believe it refers to the Holy Spirit and, therefore, as the translators of the New King James Version and many other translations have decided, the word should be capitalized. Others believe it is simply a reference to the spiritual part of man (as contrasted in Romans 8 with the physical side or the flesh) and should be lower case, spirit. Either way, the spiritual side of our being is to be led by the teachings of the Holy Spirit as revealed in the Bible.

Verses 1-17 continue the apostle's reminder that we are to focus on the things of God so that we will walk, live, set our minds on and be led by the Spirit of God. When we do that, Paul says, "you are not in the flesh but in the Spirit" (verse 9). This is what makes us "sons of God" (verse 14). Notice especially the focus on this idea in verses 5-10. No one will say that this is always easy, but it is vital for those who seek to live with God forever.

There are a couple of additional things here in Chapter 8 about this struggle between spirit and flesh. The first is that Christians have help through the indwelling of the Holy Spirit (verses 9 and 11). There are at least two non-Charismatic views of what that means. One view is that every Christian receives a personal, but non-miraculous indwelling of the Spirit when he is obedient to the gospel. This view might likely interpret Acts 2:38 – "and you shall receive the gift of the Holy Spirit" as being another reference to this type of indwelling.

The second explanation of this indwelling concept is that the Holy Spirit, who inspired the New Testament (John 14:26; 16:13; 1 Corinthians 2:10-13; Ephesians 3:3-5), dwells in Christians as the word of God dwells in us. This view would parallel Colossians 3:16 – "Let the word of Christ dwell in you richly in all wisdom" with Ephesians 5:18-19 – "be filled with the Spirit, speaking to one another in psalms, hymns..." The Bible is called "the sword of the Spirit" in Ephesians 6:17.

The second lesson about the spirit and the flesh revealed in this chapter is that when we are led by the Spirit, we are heirs of God who will receive an eternal inheritance (verses 14-17). The Spirit bears witness to our inheritance as He teaches us how to become children of God. Again, this is done through the inspired message of the gospel.

Verses 18-30 deal with the future glory of those who belong to God. Verse 18 is a favorite verse about heaven and reminds us that no earthly challenges should take us away from the Lord. Verse 24 promises us hope, one of the most positive words in all of the New Testament. Verse 28 tells us that God has and will continue to work all things together for the good of those who love Him.

Struggles and trials will confront us on every side when we seek to live for God. But God has provided for us all things we need to survive this earthly existence and live with Him forever in heaven. And no matter how many trials or difficulties we may have, we can be "more than conquerors" through Jesus and His sacrifice on our behalf. When we seek to live according to the spirit and to deny the flesh, nothing can separate us from God's love. Nothing.

## Romans 9

Paul begins Chapter 9 (verses 1-5) by expressing his sorrow that his own people, the Jews, have rejected Jesus. He refers to "great sorrow and continual grief in my heart." Of course, some Jews did not reject Jesus, but most of them did.

It was stated early in the ministry of Christ that His own people (don't forget that Jesus was Jewish also) would not accept Him as the promised Messiah of the Old Testament. "He came to His own, and His own did not receive Him" (John 1:11). Jesus told several parables to show that the Jewish people, as a whole, did not accept Him. The parables of the Wicked Vinedressers and the Great Banquet are two examples of this.

And when the Jews decided not to believe in Jesus as the Christ, the gospel was taken to the Gentiles (see Acts 13:44-47). The same idea is found in Romans 1:16 in the phrase, "for the Jew first, and also for the Greek." Paul quotes eleven verses from the Old Testament in Chapter 9. Several of them show that the Gentile nations were always intended by God to be part of His eternal kingdom. (He will quote even more verses about this in the next chapter.)

Some of the material in Romans 9 can be a little difficult, but only because we have been introduced to the Calvinistic concept of election which states that God determines ahead of time which individuals will be saved and which people will be lost, independent of their own choices and actions.

The rest of Chapter 9 (verses 6-33) shows us that this election is for groups of people, not individuals. Those in the group who choose to obey and follow the Lord are elected for salvation (here, it is primarily the Gentiles). Those in the group who choose to deny and disobey Christ are elected for condemnation (here, mostly referring to the Jews). It is God's plan for salvation that was determined before the world began, not the names of souls that would be saved and those who would be lost. We have been given free will to obey or reject.

There are three clear Biblical principles that deny Calvinistic predestination.

1. God is not a respecter of persons (Acts 10:34-35; 1 Peter 1:17).
   God does not show favoritism or partiality for groups or individuals. He doesn't care about race, gender, skin color, financial status, or any other characteristic that humans think are so important. All He cares about is that each person has an immortal soul that will live forever somewhere.
2. God wants everyone to be saved (2 Peter 3:9; 1 Timothy 2:3-4).
   The writer of Hebrews makes it clear that Jesus died for all people (Hebrews 2:9).

"And He Himself is the propitiation (atoning sacrifice, NIV) for our sins, and not for ours only but also for the whole world" (1 John 2:2). Jesus died to make it possible for anyone to be saved eternally.

3. God loves the whole world (John 3:16).
   As the song says, "Whosoever will may come." That old spiritual song is based on Revelation 22:17, "And the Spirit and the bride say, Come! And let him who hears say, Come! And let him who thirsts come. Whoever desires, let him take the water of life freely."

Unconditional Election (Calvinistic predestination) is contrary to the very nature of God. It makes Him a respecter of persons, says that He doesn't want everybody to be saved and teaches that He loves some, but not others. We can choose our own eternal home in heaven or hell.

## Romans 10

Having established in Chapter 9 that the Jews, for the most part, had rejected Jesus as the Messiah, this chapter shows that Paul still loved his people and wanted them to be saved. (We should not quickly give up on the lost people we know and love.) He prayed for the Jews; their salvation was his heart's desire. The problem was that they were ignoring God's plan for their righteousness and trying to make their own plan. God's plan for the salvation of the Jews is the same as His plan for Gentiles. They must be obedient to the gospel, not the Law of Moses.

In verse 4, Paul shows that Jesus was the "end of the law for righteousness." That doesn't mean that He ended the Old Law, although He did. But, in this case, it means that Jesus was the end result, or the fulfillment, of the Law of Moses. The New International Version (2011) says that He is "the culmination of the law." He came to fulfill the Law of Moses and He did so in every way. The Law was described as a "tutor" (schoolmaster, KJV) to bring people to faith in Christ (Galatians 3:24-25).

Everything in the Old Testament pointed people to Jesus the Messiah. From the first Messianic prophecy, found in Genesis 3:15 to God's promise to Abram that, in his seed all nations of the earth would be blessed (Genesis 12:1-3), through historical books and the prophetic writings, the single message that stands out, loud and clear, is that God was going to provide a Savior for the whole world. That Savior is Jesus of Nazareth and He is the only way to God (John 14:6).

Verse 5 emphasizes to us that the only way to be saved by keeping any law (OT or NT) is to obey it perfectly. Jesus Himself is the only accountable being in the history of the universe to do that. Because we all are guilty of sin (Romans 3:23), we must rely on the grace and loving kindness of God for salvation. We will never make it by perfect obedience.

The greatest need of Israel was to recognize Jesus as the Savior and to obey His new covenant, even though we will not obey perfectly. That's why the book of Romans begins with a reference to the gospel as "the power of God to salvation to everyone who believes, for the Jew first and also for the Greek (or Gentile, rh)" (Romans 1:16). And in the gospel is revealed "the righteousness of God," that is, God's plan for making both Jew and non-Jew righteous (Romans 1:17). Even with our obedient response to His love, we will still require God's mercy and forgiveness of our sins.

Verses 9-10 mention the importance of faith and confession. These are not the only parts of salvation, but they are important parts. I saw a yard sign once beside a highway that read, "Jesus saves" (Romans 10:9). I agree with that, but that is not all it takes. Repentance and baptism for the remission of sins are also important, but are not found in these two verses. Acts 2:38 and other passages clearly teach of the necessity of repentance and baptism for salvation.

Verses 11-13 contain a quote from Joel 2:32 (also found in Acts 2:21 and other verses in the New Testament). "Calling on the name of the Lord" is often referred to by those who believe in what some have called "the sinner's prayer." That is not a reference to praying for salvation as a non-Christian, but to obeying what the Lord's will teaches. In Acts 22:16, Ananias told Saul of Tarsus, "And now why are you waiting? Arise and be baptized, calling on the name of the Lord." Baptism is a part of calling on the name of the Lord for salvation. Jews needed to hear and believe and obey the Lord's New Testament in order to be saved, as they called upon God for salvation (Romans 10:13). In general, Gentiles were more open to the gospel than were the Jews (verse 16).

Verse 20 describes the Gentiles as those who found God as they accepted Christ. Verse 21 describes the Jews as "a disobedient and contrary people."

## Romans 11

The rejection of Christ by the Jews was never total. The majority of the Hebrew nation did not believe Jesus to be the Messiah. But some of them did accept and obey Him.

In Romans 11, Paul makes it clear that there was always a remnant of faithful Israelites, even in the dark days of the Old Testament monarchy (verses 1-4). And, in the first century, there were those in Israel who did understand the truth (verse 5). They are referred to here as a "remnant," which means it was not a huge number of people, but rather a small one. That's usually the way it is; those who obey God and His will are almost always in the minority.

For those who did not accept Jesus as the Savior, it was not too late. If they heard the truth of the gospel and were obedient to it, they could still be saved.

Verse 6 teaches again that we are not saved by works. We cannot ever do enough good things to make up for even one of our sins against God, let alone making up for the large numbers of sins we commit in a lifetime. As we have noted several times already in these notes on Romans, the only person who could ever earn or deserve or merit a home in heaven is Jesus, because He perfectly obeyed God's law with no sin at all. No one else can do that. (Perhaps it should be noted that people with the mental inability to know right from wrong, infants and toddlers who do not understand sin, and those whose minds never develop to an accountable state before God will be saved, because they do not have the ability to sin. Sin is a conscious rebellion against God, either by what we have been taught or when our conscience would convict us.)

Verses 7-10 assure us that "Israel has not obtained what it seeks" and then tells us why. Quoting Old Testament verses found in Deuteronomy 29:4, Isaiah 29:10 and Psalm 69:22-23, Paul says that the Jews have been given a spirit of stupor so that they cannot see, hear or understand. This is in the same way as God hardened Pharaoh's heart in the time of Moses. His heart was hardened in response to what God said he needed to do. He didn't want to do it, so he hardened his heart against God. God didn't make it impossible for Pharaoh (or the Jews here) to learn and obey. It was Pharaoh's bad attitude toward God that hardened his mind against the Lord. Same thing applies here with the first century Jews.

Through the Jewish rejection of the Messiah, the Gentiles were given the opportunity to hear and obey the gospel (verses 11-14).

But Jews who had initially refused to confess Christ could also still be saved if they would but turn and be converted through the preaching of the gospel. When Paul writes in verse 26, "And so all Israel will be saved," he means through hearing and obeying, anyone could be accepted by God. That's how any lost soul is made righteous before God, by our obedience and God's grace. All Israel and all Gentiles could be saved in this manner.

In verses 15-24, he compares obedience to God with branches from a wild olive tree (lost souls) being grafted into a cultivated olive tree (the saved). This is true not only of Gentiles and Jews, but of all lost people. Anyone who comes to Christ can be "grafted in" (saved) through Christ (see Ephesians 2:11-13). And he reminds us of both the goodness and severity of God (verse 22). God will accept all who believe and obey and will punish all who reject and disobey.

Verses 25-36 conclude the chapter by emphasizing the greatness of God. Verse 33 reminds us that there are many things about God that we may never understand fully in this life. We need to do the best we can. To God be all the glory (1 Corinthians 10:31).

## Romans 12

Romans 12 begins what many have referred to as "the practical part" of the letter. Some would define chapters 1-11 as "doctrinal," while calling chapters 12-16 as "practical." It would be more accurate to say that the first 11 chapters of Romans have laid the foundational principles upon which applications are then made in the final 5 chapters.

We might summarize chapters 1-11 as describing man's rejection of God and His plan to redeem mankind through His Son. Chapters 12-16 summarize man's response to God's plan.

Romans 12 is one of the most challenging chapters in all of the New Testament. It presents us with one responsibility after another in discussing our relationship with God and with each other as disciples. It is entirely possible that a Christian could spend his entire life, just trying to obey the duties outlined in this chapter.

Paul begins by telling us to completely present our lives to God. We are not to allow the world to pressure us into conformity, but rather to be changed or transformed into the image of Christ. Don't be conformed to the world; rather be transformed by the renewing of your mind. When Paul speaks of the mind, he refers to that part of man that speaks to our higher nature in contrast to the sinful things of the world (much like Colossians 3:1-2). Our logical thought process must be dominated by the message of God from the Bible. We renew our minds from the profane and worldly into the spiritual and divine realm as we focus on the things of God as outlined in the New Testament. As a part of our response to that heavenly emphasis, we present our whole being, body, mind and spirit as "living sacrifices" to God. We die to self and then live for God.

In verses 3-8, the apostle points out that we are not all the same. We all have different abilities and opportunities. But whatever our unique circumstance may be, we are to do all we can to serve God and our fellow man. He specifies teaching, serving, leading, encouraging, giving all to His glory. We are never to serve God in order to show off, to our own glory; not so we might be praised but rather that He might be honored and glorified in all that we do.

One of the challenging aspects of serving God in a way that pleases Him is that no one must "think of himself more highly than he ought to think." In other words, we must be humble. Perhaps the single most prevailing sin of man is selfishness.

Verses 9-18 get into the real life, daily practical examples of being a Jesus follower. Paul speaks of many of our personal obligations before God, including brotherly love, honoring one another, being hospitable, being a blessing to others, rejoicing and weeping with each other and remaining humble in our service to Him.

Because verse 9 begins this list of characteristics of a faithful disciple of Christ with the important principle about loving others, many have concluded that all of the other things found here are simply an outgrowth of having the right kind of love for each other. They are practical suggestions for how we can show our love for other Christians. Really, they are not just practical, they are divinely inspired. You cannot come up with a more important list than that.

The chapter ends by reminding us that we are not to be vengeful, angry people. Rather we are to be at peace with others, in every way we possibly can. God will avenge all wrong doing. We have a responsibility to overcome evil with good, not to repay evil with evil. Two wrongs never make a right. Don't be overcome by the wrong attitude; overcome a wrong attitude with the right attitude.

## Romans 13

The relationship between followers of Christ and the governments of men has long been discussed.

One of the major lessons from the book of Daniel is that "the Most High rules in the kingdoms of men" (Daniel 4:25).

When Jesus was asked by the tax gatherers about paying a temple tax, He performed a miracle with a fish to pay the tax for Himself and Peter (Matthew 17:24-27).

In Mark 12:13-17, the Pharisees and the Herodians (normally at enmity with each other) joined forces as they attempted to trap Jesus in an inconsistency. Christ's response to them was, "Render to Caesar the things that are Caesar's, and to God the things that are God's."

We have, therefore, the responsibility to obey the laws of the land. And we must obey all of them, even ones we don't like, such as speed limits and paying taxes. The single exception is if a law would require us to be disobedient to God (see Acts 5:28-29, for an example). No human relationship has the authority to cause us to disobey the Father in heaven. The Lord must always be first in our lives.

The book of Romans was most likely written right after the Jews has been driven from Rome by Claudius Caesar (Acts 18:2). Jews could not accept the fact that they could be ruled by a Gentile government. Their misconception of the Messiah was that He would come into the world as a powerful military leader for the primary purpose of freeing them from the oppression of the Roman Empire.

Romans 13:1-7 tells us that God appointed civil government for the protection of citizens and that only wrong doers need to fear those in authority. When it comes to government, the source is God; its nature is to serve God; its purpose is to punish the guilty and protect the innocent.

Verse 1 asserts that "the authorities that exist are appointed by God." This does not mean that God approves of every ruler at every level in every time period or in every part of the world. There are dictators and tyrants whose behavior obviously has displeased Him. And there are forms of government which surely do serve His goals. But government itself, intended by the Lord to achieve His general desire for law and order, is His plan.

If we violate the laws of the land, there will be punishment (verse 2). Rulers are "God's minister, an avenger to execute wrath on him who practices evil" (verse 5). "He does not bear the sword in vain" (verse 4) indicates the authority of God behind both capital punishment and carnal warfare for the protection of the innocent.

Verses 8-10 teach Christians that we are to love others, "for he who loves another has fulfilled the law" (verse 8). In quoting several of the Ten Commandments, Paul points out that adultery, murder, stealing, bearing false witness and coveting are all violations of the second most important commandment, "You shall love your neighbor as yourself" (verse 9; Leviticus 19:18).

Verses 11-14 reminds Christ's disciples to "cast off the works of darkness" by removing all ungodliness from their lives and to "put on the Lord Jesus." The apostle encourages us to walk in light, not in darkness. Verse 11 helps us to remember that, if we are indifferent and immoral, we need to awake out of our spiritual sleep. He admonishes us to walk properly and not in revelry, drunkenness, lewdness, lust, strife or envy. We belong to Christ and we must live appropriately in order to help the lost find Him.

## Romans 14

How to differ with other Christians without dividing was a controversial subject in the first century and it continues to be an important question for disciples today. Romans 14 was written to show us that it is possible for followers of the Christ to have different views on some issues, but to remain in fellowship with one another.

The first thing we need to understand about Romans 14 is that Paul is dealing with matters of judgment in areas where God is indifferent, that is, where either decision is acceptable. Doctrinal matters of right and wrong are entirely outside the content of the apostle's teaching here.

There are two specific issues that Romans 14 mentions. One was the question of eating meat that had been sacrificed to idols (verses 1-4). Some Christians thought they could; others believed they should not. Another was the practicing of "observing days" (verses 5-6). This probably was speaking of the practice of Hebrew Christians who continued to respect Jewish holidays, not as "holy days" but as civil observances. Some thought it to be a compromise (because the Old Law was finished), while others believed they could still observe those days without the religious or spiritual implications they formerly held.

There are many similar subjects today on which brethren differ, such as the woman's head covering, the observance of Christmas as a national holiday, the Bible version one uses, whether a Christian can serve in the military or as a policeman or woman, and whether Christians should go to movies or not. Paul writes, "Let each one be fully convinced in his own mind" (verse 5).

As stated above, the teaching of this chapter deals with matters of opinion or judgment, not doctrine. So this chapter does not teach that we should just accept anyone who claims to be a Christian, no matter what that person might believe, teach or practice. The teachings of passages like 1 John 4:1 apply here: "Beloved, do not believe every spirit, but test the spirits whether they are of God; because many false prophets have gone out into the world." If there is such a thing as a false teacher (and John says there are many of them), then we cannot just throw everything into Romans 14 and say that we will just agree to disagree. Paul had numerous false teachers who followed him around everywhere he went and tried to damage his influence. He was preaching truth and others were teaching error and they could not be in fellowship with each other or with God until those who taught error repented and started teaching the truth. 2 John 9 warns of those who transgress God's will and do not abide in the teaching of Christ. John's inspired admonition is that they must not be fellowshipped in their error. 1 and 2 Timothy and Titus contain repeated warnings about the importance of truth and sound doctrine and that those who taught heretical ideas must be marked and avoided.

How a person becomes a Christian (faith only vs. full obedience to the gospel) is not something that Christians can disagree about. One is right and the other is wrong. Instrumental music is not a "take it or leave it" practice. It violates New Testament teaching and those who would press for its use in the Lord's church to the point of division are wrong. (I believe in these areas, we need to study together with love for God's word and each other and hopefully, we can come to an agreement about what God wants.)

The second consideration in the chapter is the effect that such decisions would have on other Christians. One of the key parts of the chapter is verse 7 – "For none of us lives to himself, and no one dies to himself." Paul is reminding us that our actions can affect the conscience of others and we ought not to dismiss the views of others just because they disagree with us about a particular subject. If brothers and sisters love God and one another, we can find a way to work together that pleases the Lord and does not violate His Holy word.

## Romans 15

Chapter 15 continues the theme of unity in the church.

One of the greatest challenges in the early church was to unite Jews and Gentiles together in one body. It is true that Christ broke down the middle wall of separation between the two (Ephesians 2:14-16). Jesus was, after all, the "Prince of Peace" (Isaiah 9:6).

However, the reality is that this unity was not easily accomplished. After centuries of enmity between Jew and Gentile, those hard feelings did not die quickly. And other issues, such as those discussed in Chapter 14, dietary attitudes and the keeping of old Jewish holy days, caused differences between brothers and sisters, long after the Law of Moses had been done away with.

Paul places more responsibility for unity upon the stronger, than on the weaker. (That is not to be understood as saying that stronger Christians should ignore the sins of their weaker brothers. It is saying that in matters of judgment or opinion, we must consider the other person's conscience.) Our goal, as he expresses it in verse 2, "Let each of us please his neighbor for his good, leading to edification." He reminds us that even Jesus did not do things that would have pleased Him, in order that He might help others to grow stronger (verse 3), even to the point of suffering reproach in the eyes of some.

Verse 4 is another reminder that, although we are to live by the teachings of the New Testament today, there are many valuable and important lessons that come from the Old Covenant. Those things are preserved for us today, "for our learning." Through our study of the Hebrew Scriptures, we might receive learning, patience, comfort and hope.

God's desire is that we might be "like-minded toward one another," so that together we might "with one mind and one mouth glorify the God and Father of our Lord Jesus Christ" (verse 6). The church is a much happier place and our lives are infinitely better when we get along with each other. That was really challenging advice for first century

Jews and Gentiles. But Paul's statement is verse 7 is clear: "Therefore receive one another, just as Christ has received us, to the glory of God."

Verses 8-13 quote several Old Testament passages to remind us that God's intention all along was for the church of Jesus Christ to be a universal family, made up of Jews, Gentiles and even Samaritans and any one else who wants to live for and please God. We glorify Him together for His mercy and our salvation. And the God of peace fills us with "all joy and peace in believing, that you may abound in hope by the power of the Holy Spirit" (verse 13).

Paul also speaks of his future plans to travel to Spain with the gospel (verses 14-24). He hoped to visit Rome during that trip.

One of the things Paul mentions in connection with his travels has to do with his evangelistic strategy. His aim was "to preach the gospel, not where Christ was named, lest I should build on another man's foundation." Paul's plan was to preach in unreached areas, as part of Christ's commission to reach all nations with the gospel of salvation.

He also makes reference to his plans to deliver benevolent aid to "the saints who are in Jerusalem." The early church took care of her own, whenever those needs arose. He asks the Christians in Rome to pray for him and his work in the Lord. "Now the God of peace with you all. Amen."

## Romans 16

A strong local church is made up of Christians who have close, loving, godly relationships with one another.

The first 15 verses of Romans 16 list one Christian after another for whom Paul held special affection. At least sixteen of the names are female.

The first Christian named in the chapter is Phoebe, described as "a servant of the church in Cenchrea." It is also said of her that "indeed she has been a helper of many and of myself also" (verses 1-2). Some have used Phoebe in a vain attempt to "prove" that woman can be preachers. The passages says nothing at all about service in that capacity. The very idea of a woman serving as a preacher for a local church is cultural and societal, not scriptural. There are verses that strictly prohibit a woman from preaching publicly, in the presence of men (1 Timothy 2:11-12; 1 Corinthians 14:34-35). Some newer translations have referred to Phoebe as a "deacon," which again is a misunderstanding of the role of women in the church. Deacons are to be "the husbands of one wife" (1 Timothy 3:12). All Christians are to be servants, however, and Phoebe is obviously an exemplary example of one who served others well. Appreciate her commendation by the apostle Paul, but do not make her into something she was not.

Priscilla and Aquila (verses 3-5) are mentioned elsewhere in Scripture (see Acts 18; 1 Corinthians 16; 2 Timothy 4:19). But most of the rest of the people in verses 1-15 are unknown outside of this chapter.

Notice the kinds of things that Paul says about each of those first century saints. What was it that made them so special? They...

- were firstfruits of Achaia to Christ
- labored much
- were in Christ before (Paul)
- were beloved in the Lord

...among other things. All of these descriptions speak of the spiritual work that these faithful disciples performed for the Lord. Paul noticed when people work for God and so does the Lord (1 Corinthians 15:58; Hebrews 6:10).

Consider a quick word about the phrase in verse 16: "Greet one another with a holy kiss." This idea is mentioned in numerous New Testament passages: 1 Corinthians 16:20; 2 Corinthians 12:12; 1 Peter 5:14. Kissing was a common form of greeting and saying farewell in many Eastern cultures. He was not binding a specific greeting or farewell. The emphasis is on the "holy" part of the command. Such a kiss was not to be sensual in nature, but a genuine expression of love and care for others. Men kissed men and women kissed women and males and females kissed each other. It was not provocative or inappropriate (that's what kept it holy). In our time and culture, the same loving care for other disciples is expressed in a warm and friendly handshake or hug.

In verses 17-20, Paul issues a warning about false teachers who would deceive weak brethren. They were to be noted and avoided. In spite of what some thought, these were not serving Christ, but their own desires. And ultimately, Paul wanted them to know that God would crush Satan and the great deceiver would be destroyed eternally in hell.

Chapter 16 ends with a reminder that what pleases God is "obedience to the faith" (verse 26).

# The Letters of 1 & 2 CORINTHIANS

## 1 Corinthians 1

The first century church in Corinth had serious problems.

Some of the problems were things that Paul had heard about from others (1 Corinthians 1:11; 5:1). Others were questions that the church had written to him about (1 Corinthians 7:1).

Some of the specific matters that the letter deals with include division, immorality, lawsuits, marriage, meat sacrificed to idols, idol feasts and communion, the woman's head covering, questions about spiritual gifts, and the resurrection.

Paul writes to provide divinely inspired solutions to these important issues. The principles found in the letter apply to many modern problems facing churches today.

The letter begins by addressing the congregation as "the church of God which is at Corinth." The Christians who comprised the local church were "sanctified in Christ Jesus" and "called to be saints."

The author of the inspired epistle is Paul (1 Corinthians 1:1), a bondservant and an apostle of Jesus Christ. He planted the church in Corinth and some of the events are recorded for us in Acts 18:1-17.

He has several more faithful Christians with him when he pens the letter and they send their love and greetings to these disciples also (1 Corinthians 16:21, 23).

The church in Corinth has often been referred to as a dysfunctional church. They certainly have a number of problems which the apostle deals with in the letter.

Some of these problems have been described to Paul by members of the congregation, in the hope that these struggles could be corrected (1 Corinthians 1:11; 5:1; 11:18, for example).

Other problems have been mentioned to Paul in a letter which he received, in the form of questions that some of the disciples there have asked him to clarify for them (see 1 Corinthians 7:1).

The first problem dealt with is the issue of division. Various disciples are claiming to be of Paul, of Apollos, of Cephas, or of Christ. And beyond the idea of having favorite preachers, they are dividing into groups that would only listen to certain messengers, while rejecting the teaching of any others.

What could reunite the Christians in Corinth and all believers today is the message of the cross of Christ (verses 10-25). To the Jews, it was a stumbling block and to the Gentiles it was foolishness. But to the faithful, it contains the power of God to salvation.

It is unimportant whether one is wise, mighty and noble or foolish, weak and despised (verses 26-29). In Christ, anyone can have righteousness, sanctification and redemption. That's the beauty of the gospel message of salvation through the cross of Jesus. Anyone can be saved who makes the decision to surrender his or her will to God's plan for his life. The Savior, the Son of God, endured the death of the cross to make salvation available for anyone who will come to Him (Matthew 11:28-30; Hebrews 2:9; Revelation 2:14, 17). We often sing a song of invitation that says, "Whosoever will, may come." Jew or Gentile, black or white, rich or poor, educated or illiterate, from every nation, tribe, culture or language, all are welcome to become a part of God's eternal kingdom. The Bible promises eternal life to anyone who does the will of the Father through faith (Matthew 7:21-23).

"He who glories, let him glory in the Lord" (verses 30-31). We must follow Jesus, not a human teacher.

## 1 Corinthians 2

Human wisdom is never a good solution for spiritual problems. The problem of division among God's people continues to be the subject of 1 Corinthians 2.

This chapter begins with Paul's admission that preaching in Corinth made him nervous (verses 1-5). He refers to "weakness" and "fear" and "much trembling." This is an extremely immoral city and one could not be certain how the gospel was going to be received. The Lord speaks to Paul, while the apostle was in Corinth, in a night vision, to reassure him that he should continue to work in this city and not to be afraid (Acts 18:9-11).

Paul reminds the Corinthians that, even in his work among them, it was not his persuasive speech or superior wisdom that brought them into a saved relationship with the Lord. What Paul brought to them that made all the difference was "Jesus Christ and Him crucified."

If we try to convert people to anyone or anything other than Christ, we will not succeed. Jesus is the message and we must never shrink from sharing our confidence in the Savior with a lost and dying world. All that we do must be to His glory, not our own.

Jesus is the only Savior, not Paul or Apollos or Cephas (Peter) or any other gospel preacher.

Verses 6-9 deal with the advantage of spiritual wisdom from God over human wisdom. Those who are mature in the Lord realize that human wisdom will come "to nothing," whereas "the wisdom of God" is something that is "a mystery." That word does not imply that God's wisdom is unknowable, only that we can only learn it as He reveals it to us, which He has done throughout human history, in small pieces, a little at a time.

Verses 8 and 9 especially make this point. If the "rulers of this age" had realized the plan of God, they "would not have crucified the Lord of glory," for this is the means by which the Father provided for the salvation of the lost (remember from chapter 1, verse 18 that the message of the cross reveals the power and wisdom of God). Even Satan himself did not realize the plan of God to provide an atoning sacrifice for sin (the Bible often uses the word, propitiation) through the sacrificial death of His perfect, sinless Son on the cross of Calvary. When Jesus was put to death, the devil thought he had won, but on the third day, when Jesus arose, Satan began to catch on that he had made a huge mistake in thinking he had defeated God. Verse 9 makes it abundantly clear that no human genius could comprehend God's plan without help. Eye could not see, ear could not hear, the human heart could not understand the beauty of God's scheme of redemption.

There is a section of this chapter which deals with the process of inspiration (verses 10-16). Given through the Holy Spirit, the Bible came from God to man so that we might understand what God would have us to do, as we seek to serve Him in this earth life.

Verse 13 affirms that we have, in the New Testament, all that God wants us to know and that He has revealed His covenant with man, not in words of human wisdom, but as the Spirit taught, a message directly from our Creator. He says that the Bible combines "spiritual thoughts with spiritual words" (NASB, 1995).

True spiritual wisdom comes from a deeper and fuller knowledge of God's revelation. Mankind can only know God's mind when He reveals it to us. And He did that in what we now call the Bible. It is a spiritual message for people who want to know and obey God's will.

## 1 Corinthians 3

The basis for the trouble at Corinth is spiritual immaturity. Rather than growing spiritually, as all disciples should, they are still "babes in Christ." This lack of spiritual growth leads to envy, strife and divisions (verses 1-4).

They have begun to divide the church (remember his warning about that in 1 Corinthians 1:10-15?) into various groups based on which preacher they liked the best. He reminds them again that this is proof of their lack of spiritual growth and development (verses 4-9).

The preachers they are following, instead of Christ, are just ministers or servants of the Lord. We are all on the same team, all on the Lord's side.

There is an important principle in verse 6. The New American Standard Bible (1995) translates that verse in this way: "I planted, Apollos watered, but God was causing the growth." We often grow discouraged when people do not respond to the gospel and that reaction is understandable. We so want souls to be saved and we are disappointed when people do not respond. But our job is to plant and water the seed of the gospel in peoples' hearts. It is not our job to produce the results. We have not failed when we teach someone who decides not to obey. We have succeeded in giving them the opportunity to obey. They must decide for themselves whether they will obey the gospel or not. This verse reminds us that preachers plant and water the seed of the gospel, but it is God who makes the plant grow. The Lord, of course, uses human agents as "fellow workers," but we are to worship God alone, not be divisive in following men.

There is only one true foundation for the church (verses 10-15). It is Jesus Christ, the Son of God, who died on the cross to purchase the church, who said He would build the church and who continues to make intercession for the church. He is the Savior; He is the way, the truth and the life. It is all about Jesus, not about preachers or elders or teachers or scholars. It is all about Him.

"God's building" (verse 9) or "the temple of God" (verses 16-17) is the church. We are to build the church on the only solid foundation, Jesus Christ, not on human wisdom or the doctrines and commandments of men. That's where true edification comes from. If we build on anything else, we will fail. As the song says, "My hope is built on nothing less than Jesus' blood and righteousness. All other ground is sinking sand."

If we teach the truth of the gospel to people, some will obey and remain faithful, some will obey and fall away from the Lord, and some will choose to continue their life outside of Christ. If we are building on the firm foundation of Jesus Christ, we have done our job and we will not be held accountable for those who do not obey or those who initially obey but then give up.

The apostle sums much of this up in verse 19 when he reminds us of the value of true spiritual wisdom. "For the wisdom of this world is foolishness with God."

He reminds us not to "boast in men" (verse 21). Our faith is in the Lord, not in our friends and other relationships here on earth.

If we ever get the idea that we have a better way to do things than what God has revealed in His word, we will always be wrong, every time. We cannot improve on God's ways, ever. Always remember, the Bible is right.

## 1 Corinthians 4

Christians are servants of Christ. He is our Master; we are His slaves. Our lives must be spent in His service, doing His work to the salvation of souls with whom we come into contact. We should share Christ and His truth with everyone we meet.

Christians are stewards of God's blessings. We do not own the truth, for example, but we have been entrusted with the responsibility to share it with others. God's primary requirement for a steward is faithfulness. The apostle Paul said to Timothy in 2 Timothy 2:2, "And the things that you have heard from me among many witnesses, commit these to faithful men who will be able to teach others also."

Faithfulness is always tested by persecution and trials. The apostles lived "as men condemned to death." Stewards must be willing to be "fools for Christ's sake." In the first century, disciples were considered "the filth of the world."

But the problem with the first century Corinthians (one of their many problems) is that they are arrogant and puffed up about their relationship with God, not humbled by their forgiveness through the grace and mercy of the Lord. They consider themselves to be full, rich, and to be reigning as kings. They could have been powerful, effective workers for God, if they had been humble and submissive to His will.

Paul shows them that he and others (the other apostles, primarily, but anyone who serve God humbly) simply consider themselves to be servants of the Lord. Paul uses his stewardship to instruct people about how to become and live as children of God, not to rule over and dominate as inferiors. Paul refers to "my ways in Christ, as I teach everywhere in every church." This is the pattern of God's truth that is the same for everyone.

The New Testament is a pattern (many don't like that word today) for both our personal lives (Philippians 3:17) and for the things we do collectively as a church, the family of God (2 Timothy 1:13).

When you look at verse 6, this point is made clearly. Paul says that he wants people to learn from himself and from Apollos, the principle that no one should think more highly of their teachers than they do of God's message. He says, "that you may learn in us not to think beyond what is written." What is written is from God; it is His divinely inspired will. We should never trust a human teacher if he cannot show us what is written. God included everything He wants us to know and do in His written word. If it is not in there, it is absent for a reason. God didn't want us to do it. He didn't accidentally forget to include anything. He included everything we need for life and godliness (2 Peter 1:3) and what is written can make us "complete, thoroughly equipped for every good work" (2 Timothy 3:17). We don't need anything else, anything extra, anything more than what He had given us. If we could just learn to be content with knowing and learning and obeying and teaching God's will for our lives, we would be much better off.

The New Testament directs how the church is to worship; it is the pattern for us to follow today. The New Testament teaches us how the church is to be organized (Philippians 1:1); that is our pattern. The New Testament shows us what the mission or work of a local church is supposed to be (1 Timothy 3:15). In all of these areas, God has not merely given us suggestions, but a pattern that we should imitate, in order that we might please Him.

The church at Corinth needed to grow and change a number of things so that they could be acceptable to the God of heaven and earth. This letter was written to help them and us please our God.

# 1 Corinthians 5

Chapter Five begins the next section of the letter and it deals with the issue of sexual immorality. Many churches since the first century have struggled with problems of immorality among the people of God.

The first century world was highly immoral, just like our current time. Temptation was everywhere and, in Corinth, one of the disciples had taken up with his stepmother. (The Greek word for mother is not in the context, so it was not his mother, but his father's current wife.) The church was not dealing with the sin and others were in danger of being influenced by the ungodly leaven.

Paul instructs the church to purge out the old leaven of ungodliness by delivering this man "to Satan," a reference to church discipline. This would purify the church so that others would not be tempted to commit the same sin. Known sin in the church must not be tolerated.

The Lord takes the purity of the church very seriously. It is no small thing for Christians to sin in a way that causes outsiders to question what the church stands for. When I was growing up, I clearly remember older Christians who would often pray publicly during worship services that the church members would "live in such a way as to never place a blot or a blemish on the church of our Lord." There is a sense in which our imperfections do not take away from God's plan for the church, but in the eyes of our friends and neighbors, they may well believe that all the members of a local church are the same and that if one member is sinning in a public way, maybe everyone else there thinks that is acceptable. Church discipline gives us the opportunity to explain to others that while some of our members might behave badly at times, such behavior is not approved by God or by His people.

Notice in verse 5, that one of the reasons for church discipline is "the destruction of the flesh," that is, the destruction of fleshly desires. That was the problem here; the man was being controlled by physical, fleshly lusts and could only be rescued if something destroyed those evil passions. Perhaps the reality of being withdrawn from (2 Thessalonians 3:6) by his brothers and sisters in Christ would shock him into repentance.

It is not easy for Christians to remain pure while living among many who have little or no regard for godliness, purity, righteousness and morality. But while it is challenging to do the right thing, no matter what others around us are doing, we must do obey God and do only those things that will honor Him.

Paul makes a clear distinction between the people of the world (those who are outside) and those who are Christians (those who are inside). He tells them not to associate with ungodly people, but he explains to them that he is not referring to non-Christians by pointing out that to totally avoid ungodly people you would have to leave the planet. We must simply not allow ourselves to be influenced in a negative way by Christians who are not living right.

He goes so far as to say that we must not even "eat with such a person." Eating a meal together had much significance in the first century. It showed not only friendship and a close relationship with another, it indicated approval of the other as well. That is the point of the invitation of Jesus, found in Revelation 3:20: "Behold I stand at the door and knock. If anyone hears My voice and opens the door, I will come in to him and dine with him, and he with Me." He offers friendship and acceptance. It is speaking of spiritual fellowship and approval from God because of our relationship with Him. Here in Corinthians, God does not want them to engage in any behavior, with a common meal together as just one example, that would lead the other person to believe that you approve of his or her behavior. It might seem extreme, but this is a critical situation that requires serious action.

His conclusion, then, is simple. "Therefore, put away from among yourselves the evil person."

## 1 Corinthians 6

Another problem in Corinth was the issue of Christians taking one another to court. Rather than allowing stronger Christians in the local church to help solve problems between each other, they were going "to law before the unrighteous." Paul tells them to act like Christians should and "let yourselves be cheated."

This passage is not saying that matters between Christians can never be resolved in a civil court of law. If two Christians own pieces of property that are adjacent to one another and a question arises over the exact boundaries of the two properties, it would not violate the spirit of this passage to have the dividing line decided by a legal survey of the land. There would hopefully be no ill feelings toward each other shown in a situation like this, but laws need to be followed to determine legal boundaries, etc. Even if one Christian were to sell a car to another Christian, there would likely be some legal exchanges that have to take place. The issues dealt with in this chapter have to do with ugly disagreements between brothers that could spill over into the work and influence of the church in the community.

Six times in this relatively short chapter Paul asks them this question, "do you not know?" (See verses 2, 3, 9, 15, 16, 19.) That is fairly harsh language to remind them that they still have much growing to do. Remember in 1 Corinthians 3:1-3, he had told them that he had to treat them like babes in Christ, as carnal men, not spiritual people? Perhaps the apostle is reminding them that knowledge is important, but it is not the only thing. We must put our knowledge into action or else it doesn't do us much good.

The apostle also reminds them of their ungodly past. In doing so, he lists many sins that will cause people to be lost. Such lists are in the Bible as warnings to Christians in the first century and to us. When he lists the sins of verses 9-10 that he says will keep people out of heaven, we must remember that any sin can be forgiven by God. But a part of our initial pardon includes the concept of repentance. Repentance means that we not only change our minds about a particular sin, but we also resolve in our hearts to stop committing that sin. We cannot expect God to forgive us of any sin that we are unwilling to give up. We cannot claim that, because we are now Christians and forgiven by the Lord, we can continue practicing sexual sins, idolatry, stealing, covetousness, drunkenness, reviling or swindling others for financial gain. If you don't know the meaning of any of these sins listed in verses 9 and 10 (or any other similar list elsewhere in the Bible for that matter), you need to look them up in a Bible dictionary because you might be guilty without realizing it and you just might miss heaven as a consequence.

The great part about serving God is that He will wash us, sanctify us, and justify us "in the name of the Lord Jesus and by the Spirit of our God" (verse 11). One of the many spiritual blessings disciples enjoy in Jesus Christ (Ephesians 1:3) is having our sins forever taken away and never remembered again by God (Hebrews 8:12 and 10:17).

He especially reminds us that sexual immorality is a sin against the God-given purpose for our physical bodies. He describes sexual immorality (in any form) as sinning against our own bodies (verse 18). We, as Christians, are not to take the members of Christ and make them members of a harlot. We are to keep ourselves pure, body, soul, and spirit. Do not forget that our bodies are described as "a temple of the Holy Spirit," who is in you, whom you have from God.

We are not allowed as followers of Christ to use our bodies in whatever way we choose. We must use our bodies in a way that honors and glorifies Him. Rather than serving the world and Satan, disciples of Christ are to use their bodies (and their spirits) to serve God. We belong to Him because He bought us with the blood of Christ.

## 1 Corinthians 7

Chapter Seven begins a series of chapters in which Paul answers some questions that the church in Corinth had sent to him. Most of the sections where he does this will begin with the phrase, "now concerning..." (see 7:1, 12; 8:1; 12:1; 16:1), but not all of them will.

The first issue he deals with is marriage.

Everything in the chapter must be considered in the context of what Paul refers to as "the present distress" (verse 26). While there are no clues in the chapter about what that was, most Bible students believe it was most likely a reference to persecution of Christians by unbelievers.

There are two overriding principles taught in this chapter.

First, if you are not married, Paul recommends that you not get married under the current circumstances. He is not saying it is wrong (verses 9, 28), simply unwise. An unmarried person can focus on serving God without distraction. If they were undergoing severe persecution, it would be even more challenging to remain faithful for one who is married. A married person might want to compromise truth if his/her spouse was in danger.

Second, those who are married should be the best spouse they can be, even if (maybe especially if) they are married to a non-Christian. He does not tell a Christian to divorce a non-Christian mate, rather he says exactly the opposite. It was important for the disciples to realize that nothing Paul taught should be understood to weaken the marriage bond, but rather to strengthen it.

Verse 15 has often been misused as a scriptural reason for divorce, that is, the desertion of a spouse. When Paul says that one who is abandoned is "not under bondage," he is not granting permission to choose a new spouse, he is telling them that they are no longer required to fulfill marital duties for the deserter.

As I have studied and prayed about this issue of divorce and remarriage over the years, my conclusion is that there is only one scriptural reason for divorce, followed by remarriage and that is sexual immorality. The only people who have the right to marry are those who have never been married, those who have lost a spouse to death, and the innocent party who has put away a guilty party because of the sin of adultery. Both parties in a marriage relationship must fall into one of those three categories.

Many have taught that these marriage laws only apply to Christians. They believe that those who may be in an unscriptural marriage can remain married if they are baptized, which is "for the remission of sins." They argue that a person who didn't know about God's marriage should not be held accountable and that, even if they have divorced and remarried multiple times, they should stay with the person they are married to when they become a Christian. But don't forget that a person who is baptized for the forgiveness of sins must also repent of his/her sins, "Then Peter said to them, 'Repent and let every one of you be baptized in the name of Jesus Christ for the remission of sins; and you shall receive the gift of the Holy Spirit'" (Acts 2:38). If you stole something before you were baptized, would not repentance demand that you return it before you can be forgiven? You couldn't argue that, because you weren't a Christian, you didn't realize that stealing was wrong, so you should be able to keep what you took from someone else, even if it is a spouse. Re-read Matthew 19:1-9 to be reminded of these truths.

Paul also tells them that a widow (in principle, a widower as well) has the right to remarry, "only in the Lord," that is, in keeping with everything else the Bible teaches about marriage.

## 1 Corinthians 8

Chapters 8-10 deal with matters of Christian liberties. Chapter 8 speaks about the problem of eating meat offered to idols. That specific issue is not a problem today but the principles of dealing with others do still apply. One thing is clear, at least to us two thousand years later. There are no such things as idol gods and, therefore, eating meat that had been sacrificed to "nothing" is not a problem that defiles anyone.

But this chapter emphasizes to us that, even if something is acceptable to the Lord, we must always consider what impact any action would have on other Christians (verses 8-13).

Realizing that there will always be stronger and weaker Christians in every local church, those who are stronger must consider the effect that their actions will have on weaker saints. We should not use our liberty in Christ to do what we want, without some consideration of how weaker disciples might be emboldened to do something similar, but that is actually wrong or sinful.

In verses 7, 10 and 12, the apostle mentions the conscience. His main point is that stronger Christians must be careful not to ignore the conscience struggles weaker disciples may be going through. The conscience is an important Bible subject and one that many people, even some Christians, do not seem to understand very well.

It is said "let your conscience be your guide." There is value in that statement. Our conscience is that inner sense of right and wrong that God has placed within us as an influencing factor to help us do the right thing in challenging or difficult circumstances.

We should follow our conscience in every situation as this will help us to make better decisions. Many verses speak of the importance of having a good conscience. See John 8:9; Acts 24:16; Romans 2:15; 2 Corinthians 1:12; 2 Corinthians 4:2; 1 Timothy 1:5, 19; 1 Timothy 3:9; 2 Timothy 1:3; Hebrews 13:18; 1 Peter 2:19; 3:16; and 1 Peter 3:21, along with other references to having a good conscience. It is a pretty impressive list of verses.

But the Bible does emphasize the fact that it is possible for a person to have his or her conscience "seared with a hot iron" (1 Timothy 4:2). Such people become so accustomed to doing wrong that it reaches a point where it no longer bothers them anymore. They become "calloused" to their own sins. Saul of Tarsus is often used as an illustration of someone who did wrong in persecuting Christians but he later said that he had done so with a completely clear conscience (Acts 23:1). This is because the conscience must be properly taught or educated or trained to know God's standard of right and wrong or else one can do terrible things without realizing they are desperately wrong. (Enforcers for organized crime often murder and steal and torture others without a twinge of guilt.)

This section of the book is parallel in many ways to the teaching of Romans 14 (and part of Romans 15). Since Scripture is best interpreted in light of other Scriptures, we must understand all of this material in these chapters consistently.

These chapters, along with the Romans 14-15 verses, show us just how difficult it was, in the first century, to unite Jews and Gentiles together in the church. The situation is similar, in many respects, to the racial tensions that still exist in our current society. Around the world, there are racial divides that are difficult to bridge. Christians should realize that we hold the key to removing these stumbling blocks. The answer is the love of God and love of our neighbor (Matthew 22:34-40). We are part of a family and need to think about our influence and how it will appear to others.

# 1 Corinthians 9

The principle established in the previous chapter was that a Christian should not exercise his personal liberties if this would cause a weaker Christian to stumble.

In Chapter 9, Paul uses himself as an illustration of giving up certain rights, so that he would not wound anyone's conscience. The primary example he uses is that he did not take any financial support for preaching the gospel in Corinth. He did not want anybody to think that he preached simply for the money.

If you recall, Acts 18:1-17 tells us about Paul's initial visit to Corinth, when the church was established in this first century city. The first few verses of that chapter inform us that, while Paul was preaching in Corinth, he worked as a tentmaker with Aquila and Priscilla, a husband and wife team. While he had the right to be paid for his work as an evangelist, he did not want to be a financial burden to the church. (He says, in 2 Corinthians 11:8, that he was paid by other churches during part of his time in Corinth.)

He further emphasizes that his motive for preaching the gospel was to save as many souls as possible, not to make as much money as possible.

But it is important for us to remember that Paul is also saying that a person who devotes his life to preaching the gospel has the God-given right to be paid for that most important work. There are many other passages which teach this truth as well.

"For the Scripture says, 'You shall not muzzle an ox while it treads out the grain,' and "The laborer is worthy of his wages'" (1 Timothy 5:18). It is interesting that he quotes from both testaments in making his point. Deuteronomy 25:4 is the first passage he quotes and then he refers to Luke 10:7. Both verses make the same argument, that one who works deserves to be taken care of because of his work. Notice that the apostle refers to both of these verses as Scripture, meaning that they come from God. This is not something Paul is making up Himself; God said it. This original statement from Luke was stated personally by Jesus.

Verse 7 refers to a soldier who does not go to war at his own expense. It mentions a farmer who plants a vineyard and then also eats of the fruit. And he speaks of one who raises and cares for animals and also benefits from the job, he will "drink of the milk of the flock."

Verse 14 says that those who preach the gospel have the right to "live from the gospel." It is biblical to pay people who work for God.

Paul risked his life on many occasions to make disciples of Christ. He listed many of the hardships he endured for the Lord in 2 Corinthians 11:23-28. As you read that listing of his trials and difficulties, it is hard for us to realize the challenges faced by first century evangelists whose very lives were often in danger. They persevered because they kept their eyes on Christ and the ultimate reward, rather than on the hardships (Hebrews 12:1-2). That is, no doubt, also true of many godly workers in other parts of the world today.

At the conclusion of the chapter, Paul reminds the disciples that all Christians must discipline themselves and remain pure in body and spirit so that they do not fall away from the Lord. He goes so far as to say that he himself, as an apostle, might become disqualified, if he failed to practice self-control. This is only one of the many New Testament passages that deny the false doctrine known as "once saved, always saved."

## 1 Corinthians 10

Paul ends Chapter 9 by encouraging the disciples to compete for the prize, an imperishable crown of victory. The word, crown, here (9:25) comes from the Greek word, STEPHANOS, which is a symbol of victory. The other Greek word often translated as crown is diadem, which is a crown of royalty.

This chapter begins by reminding them of some Hebrew history. Paul refers to a number of Old Testament accounts to show the Corinthians that if they did not continue to be obedient to the Lord's will, they could fall from God's favor.

The specific sins and Old Testament examples of them are as follows:

- Verse 6 – Lusting for evil things (Numbers 11)
- Verse 7 – Idolatry (Exodus 32)
- Verse 8 – Sexual immorality (Numbers 25)
- Verse 9 – Tempting God (Exodus 17)
- Verse 10 – Complaining (Exodus 16; Numbers 14)

These stories are preserved for us in God's holy word as warnings about sinning against God to help us realize that He hates all iniquity. Just as many of them fell from God's grace, we can also if we persist in sin.

This helps to remind us that we can learn from bad examples, as well as good ones. We have all known good people who greatly and deeply influenced our lives. They showed us what it means to be a Christian and how a sold-out disciple can change the lives of those he or she touches. We can all be grateful for those who have gone before us and shown us the right pathway to take in life. But we can also learn what not to do and how not to live by looking at the lives of those who choose to do wrong. We often learn much by seeing the mistakes they have made and the consequences of doing the wrong thing and hopefully we have tried to avoid the mistakes they have made. It has been said that a smart person learns from the mistakes of others, the average person learns from his own mistakes, but some foolish people just never learn.

In verses 14-22, the apostle points out to them that Christians cannot be partly in the church and partly in the world. They cannot rightly partake in the Lord's table and also in the table of demons (or sin). God is never satisfied with part of our hearts; He demands the entirety of our being. James refers to those who try to hold the world with one hand and God with the other as "adulterers and adulteresses" (James 4:4).

This was clearly a problem for the first century Christians and it continues to be an issue for disciples of Christ today. It is a challenge to remain pure and holy while we are surrounded by the sinful pleasures of the world. That's why Jesus spoke about the idea of being "in the world" but not "of the world" (see John 17:14-19). We should always remember that while there is temporary pleasure in sin (Hebrews 11:25), heaven is eternal and worth any sacrifice we must make to be pleasing to God.

He returns to the idea that Christians need to be aware of their influence on other people and refrain from certain activities that might cause others to stumble into sin themselves.

Paul also reminds them of the one overriding purpose of all Christians. "Therefore, whether you eat or drink, or whatever you do, do all to the glory of God" (verse 31).

## 1 Corinthians 11

There are two major themes in this chapter.

Verses 2-16 deal with issues of authority and headship, especially as they relate to the woman's head covering. Women who had spiritual gifts, such as praying or prophesying, were exercising their gifts without wearing a covering to show their submission to male authority.

This section has been the source of much contention and even division among the people of God over the years. Sincere believers on both sides of the issue have searched for truth and come to different conclusions about whether this covering is binding on Christian women today.

There are those disciples who believe that this passage remains binding on Christians in our day and that women must wear a head covering when worshiping God.

Some Christians believe this was a local custom, a societal norm that showed a woman's subjection to a man and that, as citizens of that system, Christian women should wear the veil. In other places, where no such custom existed, it was unnecessary. Christian women who visit in many Middle Eastern countries today are often encouraged to cover themselves up more, in keeping with local customs, than they would while in the United States. There are a lot of differences, however, in what many of these cultures believe should be covered up. Some cover almost everything except the eyes, while others may allow a woman's entire face to be shown, but nothing else. Even today there can be a wide variety of views.

Others feel that this was something done only during the age of miraculous spiritual gifts and only for those women who used those gifts in the presence of Christian men. When the gifts ceased, so did the need for this symbol of subjection.

There are also those who understand this passage to teach that the covering Paul refers to is the person's hair and that he is just simply saying that men and women should be distinguishable by the hair style they wear, longer hair for women and shorter hair for men.

Some, therefore, see the covering as a matter of faith for all time, while others believe it to have been a cultural tradition for first century Corinth only.

Verses 17-34 correct an abuse of the Lord's Supper. The Corinthians had turned it from a memorial feast of Christ's death into a common, ordinary meal. Paul reminds them of its true spiritual meaning.

The importance of the Lord's Supper cannot be overstated. It can be easy for us to take things we are familiar with and treat them as routine or ritual. We must never forget the importance of the death of God's Son on the cross of Calvary. It should mean everything to us. Without God's loving sacrifice and the deliberate decision of Jesus to go the cross, we would have no hope and we would be forever lost. "But God demonstrates His own love toward us, in that while we were still sinners, Christ died for us" (Romans 5:8). The Lord's Supper is a weekly reminder for us of our salvation through God's grace.

He distinguishes here (verses 22 and 34) between items of collective worship (which the Lord's Supper is and a regular meal is not) and home activities (which normal meals are and the Lord's Supper is not). We must be careful not to confuse what we can do as individuals or as families and what the church can do in worship to God.

## 1 Corinthians 12

Chapters 12-14 deal with their misuse and misunderstanding about spiritual gifts. Each chapter has unique content.

- Chapter 12 – explanation of the gifts
- Chapter 13 – duration of the gifts
- Chapter 14 – regulation of the gifts

The nine spiritual gifts are enumerated in verses 8-10. They are the word of wisdom, the word of knowledge, faith, gifts of healings, the working of miracles, prophecy, discerning of spirits, different kinds of tongues, and the interpretation of tongues. All came from the same Holy Spirit.

The "one Lord" gave all these gifts to first century Christians for the purpose of unifying them, but they had turned them into a competition where division resulted because many felt superior or inferior to others based on which spiritual gift they had received. They were all important and needed to be appreciated as they brought the church together in harmony and unity and love.

Verses 12-31 show how the gifts worked together like the various members of the human body. Every part of the human body performs a unique function. The same principle is true spiritually.

Paul describes it as though the human body parts could have a conversation with one another. The foot might argue that it is less important than a hand and so it did not feel necessary. An ear might reason that because it is not an eye, it does not contribute as much to the working of the body. Some Christians in Corinth were discouraged because they did not feel as important as some other believers, due to the "lesser" gift they had received.

Likewise, some were touting their superiority over others. The eye cannot tell the hand that he is not needed. And a hand cannot tell the feet that they are not as important as the hand is. All the parts of the body work together to help us lead a successful spiritual life.

There are two attitudes expressed in this chapter that no one in any local church should ever have and certainly should never express to others.

The first one is "I am not important here." Many disciples of the Master unfortunately compare themselves with others who may be more talented than they are and decide that, since they can't do everything as well as someone else does, they just don't matter in the church. But everyone should realize that we are what God has made us. Remember in the parable of the talents that not everyone was the same. It would be easy for a one or two talent person to be jealous of the five talent individual and decide to just not even try to use the one or two talents that God had given them. The one talent man was not condemned for only having one talent, but rather for not using what he did have.

The second bad attitude is from those who are gifted and who may be tempted to say to others, "I don't need you." That is just not so. Even a superstar athlete cannot win a team championship all by himself. It takes everyone on the team working together to accomplish great things. If you think you don't need others, that is the wrong answer, the wrong attitude, and the wrong heart.

Every spiritual gift was important and no one gift was to be valued over the others. In the same way, each member of the body of Christ is important and no one should feel superior or inferior to any other disciple.

## 1 Corinthians 13

The "more excellent way" talked about in this chapter is love.

The first section (verses 1-3) shows us that, without love, nothing else really matters. Great talent is insignificant if it is not used to love and serve others. Helping others is important but we must serve them because of our love for God and people. Miracles were performed (in the first century) in vain if they were not offered out of a motive of love.

The second section (verses 4-8a) is the most beautiful description of love man has ever heard, because it was inspired by God. Notice these qualities of love as Paul describes them here. It would be helpful for you to study each of these characteristics carefully to make sure you understand all of them. Love suffers long, is kind, does not envy, does not parade itself, is not puffed up, does not behave rudely, does not seek its own, is not provoked, thinks no evil, does not rejoice in iniquity, rejoices in the truth, bears all things, believes all things, hopes all things, endures all things. Love never fails.

Love is said by Jesus to be the single most important identifying quality of those who claim to be His followers (John 13:34-35). Remember that 1 Corinthians 13 is written in the context of working together and getting along with each other. We must love everyone in the local church we identify as being part of. We are never more like God than when we love others.

"In this the children of God and the children of the devil are manifest: Whoever does not practice righteousness is not of God, not is he who does nor love his brother. For this is the message that you heard from the beginning, that we should love one another" (1 John 3:10-11).

"Beloved, let us love another, for love is of God; and everyone who loves is born of God and knows God. He who does not love does not know God, for God is love" (1 John 4:7-8).

The third section (verses 8b-13) reveals the duration of the gifts. They were to fail, cease, or vanish away "when that which is perfect has come." There are two basic views in the religious world about what this means.

Some believe this is speaking of the return of Christ. When He comes back, spiritual gifts will cease. Of course, this event is in the future and would therefore mean that the gifts continue even in our present time. But these gifts were given by the laying on of an apostle's hands (Acts 8:17-18) and when the apostles had all died, there was no provision for them to continue.

The other view, which is more consistent with the teaching of the New Testament, is that this refers to the completed revelation of God's word. The Greek word, TELIOS, used in verse 10, means complete or finished. The spiritual gifts are "that which is in part," meaning that they existed when the Bible was gradually, little by little, being revealed. It has been compared to a pie. Any "part" of the pie is basically the same material as the whole, completed pie. A slice of an apple pie comes from a whole apple pie. The spiritual gifts were each a piece of the whole revelation of God's will for mankind, needed while the written word was being finished.

The spiritual gifts have also been compared to the scaffolding that is used to construct a building. It has an important role to play during the building of a structure, but when the house (or office complex or hotel or whatever is being built) is completed, the scaffolding is no longer needed and is taken away. When the Bible was finished, the spiritual gifts ended. They were no longer needed.

## 1 Corinthians 14

One of the problems connected with the first century spiritual gifts was jealousy over who had the better gifts. The most popular gift was speaking in tongues. Most of those in Corinth to whom Paul was writing seemed to think that this was the very best gift. That would be a very special gift to have.

Paul shows them that prophecy (inspired preaching) was the more valuable gift. Tongues were a sign for unbelievers, but prophecy was for those who believe (verse 22). If they were to be zealous for spiritual gifts, they should excel "for the edification of the church" (verse 12; see also verse 26).

God did not give these gifts to make some disciples superior to other disciples. The gifts were all given by the Lord, through the Spirit, to equip the church so that it might function more smoothly in its early days.

Today, if there are problems in the church, we solve them by looking into the New Testament to determine God's will. But, before the New Testament was completed, they had spiritual gifts to help them know what God wanted them to do.

Another problem in the Corinthian church is discussed in the closing verses of chapter 14. Besides the misunderstanding of the importance of each gift, they also were not regulating the gifts properly.

Verses 26-40 are Paul's attempt, by inspiration, to regulate the use of these spiritual gifts in worship. It divides into four sections. The first (verses 26-27) deal with the gift of tongues. The second (verses 29-33) mention the gift of prophecy. The third section (verses 34-36) is about the conduct of women. The final section (verses 37-40) is the conclusion.

He gives the example that some were speaking in tongues (which meant that they were speaking in real foreign languages that they had never studied and could not have known how to speak without God's Spirit working in them), but they did not have an interpreter present to tell anyone what was being said. Modern day tongue speaking involves an unintelligible, meaningless gibberish that no one can interpret.

Also, many of them were speaking out of turn and, therefore, it was confusing because several people would be trying to talk at the same time. The apostle reminds them that God is not about confusion (verse 33), but about order and peace. I have visited assemblies of some religious groups that seemed exactly like what Paul is trying to avoid here in Corinth, loud, confusing, disorderly, not respectful of God, women speaking out in worship (as Paul forbids them to do), disruption on every hand. It certainly was not reverent and respectful of the Father.

In addition, during their worship services, the Christians were being loud and sometimes out of control in their exercise of these gifts. It was rather chaotic and so Paul gives them guidelines about how to use the gifts properly and reminds them, "Let all things be done decently and in order" (verse 40).

Paul does make one other very important statement in this context. "If anyone thinks himself to be a prophet or spiritual, let him acknowledge that the things which I write to you are the commandments of the Lord" (verse 37). This speaks to the fact that the writers of the New Testament (and the old as well) were delivering the mind and will of God to the people. This process of delivering that message is called inspiration (literally, God-breathed, as in 2 Timothy 3:16). "How that by revelation He made known to me the mystery (as I have briefly written already), by which when you read, you may understand my knowledge in the mystery of Christ), which in other ages was not made known to the sons of men, as it has now been revealed by the Spirit to His holy apostles and prophets" (Ephesians 3:3-5).

## 1 Corinthians 15

The Corinthians believed in the resurrection of Christ, but not in a general resurrection of the dead. Chapter 15 shows that, if one is true, the other is also true. You cannot believe in one but not the other.

The first 11 verses of the chapter mention more than five hundred eyewitnesses to Christ's resurrection. It was (and is) an established fact. Most of the post-resurrection appearances are recorded elsewhere in the Scriptures, although not all of them are. He did not appear to everyone, only to those key figures who would be carrying on His work after His ascension back to heaven.

Some legal experts have stated that if all of the more than 500 witnesses were to testify in a court of law, the result would be the most one sided court case in the history of the civilized justice system. The resurrection would be confirmed as being true, "beyond reasonable doubt."

Jesus' resurrection proves that all others will be resurrected as well (verses 12-28). It was not a one-time isolated event; it was evidence that Jesus' claim that others would be raised as He has been was actually true. This is why His resurrection is called "the firstfruits of those who have fallen asleep (verse 20).

Notice that Paul enumerates several consequences if the resurrection of Jesus is not true (verses 12-19). But Paul, who was originally an unbeliever in Jesus, assures them that Jesus is indeed risen from the dead (verse 20). That was what convinced Saul of Tarsus to become a Christian.

The rest of the chapter (verses 21-58) explains a few of the details about what and how and why of the general resurrection of the dead. He uses familiar, end of time, language to describe the return of Christ. Notice phrases like, "in a moment, in the twinkling of an eye, at the last trumpet." He tells us that, when Jesus comes back, our mortal bodies (corruptible) will be changed into an immortal one that can survive eternity (incorruptible).

Everything we believe is dependent upon the truth of the resurrection of Jesus. If He was not raised from the dead, then we have no hope. Our entire system of faith crumbles if the foundation of the bodily resurrection of Jesus is false. But Paul gives us strong assurance that He was raised and therefore, we will be raised also.

Some people have claimed that all the major world religions are the same. They all have a leader, a Messiah-type figure who starts the group and rallies followers behind his teachings. Those teachings normally center around loving others and treating people with kindness and respect (there are exceptions to that general rule, however). Some of the followers typically die to show their loyalty to the primary teachings of the leader. He then often dies in the cause he has started himself, which is also part of the Messiah mystique (sometimes the death is inflicted by others; while sometimes it is from natural causes; there are examples where the Messiah figure takes his own life). The resurrection is what separates Christianity from every other world religion. Buddha, Joseph Smith, Muhammad, and other founders of various religions have all died, but only the tomb of Jesus is empty.

He concludes with the thought that our labor for the Lord is never in vain because there is something beyond this life. God will reward the faithful. We will conquer death and the grave and live forever with the Lord in heaven. "Therefore, my beloved brethren, be steadfast, immovable, always abounding in the work of the Lord, knowing that your labor is not in vain in the Lord (verse 58).

## 1 Corinthians 16

The first four verses deal with "the collection for the saints" in Jerusalem. Paul wants to make sure that the disciples in Judea will be taken care of and the church in Corinth is going to help them. We generally refer to this work as benevolence and it can include both saints in the local church as well as Christians in other places who are undergoing physical and financial hardships. This passage is the only one in the New Testament that tells us when we are supposed to take up a collection. It makes good common sense that while the church assembles for worship and praise of God, He would have us to "lay by in store" (using the old King James language) so that the financial needs of the church can be met. Those funds that are collected are to be used for evangelism, edification and benevolence, as well as the regular expenses of the church that are connected with the work that the church is to engage in. 2 Corinthians, chapters 8 and 9, also deal extensively with the matter of contributions to the Lord. You might find it helpful to refer to those two chapters and review the principles they teach.

Verses 5-12 outline some of Paul's personal plans for his immediate future.

An open door had appeared to him in Ephesus (verses 8-9). This terminology refers to opportunities to share the gospel with the lost. "Meanwhile, praying also for us, that God would open to us a door for the word, to speak the mystery of Christ, for which I am also in chains" (Colossians 4:3). "I know your works. See, I have set before you an open door, and no one can shut it: for you have a little strength, have kept My word, and have not denied my name" (Revelation 3:8). The apostle wanted to reach as many souls for the Lord as possible. There were many adversaries, however, and the work would not be easy. Any person at any time who seeks to do great things for God is going to be opposed.

Notice the words of commendation that he includes in this letter to Corinth about several of the younger preachers, whom Paul had taught and/or discipled to maturity. He specifically gives them some direction about helping and encouraging both Timothy and Apollos.

Preachers, and especially young ones, always need to be encouraged. It is not an easy task to work full-time for God. Paul told both of his young preacher friends to whom he wrote letters, "Let no one despise your youth" (1 Timothy 4:12) and "Let no one despise you" (Titus 2:15). Without years of experience and wisdom, it can be easy for young preachers to grow discouraged and downhearted. Preaching is not easy work, in spite of all the jokes about just working 4-5 hours a week, as though the time spent delivering sermons and teaching Bible studies is all the preacher does. You can't please all the people all the time and often a young preacher (or an older one for that matter) is an easy target. Encourage those who are trying to save a lost and dying world. Lift up their hands; help them in their work. Encourage them every chance you get.

The final section (verses 13-24) contains some concluding instructions for the Corinthian Christians to consider. He tells them to be alert and to stand fast for the truth of God's word. He reminds them to love their brothers and sisters in the Lord, fellow workers in the cause of Christ. "Let all that you do be done with love" (verse 14).

And he mentions several first century disciples who had been an encouragement to him in his work for God and who could serve to build up the Christians in Corinth as they had opportunity to spend time together. He names such well known (at least to them) Christians as Stephanas, Fortunatus, Achaicus, along with Aquila and Priscilla.

He concludes with a warning against leaving their first love (verse 22) and prays that the grace of God might be with them.

## 2 Corinthians 1

Paul begins this letter by dealing with the value of suffering. He wants us to know that we can grow through difficult times and that God will help us to endure such trials.

The Lord never told us that, if we decided to follow Him, our lives would be trouble-free. We may have fewer problems as Christians than we would otherwise, but we must still deal with many of the hardships of life that everyone must face.

Paul and Timothy (and many others, before and since) were not immune from these difficulties and even thought on occasion that they might die because of their mistreatment by others. Paul considered such things to simply be a part of the Christian life.

He goes on to emphasize that a disciple of Jesus who has endured and successfully gone through trials then has the ability to help others who may be facing the same difficulties in life. The key to the whole question, of course, is trusting in "the God of all comfort."

The word, comfort, is a key word in this first section of 2 Corinthians. In verses 3-6, a form of the word is found six times. A similar word is also used in the context; consolation is contained four times in verses 5-7. Comfort comes from the Greek word often translated as exhortation; it means "a calling to one's side" (W.E. Vine) and is the term used by Jesus to describe the work of the Holy Spirit as an advocate or helper (John 14:16-18, 26). It includes the idea of encouragement that the Holy Spirit would provide for the apostles after Jesus went to heaven. It is telling us that we can receive that type of uplifting help and encouragement from each other.

The thought is that those who have endured persecution and trials can then, in turn, help others who are struggling as well. See 2 Corinthians 7:6-7, Philippians 2:1, 2 Thessalonians 2:16, Philemon 7 and Hebrews 6:18, for other passages about this consolation from God and other believers. Because we all face tribulation in this earth life, we need that kind of help. We are to be there for each other.

Someone who has lost a spouse to death or children or parents or other loved ones can encourage those who are experiencing similar loss better than those who have not. Anyone can have sympathy for others during difficult times, but those who have had similar life experiences can truly have empathy; they really know what it is like; they have been there. They understand.

One of the main criticisms against Paul from the false teachers in Corinth was that he was not trustworthy. He had promised to come to Corinth and still had not; all he was doing was making excuses. These false teachers challenged everything about Paul that they could and, in this letter, he addresses many of those complaints.

In this section (verses 12-24), he will explain why he has not yet come to Corinth and reminds the Corinthians of his personal integrity and dependability. Notice that he says his yes meant yes and his no meant no. He was trustworthy.

That's how it should be for all Christians. Our words need to be understood by others as truth, as always dependable and honest. We are to be like our God. All of His promises are faithful. Peter calls them "exceedingly great and precious promises (2 Peter 1:4). When we read the Bible, we can know that it is true because it is a revelation of the mind of God and everything that He tells us will happen exactly as He says it will. As His children, we are to be faithful and honest in all that we say and do.

## 2 Corinthians 2

The theme of this chapter is "Victory in Jesus." (That's actually a good summary of the whole Bible.)

The first section of the chapter (verses 1-11) deals with the continuation of a saga that began in the first letter. The subject is the forgiveness of a penitent person.

It shows us God's victory when one who is caught in public sin repents and begins his walk with the Lord again. The person mentioned in these early verses (1-7) is the same man who was written about in 1 Corinthians 5, the man who had "his father's wife." He was immoral and ungodly, yet they were continuing to allow him to be in fellowship with the church. Paul even said to them, "And you are puffed up, and have not rather mourned, that he who has done this deed might be taken away from among you" (1 Corinthians 5:2). The rest of that chapter had discussed the procedure and importance of church discipline.

Church discipline is an important part of being the Lord's church. Immorality, divisiveness, dishonesty, unfaithfulness all reflect negatively on what the Savior wants us all to be. The warning that "a little leaven leavens the whole lump" (1 Corinthians 5:6) is not to be taken lightly. First, it might convince others that it is acceptable to behave in an inappropriate way, contrary to the teachings of Scripture. Others may actually be encouraged to do wrong. Weak Christians don't have to look very far to find justification for bad behavior if it is allowed without consequence. Second, the world needs to know that sinfulness is not accepted. If outsiders know about the mistakes and actions of Christians who sin, they need to be told that this is not approved of and, in fact, is punished in the church by withdrawal of fellowship.

Church discipline is not a means of getting back at others. It is a purifying process that is designed by God to keep bad influences from affecting other Christians. If members of the church choose to do wrong publicly, they need to know that there will be consequences. The hope is to bring them to repentance, not to judgment. The purpose is to save their souls (1 Corinthians 5:5).

This shows us the victory of forgiveness over bitterness and resentment. Verse 8 lets them know that the best thing they could do, now that the man has repented, is to "reaffirm your love to him." Paul makes it very clear that he had personally forgiven this man and that the Corinthian Christians should do the same. If not, he warns them that Satan would take advantage of the situation to weaken the entire church.

He reminds them that "we are not ignorant of his devices." We usually realize how the devil works in situations like this to cause disciples to take sides, argue with one another over what it would include if they were to forgive this penitent man and to seek to cause division in the body of Christ. We must not give in to our lower impulses to continue to hold grudges and anger against each other.

It shows us the victory enjoyed by those who will walk through the doors that the Lord opens for them. When the apostle saw such an opportunity in Troas (we don't know exactly what that involved), he says that "I had no rest in my spirit." He could hardly wait to take advantage of a chance to further the gospel and the cause of Christ.

And it reminds us of the ultimate victory that will be experienced by those who choose the Lord (the aroma of life leading to life) as contrasted with those who reject Him (the aroma of death leading to death). He prompts us to sincerity in sharing the gospel of Christ with others.

# 2 Corinthians 3

Speaking directly to one of the issues raised by the Judaizing teachers, Paul discusses the superiority of the New Covenant over the Old.

The Judaizing teachers wanted to go back to the Law of Moses (at least for some things) and tried to influence others to do the same. Galatians and Hebrews deal with this problem in their entirety.

It is probably an overstatement to say that the goal of these false teachers was a complete return to the Old Testament. They liked many parts of both laws and their real intention was to form a hybrid of the two covenants, combining parts of each testament to suit their own desires.

They liked what Christ offered; they were just unwilling to completely let go of what Moses (and other Old Testament writers) had delivered.

In 2 Corinthians 3, Paul wants to reassure the Corinthians that the new law of Christ is "much more glorious" (verse 11) than the old Law of Moses.

The chapter begins as Paul reminds them that he is not trying to commend himself, but Christ and His law to them. The apostle refers to the believers in Corinth as "our epistle written in our hearts" (verse 2). Anyone who has taught others who then become followers of Jesus knows what a special relationship that is. We all owe a debt of gratitude to those who have shown us the way to Christ. It is likely, in most cases, to be a combination of people and influences that have touched our lives and brought us to the point of saving faith in the Messiah. For some, it began with one or both of our parents who took us to church services, including Bible study, and who showed us day by day in our home what it means to be a Jesus disciple. Others who taught Bible classes at church influenced and encouraged us to obey the Lord. Preachers, both local and visiting speakers, helped us to grow up wanting to do the right thing in our service to God. We are really a combination of many people who touched our early lives and pointed us in the direction of Jesus. Those people should always be very special to us.

Paul refers to those relationships as a letter from Christ that is written not with ink or on tablets of stone, but the result of the Spirit of God writing on the tablets of our hearts.

That is why we have such "trust through Christ toward God" (verses 4-6). He has made us sufficient to obey Him through the teaching of the new covenant. He reminds them that "the letter," which speaks of the Old Testament "kills," while "the Spirit," the teaching of the New Testament, "gives life." That is a reference to the everlasting life that is available in the gospel because of the death, burial and resurrection of Jesus Christ. He says that it is "more glorious" than anything the old covenant had to offer.

He compares a practice of following the Law of Moses to looking through a veil. The Old Testament is called "a shadow of things to come" in Colossians 2:17. The reality (the real thing) that cast the shadow (or type) is the fulfillment of those images (also called an antitype) in the New Testament.

In verses 17-18, Paul mentions one more time that the Spirit of the Lord (the New Testament) gives us liberty (remember James 1:25 where the gospel is called "the perfect law of liberty"). The will of Christ frees us from sin and allows us to be "transformed into" the image of our Savior. Romans 12:1-2 also speaks of being transformed or changed into the likeness of Jesus. And he wants them to know, without question, that "the veil (the Old Testament) is taken away in Christ" (verse 14). We are to learn and obey the New Testament today.

## 2 Corinthians 4

This chapter opens with a statement of Paul's confidence in the gospel message and, therefore, in his own ministry. Although false teachers were accusing him of deception and craftiness, it was he who had renounced such duplicity and had openly proclaimed the truth.

The thoughts expressed in verse 2 ought to describe the hearts and actions of every Jesus follower. It should be our desire to be open and honest about all of our dealings with others. We should not be known for shame, craftiness, or deceit, but rather for the truth that we both teach and try to model in our lives. But we know that not everyone lives that kind of life. There are those who major in guile and deceit.

He places the blame on "the god of this age" (that is, Satan), who had blinded the minds of many so that they did not recognize the truth when the apostle preached it (verses 3-4). Don't ever forget that the devil is a deceiver (Revelation 12:9) who will say or do anything he can to pull people away from God. He is a liar and the father of it; all lies come from Satan (John 8:44). That is why there are so many warnings in the New Testament that tell us, "Do not be deceived." In spite of the worldwide influence that the evil one has over so many people (1 John 5:19), Paul had faith that the light of God's word would penetrate the darkness and be clearly seen by those who have honest hearts.

Verse 5 is a powerful reminder to those who teach the truth (not just pulpit preachers, but everyone who wants to help others learn God's will) that our message is not "ourselves, but Christ Jesus the Lord." We are, as Paul makes clear, simply servants who desire to elevate and promote Jesus, not our own personality or agenda. It is all about Jesus, not about us.

Verse 7 says that "this treasure," that is, God's will, is given to human beings. The "earthen vessels" he mentions were initially the apostles and prophets who were inspired by the Holy Spirit with God's word, but can, in a sense, be applied to those of us today who take the written word that they compiled from God and who keep that word in our hearts and minds as we seek to live daily as lights in a dark world. We must take advantage of every opportunity to tell others about the Savior who can change their lives and their eternal destiny.

Paul discusses further the reality of hardships faced by those who would stand up for God and His will (verses 8-12). There will always be opposition from Satan and those who serve him. But to a person of faith, there is no choice. We must speak. And when we do, God will be glorified.

This great apostle had been mistreated and abused by false brothers. He describes himself as hard-pressed, perplexed, persecuted, and struck down. But he wanted these first century disciples to know that he would continue "carrying about in the body the dying of the Lord Jesus."

No matter what the hardship (verses 8-10), we must tell others of what the Lord has done for us. He wants us to understand that, those who have "the same spirit of faith," would continue on speaking God's will.

As the chapter ends, Paul reminds them of "the big picture" and encourages them to adopt an eternal perspective, not an earthly, short-sighted one. The things we can see are temporary, but Paul was dealing with things that were eternal. He makes it very clear that he considers the mistreatment he has experienced as "our light affliction, which is but for a moment." He would press on toward those things "which are not seen," knowing that God has a reward for the faithful.

## 2 Corinthians 5

Paul describes the future hope of God's people by comparing a common, ordinary tent to a mansion built by the Great Architect.

"This 'building of God' is not the believer's heavenly home, promised in John 14:1-6. It is his glorified body. Paul was a tentmaker (Acts 18:1-3) and here he used a tent as a picture of our present earthly bodies. A tent is a weak, temporary structure, without much beauty; but the glorified body we shall receive will be eternal, beautiful, and never show signs of weakness or decay (See Phil. 3:20-21.). Paul saw the human body as an earthen vessel (2 Cor. 4:7) and a temporary tent; but he knew that believers would one day receive a wonderful glorified body, suited to the glorious environment of heaven" (Warren Wiersbe, *Be Encouraged*, page 55).

He spends considerable time in this chapter (verses 1-8) comparing the time we are at home in this body and absent from the Lord with the eternity he sought, being absent from this physical body, but present forever with God.

He describes our sojourn here in this earth life as walking (living) by faith (verse 7). There are times when we might like to see some proof to clear up a spiritual question we are having, but we must live by faith. There are times when our faith may waver, but God's answer is not going to be a statement or action from above that clears things up for us. We must accept by faith what we read in His inspired word; it is all we need to make it to heaven.

In the last part of the chapter (verses 9-21), Paul gives two motivations for the work we do for the Lord.

One is the coming judgment. Paul never lost sight of the reality that all of us, Christian and unbeliever, will stand before the Lord Jesus Christ (verses 9-11) and give an answer for the things we have chosen to do in this life. There will be both a reward for the faithful and an eternal punishment for the ungodly. He says, "Knowing, therefore, the terror of the Lord, we persuade men..."

This truth can be either comforting or troubling, based on the many decisions we have to make in life, often on a daily basis. If we have chosen God and His truth, and lived a life of obedience, we can rejoice and look forward to that heavenly home. If, on the other hand, we have rejected or ignored the teachings of the Bible and not lived according to God's will, we have nothing to look ahead to except judgment and punishment.

The other motivation is the forgiveness we have received in Jesus Christ and the "ministry of reconciliation" we have been given. When one obeys the gospel (2 Thessalonians 1:7-9) of Christ, his sins are taken away. This is what makes it possible for sinful man to be friends with God again. That is the meaning of the word, reconciliation, to make friends again.

After a person's sins are forgiven, we become a "new creation." Old things have disappeared and all things have become new. Paul describes this here as reconciliation. Our old man of sin is replaced with a new, completely forgiven existence that is directed and guided by the words of God from the New Testament. This gives us hope. That is why the Lord is often called, the God of second chances.

All of this is possible through the sacrificial offering of the sinless Son of God on the cross of Calvary. "He made Him who knew no sin to be sin for us, that we might become the righteousness of God in Him." Amen.

## 2 Corinthians 6

As he further defends his reputation among the Corinthians (verses 1-2), Paul describes himself and the Christians in Corinth, as workers together with God. Surely such language would stir up in their memories some of the highlights of Paul's work in their midst. And what a thrill it should be for all of us to realize that we are workers together with Him. We are on the same team as God. It should also be an encouragement to unity in the church for us to realize that we are all on the same team. Our only enemy is the devil, not one another. We may have some disagreements from time to time, but we are all brothers and sisters in the same spiritual family.

He reminds us all that "now" (verse 2) is the only time we have and that we must, therefore, serve Him while we can. This is the accepted time and the day of salvation that He extends to us. We have no assurance of anything else. We cannot save up any of yesterday to use today and we have no promise of tomorrow (James 4:14 and Proverbs 27:1).

Paul's next appeal is to their understanding of his personal character (verses 3-10). When Paul left the comforts of his Jewish upbringing behind in order to follow Christ, he did so, not because of what he would gain, but in spite of the price he would have to pay. It might be encouraging for you to read Philippians 3:3-11 to refresh in your mind those physical lineage and heritage advantages that the apostle sacrificed so he might follow the Savior and live with Him forever in heaven.

Their awareness of the many sacrifices Paul had endured for the cause would show them again about his trustworthiness. He speaks of His patience, tribulations, needs, distresses, stripes, imprisonments, tumults, labors, sleeplessness, fasting, purity, knowledge, patience, kindness, sincere love, etc. We probably take for granted and don't appreciate how much Paul's life changed when he decided to give his life to the Master. With some exceptions, most of us gave up relatively little in comparison when we became Christians. Paul's sincerity is clearly seen in the trials he went through for Christ.

If they would only recall the open love that he showed them and received from them in return (verses 11-13). "He had spoken honestly and lovingly to them; now he tenderly asked them to open their hearts to him" (Warren W. Wiersbe, *Be Encouraged*, page 73).

The chapter concludes with a reminder not to get caught up in the sinful activities of the world (verses 14-18). As Christians, we must live in the world (1 Corinthians 5:10), but we are not to live like the rest of the world. Paul borrows language from the Old Testament to speaks about being "unequally yoked together." See Deuteronomy 22:10 which says that one should not yoke an ox and a donkey together. While both are good at pulling (and were often used in the past as hard working farm animals), their nature was so opposed to each other that they simply could not reliably be used together. A yoke joins two things together and sometimes that makes for disaster.

His point is that the nature and character of Christians is supposed to be so different from the people of the world (Romans 12:2) that it is a bad idea for them to be joined together in much of anything. There should be no fellowship, communion, accord, part or agreement between a person who is seeking to follow and obey the Lord and one who serves the devil (that is what is meant by the term, Belial, which means one who is worthless, hopeless and destined for ruin). Nothing good can come from co-operating with the children of the devil.

In verses 16-18, Paul quotes numerous Old Testament passages referring to a close, personal relationship with God, as His sons and daughters. "I will dwell in them and walk among them. I will be their God and they shall be My people." It is a wonderful blessing to be a child of God.

## 2 Corinthians 7

As a result of God's promises to walk with Christians, to dwell among Christians and to be a Father to Christians, as His sons and daughters, we are expected to seek to live pure, holy, godly lives. We do so by getting rid of "all filthiness of the flesh and spirit." That is not always easy for us to do; we have grown accustomed to enjoying certain sins, but with God's help, we can cleanse ourselves of these sinful habits and desires.

Purity of life is, of course, a major theme of the Bible. It is the whole reason for the teachings in the book of Leviticus. Over and over, Paul and Peter and John and James and Jude (and Jesus) encourage use to be holy as God is holy. That's the idea behind such New Testament words as saints, sanctified, holy, purity, godliness, and forgiveness. Jesus died for us; we are supposed to live for Him.

Perhaps the key to success in seeking holiness is true repentance. (There is not really such a thing as false repentance, except when we deceive ourselves into thinking we have repented, when we really have not.) But many people think they are repenting when they are really only sorry they got caught.

"Paul's description of true repentance is one of the most powerful passages in all of the Bible (2 Corinthians 7:8-12). The theme of comfort in suffering which was first introduced in 2 Corinthians 1-2 is fully understood in light of this passage. Often it takes confrontation, conflict, and sorrow to help us come to terms with the sins that are deeply rooted in our characters. Through love, hard talks, and facing such issues, we find God's power to overcome. We see the damage that the devil has done to us through such sins, and then we work hard because of our love for God to correct our characters and avenge the wrongs done. Evidently, Titus had visited Corinth and had reported back to Paul that the Corinthian disciples had repented of the sins about which he had written them in the book of 1 Corinthians (2 Corinthians 7:12-16)" (Preston Shepherd, *Manna for the Morning, Book 11*, page 35).

The sorrow of the world can lead to an apology or "confession of sin." But, in reality, this type of sorrow regrets only having been caught doing wrong. Godly sorrow, a proper response to the Holy Spirit's conviction in our hearts (John 16:8-11), will cause us to genuinely change our minds about our sin (that's what real repentance is) . Worldly sorrow will lead us to try and figure out more clever ways to commit our favorite sin without being discovered.

Some people have used a military term to describe repentance. It is like an "about-face" in the military when an individual or column of soldiers are heading in one direction and suddenly, they turn around and march in the opposite direction. Others have described repentance as a 180-degree change.

Paul describes repentance as including diligence, clearing, indignation, fear, vehement desire, zeal and vindication (verse 11). Godly sorrow leads to repentance which in turn leads to salvation, never to be regretted.

When Titus returned to Paul after his visit to Corinth (verses 6 and 13), he convinced Paul that the repentance of the Corinthians was genuine. Titus informed Paul that being with the Corinthians had "refreshed" his spirit. Doesn't that sound nice? To be with other Christians and be so pleased with the way they are living that the time makes you stronger is such an uplifting experience.

Verses 6 and 7 actually refer back to the first chapter of this letter when Paul states how grateful he is to be serving "the God of all comfort" (2 Corinthians 1:3-7). And so the apostle states, "Therefore I rejoice that I have confidence in you in everything."

# 2 Corinthians 8

"Chapters 8 and 9 of the second letter are given over to a discussion of and an exhortation concerning the contribution which they had promised more than a year before for the relief of 'the poor among the saints in Jerusalem.' He uses the brethren of Macedonia, who in the deepness of their poverty, had abounded in liberality and given beyond their ability for this same cause, as an example, and exhorts the Corinthians to exercise themselves in the fulfillment of that which they had obligated themselves to do in the grace of Christian liberality and as a demonstration of the sincerity of their love" (Roy Cogdill, *The New Testament, Book by Book*, page 64).

Generosity on the behalf of others is a very God-like quality. These next two chapters (8 and 9) emphasize the idea of sacrificing financially to help the less fortunate. It is a concept that is found throughout the New Testament. Here are a few examples.

"Command those who are rich in this present age not to be haughty, nor to trust in uncertain riches but in the living God, who gives us richly all things to enjoy. Let them do good, that they be rich in good works, ready to give, willing to share, storing up for themselves a good foundation for the time to come, that they may lay hold on eternal life" (1 Timothy 6:17-19).

"But do not forget to do good and to share, for with such sacrifices God is well pleased" (Hebrews 13:16).

"They desired only that we should remember the poor, the very thing which I also was eager to do" (Galatians 2:10). See also Romans 15:22-29 which describes this same benevolent spirit.

The key to this "grace of God" (verse 1) which shows itself in our hearts when we are willing to help others in need is expressed in verse 5. Those who first give themselves to the Lord are eager to show Christ living in them as they give to and for others.

It is often difficult for preachers to mention the subject of money and giving, because it can appear that they are looking for a raise. (If you will give more, he can be paid more.) But two facts made it easier for Paul to deal with the subject here.

First, he was not paid by the church at Corinth for the work he did in preaching the gospel there. His financial support seems to have come from two different sources. Initially, he worked with Aquila and Priscilla in tent making (Acts 18:1-3). That would have provided some income for him. Also at some point in his work at Corinth, Paul received wages from other churches to help the church in Corinth (2 Corinthians 11:7-8). He did not want anyone to draw the false conclusion that he was "preaching for the money."

By the way, it would not have been wrong if he had taken wages from the Corinthian church or any other church for that matter. He clearly taught in several places that "those who preach the gospel should live from the gospel" (1 Corinthians 9:14). See also 1 Timothy 5:18 and Philippians 4:15-18.

Second, the specific subject of his teaching here about cheerful giving is not preacher support, but what we commonly refer to as "benevolence." Christians in other places were suffering from famine and deprivation and the disciples in Corinth were determined to help them, "according to their ability, yes, and beyond their ability."

So Paul was not serving his own interests and needs as he reminds the Corinthians of their need to first give themselves to the Lord and then, to use their financial abilities to help others.

## 2 Corinthians 9

The first section of this chapter deals with some of the details about how the financial gift for others was going to be handled. He simply wants them to have everything ready when he returns so that no collections have to be made then (remember 1 Corinthians 16:2?).

He reminds them that their example has been an encouragement to others in this area of giving. A good example always challenges others in a positive way. He uses words and phrases of praise, like willingness, ready, zeal, and generous to describe their attitude.

A general principle of giving, either in individuals helping others or through what the local church does, is stated in verse 5 when he says that it should be given "as a matter of generosity and not as a grudging obligation" (verse 5). He continues on to say that our giving should not be "of necessity" (verse 7), that is, because we feel like we have to give but don't really want to. And, it is in that context that Paul states that "God loves a cheerful giver" (verse 7).

This chapter is a living, breathing example of those who understood the attitude of Christ when He said, "It is more blessed to give than to receive" (Acts 20:35). Children do not understand this and it is a sign of real maturity in life when we finally catch on to the blessing of helping others and quit caring about what we can get out of it.

"'Give, and it shall be given unto you,' was our Lord's promise; and it still holds true (Luke 6:38). The 'good measure' He gives back to us is not always money or material goods, but it is always worth far more than we gave. Giving is not (merely) something we do, but something we are. Giving is a way of life for the Christian who understands the grace of God. The world simply does not understand a statement like Proverbs 11:24, 'There is one who scatters, yet increases more' and there is one who withholds more than is right, but it leads to poverty. In our giving, our motive is not 'to get something,' but receiving God's blessings is one of the fringe benefits." (adapted from Warren Wiersbe, *Be Encouraged*, page 97).

We need to take a special look at verse 13. Some believe that this verse refers to benevolent help from the church in Corinth to both saint and sinner. There are two important questions that will help us to understand the meaning of this passage. Why was the money collected and how was the money used?

1. Why was the money collected?
   Every verse that deals with the collection of these funds specifies that saints (Christians) were those who would receive the help. "Now concerning the collection for the saints, as I have given orders to the churches of Galatia, so you must do also" (1 Corinthians 16:1). "But now I am going to Jerusalem to minister to the saints. For it pleased those from Macedonia and Achaia to make a certain contribution for the poor among the saints who are in Jerusalem" (Romans 15:25-26). This money (or goods or clothes or food or whatever) was collected for needy Christians. Did Paul represent it as that and then distribute it to anyone and everyone who asked? Did he collect the funds for one purpose and use them for another? That brings us to the next question.
2. How was the money used?
   Please read these verses (8:4; 8:14; 9:1; 9:12). It was in this setting that Paul mentions this sharing with them and with all. (Notice that the word "men" was added by the translators.) This obviously speaks of Christians in Jerusalem ("them") and Christians in need in other places ("all"). These other Christians probably were those in the region of Judea around Jerusalem.

## 2 Corinthians 10

Paul begins his personal defense of his apostleship in this chapter. He starts out by reminding them that we fight a spiritual battle, not an earthly one and that the weapons of our warfare are not carnal.

The Judaizing teachers have apparently been accusing Paul of using worldly, carnal tactics. The truth is that they are the guilty ones. They are making false accusations and are trying to turn the Corinthians against the inspired apostle.

Paul makes an important point in verses 3-5. He reminds them (and it is saved for us so we will realize it also) that it is not right for Christians to resort to carnal methods and worldly arguments even if we are trying to defeat error and evil. The sword of the Spirit is the word of God; the gospel is the power of God for salvation. We must always be certain to combat false teaching and false teachers with the truth of God (John 8:32) and must not lower ourselves to fight ungodliness with poor actions or motives. "The weapons of our warfare are not carnal, but mighty in God for pulling down strongholds," he says in verse 4. As we "fight the good fight of faith" (1 Timothy 6:12), we must be better than our opponents and fight powerfully, but honestly and fairly. We are trying to save souls, not merely to win arguments.

Paul reminds them of his authority as an apostle of Christ. He is not doing that to impress them or to try to destroy others, but "for edification" (verse 8), so that he can build others up to defend the gospel in his absence. Paul could not be everywhere he wanted to be, all at the same time. He had to teach others so they could and would stand up for the truth of God's word, whether he was with them or not.

In verse 10, they are saying of Paul that his letters are weighty and powerful, but they refer to his bodily presence as weak and his speech as contemptible. They are trying to do whatever they could to diminish his apostolic authority.

Paul assures them that the things he taught them and has written to them are for their edification, not for their destruction. He only wants to do those things that would strengthen the disciples in their commitment to God. The false teachers, on the other hand, are just trying to line up their own disciples and draw them away to their destruction.

Paul tells them that his gentleness with them is because he is dealing with them as a loving parent. But, if necessary, on his next visit, they would see the boldness and courage of this apostle of Christ.

The apostle makes it clear that they were not to compare themselves with other Christians, but rather with the perfect standard of Christ. We are always foolish when we try to make ourselves look stronger by trying to make someone else look weaker.

Paul says that he did not overextend his authority when he preached the gospel to the Corinthians. It was his goal to take the gospel of Christ to areas of the world where it had not been preached. He does not want to take credit for the work that others have done in bringing people to faith in Jesus (boasting in other men's labors or in another man's sphere of accomplishment). His motives were genuine and pure and he wants to assure these early Christians that the gospel message is trustworthy. In verse 17, he quotes from Jeremiah 9:24 and tells them that, as Christians, we should only "glory in the LORD." It is all about Him, not about us and we must be careful to, as preachers of my youth used to say it, hide behind the cross of Jesus, so that He gets all the glory.

The criticisms against him were unfounded. He knew he could not convince the false teachers, but he did not want to lose the Corinthians themselves to the devil.

## 2 Corinthians 11

In challenging those who were questioning his apostolic authority, Paul pulled no punches. He wanted the Corinthians to know that the false teachers were messengers of Satan who would destroy the Lord's church. Of course, they did not see themselves or present themselves in that way. False teachers do not come with a name tag identifying themselves as such.

The Judaizers had so bragged about themselves that many of the Corinthian Christians had believed them and begun to follow them and their teaching. It has often been said that if you repeat a lie enough times, people will begin to believe it. That seems to be what was happening to Paul's reputation in Corinth.

Although Paul considered it to be foolishness, he realized that he needed to do some boasting of his own in order to persuade the Corinthians of his credentials.

His reference, in verse 2, to the church as "a chaste virgin" was a reminder to them that the will of God is their most important priority. The church and its teaching must remain pure (chaste) against false teaching and the ungodliness and immorality that are so prevalent in the world, even in the first century. They were willing to put up with those false teachers, but they were preaching another Jesus, a different spirit, a different gospel. The Corinthians had accepted the true gospel (there is only one real standard of good news, the salvation of souls through the death and resurrection of the Son of God).

And so reluctantly, he warns them against being deceived (verses 3-4) by those who would make false accusations against him, with no proof. He was innocent until proven guilty.

Paul's apostleship was in question because he was not one of the original twelve. He came along later, but we know, of course, that he became an apostle (as one born out of due time, he says, in 1 Corinthians 15:8) because Jesus appeared to him as he traveled to Damascus and called him to this important work. He would later be described as the apostle to the uncircumcised (Galatians 2:7-9). That was what upset so many of the false teachers, that Paul was preaching to and converting myriads of Gentiles. They were concerned that this violated God's will. That middle wall of division between Jew and Gentile was broken down by Christ (Ephesians 2:14), but it took quite a while for many Jews to realize and accept that truth.

He also reminds them that he was not preaching simply for the money (verses 5-10, he had probably been accused of that by the Judaizers). He had not taken financial support for his work in the gospel at Corinth primarily so such a false claim could not be made against him.

Paul gives them a warning against being deceived, not only by Satan himself, but by those false apostles whom the devil had sent into their midst (verses 12-15).

To assure them of his faithfulness to God and not to money, he then recounts the tremendous suffering he had endured because of his devotion to Christ (verses 22-33). They knew all of these great hardships he had gone through for them and the sake of the gospel. When you read this list of persecutions and trials that Paul endured for the cause of the gospel, it should make us grateful for his faith and his godly example. No matter how severe these difficulties were, Paul would not allow anything to deter him from his mission. God had called him to take the gospel to people who did not know the Messiah. Would he have gone through what he had to endure if it was all a fake, or if Jesus had not really called him to this work? Surely they would realize the truth when they saw it clearly.

## 2 Corinthians 12

"This section is the climax of Paul's defense of his apostleship and his love for the believers at Corinth. He was reticent to write about these personal experiences, but there was no other way to solve the problem. In fact, to avoid exalting himself, Paul described his experience in the third person rather than the first person" (Warren Wiersbe, *Be Encouraged*, page 132).

The apostle refers to one who was taken up into the third heaven (the realm of God) and had seen "the abundance of the revelations" from God. He had seen and heard things which it was "not lawful for a man to utter." He wanted them to judge his faithfulness based on the truth that God had revealed to Paul and that he had delivered to them.

This passage (verse 2) uses the phrase, "the third heaven," which is not found anywhere else in the Bible. This refers, of course, to the area where God dwells (and where we all hope to go some day). Paul was given a glimpse into heaven. There are other times in the Bible where the term "heaven" is used to speak about our atmosphere, the air we breathe, the area where humans dwell. This is the first heaven. Then there are times when the Bible uses that term to refer to the whole universe, what we commonly refer to as outer space. Our galaxy and others in the outer atmosphere could be referred to as the second heaven. Paul got to see God's heaven. That makes him special, because few people have had that blessing.

He makes a brief reference to his "thorn in the flesh" from Satan that God used to keep him humble. He had pleaded with the Lord to remove it, but God would not, choosing rather to help Paul work through his challenges than to take them away. (That is a hard lesson for all of us to learn, isn't it?)

God makes the statement to Paul, when he appealed to Him to take away this hardship, that "My grace is sufficient for you." God wants us to reach the point spiritually where we realize that, when we have God, He is all we need. If God is for us, who can be against us? (Remember Romans 8:31?) When we are in Christ, we are safe. Nothing can hurt us. Nothing can slow us down spiritually. Everything is alright when God is on our side.

Paul tells the Corinthians that he just wants them to recognize him for what he was, an apostle of Jesus Christ. He did not take from them the financial help he had a right to because he did not want them to misjudge his motive for preaching. He makes the clear statement, in verse 15, that he had done this to care for their feelings on the matter and, as a parent who loves his children, was willing to spend and be spent for their salvation.

There is a special statement in verse 19 where the apostle wants to assure them that "we do all things, beloved, for your edification." Edification is the term used in the New Testament to speak about building up Christians, about helping other disciples to grow spiritually and become more like their Savior. Paul says that everything he (and his co-workers) did was to make people stronger in the Lord. And notice that he calls them, "beloved." That shows his great love for their souls.

Reminding them of his upcoming visit to Corinth, he says that he still will not accept any money from them. Even though Paul was "in nothing," any less than "the most eminent apostles," he was not boasting in order that he might receive personal gain or benefit from them. He even asks their forgiveness in this area.

He concludes the chapter by insisting that they needed to repent of all ungodliness so that the trip would not cause him even greater sorrow.

# 2 Corinthians 13

Socrates once said, "The unexamined life is not worth living." (He probably said it more than once, to be honest.) But I fear that most people never spend much time thinking about what they really are, especially in the sight of God. Many are more concerned with what other people think about them.

As Christians, we most certainly recognize the importance of self-examination. It is all too easy to drift into bad habits and attitudes that would lead us away from the Lord. "Therefore we must give the more earnest heed to the things we have heard, lest we drift away" (Hebrews 2:1).

Especially are we in danger when we have been influenced by false teachers, as had the Corinthians. They had listened to the Judaizing teachers and had fallen prey to their evil leaven. They had been the victims of a "spiritual con job" and did not even realize it. Did you notice that Paul said to them, "since you seek a proof of Christ speaking in me?" He said that because it is exactly what they were doing, looking for evidence that Paul was a genuine apostle. The false spirits among them were telling the Corinthian disciples to believe in their words, not in Paul's teaching. Believing false teachers would cause them to fall away from the truth of the gospel and be lost.

This should be a grave warning to us today. Earlier the apostle had written to these Christians, including this warning: "Therefore let him who thinks he stands take heed lest he fall" (1 Corinthians 10:12). This is an interesting passage in view of the prominent false teaching in the religious world that one cannot fall from God's grace. Paul says you can and you need to "take heed" that it not happen.

Paul says that he trusted that they will not find themselves out of favor with God and be disqualified. But, in order that this would not happen, they needed to listen to what he has written them in both of these inspired letters and make changes in their lives and their relationship with God. Without those changes, they might easily be disqualified.

Paul acknowledges what he refers to as weakness in his life (verses 7-9). He is admitting that he is not perfect, but wants them to realize that his message is perfect. He refers to it as "the truth" and truth is not weak or imperfect in any way. He doesn't even mind if they think of him as weak and themselves as strong. What matters to him is that they will "be made complete," which is talking about spiritual maturity and growth. He was praying for them to go on from immaturity to spiritual growth and completeness in Christ. See Hebrews 5:12-14; 1 Peter 2:1-3 and 2 Peter 3:14-18 for other references to this spiritual maturity.

He wrote these things to them, not to make a show of his apostolic authority, but for their "edification and not for destruction" (verse 10). We are in the church so that we might gain strength from the encouragement of one another.

As Paul nears the end of his comments, he writes, in verse 11, "Finally, brethren, farewell. Become complete. Be of good comfort, be of one mind, live in peace and the God of love and peace will be with you." He is urging them to accept the truth of God's revelation (as he and other faithful preachers had been instructing them) and to remain true to the principles of right and righteousness that would lead them to heaven when this life is over. False brothers would try to take that from them. Paul doesn't want that to happen to them.

Because the same thing could happen to us (that we might be led astray by false disciples), we must be constantly on guard, never forgetting that these false teachers appear as "ministers of righteousness" (11:15).

# The Letters to the GALATIANS, EPHESIANS, PHILIPPIANS, & COLOSSIANS

## Galatians 1

The great apostle Paul is under attack. Judaizing teachers, who wanted to return to at least part of the Old Law, needed somehow to discredit Paul and his apostleship. Their influence was leading many away from Christ to a perverted gospel which would only condemn their souls. Galatians is Paul's attempt to reaffirm the truth of the gospel in their lives.

The book of Galatians can be divided into three major sections:

- Chapters 1-2 – Personal
- Chapters 3-4 – Doctrinal
- Chapters 5-6 – Practical [applications of the truth]

Paul opens the letter by wishing God's grace and peace upon them (verse 3). This is a common greeting that he often starts his epistles with. He is asking God's richest blessings for them. In this case, and in other letters as well, he both begins and finishes with these words (see Galatians 6:16 and 18). Also, right up front, Paul reminds them of what bound them together, the death of God's Son and our forgiveness that comes through His sacrifice (verse 4). The Galatian Christians, the apostle Paul and all of us even today are united because of the death, burial and resurrection of Jesus the Messiah for our sins. We are "one body" (Ephesians 4:4) in Christ Jesus (Colossians 1:24; 3:15).

The first ten verses of this opening chapter are a defense of the gospel in its purity and simplicity. The apostle makes it quite clear that no other gospel than the one he had preached to them was acceptable. Even if an angel tried to change the message of the gospel, they were not to listen to any false teaching. Those who preach a different gospel (which he says is not another true gospel, but a perversion of the only true will of God) are under a divine curse from the Lord (verses 8 and 9). Most translations say that such a false teacher is "accursed." Some versions say that he is "anathema." This means that the curse comes from God Himself.

The apostle was surprised ("I marvel") that some were abandoning the truth of the gospel so soon after first accepting it. It had been somewhere around three years before that they had become Christians and now many of them are having second thoughts about their relationship with God through Christ. This shows us that false teachers can have a devastating effect on those who are weak and unstable spiritually. We must do what we can to help strengthen new disciples so that they are not easily confused by those who would lead them astray.

In verses 11-24, Paul clarifies and reminds them that his message came through the inspiration of the Holy Spirit, not from mere men. This is a fulfillment of the promise from Jesus that He would send the Helper (Comforter, KJV) who would reveal all truth (John 14:26; 16:13).

False teachers (Judaizing teachers) sought to minimize Paul's influence on Christians by claiming he was not a true apostle of Christ. If he was a false apostle, his teaching could be ignored. In this section, Paul refers to his pre-Christian background and then to his conversion and his inspiration from God.

The account of Paul's conversion from Judaism is one of the strongest proofs for the validity of Christianity that there is. Why would he change so suddenly from being a persecutor of Christians to one who preached that Jesus was indeed the Christ and the Savior of the world? He explains it in several places by telling them that he personally saw the resurrected Lord after he knew He had been put to death. He could no longer deny that Jesus of Nazareth was the promised Messiah of Old Testament prophecy.

## Galatians 2

The events mentioned early in Galatians 2 probably occurred in Acts 15. Paul found it necessary to go to Jerusalem to help clarify the issue of circumcision in the early church. It would be helpful to read Acts 15:1 31 in connection with this chapter.

As those great men of faith gathered in Acts 15, they came to the realization that circumcision was strictly an Old Testament requirement and that, once the Law of Moses was replaced with the gospel, circumcision was no longer an ordinance of God. It has been nailed to the cross. People could still circumcise their male children if they wanted to, but it was not necessary to please God.

Both the circumcised and the uncircumcised could join hands in fellowship with God and with one another. This was a huge test in the first century church. Once they got past this issue, real spiritual and numerical growth could occur.

It is probably difficult for most of us to appreciate how much of an issue this whole circumcision question was in the first century, because we are so far removed from it today. For about 1500 years or so, the children of Israel had practiced circumcision as a part of the Law of Moses. It actually went back further than the Law to the time of Abraham. So for a long, long time, it had been a regular part of Hebrew culture. To them, it was an issue of cleanliness. If you were circumcised, you were spiritually clean and therefore, acceptable to God. And that also meant that one who was not circumcised was unclean and therefore, not acceptable to God. It was that clear and easy to understand.

Now that Jesus had broken down the wall of division between Jew and Gentile (any non-Jew), they were both becoming Christians and were added to the one body of Christ (1 Corinthians 12:13). But centuries of separation and hatred between the two groups (and it was mutual, both sides hated the other) were not easily removed. They could not imagine sitting beside one another in a worship service and considering the other group to be their brothers and sisters in Christ. Old, long held prejudices do not die quickly. It took a long time.

Verse 10 also gives a brief, but important reminder to Christians to help those who are less fortunate. Do not underestimate the value of helping others.

In verses 11-14, Paul recounts an occasion when he had to confront the apostle Peter to the face because he had not handled an encounter with Gentiles in a proper way. Peter had come to Antioch and was eating with Gentiles, according to the agreement reached in Acts 15. But when a group of Jews from Jerusalem ("certain men came from James") came there, Peter withdrew himself and would not associate with the Gentiles, while his Jewish brothers were there. Paul says that they "were not straightforward about the truth of the gospel."

Notice Paul's statement in verses 16 that makes it crystal clear that we are under the New Testament and not the Old. "...that we might be justified by faith in Christ and not by the works of the law." This truth is taught multiple times in the gospel of Christ and it is the main theme of this book of Galatians. One of the hardest lessons for the first century Jews to learn was that Gentiles who were converted to Christ were full heirs of God and not subject to Old Testament Jewish customs and practices. It was not easy for them to set aside hundreds of years of traditions.

Galatians 2:20 is a key verse in this chapter that reminds us that our "old man" was put to death ("crucified with Christ") when we were baptized into Him. His life is to be lived through us as we shine as lights to a lost and dying world. It might help you to memorize this verse.

# Galatians 3

Chapter 3 is a clear explanation of the subject of salvation and the law. It divides into three major sections:

- Verses 1-14 - Salvation is not through the law of Moses
- Verses 15-18 - The law of Moses did not annul the promise
- Verses 19-29 - Why then was the law necessary?

In verses 1-14, Paul discusses again the reality that the Old Law was done away with and replaced by the gospel of Christ. He refers to their having begun their walk with God "by the hearing of faith," but now they are trying to maintain their relationship with God through "the works of the law."

One of the primary lessons from the book of Galatians is that we cannot earn ourselves a home in heaven by our good works. We are expected to obey God and do those things He reveals in the New Testament, but never with the thought that we will so perfectly carry out the will of God that He will owe us an eternal reward. The only way anyone will be saved is through God's grace.

This idea of earning our salvation is sometimes called "works salvation" and sometimes it is called "legalism." So many different ideas are thrown into that word, legalism, that I hesitate to use it at all. To me, legalism is not law keeping, but law depending, that is, believing we will do it well enough to justify our salvation. We are always going to need the mercy and loving kindness of God.

As we look at verses 15-18, the apostle deals with the relationship between the Law of Moses and the promise of God to Abraham. The promise to Abraham (verse 16; see Genesis 12:1-3) of salvation through Christ was given long before the law was given through Moses. The question in the minds of many seems to have been, did the Law of Moses make the promise void? The answer, of course, was no. He says, in very clear terms, that the Law, given hundreds of years after the promise, did not annul, or make void, the covenant with Abraham. Salvation through Christ was not nullified by the giving of the Law of Moses.

But, if that was the case, why was the law necessary (verses 19-29)? This section answers that question and shows how the Promise and the Law fit together.

First, the law did not replace the promise, but rather was "added" to it. That means that during the Mosaic Period, there were two laws of God existing at the same time, one for Israel and one for everyone else.

Second, the law was added "because of transgressions." Something needed to be done to help the bloodline of the Messiah remain pure. God's solution was the Law of Moses, for the Hebrews alone (the descendants of Abraham). The Law of Moses served as a tutor, to bring people to faith in Jesus.

Verses 26-29 are rich in meaning and application. He reminds us that we are "sons" (some versions say, "children" which would include men and women) of God through faith in Christ Jesus. Hebrews 11:6 tells us that "without faith it is impossible to please

Him" and Mark 16:16b says that "he who does not believe will be condemned." Faith motivates all of our obedience to God, including being "baptized into Christ" (verse 27). This is how we "put on Christ," or how we start our journey of becoming more and more like Him.

Verses 28-29 emphasize our unity in the Lord, that we are all equal, no matter what our station in life might be. People will always look at us differently, through cultural glasses. God sees us all the same.

## Galatians 4

In this chapter, Paul uses three word pictures to show the difference between the old law and the gospel.

In verses 1-7, he compares it to childhood and adulthood. Childhood, for both slave and heir, is a time of being under "guardians and stewards." Paul refers to the Old Law as a time when the Jews were "in bondage under the elements of the world."

But, in "the fullness of the time," according to God's divine timetable, He sent His Son into the world. Jesus was "born of a woman," a reference to the virgin birth of the Messiah, with no earthly father. Christ came into the world to redeem those who were under the Law of Moses from that bondage. He says, in verse 7, "therefore you are no longer a slave but a son," an heir of God through Christ. The old has been replaced by the new.

In verses 8-20, he contrasts bondage to freedom. There are several Old Testament practices that Paul was concerned that the Galatians might be involved in, even after the Law of Moses had been replaced. He specifies his concern about their religious observance of "days and months and seasons and years." This is speaking of the various feast days, sacrificial days, including the weekly Sabbath. It also reminds us that under the New Testament system, the only special day is the first day of every week. There are no annual, quarterly, monthly or other special days in Christianity. There is no New Testament teaching to observe popular "Christian" holidays, such as Easter or Christmas, including lent and other common man-made practices. This is the type of practice that Paul refers to as "bondage."

Paul reminds them that his work among them was designed to make certain that "Christ is formed in you." He wanted all disciples to be like their Master (Luke 6:40).

In verses 21-31, he refers back to the Old Testament story of Hagar, Sarah and their children. Many Bible translations call this comparison an allegory. He reminds us of the relationship between Hagar and her son Ishmael and the God approved family of Sarah and Isaac. Hagar was a bondwoman (household servant) while Sarah was Abraham's wife. Hagar and Ishmael are compared to the Old Testament (bondage) and Sarah and Isaac are compared to the New Testament (freedom from the Old Law). Paul also uses the familiar language of the flesh (OT) and the spirit (NT).

We are often accused of not believing in the Old Testament. That is simply not true. We believe the Old Testament is just as inspired by God as the new. We believe there is great value in studying the old law. And frankly, we believe you cannot completely understand the new if you don't know the old also. This story of Abraham, Sarah and Hagar is an excellent illustration of this principle. If you only had the New Testament and knew nothing at all about the old, how could Galatians 4 make any sense to you? You need to know the original story so that you can understand how Paul is using the allegory here. There are literally hundreds (several hundred) of Old Testament stories like this one that are referenced in the New Testament.

You can read the final couple of chapters of a book and know how it ends. But those last chapters make a whole lot more sense when you have read the entire book. The Bible is like that also. It is one continuous story of human rebellion (sin) and divine redemption (salvation). It is true that we are not bound by the laws and regulations of the Old Testament. But seeing how God has dealt with people throughout human history helps us to see and understand what He expects of us today.

## Galatians 5

Paul returns to his previously used illustration to drive home his major point that we are not under the Old Testament, but are living under the teachings of the New Testament. He speaks of the Old Law as being a form of bondage and the New Testament as liberty. (Remember that James also refers to the gospel as "the perfect law of liberty" in James 1:25.)

The apostle specifically mentions the first century issue of whether Christians from a Gentile background had to be circumcised and he lists two consequences of answering in the affirmative. First he says that Christ will profit you nothing and second, you will be required to keep the entire Old Law. (Do you recall that the Judaizing teachers wanted to bind a hybrid law, combining their favorite parts of both testaments?)

Our freedom from the Law of Moses is never to be interpreted as liberty (or license) to sin. The Judaizers were turning people back to the law with its detailed instructions and codified nature. Some thought they needed such detail to remain faithful. Paul wanted them to see that such a move led people away from Christ.

Paul warns them in verse 15 that if they continued to argue and debate and quarrel over this matter, they would consume one another and Satan would be the only winner.

In verses 19-21, Paul lists an impressive number of sins that he refers to as "the works of the flesh." It is vital that we realize what each of these sins includes. Although some of them are words or phrases with which we are not familiar, they involve attitudes or actions that can keep us out of heaven. If you do not recognize any of these words or sins, it is important that you learn what they include so you will not lose your soul over them.

Then, in verses 22-23, he names what he calls "the fruit of the Spirit." These are nine positive qualities that we should strive to possess. Notice that he uses the singular word, fruit, here not the plural, fruits. This is because these nine characteristics all meld together to form a single type of character that God wants us to have. If we leave any one of these qualities out of our lives, we are not complete. We are missing an important ingredient in the life of a Jesus follower.

The fruit of the Spirit comes from the seed of the word of God (Luke 8:11). If we are led by the Spirit, as He leads us through the word, we will produce these characteristics in our lives (Colossians 1:5-6). All men have the choice of bearing good or bad fruit (Matthew 7:15-20; John 15:1-6).

It is important to realize that these qualities are not miraculous. The Holy Spirit does not take control of our lives and force us to be the kind of people that God wants us to be. It is a matter of personal choice and decision we have to make. Each of these characteristics can be learned and developed in the life of a Christian who desires to serve God.

This chapter concludes with a reminder to walk in the Spirit's teaching and to put to death the sinful desires of the flesh. This is a consistent idea throughout the New Testament, that our old way of life is to be crucified (remember 2:20?) so that the new way of a God-pleasing life can be ours. If we still have too much of the old life in us, there is not room for the newness of life in Jesus. The Lord Himself taught this important lesson when He said, "No one can serve two masters; for either he will hate the one and love the other, or else he will be loyal to the one and despise the other. You cannot serve God and mammon" (money). Notice He did not say it is difficult; He says, "you cannot." Period.

## Galatians 6

Paul concludes the Galatians letter with some practical applications of their faith.

He speaks first of their relationships with each other. The chapter opens with words about helping those who struggle spiritually to overcome and defeat sin in their lives. He particularly addresses "you who are spiritual," referring to those who remain faithful to God. He points their attention and concern to those Christians who have been "overtaken in any trespass." We all know of our fellow disciples who at times have found it difficult to overcome temptations and have, therefore, surrendered to them. Paul wants the strong to help the weak, which is a common theme of his writings.

His advice (inspired, by the way) is to bear each other's burdens, that is, to help others where we are strong and they are weak. In turn, in areas where they are strong and we are the weaker, they can assist us in remaining true to the Lord. It is rarely a one way activity. You may be stronger today and I may be stronger tomorrow. Or it may be that I struggle with a sin that you have conquered and you can help me to do better. We are a family of faith and instructed by our Master to exhort and encourage one another as we have the opportunity to do so.

In verses 3-5, he reminds us that we will be judged personally. As individuals, we can help each other to live better, but ultimately, I am responsible for me and you are accountable for you, so we need to make certain that we are doing the best we can. If I need help in an area of my life, I may need to go to someone who can provide the strength I need to make it through the struggle and ask for their aid.

Verses 6-10 are filled with individual responsibilities to carry out with loyalty to God and His cause. We should share physical blessings with each other, especially with those who help us to learn, know and obey the truth (verse 6).

He speaks of the importance of remembering that we will reap what we sow in life, whether good or bad (verses 7-8). Sometimes we act as though we forget that there will be consequences to our actions. A similar idea is contained in the Old Testament in Numbers 32:23 where God warns some of His people, "But if you do not do so, then take note, you have sinned against the LORD; and be sure your sin will find you out." The context is something very different, but the warning is universal. We should never believe that God won't know about it when we violate His will. (See Psalm 11:4; Proverbs 15:3; Hebrews 4:13, for example.) Notice Paul warns us "do not be deceived" about this; Satan will try to convince us otherwise.

And we should not grow weary or discouraged in doing the right thing in every circumstance of life (verse 9). It is not easy to stay strong and that is why the New Testament seeks to encourage us to remain faithful at all times. Never let down your guard.

Verse 10 reminds us again that Christians are to be benevolent, thoughtful people toward those who are less fortunate and less blessed materially. And that includes both fellow believers and non-Christians, as well.

Verse 11 begins the concluding section of the text and Paul spends a little more time reminding them that we should do all that we do to the glory of God. If we have any basis for boasting, it is only in those things that God accomplishes in us through the sacrificial cross of Jesus. Without Him, we are and can do nothing. He ends this great letter with a prayer that the grace of Jesus Christ might with them. What a blessing to know that this is so.

## Ephesians 1

God had a plan in His mind before the world began, a grand scheme to redeem mankind from sin. This scheme of redemption is the theme of the Bible, the single thread that runs from Genesis to Revelation and ties the entire Bible together. When Adam and Eve sinned in the Garden of Eden (Genesis 3), God had three alternatives – to abandon man, to destroy man or to redeem man. He chose to save us.

More than any other book in the Bible, Ephesians summarizes the eternal plan of God for human redemption.

The first few verses (verses 1-14) emphasize the spiritual blessings that are only available in Christ Jesus our Lord. He speaks of our adoption by God, of our redemption through His blood, of our forgiveness of sins because of the grace of God. And he promises us that we are sealed with "the Holy Spirit of promise."

He uses the term, predestined, to describe our adoption into the family of God (verse 5) and says that this was all determined "before the foundation of the world" (verse 4). This is referring to the plan of God for human salvation that was predestined, not that we were chosen as individuals for salvation (or condemnation) before we ever made any decisions about whether we would obey or disobey God. This would mean that God shows personal favoritism (what the King James Version calls "respect of persons") in deciding ahead of time who would be saved and who would be lost (the Calvinistic doctrine of predestination). God predestined the scheme or the plan, not the individuals. If not, then all the statements about obeying, serving and following God would make no difference.

The other side of the coin is that obedience to the plan of God and the forgiveness of sins that comes from doing His will does not mean that we earn or merit our salvation by our good deeds. The wages we earn by our foolish and sinful decisions in life earn us "death" (Romans 6:23a). That is what we deserve. But the grace of God and the gift of salvation are not something we deserve or earn, rather they are an undeserved gift (unmerited favor) for those who, of their own free will and not because they are forced to accept Him by an irresistible grace, chose to follow and obey God's will. Faith without works is dead; only those who "obey the will of Father" (Matthew 7:21) will be saved. Although there are likely people who do believe that God will owe them a home in heaven because they have been so good, I have never met anyone who misunderstands the plan of God so badly. Salvation will only be a free gift from God.

In verses 15-23, we read of Paul's sincere prayer on the behalf of the Ephesians.

One of the most impressive things that really stands out when you read Paul's letters to both churches and individuals is how much he speaks of praying for others. Called prayers of intercession, they refer to Christians who spend much time helping others by praying for them. Paul's relationships with other disciples were so strong that he constantly thanked God for them and continued to ask the Lord to bless them in many ways in their future.

Here, he prays for these first century disciples that they will be given "the spirit of wisdom and revelation in the knowledge of Him," and that the eyes of their understanding might be enlightened to recognize the exceeding greatness of God's power.

In verses 20-23, Paul also emphasizes the preeminence of Christ in God's plan. All things have been placed under His authority. And the same power that raised Jesus from the dead can also work in those of us who believe.

## Ephesians 2

Man was lost and unable to save himself. God loved us and didn't want us to go to hell for eternity. So, in His love and because of His mercy, He sent Jesus Christ to pay the penalty for our sins so we could not have to pay our own price ("the wages of sin is death"). We were dead and God made us alive in Christ. This is the key point of Ephesians 2:1-10.

"For we ourselves were also once foolish, disobedient, deceived, serving various lusts and pleasures, living in malice and envy, hateful and hating one another. But when the kindness and the love of God our Savior toward man appeared, not by works of righteousness which we have done, but according to His mercy He saved us, through the washing of regeneration and renewing of the Holy Spirit, whom He poured out on us abundantly through Jesus Christ our Savior, that having been justified by His grace we should become heirs according to the hope of eternal life" (Titus 3:3-7).

When Paul refers to salvation by grace through faith (verses 8-9), he lets us know that we cannot and do not earn a home in heaven for ourselves by our good works. This does not negate the reality that God separates the righteous from the unrighteous by setting conditions of obedience for mankind.

There are many good works that God wants His people to do. He wants us to study the Bible, pray regularly ("without ceasing"), give to the church and to help others in need, bear one another's burdens, be kind to others, attend worship services faithfully, praise Him in song, try to teach our lost friends and neighbors the gospel, build up our brothers and sisters in Christ. Those things are part (certainly not the whole picture) of being faithful to the Lord. But those things can all be done by decent people in the world who have never given their hearts to Jesus. They are not proof of salvation and say nothing about the kind of person we really are on the inside. We don't do those things so God has to save us. We do them because we want to please Him.

It is not by mere mental assent to a set of facts that we are forgiven, for James makes it clear that faith without works is dead (James 2:14-26).

But it is also important for us to understand that our obedience to God does not mean that He owes us an eternal reward. It is a gift of His grace (Romans 6:23) as we studied in Ephesians 1. Ephesians 2:10 even states clearly that God has appointed us to do good works. Those are the kinds of things that God wants us to do. But we will only be saved by the grace, mercy and lovingkindness of God, not by our good deeds.

The following verses (Ephesians 2:11-22) discuss another aspect of God's scheme of redemption, the inclusion of the Gentiles into God's plan. His plan brings everyone into an equal basis before God.

"For you are all sons of God through faith in Christ Jesus. For as many of you as were baptized into Christ have put on Christ. There is neither Jew nor Greek, there is neither slave nor free, there is neither male nor female; for you are all one in Christ Jesus. And if you are Christ's, then you are Abraham's seed, and heirs according to the promise" (Galatians 3:26-29).

When you read the New Testament all the way through, you get a clear picture of how difficult it was to merge Jews and Gentiles together in the first century church. They had despised one another for hundreds of years (at least 1500 years). But they were all baptized into one body, one church. Christianity is a universal religion. There is no partiality with God. People from every race, language, country and cultural background are all equal in the Lord's kingdom.

# Ephesians 3

Verses 1-13 serve to show us how the Bible, the revealed will of God, fits into the big picture we have referred to as God's scheme of redemption.

Previously a mystery (that which is unknown, but knowable), it was revealed piece by piece through God's Holy Spirit. In some ways, it is like a jigsaw puzzle that comes together one puzzle piece at a time until eventually you can make out the entire picture.

The Bible is made up of sixty-six books, but really it is one story. It begins with the creation of man, then progresses into the account of the first human sin and everything in the Old Testament, from that point on, is taking us to the life of Jesus. The gospel accounts tell us of His life, teaching, example and His trial and crucifixion and then end with the story of His death, burial and resurrection. The book of Acts informs us about how to become a Christian and the rest of the New Testament tells us how to live as a disciple of Jesus as we await His return and the Day of Judgment. The entire Bible is given by inspiration of God (2 Timothy 3:16-17).

Paul says that as he and other inspired writers received the message from God, they wrote it down and when we read it, we have the ability to understand it. He makes the same point in Ephesians 5:17 where he plainly says that we can understand the will of God. It was written for the common person, just like you and me. He calls this process, revelation, which means to uncover or explain something that had not been known up to that time.

So in the Bible, we have the mind of God made known to mankind. The Scriptures are inspired, breathed out by God for our eternal salvation.

"For who among men knows the thoughts of a man except the spirit of the man which is in him? Even so the thoughts of God no one knows except the Spirit of God. Now we have received, not the spirit of the world, but the Spirit who is from God, so that we may know the things freely given to us by God, which things we also speak, not in words taught by human wisdom, but in those taught by the Spirit, combining spiritual thoughts with spiritual words" (1 Corinthians 2:11-13, NASB, 1995).

In verses 14-21, Paul begins to remind these first century disciples of the love of Christ for the world. Those who are His can comprehend its "width and length and depth and height."

In the Bible, we learn of the great love that God has for His ultimate creation, people. We have been created in His image, we have gone our own way in choosing to rebel against God (Romans 3:23), but He loves us so much that He sent His only begotten Son into the world to die for our sins (John 3:16).

Being a Christian means being more like Christ. The real qualities of personal, spiritual strength are inner, not outer. Having Christ to live in us helps us to be more patient, gentle, kind, humble, pure and loving. People around us should be able to see the difference that Jesus makes in our lives. He makes us better, stronger, more faithful. God is able to use us to accomplish great things in His kingdom, more than we ask or can even imagine. "I have been crucified with Christ; it is no longer I who live, but Christ lives in me; and the life which I now live in the flesh I live by faith in the Son of God, who loved me and gave Himself for me" (Galatians 2:20).

The chapter concludes with a forceful statement about God's power working in His people to accomplish more than we can ask or even imagine (verses 20-21). This power, He says, is released when His church does all things to His glory.

## Ephesians 4

Jesus wants His church to be united and at peace. He desires that we live, love, work and worship in harmony. Paul speaks here of two vital components of unity – attitudes and doctrines. We must not only believe the same things (verses 4-6), but it is also essential that we maintain the proper internal attitudes in our hearts (verses 1-3).

There is a certain behavior that is appropriate for the Christian. We are children of God and ought to act like it. If we would all behave as disciples of Christ should behave, there would be far fewer problems in local churches. He especially points out the importance of humility, gentleness, patience, and bearing with one another. Sometimes we just need to try harder to get along. Paul describes this as walking or living "worthy of the calling with which you were called."

We can only have "the unity of the Spirit" when we have the spirit of unity within our hearts. That's where good things and bad things begin (remember the teaching of Jesus in Matthew 12:33-35?).

And doctrinally, too many religious people just ignore the significance of the seven "ones" that the Holy Spirit lists here, one body (the church), one Spirit (the Holy Spirit Himself), one hope (of eternity in heaven with the Savior), one Lord (Jesus the Christ), one faith (the singular body of truth revealed one time for all time), one baptism (in water for the remission of sins), and one God (our loving and all powerful heavenly Father).

The various teaching functions in the church were appointed by God to help us all grow to spiritual maturity. The first two (verse 11) were miraculous; there are no longer any apostles or prophets (except as we have their inspired teaching in the New Testament). But the others are simply gifted Christians who challenge us to live up to our spiritual potential and grow the one body, both numerically and in spiritual strength.

Notice that he uses such phrases as "till we all come to the unity of the faith," and "of the knowledge of the Son of God." He wants us to be "perfect" (complete and mature in the Lord) and to seek to measure up to "the stature of the fullness of Christ."
In verses 14-16, he warns us about being deceived by false teachings, the trickery of deceitful men and the cunning craftiness of the wicked. The solution to those things is "the truth in love." And we must not forget that, as the spiritual body of Christ, each of us has a function to perform in His service so that the church will be edified.

Beginning in verse 17 and continuing through the end of Chapter Four, Paul deals with the appropriate conduct of all believers.

What does it mean to walk as a Christian? What is proper behavior and what is not? How should we conduct our lives in front of an unbelieving world? In this section, Paul deals with all these questions and more. He contrasts the old man and the new man. This passage shows the difference in what we used to be and do and what we now are and do. This admits the fact that, in our past, we all have done things we shouldn't do (see also 1 Peter 4:3-4). That's why we needed a Savior in the first place. But he also discusses how we should live now in Christ Jesus. He gave us a second chance. We should walk in godliness and true holiness.

Verses 31-32 conclude this chapter with two of the most beautiful verses in the whole Bible. If we could just practice these two verses, both the church and the world would be better places to live.

## Ephesians 5

In one sense, verses 1-21 are a continuation from Chapter Four, emphasizing the differences between the old man and the new man. This section, however, deals almost exclusively with "old person" actions, sins that must be repented of and stopped. He encourages them to avoid immorality and specifies several sins and areas of the world to forsake.

The New International Version says that there should not even be a "hint" of immorality in our lives. He especially reminds them that "because of these things the wrath of God comes upon the sons of disobedience. Therefore, do not be partakers with them." Some things are so obviously improper for those who claim to be following the Lord that they should almost go without saying. But there are always those for whom these reminders are necessary.

Verse 6 is a clear reminder of God's judgment on sin. Many today take such a casual attitude toward grievous sins that they can rationalize almost anything in the right circumstances. But God says here, don't be deceived by the empty words of others. There is no way that sin and its consequences should be minimized to act like God doesn't really care what we do. The "wages of sin" is death (Romans 6:23), which means that those who commit such things will be lost. And Jesus paid the ultimate price of giving His life for human sins so that we might have the opportunity to be forgiven and live forever in heaven. Sin is a big deal; don't be fooled by those who try to come up with excuses to justify bad behavior.

He refers to the old man and the new man briefly in verse 8 where he uses the common Biblical analogy of darkness and light. As children of the light, we are to possess certain qualities (what he calls the "fruit of the Spirit," remember that phrase from Galatians?). And at the same time, we must not only have no fellowship with evil, but it is our responsibility to expose those things that are shameful to even speak of. Did you notice that he says, "have no fellowship with the unfruitful works of darkness?" He means that. Two things are important, don't do wrong things, but do good things. That is not always easy when we are surrounded by a world of wickedness, but it is vital that we do what pleases the Lord.

Verse 15 begins a short discussion of walking wisely in the world. To do that, we must make the most of every opportunity to do good (that's what he means by redeeming the time, using it wisely) In verse 17, he states again that we not only can understand the will of God, but we must.

All of this is what he opens the chapter with by reminding us that we are to "walk in love," as the Lord desires.

In verses 22-33, he changes the subject, by getting more specific about how spouses are to treat each other. The church is the bride of Christ (2 Corinthians 11:2; Revelation 21:2). And no bride ever had a more loving husband. The relationship between Christ and His church is so perfect in its design that the Lord uses it as an illustration and model for the roles of all husbands and wives.

Christ is head of the church and the husband is head of the wife. The wife is to be subject to her husband as the church submits to Christ. Christ sacrificed Himself for the church and the husband must be willing to do the same for his wife.

There is mutual respect and love between Christ and the church and the same love and respect should exist between every husband and wife. "This is a great mystery, but I speak concerning Christ and the church. Nevertheless let each one of you in particular so love his own wife as himself, and let the wife see that she respects her husband" (verse 33).

## Ephesians 6

There are numerous relationships that most/many people sustain in life. Ephesians 5:22-33 dealt with the husband and wife relationship. In verses 1-9, Paul describes some of the duties and obligations of four groups – children, fathers, bondservants and masters.

Many of these responsibilities can be summarized by a look at the verbs used in each situation – obey, honor, do not provoke, bring them up, be obedient, and do the same.

Children are taught to both honor and obey their parents, as God would have them to do.

Fathers, while rearing their children as the spiritual head of the family, should be careful not to anger them, in case that might cause them to rebel against both the earthly father and God. The New International Version says that fathers must not "exasperate" their children. A father's goal is to train his children to love and serve God, not to run them away by harshness and inconsideration.

Bondservants are encouraged to obey their masters in all things that are right and good. He uses words like sincerity, with fear and trembling and tells them not to be men-pleasers, but willingly and freely serve their master on earth. He does tell them that they will receive a good reward for being the kind of servants the Lord would have them to be.

And he admonishes masters to treat their workers properly. He reminds them that they (the masters) also have a Master in heaven to whom they will answer some day.

The next section of the chapter, verses 10-20, calls us to be faithful and true soldiers of Christ, in the spiritual battle we wage against sin and wickedness. Paul encourages us to "be strong in the Lord and in the power of His might." He wants them and us to "stand against the wiles (the clever and deceitful ways) of the devil." He reminds us that there is wickedness all around us in the world and that we are fighting a spiritual battle against all ungodliness. Notice that he uses the word, "stand," several times in this context to build us up so that we do not lose heart in this battle. This is a war for souls, both our own and those of people we love.

It is not easy to be a Christian. Sin, the world, temptation, and Satan are very real and very difficult to overcome sometimes. We are in a war against the devil and all of his forces of evil. In another place, Paul reminds us to "Fight the good fight of faith" (1 Timothy 6:12).

There is much we could say about "the whole armor of God" that Paul describes for us in verses 13-18. Truth is to be the belt or sash around our waists. Our breastplate is righteousness and it protects our heart. Our feet are quick to run with the gospel of peace. Our shield is faith that helps to keep us safe from arrows and spears of error. Our head is protected by a helmet of salvation. Our offensive weapon is the word of God, which is a two-edged sword (Hebrews 4:12). And we are to be people of prayer, which is like an "on button" that activates all the other pieces of equipment.

Left to our own defenses, we don't do very well (Romans 3:10, 23). However, we must never forget: "If God is for us, who can be against us?" (Romans 8:31). When we learn to properly utilize "the whole armor of God," there is no evil power that can overcome us. We can win every battle. We will be victorious, eternally.

Verses 21-24 close out the book with some compliments about Tychicus and a prayer that God's peace and grace will be with them.

## Philippians 1

The theme of the book of Philippians is joy. In what has been called the most positive book of the New Testament, Paul encourages them (and us) to realize the overwhelming joy of living for God.

This is all the more interesting when you realize that this letter was written while Paul was in prison for his faith. There are four letters that are commonly referred to as "prison epistles." They are Ephesians, Philippians, Colossians, and Philemon.

Paul had fond memories of the Philippian Christians and longed to see them. The church had done well since its planting and they had matured to the point of appointing overseers and deacons. This is always a positive thing in the life and history of a congregation. He had been touched by their love and the joy that comes from this mutual relationship in Christ.

Rather than painting a picture of gloom and despair, Paul proclaims victory for the cause of Christ. His imprisonment was not going to bind the gospel. In spite of circumstances and mistreatment that would cause many to give up, the apostle Paul was greatly encouraged (verses 12-18).

Some were preaching Christ out of good will. Others were doing so out of envy and strife, desiring glory and recognition. They were jealous of Paul and hoped to cause him some additional problems. However, they were preaching truth, not error. Those who were converted by their message were genuine Christians and their purity was not compromised by the less than pure motives of their teachers. Paul was grateful they had become disciples of Christ. And his own faithful example was encouraging many others.

No matter what others do, always serve God faithfully. Jesus did not allow the hypocrisy of the Pharisees and scribes to make Him quit. The other apostles did not leave the Lord because Judas fell away. Paul did not give up because others fell short.

But Paul was "between a rock and a hard place." He couldn't decide whether he would rather live or die.

Verses 19-26 teach us that the overriding principle of Paul's life was "to live is Christ." Whatever else happened, he was a servant of the Lord, a disciple of Jesus Christ. Knowing the power of a positive influence, he was determined that, in everything he did, Christ would be exalted. And because Paul lived every day for Christ, he knew that "to die is gain." Paul did not fear death. He knew the separation of his body and spirit would allow him to live in the presence of the Savior forever.

In verses 27-30, Paul conveys to these first century disciples that their conduct must always "be worthy of the gospel of Christ." The only way that happens is when Jesus followers are living by the principles taught in the New Testament. Verse 27 says that this includes "standing fast in one spirit, with one mind striving together for the faith of the gospel." The phrase "striving together" is athletic language and carries the idea that as members of the family of God, we must see ourselves as a team playing together in cooperation in order to achieve a victory. A team that is fighting amongst themselves is not going to work together well enough to win. We are on the same team with each other. Satan is the enemy, not other believers. We should work out our internal issues so we can obtain the eternal victory over sin and death. Paul will have more to say about unity in the next chapter.

The apostle hoped to visit the Philippians soon (Philippians 2:24). But, of course, he was still a Roman prisoner and could not know for certain that he would have that opportunity. So he wanted to encourage them to live godly lives, even in his absence.

# Philippians 2

Unity in the Lord's church is absolutely essential. To please God, there is no other option.

Unity begins with one's attitude (verses 1-4). If we have the proper attitude toward other Christians, division will not be impossible, but it will be rare. The so-called "Golden Rule" is not just good advice. It is a matter of obedience or disobedience. "Therefore, whatever you want men to do to you, do also to them, for this is the Law and the Prophets" (Matthew 7:12). Treat other people, and especially fellow disciples, the way you want to be treated, with dignity and respect and honesty.

Verses 3 and 4 are especially powerful. It reminds us that life is not all about us; it is about helping and serving others, primarily here he speaks of fellow believers. We have all met people (and probably been annoyed by them) who only think of and want to talk about themselves all the time. They always have a better story than yours or a funnier joke or superior children who have done much better things than your children have done. Their spouse is much more considerate than yours is and they love to have the last word about any subject that you talk about. People like that not only think too highly of themselves, they rarely think about other people at all. Paul seems to be warning us that this can be a part of human nature if we are not aware of it and if we don't work to try to be one who thinks about the needs of other people. One of the main problems of many people, perhaps of many Christians also, is selfishness. The world revolves around them (in their little minds) and they want everyone to serve them without thinking about how they could help meet the needs of others and help them grow as Christians.

Jesus is the perfect example (of course) of the selfless attitude we must have (verses 5-11). Christ had every right to remain in heaven, but He left those glories behind to serve the needs of others, a dying mankind (us!). It required humility and selflessness. We must have the mind (attitude) we see in Jesus Christ.

In verses 12-18, Paul describes what he means by "work out your own salvation."

"But God be thanked that though you were slaves of sin, yet you obeyed from the heart that form of doctrine to which you were delivered" (Romans 6:17). Man (the creation) is expected to obey God (the Creator). This obedience from the heart is one of the ways we demonstrate our faith (James 2:14-26) and our love for the Lord (John 14:15). One who does not obey the gospel of Christ will be lost eternally (2 Thessalonians 1:7-9; Matthew 7:21).

As Christians, we are to shine as lights in a dark world of sin. The greater the wickedness (the darkness), the greater is the need for light. If Christians do not let their lights shine, how will the lost world see the Lord in us?

Earlier in this chapter, Paul uses Christ as the example of selfless humility. The Son of God became the Son of Man to serve dying humanity's need for salvation. In all areas of life, the Lord is our perfect role model and we must seek to be like Him in this area as well.

In verses 19-30, Paul describes two other excellent examples of this type of attitude. He first mentions Timothy, his "son in the faith" who had proven his character and purity of heart by the way he served others. Paul says he has no other companion and fellow worker like Timothy.

Then he brings up Epaphroditus who had risked his own life to serve Paul's needs. You never forget someone like that. The impact we can have on others can be powerful when we show our love for them by serving them, whatever those needs might be.

## Philippians 3

One of the most common problems in the first century church was the question of circumcision, an Old Testament sign of purity. Judaizing teachers (those who wanted to keep parts of the old law) kept trying to bind it, while the apostles insisted that it was not essential.

Paul reminds his readers that, if anyone had a right to trust in his fleshly heritage, he did. After describing his Jewish credentials, Paul tells them that he had not only abandoned these things to follow Christ, he counted them as rubbish, totally unimportant compared to eternity (verses 1-11).

Paul's Hebrew background is really quite impressive. He not only possessed impeccable Jewish qualities, he had done all he could to oppose Jesus as the supposed Messiah of Old Testament prophecy. He had persecuted the church (we have read about much of that in the book of Acts (chapters 7-9) and there is likely much more he did along those lines that is not recorded for us. We have read enough to be impressed with his zeal for Judaism and that is why it is surprising in some respects to read of Jewish opposition to him now. But to many first century Jews, Paul was nothing but a traitor. To Paul, once he saw the resurrected Jesus, he had no choice. He knew beyond any doubt that Jesus had died on that Roman cross at Golgotha, but when the Lord appeared to him as he traveled to Damascus, he could no longer deny that Jesus of Nazareth was the promised Messiah. He was the One.

But Paul gave up his family religious connections and friendships and destiny (he probably would have ended up on the Sanhedrin Council) to follow an itinerant carpenter and His fishermen disciples in a movement that would change the world.

All of Paul's life could now be described by the phrase, "one thing I do." Forgetting all else, he pressed forward in pursuit of his goal, heaven. In verses 12-14, Paul uses the illustration of a runner in a race who has not yet reached the finish line. He would not look back. He would not quit short of the goal. He would press on, reaching forward to win the prize. His goal, and it should be ours as well, is the "prize of the upward call of God in Christ Jesus" (verse 14).

Beginning in verse 15, Paul reminds us that we are all at different stages of spiritual maturity. Wherever we are, there we ought to do all we can, using our abilities and taking advantage of our opportunities. (By next year, we should have grown enough to do more.)

Enemies of the cross, the worldly minded, will do all they can to oppose our efforts to serve the Lord. Paul makes it very clear that their "end is destruction." We must not love the world (1 John 2:15) and must not allow ourselves to be caught up in the sinful pleasures that the world offers. Any pleasure in wickedness is temporary and not only will it not last, it will cause our souls to be lost throughout eternity.

He uses four phrases to describe those who would oppose Jesus and His followers. He says, "whose end is destruction," starting off with a reminder that they would be lost eternally. He tells us their "god is their belly" (meaning that they focus on this world, not spiritual things). He reminds us that false teachers "glory in their shame;" they are often guilty of gross immorality, and they "set their minds on earthly things" as contrasted with the things of God.

In contrast, as Christians, we are to set our minds on things above. We face daily choices about right and wrong. Our citizenship is in heaven, not on this temporary world. Realizing that "this world is not our home," we must love God and the things of the Spirit, not of the flesh. As we eagerly anticipate the return of Christ, let us submit to the Lord in all things.

## Philippians 4

Verses 1-3 contain the only rebuke found in the book of Philippians. It is directed at two women, Euodia and Syntyche, and shows that Christians need to live and work together in love. If there are problems between you and another Christian, please go to that person, talk it out and pray together about the problem.

In verses 4-7, there are two key thoughts, joy and peace. Both are described in other places as "fruit of the Spirit."

Joy is the theme of this letter. Christians are to rejoice in all things, even in times of suffering. Christianity alone can teach us how to properly enjoy life.

Peace is that quality of mind and attitude that enables us to live calm and tranquil lives, free of anxiety and fear.

The key to having such joy and peace is found in verse 8. Having the right attitude and thinking on those things that are true, noble, just, pure, lovely and of good report will bring the peace of God into one's heart. It might be challenging, but if you can memorize this verse, and then actually call it to mind when you are faced with temptation, it might help you to do the right thing more often and the wrong thing less frequently. This is one of the problems caused by pornography, movies and television programs which promote ungodliness and sexual immorality, listening to inappropriate music or comedy, being around people who tell filthy jokes or use bad, sinful language, including taking the Lord's name in vain, those who would blaspheme God and His will. Once these sinful thoughts, words or images, get into our minds, it is difficult to remove them.

When the apostle wrote Romans 12:1-2 about presenting our bodies as living sacrifices to God and being transformed into the image of His Son, he told us that the method through which those positive actions come about is "the renewing of your mind." We need to think about good things so that we will do good things.

In verses 10-23, Paul turns to the subject of contentment with the physical blessings that the Lord has given us.

The brothers at Philippi were concerned about Paul's material welfare, as they should have been. In the past, they had been blessed with opportunities to help Paul in his work of spreading the gospel. At the time of the writing of Philippians, they had no such opportunity.

Paul wanted them to know that he was going to be all right. God would take care of him and, whether he had much or little, he was content. He had been instructed by the harsh realities of life and had come to the realization stated in verse 13, "I can do all things through Christ who strengthens me." Paul did not write about this subject to the Philippians so they would send him money (verse 17). He was thanking them for those times in the past when they had "shared in my distress" (verse 14).

The apostle points out to them that, when they helped him financially, the fruit that resulted would be credited to their account. Their financial support would result in souls being saved eternally and God would remember their sacrifice and faithfulness in the Day of Judgment.

## Colossians 1

Colossians is one of Paul's prison epistles (Colossians 4:18), along with Ephesians, Philippians, and Philemon.

There is no evidence that Paul had ever been to Colosse (Colossians 2:1). In all likelihood, the church was started by a man named Epaphras (Colossians 1:7 and 4:12-13), perhaps when Paul was nearby in Ephesus (Acts 19:8-10).

Colossians contains numerous parallel passages with Ephesians. Both deal with God's eternal plan to save man. But while Ephesians focuses on the church in God's scheme of redemption, the book of Colossians emphasizes the role of Christ in that plan. There are several references to the influence of "Judaizing teachers" in Colosse. These false teachers sought to combine parts of the Old Law with New Testament teaching.
Colossians begins with Paul's typical greeting to churches. He identifies himself, tells who is with him, tells to whom he is writing and then pronounces God's grace and peace upon his readers (verses 1-2).

Verses 3-8 contain a prayer of thanksgiving. Paul was grateful for the disciples of Christ to whom he was sending this inspired letter. Again, this is typical of his epistles. Not in all of his letters, but in most of them, he lets them know that he has been praying for them and why.

Paul was grateful that the gospel was bearing fruit everywhere around the world. He was especially thankful, as he expresses here, that the people of Colosse were being brought to Christ by the preaching of the gospel.

In verses 9-18, Paul deals with the preeminence of Christ. Jesus is the Head of the church (verse 18). This is true for many reasons.

He has all authority in heaven and on earth (Matthew 28:18) and said He would build His church (Matthew 16:18). Christ adds those who are being saved to the church (Acts 2:47) and purchased the church with His own blood (Acts 20:28). The church is His body (Colossians 1:18).

Reconciliation (verses 19-23) is one of the many word pictures of salvation used in the New Testament. Reconciliation refers to the process of restoring a broken friendship between two people. In the spiritual realm, of course, reconciliation refers to a reuniting between sinful man and a perfect God. Separated from a holy God because of our sins (Isaiah 59:1-2; Romans 3:23), the Lord made it possible for us to be brought back into fellowship with Him. This reconciliation was accomplished through the death of His Son on the cross.

As disciples of Christ, one of our responsibilities is to take the gospel of reconciliation to a lost world (2 Corinthians 5:14-21). The first century Christians took the gospel to the entire known world of their day (Colossians 1:23). If they could take the gospel to their world with none of the modern advantages we possess, then surely, if we were really determined to do so, we could use the current technology and advances we have to spread the good news of salvation to our whole world. Maybe the difference is in our desire to accomplish that, compared to theirs? Why do you think we haven't done it in our time? Perhaps we just don't care as much about lost souls as they did.

The goal of all spiritual activity should be to develop "Christ in you," that is, in every Christian (verses 24-29). Let us work toward the goal, then, of helping each member of the Lord's church to be more like the Master in all things.

## Colossians 2

God desires that all Christians grow spiritually. We begin as babes in Christ (1 Peter 2:1-2; 2 Corinthians 5:17) and over time, we are to grow to "perfection" (Hebrews 5:12-6:3; Colossians 1:28).
Paul refers to this spiritual completeness or maturity with several phrases – good order, the steadfastness of your faith, rooted and built up in Him, established in the faith, abounding in it with thanksgiving (verses 1-10).

He did not want them to be deceived "with persuasive words" by false teachers, such as the Gnostics or others (verse 4).

Verse 8 is a key verse in this chapter. "Beware lest anyone cheat you through philosophy and empty deceit, according to the tradition of men, according to the basic principles of the world, and not according to Christ." Notice the emphasis there on the traditions of men and the teaching of Christ. It is the same basic question Jesus asked all the way back in Matthew 21 to the chief priest and elders of the people about John's baptism. "Where was it from? From heaven or from men?" (verse 25). That ought to be the question we ask whenever there is controversy or disagreement about any subject. What did God have to say about it? That's really all that matters. My opinion, your opinion, the thoughts of famous preachers or television personalities or politicians, or other influential people in any area of life, really do not matter. What is important is what God tells us about it in His word. The Bible is always right.

The solution to spiritual immaturity and the path to growth is "Christ Jesus the Lord" (verses 6-7). "You are complete in Him" (verse 10). Christ is what we need. And He is all we need. He is our Savior and will supply all of our needs (Philippians 4:19). No one can come to God, except through Jesus Christ (John 14:6).

Verse 9 is an inspired reminder of the Deity of Jesus of Nazareth. "In Him dwells all the fulness of the Godhead bodily." He is incarnate Deity (God became man). There was nothing about Him that makes Him less divine than God the Father and the Holy Spirit. If it is true of God, it is also true of Jesus.

Verses 11-23 discuss further the struggle between human and divine wisdom.

For some reason, human beings have historically had a tendency to want to change what God has revealed to suit themselves. God has often found it necessary to remind people that they are not allowed to add to or take away from His word (see, for example, Deuteronomy 4:2 and Revelation 22:18-19).

The prophet Jeremiah reminds God's people of his day in Jeremiah 10:23, "O LORD, I know the way of man is not in himself; It is not in man who walks to direct his own steps."

The Pharisees were often warned by Christ Himself that they must be content with God's will and not to exchange it for "the doctrines and commandments of men" (Matthew 15:8-9). To do so would make their worship "vain" or worthless.

They were never condemned for strictly obeying God's revelation (as many claim today), but for adding their own human regulations and elevating those man-made rules to the status of divine revelation (or even considering their rules and traditions more important than God's ways).
Let us learn to "speak as the oracles of God," nothing more, nothing less and nothing else.

## Colossians 3

Man is a dual being, one part physical body and the other part, the spirit or soul. Those two aspects of man are often at odds with each other. This is the eternal struggle of the spirit against the flesh (Galatians 5:16-17; Matthew 26:41).

The "things which are above" are the things of God, as He has revealed them to mankind in His word, the Bible. The "things on the earth" fall into two distinct categories, both of which we must be constantly aware. The first category would be sinful things. There are many lists of these ungodly actions and attitudes in the New Testament (verses 5-9 are one example). The second area would be those things that are not sinful, in and of themselves, but which can occupy so much of our time that we fail to serve the Lord. As a Christian grows spiritually, he focuses on "those things which are above" and is not caught up in the world and its temptations.

The primary difference between those who do right and those who do wrong is how they think. Which of these two groups of "things" dominates your thinking, things of the world or the things of God? It is a personal choice and every person has the ability to train his or her mind to think about whatever that person decides. It is not always easy to think about the things above, as the things on the earth are visible and tempting and appealing to us at times. It is more challenging for us to walk by faith, rather than by sight when we are constantly bombarded with material and carnal things in the world.

Paul reminds Christians that "you died, and your life is hidden with Christ in God." This refers to repentance when we change our minds about those things in the world that have separated us from God when we have chosen to sin (Romans 3:10). We no longer make decisions solely based on what we see and like and want; we make decisions based on what a disciple of Jesus should participate in. We know that, just because we might want something, doesn't mean that God wants us to have it. There is sacrifice involved in the life of a Jesus follower. But we should never forget that God will reward us and repay us for those hard choices we have had to make.

There is also a reminder in verses 6-7 that there is a punishment for those who make the wrong decisions in life. He mentions "the wrath of God," a phrase that ought to get our attention. When you know the stories of the Bible where God has punished those who ignore His will for their lives, we should not want any part of that. Sometimes those punishments have come in the form of consequences of bad decisions. Sometimes they point further to eternal punishment and separation from God in the place referred to in the Bible as hell. Both thoughts should motivate us to do the right thing and shun all things evil. Many of those Bible passages, both Old Testament and New, have been preserved to help encourage us to live our lives in a way that pleases God. We want no part of His wrath.

The Christian, who is walking in the light of God's truth, develops many qualities, discussed here in verses 12-17, which are commendable both to God and in the sight of all men. He is tender, kind, humble, patient and forgiving. He also grows in his love for his fellow sojourners and pilgrims. A disciple will develop and mature to be like his teacher (Luke 6:40).

The best thing about being a faithful Christian is that we will get to live in heaven with the Lord forever. But another benefit of obeying God's will is that this makes life on the earth better. That is especially true about our relationships in this life. Paul discusses some of these in 3:18-4:1. He speaks of wives (verse 18), husbands (verse 19), children (verse 20), fathers (verse 21), bondservants (verse 22) and masters (4:1).

# Colossians 4

One of the things that Paul asked the Colossians to pray for on his behalf was "that God would open to us a door for the word." A door can be an impediment to progress. That's why most of us lock the door to our houses when we leave home. We don't want someone to go through our door and have free access to our possessions. But an open door is another matter. An open door invites one to enter. A door for the gospel represents an opportunity to share the message of salvation with others.

In 1 Corinthians 16:9, Paul says that a great and effective door for the gospel had been opened for him. When a door opens, Satan will make certain that there are many adversaries who will oppose the gospel.

In Revelation 3:8, the Lord had opened a door for the small, but strong church in Philadelphia. When He opens a door, no one can shut it (verse 7), but many times as Christians we are fearful to walk through those open doors. We should use all such opportunities and not waste them.

In verses 5-6, Paul tells them to walk in wisdom toward those who are outside. We need to always be aware of our example in front of non-believers. If they see anything they can criticize, they usually will. Our lifestyle and purity must not come across to others as a "holier than thou" attitude, which turns people off and may drive them away from the Lord. People will often misjudge us and say untrue things about God's people. We really can't do much about that, but we need to make certain that we do not give them a legitimate reason to criticize the church and God because we are doing something wrong that they will use against us.

The phrase, "redeeming the time" (verse 5), is translated in some versions as "making the most of every opportunity." We pass up a lot of good opportunities to help people come to know Christ because we are fearful or just not paying attention of a chance to talk to someone about the Lord. This is where sins of omission (failing to do right) come into play (James 4:17).

Verse 6 reminds us to be careful what we say around others, especially non-Christians because, again, they may be looking for something to find fault in us and we must be aware of that and be cautious about how we speak to others.

As Paul writes his final farewell to the Colossians (verses 7-18), he also sends greetings to the disciples from others who were with him. Tychicus was a messenger to both Ephesus (Ephesians 6:21-22) and Colosse, who would share information about Paul. Onesimus will accompany Tychicus to Colosse and will be a prominent character in the book of Philemon.

Many Bible students believe that Archippus was the local preacher for the Colossian church and that his parents were Philemon and Apphia (Philemon 1-2). The church there met in their home.

Epaphras was a member of the church at Colosse and labored fervently for the church in prayer. It is important for a church to have people pray for them.

Notice, in verse 16, that this letter was to be read not only in Colosse, but to the church at Laodicea, as well. In turn, a letter to Laodicea was to be read to the Colossians. Before the completion of the New Testament, epistles like this one were to be shared with other Christians. In the book of Revelation, that inspired message was to be passed around through the seven churches of Asia Minor. In that sense, while they had a primary recipient (a person or a local church), they were circulated to others who could benefit from the teaching contained in the letter.

# The Letters of 1 & 2 THESSALONIANS

## 1 Thessalonians 1

The church in Thessalonica was planted as a part of Paul's second preaching journey (Acts 17:1-10). He spent three Sabbath days, teaching in the Jewish synagogue. He may have spent more time in Thessalonica, teaching some of the "devout Greeks" in places other than the synagogue.

But he had to leave prematurely due to persecution. Acts 17:5 tells us that "the Jews who were not persuaded, becoming envious, took some of the evil men from the marketplace" and started a riot against Paul and his companions. They accused them of "turning the world upside down." Actually, the world was already upside down because of the influence of sin and Paul and others were trying to turn it right side up again. These wicked men were able to influence both the crowd of people and the rulers of the city with these false statements about the disciples. Paul and his traveling co-workers were forced to leave Thessalonica. They went on, in Acts 17, to preach the gospel and establish local churches in both Berea and Athens.

Naturally, having to leave these new Christians so quickly after their conversion was troubling to Paul and so he wrote 1 Thessalonians to strengthen these young Christians in the faith. According to 1 Thessalonians 1:9-10, many of them had been involved in idol worship prior to learning about the living and true God. That would not be an easy or automatic change for them to make. They needed further instruction.

In verse 3, Paul refers to these relatively new disciples as a hard-working group that just didn't quit. They did not let their problems get them down. Remember that the Jews who had run Paul out of town were still there. These young followers of Jesus could easily have been favorite targets of these persecutors. And yet they kept going. They did not give up just because they faced opposition. Paul mentions their work, their labor and their patience or perseverance. What praiseworthy qualities those are. Every church needs dedicated, self-surrendered workers who have devoted themselves to do the Lord's will. The New International Version translates this verse to commend the Thessalonians in this way: "your work produced by faith, your labor prompted by love, and your endurance inspired by hope." Do you see faith, hope and love (1 Corinthians 13:13) in that verse? Faith results in work; love brings about labor; hope inspires endurance. May it be so for all of us.

In spite of their "newness" in the faith, they seem to have grown well in these early days, so that they showed their willingness to receive "the word in much affliction" and they were doing so "with joy of the Holy Spirit." And he tells them that they had become "examples" of faithful devotion to God in a way that was motivating and encouraging others who had heard about their faith. They had become a "model" (NIV) for other churches to imitate. As we seek to restore New Testament Christianity in our time, we need to be familiar with the various first century churches and seek to follow their examples when the Lord praises them, churches like Jerusalem, Philadelphia, Smyrna, Philippi and Thessalonica.

Verse 8 assures us that these early Christians were quite evangelistic. They "sounded forth the word" locally and in other places. They had a reputation for that and it motivated others. They were so moved by God's grace that had freed them from sin that they wanted to share the good news of salvation with others. It should be on the heart of every Christian today to take the message of Jesus of Nazareth to every lost soul we know so that more people can be saved eternally. If we don't, who will?

Their primary issue seems to be some confusion about the return of Christ, which many of them believed to be in their very near future (people are still confused about that even in our day). So much of what he writes in this epistle had to do with answering some questions about the second coming.

## 1 Thessalonians 2

There are several recurring themes in these two letters. The most obvious one is the second coming, which is mentioned in every chapter. He also frequently comments about persecution and afflictions, a common problem for first century disciples who lived in an ungodly world.

Another major theme deals with the relationship between a preacher and the congregation. The principles revealed here (verses 1-12) apply to elders, deacons, class teachers, small group teachers, or any Christian who is trying to help other disciples to mature in the faith.

He begins the chapter by speaking about some of the trials that "we" (Paul, Silvanus and Timothy, see 1:1) endured in bringing the gospel to Thessalonica. Remember the almost immediate persecution from jealous Jews when the gospel began taking root in the lives of the local citizens? He mentions being "spitefully treated at Philippi" and then, when they came to Thessalonica, they delivered the gospel "in much conflict." We read about some of that in the Acts 17 account of the beginning of this church.

After speaking of being persecuted at Philippi, Paul reminds these Christians that he (and those who were traveling with him) had been bold to preach the truth, in spite of the difficulties. He knew that they have been entrusted with the gospel and so they encouraged others to obey God's word and did not participate in error, uncleanness or deceit (verse 3). Their purpose was to please God, not men. It can be tempting for preachers to deliver lessons that will make people feel good and avoid anything that might be unpleasant, but it is our responsibility as teachers of the gospel to bring "the whole counsel of God" (Acts 20:27), not just the parts they already like to hear. Sometimes that means preaching hard to hear, but necessary, lessons that will bring us to full maturity and completeness in Christ. If we "seek glory from men" (verses 5-6), we will not be pleasing to God (Galatians 1:10). It is comforting to know, however, that faithful Christians want to hear all of God's truth, not just the easy parts.

Then, in the next few verses, he makes comparisons between his work in their midst and the gentle, loving care of a mother (verses 7-9), along with the strong comfort and encouragement from a father (verses 10-12). His exhortation is for them to continue to walk worthy of their Lord's example. Notice, again, that Paul emphasizes here (especially verse 10) that he and Silas and Timothy behaved "devoutly and justly and blamelessly." What a blessing that was for the disciples in Thessalonica to have heard the truth and seen it in action in the genuine and godly lives of those who planted the church there.

Verses 13-20 speak of the relationship between truth and error (and those who stand for each). They affirm the inspiration of Paul's message and that its source is in God. Verse 13 is one of the most beautiful passages about the inspiration of Scripture and its value in our lives. They received the word of God as truth (John 16:13; it is all truth) and not merely as the words of men. And notice that he tells them the word of God "effectively works in you who believe." There is power in the gospel, not only to save us, but as it instructs us how to live as Christians after we obey the gospel. You can never go wrong when you are following and obeying the Bible.

There is also a description of how God looks at false teachers (verses 14-16; see also Titus 1:15-16). It reminds us that false teachers, in both old and new testament times, have gone so far as to kill the prophets who have brought the word of God to them. What a contrast between the false teachers (who even killed Jesus) and Paul, who along with his companions, brought them the truth.

He concludes this chapter with a return to their close relationship to one another (verses 17-20). Paul's hope for them was that they would be prepared when the Lord returns.

## 1 Thessalonians 3

Paul ended the last chapter by saying that he wanted to come and see them, but had been unable to do so (1 Thessalonians 2:17-18). He is still on the same subject in Chapter 3.

Unable to come to Thessalonica himself, Paul has sent Timothy to "establish and encourage" them in their faith. There were several reasons he was concerned about them.

They were relatively new in the faith and, as a result, they had very little knowledge. If a brand new Christian today wants to learn fast, all he has to do is read and study the New Testament. I have heard of new disciples who have read the entire New Testament in three days. But the New Testament was not yet completed. (Actually, it was barely even started; 1 Thessalonians is one of the earliest books written.) Their exposure to the word of God was limited, although, as an apostle, Paul could have laid his hands on some of the members there and imparted spiritual gifts to them, which would have given them some degree of teaching ability. (To review what the basic spiritual gifts were, see 1 Corinthians 12.) So they were not left totally alone in this area, but it wouldn't have been the same as if Paul had been able to stay there longer.

And persecution was still prevalent. There are references in this chapter to the trials that these young disciples were facing. He mentions "these afflictions" (verse 3), "tribulation" (verse 4) and "the tempter" (verse 5). He was naturally concerned about their spiritual well-being and says that he "could no longer endure" not knowing how they were doing. We should never get the idea in our minds that the first century Christians had an easy life. It is true that the early church grew and spread to the entire known world of their day, but that was because so many Christians were devoted and determined to take the gospel everywhere; it was not because there was no persecution and trials. It was hard to be a Christian then, just as it is in many parts of the world today. There are several references in the Bible to those who died for their faith; they are called martyrs. Stephen was one (Acts 7; 22:20). Antipas is also named (Revelation 2:13). The plural word, martyrs, is used in Revelation 17:6. Hebrews 11:33-38 gives us a graphic, vivid description of just some of the types of persecutions that old and new covenant believers endured for God.

So the apostle sent Timothy, his son in the faith, to help them and determine how they were faring spiritually. Verses 6-10 tell us that Timothy brought back good news of their faith and Paul was comforted by the news. In verse 8, Paul tells them that their endurance helped to give him the courage to continue on and to live a life of joy and contentment. He was so grateful that they had not allowed the hardships they were facing to cause them to give up and quit serving God. He tells them that he will continue to remember them in prayer and thanksgiving to the Lord for their faith (verses 9-10).

He makes it clear that he still hoped to return and be able to spend some time strengthening them (verses 11-13). He tells them to love each other and to increase in that love. And he prayed that they might be blameless and holy at the coming of Christ.

Perhaps the key thought in this chapter is that Paul wanted to do whatever he could, in his absence from them personally, to "establish" (verse 13) their faith. He had been forced to leave them before he wanted to do so, but he didn't want them to think that his absence meant that he had abandoned them to survive on their own. He couldn't be there right then to help them, but he was interested in doing whatever he could to strengthen and build them up in the faith. As was often the case, when he could not be with a church personally, Paul writes them a letter to strengthen their faith. That is exactly what this epistle is all about.

## 1 Thessalonians 4

Verses 1-12 discuss living a life that pleases God. The apostle deals with three major areas:

- verses 1-8 – walking in holiness
- verses 9-10 – walking in brotherly love
- verses 11-12 – walking in honesty and integrity

Remember that they had previously had a problem with idolatry (1 Thessalonians 1:9). Immorality always follows idolatry, because, when God's moral standards are no longer being followed, then anything goes. You can make up your own rules and decide for yourself what is right and what is wrong (and sometimes people decide that nothing at all is wrong).

Two important things that most distinguished first century Christians from their society was their moral purity and their love. So Paul addresses those subjects here.

He reminds them of the need for personal purity and holiness in the first eight verses of the chapter. He makes certain that they understand the immorality of fornication and adultery. Those are tragic sins against the Lord and will be devastating to His people, both personally and collectively.

Paul uses the word, sanctification, in verse 3 to describe the moral purity of God's people. This word, in the original Greek language of the New Testament, means "separation to God" (Vine). It pictures the course of life that is appropriate for those who have been separated from the world to service for God. That is why the word, saint, is often used to refer to all Christians. It is also sometimes used as an adjective and is translated as "holy." As Christians, we are to separate ourselves from all ungodliness. That doesn't mean we will do so perfectly, but that should be our goal as Jesus followers. His perfect life is our perfect example.

Multiple applications of that principle should show us that self-control is an important characteristic of the Lord's children. We must learn and know how to say "no" to the many temptations of the world and that is not always easy. Paul makes the vital application here, primarily, to sexual sins and temptations. He wants us to never forget that "God did not call us to uncleanness, but in holiness" (verse 7). Many churches have suffered the ill effects of immorality in preachers, elders and other Christians. We should know better and act better.

Paul also wants to assure that they will continue to be loving toward one another. They were doing well in this area but he wanted them to "increase more and more." He says that we have been "taught by God to love one another" (verse 9). What is often called the golden verse of the New Testament, John 3:16, reminds us that "God so loved the world that He gave His only begotten Son."

He also wants them to be people of honesty and integrity and to work hard so they can be a good example for the world and share with others. He tells us we should "aspire to lead a quiet life, to mind your own business, and to work with your own hands, as we commanded you, that you may walk properly toward those who are outside, and that you may lack nothing" (verses 11-12).

As we come to verses 13-18, Paul addresses the subject of the second coming. Their main concern seemed to be for their deceased loved ones. Would they go to heaven? Or did they miss their chance since they had died before the Lord's return? Paul seeks to relieve their fears. His description of the second coming is at once exciting, terrifying and comforting. Perhaps the key question here is this, is the thought of the judgment day a comforting one for you?

## 1 Thessalonians 5

Chapter Five continues the theme from the end of Chapter 4 about the second coming. Paul discusses two major aspects of our Lord's return.

- We don't know when it will be
- We need to be ready for it at all times

He is telling them that belief in the second coming should improve the way Christians live (verses 1-11). A constant awareness that Jesus could come back at any time should cause us to think twice before we do anything that might be questionable. (If you are considering doing "something" that you are unconvinced is right, ask yourself if you would be willing to be doing this thing when Christ returns. If not, it is probably a bad idea to do it at all.) The phrase, the day of the Lord, is used throughout the Bible to describe a coming judgment from God upon the sinful. The New Testament uses it to refer to the end of the world and the final judgment on all people (Matthew 25:31-46).

He compares the Lord's return to "a thief in the night" (verse 2). A thief strikes suddenly and often when least expected. He also uses the illustration of labor pains coming on a pregnant woman suddenly and sometimes without much warning.

Verse 3 shows that there will always be unbelievers around. They will preach the gospel of "peace and safety" when disaster could be imminent. The book of Jeremiah deals with this kind of person, one who doesn't want to face the reality that all is not well and we should not continue to live any way we want to and believe there will be no consequences for bad behavior. (See Jeremiah 4:10; 6:14; 8:11; 14:19 as well as others.)

As sons of light, we should not be surprised by His return (verse 5). We have been warned. A wise person takes such warnings seriously and makes preparation. Only those of "the night" or "of darkness" should be unprepared to stand before the Christ in judgment. The apostle encourages them to "be sober," that is, to take these warnings of coming judgment seriously. We need to be serious about our relationship with God and realize that the daily decisions we make will affect our eternal destiny.

In verse 11, Paul tells us to comfort and edify (build up) one another. We should be working to promote mutual growth and spiritual development. We are here to help each other.

Similar to the end of many of Paul's letters, verses 12-28 contain miscellaneous instructions and some practical advice about preparing for Jesus' return. There is no need for those who are believers to be unprepared. But just because these subjects are miscellaneous, this does not mean that they are unimportant.

He speaks of the responsibility of every Christian to work in harmony with the shepherds (or elders) of the local church (verses 12-13). The Lord desires peace to exist in every congregation.

Paul also addresses many of the duties of a child of God in relationship with each other and with the Savior (verses 14-15). We must "test all things" and only seek to do those things that will help us and others to make it to heaven, not those things which would turn us away from the Master. We need to pray and be grateful for all we have been given by God (verses 16-23).

"Watch therefore, for you do not know when the master of the house in coming—in the evening, at midnight, at the crowing of the rooster, or in the morning—lest, coming suddenly, he find you sleeping. And what I say to you, I say to all: Watch!" (Mark 13:35-37).

## 2 Thessalonians 1

Very little time has passed since Paul wrote 1 Thessalonians, perhaps only 2-3 months. The circumstances described in both letters are almost identical. These Christians remain troubled by outside persecution and are still confused about the second coming.

There have been apparent misunderstandings about Paul's message in the first letter. Some think a forgery letter had been sent (2 Thessalonians 2:2), so Paul makes it even clearer now with further instruction.

And he speaks even stronger words of rebuke to those who were causing problems by their actions. He makes it clear in this chapter that the Lord is aware of their "patience and faith" in the face of the "persecutions and tribulations" that they were enduring. He states that this shows them to be "counted worthy of the kingdom of God" for which they were suffering.

He promises two things. First, that God would give the faithful rest from their trials. Second, that He would "repay with tribulation those who trouble you."

Imagine yourself to be a Christian in the middle of the first century when persecution came from multiple directions. The Roman Empire still had a vice grip on the world and while most of the time, they were willing to live and let live, if they considered anyone to be a threat to the "Pax Romana," the Roman peace, they would come down hard on those who were disturbing that peace. And the Jewish persecution of Christians continued as well. They still looked at anyone who believed Jesus was the Messiah as deluded and so, until the destruction of Jerusalem in A.D. 70, they did not hesitate to cause hard times for Christians. Plus, internally, there were false teachers, Judaizers, Gnostics, some who were teaching false things about the resurrection, etc. They denied Paul's apostleship and just in general, caused a lot of trouble. And it would have been easy for them to give up, but Paul is promising that if they will hang in there, God will give them rest at the end of their journey. Their labor was not in vain (1 Corinthians 15:58); the Lord would not forget their hard work (Hebrews 6:10).

He says that the final reckoning of these matters would occur "when the Lord Jesus is revealed from heaven with His mighty angels." The description of the punishment of the ungodly that he gives here is striking. Notice verses 8 and 9. "...In flaming fire taking vengeance on those who do not know God, and on those who do not obey the gospel of our Lord Jesus Christ. These shall be punished with everlasting destruction from the presence of the Lord and from the glory of His power." Any questions about the reality of the place that is elsewhere called hell?

And then, speaking about the disciples in Thessalonica, Paul writes that "in that Day," Christ would be glorified by the faithfulness of His people and he expresses his personal gratitude that they had believed and obeyed what Paul, Silvanus and Timothy had taught them.

Paul also mentions in verse 11 that "we" (himself, Silas and Timothy, verse 1) "pray always for you." How amazing would it be to have someone like the apostle Paul (I guess there really is no one else exactly like him) to pray for you? That had to be so comforting for them, so reassuring to know that he had not forgotten them and continued to speak to God on their behalf on a regular basis. He prayed that God would "fulfill all the good pleasure of His goodness and the work of faith with power" in their lives.

Obedience always glorifies the Lord and He wants them to know that the persecutors and injurious ones who have troubled them will be punished. Mark that down; it is certain.

## 2 Thessalonians 2

In view of their preoccupation with Christ's second coming, Paul reveals some things that would happen before the Lord's return. He predicts a great apostasy, a major rebellion against God. Since the first century, there have been many spiritual rebellions against the Creator.

Even in the first century, there were "many antichrists" already in the world (1 John 2:18). 1 John 4:3 speaks of "the spirit of the antichrist" (NASB, 1995) and reminds God's people that "greater is He who is in you than he who is in the world" (1 John 4:4).

In the course of human history, there are many people, both individuals and groups, who could be described by the language Paul uses in this chapter to describe "the man of sin." They oppose the Lord and all that is good and right. They promote themselves and elevate themselves, sometimes even to the point of expecting the worship of their followers. There are at least three (probably more) popular explanations of that passage.

The first possibility is that he is referring to the Roman Caesar. He fits all of the descriptions of this person. He was wicked (the son of perdition). He opposed and severely persecuted Christians. He exalted himself above God. As a matter of fact he claimed to be deity himself and demanded to be worshiped (sitting in the temple of God and showing himself to be God).

The second common explanation is that this passage is speaking of the Roman Catholic pope. Again, he fits the description. He persecuted all of those who would not submit to his rule as the earthly head of the church (we usually call that persecution "the Crusades"). He claims to be the "vicar of Christ" on the earth, meaning that he is claiming as head of the church some degree of divinity.

Explanation number three, of course, is the premillennial view. This view holds that this is some kind of person near the end of the world who presides over a reign of terror against Christians and all that is good and right. He is usually called "the Antichrist." The Bible does teach that there were many antichrists present even in the first century (1 John 2:18). Anyone who opposes Christ and his teaching was/is an antichrist.

Which of these views makes the most sense? I believe it is the first view because this would have meant much more to the first century Christians to whom the book of 2 Thessalonians was written. What would it mean to them that at least 2000 years from their time other Christians would be troubled with such an individual? Doesn't it make more sense that they were concerned with persecution in their own day and time, rather than something that would occur hundreds or thousands of years later?

Deception is one of Satan's favorite schemes. But those who take "pleasure in unrighteousness" are often easily deceived. Paul says that the false teachers/prophets would come with "all power, signs, and lying wonders" and with "all unrighteous deception." Their followers' reaction to error shows where their hearts really are. God has often used evil people to accomplish His will.

Paul encourages them to hold fast to the apostolic teaching (he calls them "the traditions," which literally means, something handed down). It is only when we remain faithful to inspired truth that God will be pleased with us. Truth will always prevail over error, in the long run.

There are three important lessons we can learn from this chapter. First, there is evil in the world. Second, God is still in control. And third, God will ultimately win. So don't give up. Be faithful to the Lord, no matter what.

## 2 Thessalonians 3

Paul begins this section, verses 1-9, by asking the Thessalonians to pray for him (and Silas and Timothy) in order that their work in the gospel might prosper.

He includes a request, in verse 2, that these disciples might pray that he and his companions might "be delivered from unreasonable and wicked men." There will always be those who oppose the preaching of the truth, for a variety of reasons. But this should be a warning to us to expect that kind of sinful behavior from people, even in our time. As Paul says, "not all have faith." There are many unbelievers who will do anything they can to stop the progress of God's will throughout the world. We must be vigilant and alert.

He also asks them to pray that the word of the Lord might spread rapidly. That was important in the first century world and equally vital for us today. We just don't know how many more opportunities we will have in our lifetime or how much time we have before the Lord returns and we need to use our time wisely and profitably to tell others about the salvation that is available in Jesus.

They were facing opposition from unbelievers who were determined to undermine the disciples' influence. Satan has many powerful followers who will do what they can to defeat the Lord's work. Ultimately, they will lose, but in the meantime, they can do much damage and we must fight the good fight of faith to stand for and with God. Let's work hard until our time is over.

He warns them, in verse 6, of the need to discipline unfaithful members ("every brother who walks disorderly"). This is a military term to describe those who are out of rank, those who have fallen away from the Lord and those who remain but are not living according to biblical standards.

In verses 7-9, he points to his own example as one who worked hard to provide for his own needs so as not to be a burden to others.

In earlier passages in these letters, we have noted that some of the Thessalonian Christians had quit working so they could simply await the Lord's return, which they considered to be imminent. Two thousand years later, we know they were wrong.

Perhaps that should give pause to those today who believe He will return in our own lifetime. He might, but He might not. Nobody knows for sure (Mark 13:32-37). In this last section of the book, Paul gives final instructions for faithful, prepared living.

He teaches in verses 10-12 that a person should work for a living and, if he is not willing to do so, he doesn't even have the right to eat. He is not talking about someone who is physically unable to work, but about those who simply chooses not to work and support his family. This subject will also be dealt with in 1 Timothy 5.

Verses 14-15 remind us that, if a person has been "withdrawn from" (verse 6), he is not an enemy, but should be treated as a brother and encouraged to do the right thing. Do not avoid such people, but try to help them get things back in order with God.

In verse 13, Paul encourages them, and also us, not to "grow weary in doing good." It is often easy to grow discouraged and the Lord wants us to keep on doing the right thing.

Jesus is coming again. Do you love His appearing (2 Timothy 4:6-8)? Are you ready?

# The Letters of 1 & 2 TIMOTHY, TITUS, & PHILEMON

## 1 Timothy 1

1 and 2 Timothy and Titus have been described as "God's preachers' manual." They contain inspired advice from the Apostle Paul to two young evangelists, from a veteran preacher (one who has been around for a long time) to younger men (still learning and growing). These three letters emphasize the importance of standing for the truth. There are two sides to this vital work. One is the preaching of the gospel, the good news of salvation through Jesus Christ. Paul tells Timothy and Titus to teach only "sound doctrine." The second aspect of an evangelist's work has to do with opposing error. The world is always filled with false teachers who turn aside from sound teaching to idle talk.

In verses 1-11, Paul has much to say about the important work of a gospel preacher. After a brief introduction in which the apostle refers to Timothy as "a true son in the faith," he wishes upon his young friend, "Grace, mercy and peace" from both God and Christ.

In verse 3, Paul mentions that he had sent Timothy to Ephesus to be the preacher for that local church. This, of course, is the same Ephesus that received the book of Ephesians from Paul and the church that was included in the seven churches of Asia that received messages from Jesus in Revelation 2 and 3 (and the rest of the book of Revelation also).

Paul immediately warns Timothy to beware of the negative influence of those who would teach "other doctrine," that is, things contrary to the gospel of Christ. He specifically mentions those who were teaching fables, involving "endless genealogies," and said that these things would cause disputes and not godly edification (verses 3-4). He also says that some false teachers had strayed from the truth and turned aside to idle talk, although he says that they did not even understand what they were saying (verses 6-7).

As he issues these pronouncements against error, he also encourages Timothy to remain true to God's will and to maintain a pure heart, a good conscience, and sincere faith (verse 5). A man of God must be a person of integrity, conviction and godly character in all things.

Verses 8-10 remind us of the importance of following and obeying God's law and then lists a number of sins that those who do not obey God will often be guilty of. This is not a complete list of every possible sin, but is comprehensive enough to help us realize that the Lord takes sin very seriously. After listing fourteen specific sins, Paul also includes "any other thing that is contrary to sound doctrine" (verse 10). Remember that Jesus came to the earth to save us from sin. We are forgiven of those sins by obeying the gospel of Christ (believe, repent and be baptized for the forgiveness of sins) and, as disciples of Jesus, we must continue to live pure and godly lives. That's the good news: that we can be saved and live eternally with God in spite of our rebellion against Him (verse 11). We are saved by God's grace.

Then, Paul begins to tell his own story of conversion and how God forgave him and not only made him right with God, but commissioned him to preach that same gospel to others (verses 12-17).

Paul starts back at his pre-Christian days, as a young Jewish man, to his blasphemy and disobedience to God (he calls himself the "chief" of sinners). But through the grace, love and mercy of God, he was forgiven. He says that he is "a pattern to those who are going to believe on Him for everlasting life." In effect, he is claiming that, if he could be saved after what he had done, everyone can be saved.

Verses 18-20 contain further warnings about those who have shipwrecked the faith and would blaspheme the name of God. Timothy (and all preachers) was expected to oppose those who oppose God.

## 1 Timothy 2

Prayer (verses 1-7) must be a top priority in the life of a preacher (and others). The apostles devoted themselves to prayer and to the ministry of the word (Acts 6:4; notice which one was listed first). It is part of the Christian's armor of faith that protects believers from the attacks of the devil (Ephesians 6:18). And it is so important that Paul, in 1 Thessalonians 5:16-18, told Jesus followers to "pray without ceasing."

Chapter 2 begins with a discussion of prayer, with a list of various types of prayers, including supplications, petitions, intercession and thanksgiving. We are encouraged to pray for rulers "that we may lead a quiet and peaceable life in all godliness and reverence" (verse 2). When you realize the troubled times in which the first century disciples lived (don't forget that Nero was the Roman Caesar then), we can see that prayer remains vital for us in the perilous times in which we live today.

He speaks about our Mediator in prayer, Jesus Christ (verse 5). He is our Savior and wants all people to be saved (verse 4). He is also described as our ransom (verse 6), the one who paid the redemption price to free us from our sins (see also Matthew 20:28).

There are multiple passages in the New Testament that describe Jesus as our Mediator, the One who delivers our prayers to God. This touches on the unique position of Jesus as the Son of God and the Son of Man, both divine and human. He was called Immanuel (Matthew 1:23), which means "God with us." 1 John 2:1 tells us that He is our Advocate with the Father, so that when we sin and ask for forgiveness, He pleads our case before the Father. Hebrews 7:25 promises us that "He always lives to make intercession for us." And the book of Hebrews refers repeatedly to Christ as our High Priest, according to the order of Melchizedek. The High Priest under the Law of Moses was the one who offered the sacrifices for the sins of the people on the annual Day of Atonement. Priests in general served as the mediators between God and the people. For this reason, as our High Priest who was tempted in all the same ways we are, but without sinning, the Hebrew writer encourages us: "Let us therefore come boldly to the throne of grace, that we may obtain mercy and find grace to help in time of need" (Hebrews 4:16).

Verses 8-15 deal with the distinct roles and responsibilities of men and women in the work of God.

Verse 8 focuses on the leadership role of men in the plan of the Lord. (This doesn't mean that women are inferior or less important, only that God has given them different functions.) When Paul writes that "men" are to pray everywhere, the term he uses does not refer generically to all people, but rather specifically to males. When both men and women are present, especially in public gatherings, the men should be the ones to lead the prayers on behalf of the group. Obviously, that leaves plenty of circumstances in which women may pray as well, but not publicly in front of men. The prayers of these men are to be accompanied with a consistent, godly life (he is not saying that men literally have to raise their hands when they pray, although there is nothing wrong with that, if the prayer leader decides to do so). If there are matters of dissension and arguments, wrath and doubting, these issues should be resolved so that our prayers are not hindered by such contention.

Verses 9-15, in short, say that women are to submit to that male leadership. That isn't popular in many circles today, but God said it and that should settle the question. He specifies two areas of life where this principle should be applied. First, he teaches women to dress modestly (verses 9-10), in a tasteful, well arranged, respectful, feminine and godly manner. Overdressing (for show) and underdressing (too much show) are both inappropriate. Second, he expects the woman to learn submissively (verses 11-12). They should not put themselves into situations where they would be in positions of authority over men. Woman's crowning glory, however, is her ability to bear and raise children who will love God.

## 1 Timothy 3

Chapter Three begins with a listing of the qualifications for elders in a local church (verses 1-7).

These qualifications are strict, but not impossible to attain. They are demanding, but not unreasonable. These requirements assure that the church will be led by a plurality of spiritually mature, godly men, approved by the Holy Spirit, who will diligently watch out for the souls of the members.

You will notice the listing begins with a reference to "the position of a bishop." Most other translations now render that Greek term as "overseer," both here and in other passages. That is a helpful and comprehensive term to describe the work of elders. There are several terms that are used in various versions and verses to refer to these men: elders, overseers, bishops, presbyters, shepherds, and pastors. Many people, from denominational groups, may be surprised to learn that, in the New Testament, a pastor is not a preacher, but an overseer. It is synonymous with the word, "shepherd," and is rendered that way in some versions. Many who serve as "pastors" in churches today do not meet the requirements that Paul, by inspiration, sets forth here. Many of them are unmarried; if married, they may be with or without children. (Increasingly, some are even women, in direct violation of numerous verses and principles in the Bible. Spiritual decisions are to be made, even in difficult areas, not by the whims of society, but by the statements of God's word. An overseer or pastor MUST BE the husband of one wife, says God, and no human being has the right to change that.) A pastor is a church elder and a preacher is just that, a preacher, a minister or an evangelist. A preacher might be one of the pastors in a church, if he meets these scriptural qualifications, and many have served in both roles over the years.

Each of the qualifications needs to be studied carefully and understood well, both by the men who would serve in that capacity and by the flock over which they would rule. A helpful way to study these qualities might be to divide them into three categories: his spiritual life, his family life, and his moral life.

In verses 8-13, Paul tells Timothy about the importance of the deacons' qualifications. Deacons are assistants to the elders, who help take care of some of the spiritual and physical needs of the church, as overseen, assigned and directed by the shepherds. They are spiritually minded servants, who meet the qualifications outlined here and who have proven themselves dependable, faithful and trustworthy.

One of the duties of an evangelist in a local church is to train and appoint men to serve the Lord as elders and deacons.

Proper behavior in the church, for both preachers, like Timothy, and other Christians is the next subject in the chapter (verses 14-15). In many ways, 1 Timothy 3:15 describes the theme of the book. It tells us the proper conduct for a disciple of Christ Jesus and also contains special instructions for an evangelist that help to equip him for his work. The verse describes the spiritual work of God's people (that's what the church is) to be "the pillar and ground of the truth." Our two fold responsibility as the church is to bring people to Christ and then to teach them how to live as disciples of the Messiah.

Verse 16 is a beautiful and touching description of Christ. There are six facts about Jesus found here. These phrases summarize the entire earthly life of our Lord. "God was manifested in the flesh, justified in the Spirit, seen by angels, preached among the Gentiles, believed on the world, received up in glory." Paul refers to this as "the mystery of godliness." It was something from God to man that was revealed little by little, clue by clue, a step by step summary of the gospel story. The whole Bible is a love story about God and man and how, in spite of our rebellion against His will, He cared so much for human beings, created in His image, that He sacrificed His Son on the cross so that we might be saved eternally. Praise the Lord.

## 1 Timothy 4

The theme of First Timothy is the proper conduct of a Christian (1 Timothy 3:15). It contains special instructions for an evangelist, to equip him for his work. Many of those specific responsibilities are described in this chapter.

Verses 1-5 warn of a coming apostasy. False religious teachings did not originate in our time, although we are surrounded by people who claim to be following Jesus, but whose ideas are wholly foreign to the New Testament. There is no part of biblical teaching that has not been twisted and changed from what the Bible really says. In "latter times" (verse 1), some would depart from the faith. That is not talking about the end of the world, but rather "the last days," the final dispensation (often called "the Christian Age"), which began on the first Pentecost after the resurrection and will continue until the end of time. There are several colorful phrases that Paul uses to describe these false teachers, "deceiving spirits," "doctrines of demons," "speaking lies in hypocrisy," and "having their own conscience seared with a hot iron." It is not a pretty picture that the apostle paints here.

There were two major errors that he specifically mentions. The first was "forbidding to marry" and the second was "commanding to abstain from foods." In some ways, those sound much like Roman Catholicism with its emphasis on the celibacy of the priesthood and its prohibitions for many years on eating meat on Fridays. To the first century reader, it would have reminded them of two key tenets of Gnosticism, a growing movement among the early Christians. The answer to these two issues, then and now, is found among "those who believe and know the truth." God's truth is always the right answer.

In verses 6-16, Paul emphasizes the need to teach truth and oppose error. You really can't do one without the other; a balanced approach is important. Instruct people to know what is right and to distinguish between truth and falsehood. An evangelist is told to "instruct" the brothers and sisters in these important truths. At the same time, to please God, we must avoid "profane and old wives' fables."

Verse 8 is especially poignant. It focuses on the worth of the spiritual over the physical. There is some value in bodily exercise (it profits a person "a little"). But godliness, the Holy Spirit reminds us, profits much ("all things"). The benefits of godly living help us in this life ("the life that now is") as well as for "that which is to come," referring to eternity. Being a Christian is the best life there is and it leads us to heaven throughout eternity.

Verse 10 teaches several key principles of Christianity, including laboring for God, being willing to suffer reproach for Him, trusting in God. He states clearly that Jesus is the Savior of all men and of the importance of true faith in Him for salvation.

Verses 12-16 contain some important, personal applications and principles for Timothy in his life as a gospel preacher. Timothy, even as a young Christian, was to provide a godly example for other Christians. Others are looking for positive, righteous role models to follow. Serving God is not a compartment of your life. Your relationship with God must regulate everything you do (verse 12).

You will notice that this chapter uses the word, doctrine, four times. Verse 1 warns against false doctrines ("the doctrines of demons"). Verse 6 shows that teaching "good doctrine" is essential to being a faithful servant of the Lord. Verse 13 warns the preacher to pay close attention to his teaching (doctrine). And verse 16 reminds Timothy (and all evangelists) to watch carefully both his life and doctrine. That concept of teaching sound doctrine is an emphasis in all three of these letters (1-2 Timothy and Titus).

## 1 Timothy 5

Relationships within the church are an important part of the Lord's work. Chapter Five deals with several of these relationships.

The first two verses speak about a preacher showing the proper respect for all other Christians in the church where he works for God, both younger and older, both men and women. There should be mutual love, respect and devotion. As an evangelist, Timothy had to be careful to treat each group of people properly. It is important for the preacher in a congregation to deal with everyone from all age groups equally and not to play favorites. Paul tells Timothy to encourage others and to be certain to treat young women with purity.

Verses 3-16 deal with widows in the church. Many churches have more women than men, especially as families age. It is not uncommon for husbands to pass away before their wives and therefore, there are often significant numbers of elderly women who have special needs and who should be cared for by the church, in a variety of ways.

These verses tell us of four different "kinds" of widows – those with no family, those with family, those who are carnal and those who are to be cared for on a permanent basis.

The first group are referred to as "widows who are really widows," The King James Version calls them "widows indeed" (verses 3, 5). These are women who have no family to help with their care. Perhaps they never had any children or they have passed away before their mother or they are not disciples and therefore, they do not show much interest in their aging mother. Paul describes this godly woman as one who is "left alone" and has no visible means of support. The church can and should help in such situations.

Then there are those who do have family to help (verse 4 mentions children or grandchildren). Paul makes it clear that the primary responsibility to care for such godly women falls on the family. Verse 8 says that a person who will not take care of his own family "has denied the faith and is worse than an unbeliever." Notice also verse 16: "If any believing man or woman has widows, let them relieve them, and do not let the church be burdened, that it may relieve those who are really widows."

Verses 6 and 11-15 describe those "younger widows" who are carnally minded and do not conduct themselves as a Christian should behave. They are taught to get married, repent and take care of their own needs in a godly manner. The church should not support those who are worldly minded.

Verses 9-10 deal with the situation, in days before government programs, etc., where some widows are taken care of by the church on a permanent basis. Notice that this widow has qualifications to meet, similar to the qualifications of elders, before such a lady can be "taken into the number," that is, provided for wholly by the church. In such cases, there was no one else to care for them.

Verses 17-22 give some specific instructions about the important relationship between an evangelist and the elders. He begins by pointing out the proper respect and honor that is due those who are overseers in the local church. Verse 18 states that some elders are worthy of financial support so they might devote their time to shepherding the people of God. There are warnings about receiving accusations against godly elders (verse 19), although they can be disciplined if they are living improperly (verse 20). It is important for an evangelist to be impartial in dealing with pastors (verses 21-22).

Verses 23-25 contain some important concluding remarks. Read this section carefully and think about it.

## 1 Timothy 6

The last chapter of First Timothy contains some final important thoughts from the aging apostle Paul to his young apprentice, Timothy the evangelist.

Verses 1-2 tells the Christian to be a faithful servant, not only to God, but also to an earthly master, for those who had one. The emphasis is to do a good job and be a good example to others. Show them that you take being a disciple of Jesus very seriously and that this includes being a good worker on the job. He also reminds them that the master/employer/supervisor is worthy of respect and should be treated properly by the Jesus follower, so that God will not be blasphemed (compare these thoughts to those in Ephesians 6:5-8).

Verse 2 adds an interesting dimension in that, in some cases, the master/employer is a fellow believer. His encouragement is: don't despise them, rather serve them faithfully and loyally.

Verses 3-5 speak about church troublemakers. The primary subject of the chapter is how an evangelist must deal with those who would trouble the people of God, His church. There have always been those who would cause strife and division among the disciples. It is not simply a current problem; it has been around since the first century.

The apostle Paul uses numerous words and phrases to describe the influence of those who are obsessed with causing division and strife among believers. He warns that their work will result in envy, strife, reviling, evil suspicions, useless wranglings. He says such people have "corrupt minds" and that they are "destitute of the truth."

If such false teachers are not dealt with in the proper (that is, scriptural) way as God would have them handled, only more trouble will arise (verse 5). The New King James Version adds "From such withdraw yourself." Other translations do not include this phrase, but clearly that is the idea behind why Paul is warning Timothy about these false prophets, not to be influenced by them negatively.

Paul points out (verse 5) that the motive for many of these church troublemakers is their feeling that "godliness is a means of gain." Not every false teacher is in the preaching/teaching business because of the hope of financial gain. But many are and so he issues some strong words against the sin of covetousness (verses 6-10).

Paul compares a covetous man to a person who is drowning. Death is near. Greed is a serious sin in the Bible and we need to beware of its influence and power in our lives today as well. We live at a prosperous time in a wealthy nation and the dangers of covetousness are very real. It can cause heartache, anxiety, bitterness, resentment and worry. Verse 10, often misquoted, warns us that "the love of money" (not money itself) is the root of all kinds of evil and sinfulness. In contrast, Paul encourages us to be content, satisfied with the physical blessings that God has already given us. We need to learn when enough is enough and not constantly be wanting more. Verses 17-19 tell one who is already rich not to trust in his material possessions, but in God.

Verses 11-16 and 20-21 speak to a man of God (a term in the Old Testament that often referred to a prophet; in the New Testament usually to a preacher, but in principle can be applied to every Christian) about fighting the good fight of faith and standing up for God. We must avoid greed and arguing about unimportant matters and live up to our confession in Jesus as the Son of the living God. We must remain faithful to Him until He comes again.

# 2 Timothy 1

Second Timothy was written under very different circumstances than First Timothy.

Paul was imprisoned at Rome on two occasions. During his first imprisonment, he wrote the four "prison epistles," Ephesians, Philippians, Colossians, and Philemon. After his release, he wrote several letters, including First Timothy and Titus. If he wrote Hebrews, this was probably also when he did that. He was free for approximately 2-3 years. Now he is back in a Roman prison and he writes what will prove to be his last letter. (We see, in 2 Timothy 4:6, that Paul is ready for his death.) There are some important, final things he wants to say to his younger protégé.

Verses 1-7 show us the closeness of the relationship between Paul and Timothy. The young Timothy was more than a student, more than a co-worker. He was a dear friend, "a beloved son" in the faith. He was, perhaps more than any other, the next generation preacher to whom Paul is passing the torch. Paul had many sons in the faith (he calls Titus that in Titus 1:4) and they were all important to him, but there was no one else like Timothy; see Philippians 2:19-22.

As you read these verses, it becomes clear how intense the relationship was between Timothy and Paul, in both directions. Paul prayed regularly for Timothy. Timothy was young and some believe he was in ill health and perhaps quite shy in personality. His old friend is about to die and yet his final thoughts are "I am praying for you and I greatly desire to see you one more time." He knew Timothy's faith was genuine and that he had never let Paul down in any way.

He comments about Timothy's family. Timothy was at least a third generation believer in God. This is often a dangerous generation and people can easily "inherit" their faith, but this is not necessarily so. Timothy's trust in and love for God was the real deal. His family was divided religiously (Acts 16:1) which can also be a threat to children, but it had not negatively affected Timothy. There are many godly women like his grandmother Lois and his mother Eunice who stand true for God, even without the help of a believing husband. They started young with Timothy (2 Timothy 3:15) and he never disappointed them.

Paul encourages Timothy to be bold in his faith, not timid or fearful (verse 7). A preacher often feels alone and without much support in his work, but Timothy was a righteous young man who didn't give up on what he believed, even if he had to fight alone.

Being a Christian will often bring challenges and hardships (verse 8), but Paul prompts him to continue true and steadfast in his love for the Lord and the lost (verses 8-18). Faithfulness to God's plan (verses 9-10) would bring eternal life for Timothy and others he worked with. God's plan for human redemption was in His mind "before time began." Through His grace we can be saved.

Paul confidently affirms, "for I know whom I have believed and am persuaded that He is able to keep what I have committed to Him until that Day" (verse 12). He wants Timothy (and all gospel preachers for all time) to hold fast to the truth (verse 13 – "the pattern of sound words which you have heard from me," he says).

There have always been, and will continue to be, those who oppose the truth and seek to turn others away from the faith. Paul names two from Asia who had done that, Phygellus and Hermogenes. But he also expresses his appreciation for "the household of Onesiphorus," who had refreshed his weary spirit. These were difficult times for Paul. He knew his death was approaching and his life's race was almost completed. He was grateful for those who stood beside him.

## 2 Timothy 2

In Chapter Two, Paul continues to give final instructions to the young evangelist, Timothy. They have been fellow soldiers for a long time now, since Timothy's own conversion to Christ during Paul's first preaching journey. He traveled with Paul on the second journey (Acts 16:1-5) and they have been close friends ever since.

In verses 1-13, Paul's words to Timothy encourage him to "be strong" in the Lord. He ties the Christian's strength to God's grace (verse 1). A proper understanding of God's grace makes a disciple stronger in the Lord. Realizing that God loves you so much that He sent His Son to die for you allows one to be bold, aggressive and confident.

Grace is God doing something for us that we could not do for ourselves. We were lost in sin with no hope of being saved; nothing we could invent or try would work (Jeremiah 10:23; Proverbs 14:12). So God came to the rescue and His plan began to unfold. Salvation would be possible because Jesus paid the penalty for the sins of the world (Ephesians 2:12-13).

Some people have the idea that God's grace means you can do whatever you want to and it's no big deal. We must never forget that sin is what separates souls from God (Romans 6:23), including the on-going sins of a Christian. God's grace should be an encouragement to us not to sin and in no way should we be lax or loose in our thoughts about sin. Unforgiven sin will cause souls to be lost eternally.

In verse 2, Paul tells Timothy to teach that important truth to others, to make certain that God's grace isn't forgotten (that's not all this verse means, but it is included in "the things that you have heard from me"). Notice the multiplying effect of this verse. Teach others who will teach others who will teach others. This assures continued faithfulness in following generations.

Verses 3-7 contain three illustrations of what it means to be a Christian. Each example says something different about serving God and approaches from a new angle of what is involved. A Christian is a soldier (verses 3-4). He emphasizes two things. Endure hardship and stay out of the world. When in the heat of a battle, any distraction could be fatal. A Christian is an athlete who must play (live) by the rules or be disqualified (verse 5). And the Christian is like a farmer, who enjoys the benefits of his hard work as he provides for himself and his family (verse 6). Paul prays that God would give Timothy a better understanding of these principles (verse 7).

Verses 8-13 promise us that God will reward those who remain faithful to Him. God will always do the right thing.

Verses 14-26 describe the firm (solid) foundation on which a servant of the Lord rests his hope. Paul encourages Timothy (and us) to study God's word carefully, to not engage in foolish and ignorant disputes and to humbly correct those who oppose the truth.

Some Christians (including some who are preachers and some who are not) get so wrapped up in their "hobbies," their favorite arguments or doctrines that they don't seem to care that lost souls are dying without Christ. (Nobody thinks it is a hobby when it's them, by the way; that's something other people do, but not me.) Paul warns that this attitude will lead to more ungodliness (verse 16), is like a cancer in the spiritual body (verse 17), and will overthrow the faith of some (verse 18).

Verses 24-26 are inspired words to every preacher about the proper way to conduct himself during times when the church may be struggling with divisive types of issues. Handling problems wisely can be quite challenging. The goal is not simply to be "right," but to save and restore those who are lost.

## 2 Timothy 3

In this chapter, Paul warns Timothy about the dangers he would face from false teachers who would seek only what was best for them. They are described as "lovers of themselves" in verse 2 and all of the other unflattering descriptions of their character flow out of that characteristic.

These "perilous times" are said to occur "in the last days." Many people have been taught that this phrase refers to the period of time immediately preceding the return of Christ. But, in the New Testament, this idea of "the last days" refers to what is sometimes called the Christian Dispensation or Age. (The final segment of human history that followed the Patriarchal Age and the Mosaic Age.) The last days began on the first Pentecost after the resurrection of Jesus and will continue until the end of time. Acts 2:17 tells us that the last days began on that day in A.D. 33. Jesus speaks to us in the last days (Hebrews 1:1-2), which means for the entire final age before Jesus comes back for the Day of Judgment. That is why we obey and follow the New Testament. It was a New Law for a new period of time. So when Paul warned Timothy about these things, they were already living in those perilous last days.

In verse 5, Paul says that the false teachers he is speaking about have "a form of godliness," but they deny its power. They are hypocrites, play actors, people who pretend to love God, but in truth, they only love themselves. He commands Timothy (and everyone else) to turn away from such pretenders; they will only bring sorrow and heartache to true believers. Read and study each of the characteristics of these ungodly people so that you will know what to look for, even today.

They are immoral (verse 6) people who try to "make captives of gullible women loaded down with sins, led away by various lusts." They are sensual, not spiritual.

Such false disciples are "never able to come to the knowledge of the truth." Paul mentions, in verses 8-9, by name, Jannes and Jambres. These two men are not mentioned by name anywhere else in God's word, but most Bible students believe they are the magicians of Egypt from Exodus 7:8-13 who tried to duplicate the miracles of Moses and Aaron before Pharaoh. They will eventually show their true colors, even if they appear righteous at first. Time often reveals the truth and separates the true followers of God from the false (See 1 Corinthians 11:18-19; 1 Timothy 5:24-25; 1 John 2:19).

In contrast to following and imitating people like those he has been describing, Paul now has some personal advice for Timothy (verses 10-17). The best way for Timothy to succeed as a man of God was to follow Paul's godly example and the teaching of the inspired Scriptures. The best teacher is one who helps you learn from the Bible and also shows you the way to live in his personal life.

Paul not only taught the truth to Timothy but he also modeled the truth in his life. He encourages his young friend to "carefully follow" (to remember and copy his example) many things about Paul. His integrity has been proven over time. Even those who originally doubted his conversion could look at his example and realize that he has shown himself to be faithful time after time. His service to God included not simply teaching what is right (purpose, faith, patience, love, endurance), but also could be seen in his trials and persecutions and afflictions caused by his unwavering stand for God and His will. Paul points out that everyone who is faithful to the Lord will, at times, have to endure some forms of persecution (they may vary in form and intensity). This is the price for godly living in an ungodly world.

Paul realizes that Timothy has been taught the Scriptures from his childhood (from grandmother and mother) and they have always pointed him to Jesus. The God-breathed (inspired) Word of God will provide him with all he needs to continue faithfully serving his Lord and Savior.

## 2 Timothy 4

It is generally agreed among Bible students that Second Timothy is the aged apostle's final letter. He has walked "the last mile of the way," as the song says. His final thoughts have to do with encouraging Timothy's faithful proclamation of the gospel.

Verses 1-5 outline the work of an evangelist. Of course, the most important statement in these five verses is "Preach the word." That sums up the primary responsibility of a gospel preacher; he is to tell others the good news about the salvation which is in Christ Jesus. A person wastes his time if he spends it sharing opinions, traditions of men, or human philosophies. Only the gospel will save (Romans 1:16).

"Be ready in season and out of season." That simply means to preach the truth always. When it is popular and when it is not. When the crowds are big and when they are small. When you feel good and when you feel lousy. When they cheer what you say and when they throw stones. When you get paid and when you don't. When it's easy and when it's hard. Always. Faithfully. Without compromise. Preach the word.

"Convince, rebuke, exhort, with all longsuffering and teaching" (NKJV). The New International Version gives it like this. "Correct, rebuke and encourage – with great patience and careful instruction." Some of this teaching sounds like 2 Timothy 2:24-26 where Paul makes it clear that the purpose of this preaching is to help souls make it to heaven. Our goal in all of the work we do for God, both public and private, is to do what we can to take others to heaven with us. That requires great patience and an attitude that helps us to realize that this is the most important work in the whole world.

Verses 3-5 show us that there will often be opposition to the work we are seeking to do. People often want their "itching ears" to hear happy thoughts, pleasant words that do not convict of sin, but promise great reward. Jesus came to save lost souls (Luke 19:10). We needed a Savior because "all have sinned and fall short of the glory of God" (Romans 3:23). And we must never forget that "the wages of sin is death, but the gift of God is eternal through Jesus Christ our Lord" (Romans 6:23). There can be no conversion, no salvation for those who are unwilling to repent of their sins against God and faithful preaching will bring that conviction to honest hearts. That's not always easy, but it is always necessary.

Paul's life before God has been poured out like a drink offering and the pitcher is almost empty (verses 6-8). His soul is calm, his heart is steadfast, his eternity is secure. He wants to spend his last words to his young friend encouraging him to remain faithful unto death.

Notice that Paul describes his eternal reward as "the crown of righteousness." This is the same as "the crown of life" that James mentions in James 1:12. It is the victory crown of one who has finished his race in life. It is available to "all who have loved His appearing."

Verses 9-22 conclude the chapter and book with some personal notes, comments and observations.

Paul shows his interest in the work of others (Luke, John Mark, Tychicus, Onesiphorus, Aquila and Priscilla, Erastus, Trophimus) in the greatest cause on the earth, the faith of his Lord and Savior. He sends greetings from Eubulus, Pudens, Linus, Claudia and others. There are words to uplift Timothy and others and words of warning about dangers that could lie ahead.

The apostle is hoping that he will have the opportunity to see Timothy one last time before his death (verses 9, 11, 13, 21). Remember that he has committed everything to God (2 Timothy 1:12).

# Titus 1

Paul writes this letter to another young preacher, Titus, to whom, like Timothy, he refers as his "true son in our common faith." The name, Titus, means "honorable" and he certainly was an honorable man.

Verses 1-4 serve as a brief introduction to this personal letter between the aged apostle and his young student. Paul refers to himself in verse 1 as both "a bondservant of God" and as "an apostle of Jesus Christ." All Christians are to be servants of the Lord and, in an unofficial sense, we are all sent out with the message of salvation to share with our lost and dying world.

Did you notice that Paul reminds Titus of our "hope of eternal life" (verse 2) and says that this promise was made "before time began?" This is strengthened by the statement that God cannot lie. There are certain things that are impossible for God, all of them things that would be inconsistent with the nature and character of Deity. (Another example would be that God cannot die or cease to exist.) Paul reassures us, in this passage, that God designed the scheme for human salvation even before the world was created. It was accomplished in Jesus the Messiah, of course, and that was to be the basis for the preaching that Titus was to do in the first century and that every faithful Christian is supposed to be engaged in (verse 3). We all have the responsibility of sharing the message of salvation with the lost souls we meet. This is a "commandment of God our Savior." Paul took his obligation to share the gospel with others very seriously. We should as well.

Verses 5-9 outline the spiritual work that Titus was to engage in on the island of Crete. His work is defined in two specific areas. First, he was to "set in order the things that are lacking." Every local church has areas of weakness that can be strengthened and part of the work of an evangelist is to complete much of that unfinished business. Even strong churches have things that can be improved and we will never run out of lost souls that need to be saved. There will always be unfinished work for God's people.

Next, Paul tells Titus that he also needs to appoint elders in every city, that is, in each local church. A scripturally organized church leadership consists of elders who lead and deacons who serve, along with the members (saints) in each congregation (see Philippians 1:1). Notice that each church needs a plurality (at least two) of elders (compare to Acts 14:23).

Verses 6-9 contain a list of the qualifications of elders. This list is very similar to the one given in 1 Timothy 3:1-7, although there Paul uses the term, bishops (or overseers), to describe this important leadership role in the church. They are referring to the same group of people, the shepherds in each local church.

Titus is preaching on Crete, an island southeast of Greece, which apparently had multiple cities with congregations of the Lord's people. His dual responsibilities include putting in order some things that were unfinished and appointing elders in each local church. The contents of this letter would equip him to do both of those things. This would help secure the future of God's people on Crete.

Verses 10-16 issue some vital warnings about false teachers. These enemies of the faith were a danger to the first century disciples and we must still be on the lookout for their influence today. He sums up their wicked influence by saying that they "teach things which they ought not" (verse 11). The problem is that sometimes people believe them and their error. They were ruining the faith of entire families. They claimed to know God, but in their works, they denied Him and His inspired message. The churches on Crete, as well as others everywhere, need elders to oversee and evangelists to teach the truth so that these false teachers would not take over and destroy the work of God.

## Titus 2

As a local church grows and develops, one of the important aspects of securing the future is the handing down of the faith from one generation to the next. It is like the passing of the baton in a relay race or like Elijah passing his "mantle" of prophecy on to Elisha (2 Kings 2:1-15). It is the responsibility of the older generation to pass "sound doctrine" (verse 1) on to the younger disciples.

Verses 1-10 deal mostly with the older teaching the younger.

He starts with older men (verse 2), the leaders in the church. Their qualities of reliability are discussed in this verse, including being serious about serving God, being self-controlled and full of faith and love. They are to exhibit patience and wisdom in their lives. Remember that he is discussing what he referred to as "sound doctrine." Such teaching includes both what is said to the younger men and the kind of example that these mature disciples are supposed to model in front of others. They say and do what is right consistently. Lifestyle and doctrine are closely intertwined here as they teach and live the truth.

Next he addresses "older women" (notice Paul is wise enough not to state at what age that begins). They are to be reverent teachers of those who are younger. Again, we can see the value of their years of experience here and of God's desire that this type of godly behavior be passed down from one generation to the next. It can be done in the home and family setting, but realizing that not every one (then or now) has a stable home environment, it also falls upon those in the church context to help others who may or may not be getting what they need from their biological families. They are to be teachers of the younger women and to instruct them not to be slanderers of others (that can always be a temptation for some) and not given to wine. Alcohol will not produce godliness and Paul wants them to encourage their younger sisters to avoid the possible problems that can result from alcohol use.

Verses 4-5 tell us some other things that should be passed on from older ladies to younger ones. They need to be taught to be discreet (not immodest), chaste (keeping themselves morally pure), homemakers, to be obedient to their husbands, to love and nurture their children.

Verses 6-8 focus on the behavior of younger men. They are to be "sober-minded" and to show themselves to be men of integrity and reverence and incorruptibility. In them, others should be able to see "a pattern of good works" as they devote their lives to serving God. Verse 8 reminds them that others, especially non-Christians, are watching them and that many will believe that every other Christian is just like you. Show them what they need to see, a life that glorifies God (Matthew 5:14-16).

He shifts slightly in verses 9-10 as he addresses all Christians who are bondservants. They are to be obedient to their masters and to please them with the quality of work they do. They are not to be rude verbally to their bosses and not to steal from work. They should be loyal and faithful to the employers so that they see the value of Christianity and the difference that being a Jesus follower makes in a person's life (see also 1 Peter 2:18 and Ephesians 6:5-8).

The second section of Chapter Two, verses 11-15, emphasizes that God's grace and salvation are available universally. God "desires all men to be saved" (1 Timothy 2:4) and His grace as shown in the sacrifice and resurrection of Christ is extended to all people. But in order to be saved, everyone must obey the Lord, including putting away all ungodliness and seeking to live a pure and holy life.

Verse 14 reminds us that, as Christians, we are special people. Jesus gave Himself for us, to redeem us from every lawless deed and to purify for Himself those who are zealous (excited, eager) for good works. Faithful gospel preaching should encourage us to live up to our spiritual calling (Ephesians 4:1).

## Titus 3

Paul begins to conclude this letter to Titus by reminding him to tell other Christians of their duty to God. Don't we all need occasional reminders of things we already know? He emphasizes the overall importance of repetition in the whole teaching process (verses 1-2). That's how we memorized the multiplication tables and learned how to spell words and how we remember certain important dates in human history. That is even how we learn to talk, by repeating words and phrases over and over. The same principle holds true in learning and applying spiritual lessons as well.

He speaks of general behaviors in life that ought to characterize every single Christian. As we read these reminders from the Holy Spirit, none of them should surprise us at all. We should respect and obey the laws of the land (at every level, by the way, national, state, local), to do good things for others, to be kind and considerate, peaceable and gentle, and humble in our dealings with others.

There is a sense in which verses 3-7 are a summary of the whole Bible story. Man is separated from God by our sinful choices, we cannot do anything to save ourselves without God, and God's mercy provides forgiveness and salvation for us.

The emphasis is on God's grace once again, on salvation through Christ. Verse 3 shows us how God sees a sinner. It isn't a pretty picture. While comedians make jokes about sinners and sin and everyone has a good laugh, there is really nothing funny or appealing about sin from God's perspective. Notice how he describes a sinner: "foolish, disobedient, deceived, serving various lusts and pleasures, living in malice and envy, hateful and hating one another." What an ugly list of attitudes and actions. But don't forget that the Bible says we are all guilty of sin (Romans 3:23) and that is why we deserve to be lost eternally (Romans 6:23; James 1:13-15).

Verses 4-7 give us a heavenly description of what salvation looks like. What we deserve and what God makes available to us are two very different things. Often we use the words, grace and mercy, as synonyms and it is true that both of them deal with the spiritual blessings of God, given as gifts to those who obey Him. But there is a difference in the two. Grace is God giving us something (salvation) that we don't deserve. Mercy is God not giving us what we do deserve (damnation).

He attributes our salvation to the kindness, love and mercy of God (see also Titus 2:11-14; John 3:16; Ephesians 2:8-10; Romans 2:4 and many other similar passages). It is through His undeserved kindness that we can be "heirs according to the hope of eternal life." It is not because we have earned a home in heaven through our works of righteousness, but solely through His grace that we can be saved. (At the same time, God commands us to obey and serve Him to be saved – James 2:14-26; Ephesians 2:10; Matthew 7:21). But we will never do enough good things to earn heaven; it will forever be a gift. We are taught to do the will of the Father, as a means of expressing our faith by our deeds.

And "the washing of regeneration" mentioned in verse 5 is speaking of water baptism for the remission of our sins (see Acts 2:38; Acts 22:16; Ephesians 5:26; Hebrews 10:22; 1 Peter 3:21). After we have done all those things, we will still be saved by God's grace.

Paul needs to spend some time teaching Titus how to deal with false teachers, those who would divide the people of God with their unprofitable and useless doctrines (verses 8-11). Titus, as a preacher, needed to be prepared to defeat such challenges to the faith. He would do so by remaining faithful to God's will as revealed on the pages of the New Testament. After a few personal references, Paul closes his letter to his young preaching friend.

## Philemon

Although this is one of the shortest books in the New Testament, we do have quite a bit of information about the man for whom this book is named. The first seven verses focus on Philemon himself.

He was a family man from the city of Colosse. His wife's name was Apphia. Their son was Archippus, whom many Bible students think was the preacher for the Colossian church.

Philemon was a wealthy man. The book tells us that the church met in his house and that would imply a house of considerable size, which would also indicate substantial wealth. Most homes of the first century were small and could not accommodate a congregation of any size at all. Philemon's home was likely large and, therefore, expensive.

Paul describes Philemon as a beloved friend, fellow laborer and brother in Christ. Philemon was also a disciple of the Savior who shared his faith with the lost. Paul prayed for Philemon in his work, which we commonly refer to as personal evangelism. He wanted Philemon to be "active in sharing your faith" (NIV).

Paul was a good friend of Philemon and referred to his companion in the gospel as a man of "love and faith." What an honor it would be for all of us to be so considered.

Verses 8-25 introduce us to Onesimus and tell us why this letter was written.

A slave named Onesimus runs away from his master, Philemon, and finds himself in the city of Rome. While he is there, he meets the apostle Paul, a long-time friend of Philemon, who is under house arrest in Rome (Acts 28:30-31).

Paul, even while in prison, preaches the gospel to anyone who will listen and Onesimus hears the truth and obeys it. Paul says, in Philemon 10, of Onesimus, "whom I have begotten while in my chains."

The apostle is now sending Onesimus back to his master. Onesimus is probably the one who carried the epistle to the Colossians, along with Tychicus (Colossians 4:7-9).

Paul asks Philemon to receive his former slave back as a brother in Christ. He tells his friend that, if Onesimus owes him any money, to charge that to his own (Paul's) account and he will repay the full amount. Perhaps this indicates that Onesimus stole something from Philemon before he ran away?

Was this all just a big coincidence? Or does it show us that there is no such thing when it comes to God? He controls all things and we would do well to realize what great changes in our world can be brought about by sincere, fervent trust in God.

There are several valuable lessons for us in the short letter to Philemon.

We are taught about reconciliation, both with God and with our fellow servants of the Lord. Things happen between Christians sometimes and we must be quick to forgive and forget the sins of others.

He also teaches us about the importance of spiritual family. We, as children of God, are brothers and sisters in Christ and we need to see one another in that light, no matter our station in life.

Above all, Paul teaches us to trust in Christ and to follow His example in how we love and treat each other. This is a personal and intimate look into the apostle's heart and how much others meant to him.

# The Letter to the HEBREWS

## Hebrews 1

This letter was written, by an unnamed author, to convince these Christians that they had done the right thing in obeying the new covenant. He reminds them that the Old Law was being taken out of the way (Hebrews 8:8-13) and had been replaced by a better way, the gospel of our Lord Jesus Christ. We commonly call this the New Testament. The theme of Hebrews is "don't turn back."

This first chapter has two major sections.

Verses 1-3 point out the superiority of Jesus over the Old Testament prophets. Though God revealed His will "in time past" at various times and through many different ways, the primary source of His revelation was prophets. These were inspired spokesmen of God. Sometimes they revealed the future, but that was not the focus of their work. Ultimately, they were men (and a few women) who, by the process called inspiration (a God breathed message), told the people to whom they were sent, what the Lord wanted them to do. Today, God's primary spokesman is His Son. Jesus, when He returned to heaven, sent the Holy Spirit to deliver His message through apostles and other prophets (John 14:26; 15:26; 16:13-14).

There are seven key phrases that the writer uses to describe Jesus in these early verses of the book.

- Whom He has appointed heir of all things – Jesus is the One that all Old Testament prophecies pointed to (Romans 10:4)
- Through whom also He made the worlds – Jesus is the Creator (Colossians 1:16)
- Being the brightness of His glory – reflecting the glory and majesty of God
- The express image of His person – Jesus is deity in every way (John 14:9)
- Upholding all things by the word of His power – holds the universe together (Colossians 1:17)
- He purged our sins – cleansed by His death on the cross
- Sat down at the right hand of the Majesty on high – to rule His spiritual kingdom from heaven

Verses 4-14 remind us that Jesus is superior to ("so much better than" – verse 4) the angels. The angels were heavenly spokesmen for the Lord. The word, angel, simply means "messenger." They were "ministering spirits" sent to help the people of God on their way to salvation.

But Jesus is far better than all the prophets and all the angels put together. He is the One through whom God has revealed His final will for mankind, in the dispensation called "the last days" or the Christian Age. Jesus taught that His words will judge us in the last day (John 12:48). His gospel is the power of God for the salvation of all people (Romans 1:16). We are warned not to add to His word or to take anything away from it (Revelation 22:18-19).

There are five reasons that the writer describes Jesus as "better" than the angels. Notice all of the Old Testament verses that are quoted to make his point:

- Christ is the One whom God called "My Son" (Hebrews 1:5). Not once did He say that to any angel.
- He is the One who is worthy of worship, not the angels (verse 6).
- Jesus is the king on His eternal throne and righteousness is the scepter of His kingdom (verses 8-9). To be like Him we must be holy and pure.
- He is eternal. "Your years will not fail" (verse 12). This is a reference to His deity.
- He is at God's right hand (verses 13-14); repeats this point from verse 3.

That's why the Bible calls Him Savior.

## Hebrews 2

Verses 1-4 emphasize the importance of Christ's message, due to His superiority over the Old Testament prophets and the angels, as discussed in Chapter One.

We must pay close and careful attention to the things that Christ has taught, either personally (the red letter parts) or through His inspired apostles and prophets. Salvation is available through the gospel of Christ which was accompanied by miraculous signs and miracles as proof of its validity. That is what is meant in verse 4 where the writer uses the word, confirmed, to show that the miracles verified the teaching of the apostles as true.

Those who obey will be saved, while those who disobey will be punished.

In verses 5-8, the author pauses to talk about the relationship between human beings and the angels. Men were created a little lower than the angels (Psalms 8:4-6). But the inhabited world was made subject, not to angels, but to human beings (Genesis 1:28). God cares for us and, though we are lower than angels in power, we have been given an important position in God's plan, that of dominion over His earthly creation. The earth is under man's dominion, not that of angels.

In verses 9-10, he applies Psalm 8 to Jesus, who was also made lower than the angels, when He became a man and then was subjected to physical death. But He too had an important position in God's plan as the Savior of the world and therefore, is crowned with honor and glory. He became the captain of human salvation, something angels could not have accomplished. Verse 9 shows us that Jesus was crowned with glory and honor because He tasted death for all people. The good news of salvation is available to all souls.

In verses 11-13, we learn the truth that we are brothers and sisters (fellow members of the family of God) with Christ. The One who sanctifies (the Lord) and the ones who are sanctified (faithful disciples/ Christians) are "all of one." We are in the same body, family, church. Verse 12 is a quote from Psalm 22:22, saying that Jesus is not ashamed to call us brothers (and sisters). We are the children God has given to Christ (verse 13).

Verses 14-16 teach an important truth. Jesus took upon Himself bodily form, humanity (this is sometimes called "the incarnation") in order that He might destroy (to ruin utterly) the one who had power over death (1 John 3:8). Previously Satan had power over the realm of death; now Jesus does. It is ironic, but Jesus died (and rose again) to destroy death.

This was done to deliver us from bondage (of sin). Verse 16 says that He didn't do that for the angels who sinned, but for the people who sinned.

Verses 17-18 continue to remind us that Jesus became like us (He was one of us/with us), His brothers and sisters. He made propitiation (atonement, KJV and NIV) for our sins. That means He became the atoning sacrifice who paid the price for our sins (1 John 2:2; 4:10).

His major point in all of the information given to us in Chapter 2 is that it was Jesus who did all of this, not an angel. He is the Savior of the world. Angels have had an important part to play in human and divine history, but do not lose sight of the central truth that Jesus died to save us from our sins. This is why we can have hope in Christ. He controls death and will continue to help and aid us in our feeble attempts to serve God acceptably. Do not give up.

## Hebrews 3

There was no one more important to the Hebrew people than Moses (unless maybe it was David). Moses was the great Old Testament Lawgiver, the leader of the children of Israel during the wilderness years. He stood in the presence of God while receiving the Law and his face continued to shine brightly for several days (2 Corinthians 3:7-13; Exodus 34:29-35). The Messiah was to be a Lawgiver (James 4:12), "like me," according to Moses himself (Deuteronomy 18:15-19; Acts 3:22-23).

Now the author of Hebrews reminds them that Jesus is to be "counted worthy of more glory than Moses" (verse 3). Both were faithful to God. Moses was faithful to the Lord in his house as a servant, while Christ was faithful over His own house as the Son of God. Jesus is God's only begotten Son (remember Hebrews 1:5?).
The first two chapters focus on the superiority of Jesus over the Old Testament proph-

ets and the angels. Chapter 3 now reminds the concerned Hebrews that Jesus is "better" than Moses. The major point, of course, is that the old covenant has been replaced with a new covenant. It would be a mistake for them to return to the Law of Moses, since it has been fulfilled and replaced with the gospel of Christ.

Two important roles of Jesus are mentioned in verse 1. He is called "the Apostle and High Priest of our confession." The word, apostle, means "one who is sent." We are most familiar with the twelve apostles, men whom Jesus chose out of hundreds, perhaps thousands, of disciples who were following Him. They were Simon Peter, Andrew, James, John, Philip, Bartholomew, Thomas, Matthew, James, Labbaeus (also called Thaddaeus), Simon the Canaanite (or the Zealot) and Judas Iscariot. After the death of Judas Iscariot, Matthias was chosen to take his place (Acts 1). And later (as one born out of due time, 1 Corinthians 15:8), the Lord called Paul to become the apostle to the Gentiles (Acts 9). However, there are other servants of God who were "sent" at various times and for different reasons, on missions for God and sometimes, they were referred to as apostles also. They were not "official apostles" (my term, rh) but were simply men of God asked and sent to accomplish certain things for God. See Acts 14:14 and Galatians 1:19 as examples.

The other term used to refer to the Savior here is "High Priest" of our confession. Beginning in Chapter 4 and continuing for several chapters, the writer will spend a large section of the letter explaining why Jesus is superior to the priests and high priests of the Law of Moses. To those who were concerned about leaving the long important priestly system of the Old Testament, the author wishes to show over and over that Jesus and His one time, for all time sacrifice and priesthood far surpasses the one found in the Old Law.

In verses 7-13, they are reminded of Israel's historical failure to remain faithful to God, referring especially to the time in "the wilderness" (verse 8). He quotes Psalm 95:7-11 several times in this chapter and the next to emphasize the importance of trusting God and not rebelling against Him. During that forty year journey, their fathers rebelled often against God and His chosen leader, Moses. Those who hardened their hearts and forsook the Lord died and their "corpses fell in the wilderness" (verse 17). Those who persevered were allowed to enter the Promised Land. We need to help each other to remain faithful (verses 12-13).

So once again (and not for the last time either), the Hebrews are told to keep their faith strong in Christ and not to revert to the Old Law. He says to "hold fast the confidence and the rejoicing of hope firm to the end" (verse 6) and to be "steadfast to the end" (verse 14). What does that mean to us today? We must not go astray in our hearts and turn from serving God. Do not rebel against His will for your life. The consequences will be eternal.

# Hebrews 4

How can two people hear the same sermon and one is drawn closer to God while the other leaves unaffected by the message? The first listener had faith in God, but the second one did not (verses 1-3).

The chapter begins with the word, therefore. This means that these thoughts are a conclusion (or necessary inference) based on what was discussed in the previous chapter (remember that the chapter and verse divisions are man-made). Chapter 3 had emphasized the importance of listening to Christ, not Moses. It also warned of serious consequences for those who reject the word of the Lord through unbelief. The writer does not want these Hebrew Christians to "come short" (verse 1) of heaven, but to "hold fast our confession" (verse 14).

Do you really believe what you read in the Bible? Do you believe there is a heaven to gain and a hell to shun? The point being made here is that Old Testament Israel did not listen to God. We must not make the same mistake.

In verses 4-11, he emphasizes that the Promised Land of the Old Testament (and the rest it offered) was not the ultimate rest promised to those who remain faithful to God. Joshua did not provide them with that final rest, although they did conquer the nations of the Promised Land and take possession of it (see Joshua 21:43-45; that's really the message of the entire book of Joshua). The final place of rest (Revelation 14:13) is heaven and this ought to be the top priority of every disciple of Christ, to live in such a way that we can live with Him forever (verse 11).

(By the way, Joshua is the Hebrew equivalent of the Greek name, Jesus. Both mean "Savior" – see Matthew 1:21.) Joshua delivered his people into the Promised Land and Jesus will deliver His followers into the final promised land of heaven.

Looking into God's word can tell us whether we are pleasing to Him or not (verses 12-13). How can we know if we will receive the eternal rest of heaven? God's word tells us. The Bible is described in verse 12 as living and powerful, sharper than any two-edged sword. It is said to pierce even to the division of soul and spirit, and of joints and marrow and it is a discerner of the thoughts and intents of our hearts. The Bible is the most important book ever written (2 Timothy 3:16-17; John 12:48). We must not ignore its teaching; we must live as it teaches us to live. Verse 13 speaks of the omniscience of God; He is all-knowing. Nothing escapes Him and He doesn't forget either.

In verses 14-16, the author shifts to another comparison between the old and the new. Jesus is our High Priest today and He will be described as superior to the Levitical priests.

Verse 14 states that Jesus is a great High Priest; let us hold on to our faith. We must never abandon Him.

Verse 15 tells us that Jesus is our perfect example in overcoming temptation. He was tempted in the exact same ways that we are, yet He never sinned. This means that

Satan used the same areas of temptation on Jesus that he uses on us, the lust of the flesh, the lust of the eyes and the pride of life (1 John 2:15-17). Jesus responded by reminding the devil "It is written," telling us that knowing and living the Bible is the key to victory over sin.

Verse 16 promises us that we can turn to God in prayer with boldness and confidence that He will help us, as well as forgiving us when we do wrong.

The Hebrews who were in danger of returning to the Old Law needed to be convinced that everything about Jesus is better. Chapters 5-9 will go into much more detail about Jesus as our High Priest.

## Hebrews 5

The first reference to Jesus as High Priest in Hebrews is 2:17. The second is Hebrews 3:1. Then we come to Hebrews 4:14-16. We learn that He is a perfect High Priest and so, let us hold on to our faith, our confession that He is God's Son. We are also taught that He can sympathize with us (because He was tempted, although He did not give in like we often do). And we can go to God in prayer with boldness and confidence that He will hear and forgive and help us.

The author now continues the comparison between Jesus and the Old Testament priests (sometimes he speaks of similarities and sometimes of differences).

In verses 1-4, the unknown writer tells us that the compassion of the Levitical high priest toward others came from the priest's own weaknesses. He had to offer sacrifices first for his own forgiveness and then for the sins of others. These high priests were not self-appointed, but rather were chosen by God, beginning with Aaron, the first high priest of the Mosaical Dispensation.

He points out that Aaron did not apply for the job as high priest and promote himself until God decided to give him the job. He was "called by God" to serve in this important role. His sons after Him were chosen by God in the same way. That's what it means that "no man takes this honor to himself."

In the same way (verses 5-11), "Christ did not glorify Himself to become High Priest." Jesus was glorified by God in two distinct ways.

First, He is God's Son. Verse 5 quotes Psalm 2:7, a well-known Messianic psalm. Jesus was born in the flesh as God's Son, lived as the chosen Savior of the world (Messiah means "anointed one") and was raised from death by the power of God.

As the Son of God on earth (God with us – Matthew 1:23), Jesus learned obedience to God through the trials and sufferings He endured. Being perfect (never sinning) through those trials, Christ became "the author of eternal salvation to all who obey Him" (verse 9). This brings the impact of salvation down even to us today. Notice that the writer does not say salvation is for the select few whom God chose before the world was created while everyone else will be lost eternally. That is the false Calvinistic doctrine of Unconditional Salvation (or Calvinistic predestination). A human response of acceptance or rejection will determine our eternal destiny, according to God's grace. Anyone can choose to "obey Him" and be saved. Those who choose not to obey the Lord and His gospel will be lost.

Second, Jesus is "a priest forever according to the order of Melchizedek" (verse 6; see also Psalm 110:4). The next few chapters will be devoted to the superiority of "the order of Melchizedek" over "the order of Aaron" (or the sons of Levi – 7:5). He will have much more to teach them about Melchizedek, in Chapter 7.

In verses 12-14, the author pauses to remind the weak Hebrew disciples that part of their problem was that they had not grown spiritually. They should have grown to the place where they could teach others, but they still did not even understand "the elementary principles of Christ" (6:1).

Spiritual immaturity is, and has always been, one of the greatest failings of the people of God. Too often people are baptized into Christ, become a "babe in Christ," and never advance beyond spiritual infancy. These verses show us that God wants all of us to grow spiritually "in the grace and knowledge" of God.

## Hebrews 6

Hebrews 5:12-6:20 is a parenthesis, a brief insert of very important information. The author has brought up Melchizedek and wants to say more, but is struck by the Hebrews' spiritual immaturity. He addresses that lack of growth in this short section and then returns to Melchizedek in Chapter Seven.

At the end of Chapter 5, the writer contrasted milk with solid food. Here at the beginning of Chapter 6, he points out that those who grow to maturity must leave "the elementary principles" of the gospel, what he calls "the milk" (see also 1 Peter 2:2) and move on to maturity, which includes "solid food" or, as the KJV words it, "strong meat."

The basic and fundamental first principles of God's word are vital to the Christian's life, but we must advance to more difficult and mature subjects as we grow in Christ. Many of the Hebrew Christians had not matured, although they had been disciples of the Lord for some time (Hebrews 5:12).

When a Christian leaves his commitment to Christ behind and falls from the faith, either to the world or to his old way of life in false or outdated religion, he can be difficult to restore. The writer says it is "impossible," because there is nothing new we can say to that person that he doesn't already know. Sometimes a reminder of the truth he knows will touch a soft place in his heart and bring him back to God. But if he doesn't want that, however, it will never happen.

This should be a clear warning to those who believe in the false teaching called, Once Saved, Always Saved. There are so many straightforward verses in the New Testament that show a person can lose his or her salvation, if they do not continue to faithfully serve God.

The old dodge is that one who seems to be falling away from God was never really saved in the first place. But the context of Hebrews 6 shows that this is not true. (Many of the other verses that show us it is possible to walk away from God, after accepting Jesus, also make it clear that some really are saved, but then really are lost.) Notice, here in Hebrews 6, that the one being spoken about was "enlightened," has "tasted the heavenly gift," was a partaker "of the Holy Spirit," had "tasted the good word of God and the powers of the age to come." This is not a pretender; this is one who begins the race but does not finish. Even the apostle Paul said that he pressed on, disciplining his body and keeping it in subjection so that he would not "become disqualified" (1 Corinthians 9:27).

In another passage that describe this descent back into sin, 2 Peter 2:20 tells us of some who "escaped the pollutions of the world through the knowledge of the Lord and Savior Jesus Christ" (if they have escaped, that means they are no longer in those pollutions), but then they are "again entangled in them and overcome." Peter is talking about people who have become Christians, but then do not continue in that commitment and go back into the world from which they were saved. It is said of them that "the latter end is worse for them than the beginning." They had a chance at heaven, but could not or did not control their lives and will end up lost. How sad.

The author reminds these first century followers of Christ that God will never forget the good deeds done for the Lord. He speaks of "your work and labor of love which you have shown toward His name" (verse 10). They had sacrificed much and given their all to the Messiah and now were in danger of leaving Him. He tells them they needed to show diligence and patience, and not to become "sluggish" in their service to the Christ. Verses 13-20 encourage our faithfulness to a trustworthy God.

The only hope of the world is Jesus Christ. Our genuine hope in our Savior is what enables us to have the strength to persevere to the end.

## Hebrews 7

Melchizedek, the mystery man of the Old Testament, was a "type" of Christ. The Old Testament is filled with types and shadows, which were people, places, events, etc. that foreshadowed the coming realities of the new (and better, verse 22) covenant.

After the insert (5:12-6:20), when he reminds them of the importance of going past the first principles, the writer returns to his original discussion, which was the high priesthood of Jesus and the comparison between Christ and Melchizedek. (One comparison is that Melchizedek was both priest and king as was Christ. No one could be a priest and a king under the Law of Moses, because those appointed to these offices had to be from two different tribes, which was impossible.)

Melchizedek preceded the Levitical priesthood by many years. The time of Melchizedek is Genesis 14, during the lifetime of Abraham. The Levitical priesthood was not established until many years later during the time of the Exodus. Hebrews 7 shows us that the priesthood of Melchizedek is superior to that of Aaron (or Levi). It would be helpful for you to read again the account in Genesis 14:1-24. The part specifically about Melchizedek is found in verses 18-21 but please read the entire chapter for context.

Hebrews uses two lines of reasoning to prove this. First, Melchizedek received tithes from Abraham, the father of the Levitical priesthood and second, Melchizedek (the better) blessed Abraham (the lesser).

Of course, Jesus could not be a priest under the Law of Moses, because that covenant specified the tribe of Levi. So for Christ to be a priest, the law had to be changed (verses 11-14). Notice again, that this is an example of God's silence prohibiting something from being done. There are no passages that say, "Do not appoint priests from Judah." Or "do not appoint priests from Ephraim or do not appoint any priests from Issachar." God didn't have to say that, because He already said, "Levi." That is sometimes called "the law of exclusion," since specifying the thing God wants us to do automatically eliminates everything else. God never said, "Do not use lamb and milk for the Lord's Supper." He did not need to say that because He said, bread and fruit of the vine. Silence is never permission; it is always prohibition.

Some of the Hebrew Christians were considering returning to the Old Law and that would have been an eternally fatal error. The contrast is between "the law of a fleshly commandment" (the old) and "the power of an endless life" (the new). The Old Covenant was annulled due to weakness and unprofitableness. That doesn't mean the Law of Moses failed. It did exactly what it was designed by God to do. The Old Testament fulfilled its purpose and the New Testament brought in a new, better hope.

Here are four possibilities for who Melchizedek was. (Choose one or some other better option.)

- A normal man about whom we have little information, no lineage, no recorded beginning or end of life, etc.
- An angel sent for a specific purpose
- A specially created man who was then removed from earth without death (like Enoch and Elijah)
- A pre-incarnation appearance of Jesus Himself

Christ is the superior High Priest. He is described in verse 26 as "holy, harmless, undefiled, separate from sinners, higher than the heavens." Because He lives forever, unlike the Levitical priests, He has "an unchangeable priesthood." And His current role is to make intercession for the people of God. His "once for all" sacrifice made our salvation possible.

Can you see how the writer of Hebrews is elevating Jesus, one point at a time, to increase their devotion to Him so that the readers of the book would never want to abandon the only true Savior of the world?

# Hebrews 8

What Jesus brought into the world was a new covenant, a better covenant, which contains better promises (verse 6). Chapters 8-10 are "summary chapters" concerning Christ's priesthood. He begins by saying that our High Priest is "seated at the right hand of the throne of the Majesty in the heavens." This is why He "lives to make intercession" for Christians today (7:25). He is the perfect High Priest.

Verses 1-5 start these conclusions about the priesthood of Jesus with a comparison to the way in which people served and worshiped God under the Law. "Now this is the main point of the things we are saying: We have such a High Priest, who is seated at the right hand of the throne of the Majesty in the heavens." Can you see that the writer is not talking about Moses or Aaron, but about Jesus Christ? He is reminding them (and us) that what we have because of Jesus is better now, a better sanctuary, a better tabernacle, better gifts and sacrifices.

The items of service and worship under the Old Law are referred to as "the copy and shadow of the heavenly things" (verse 5). They were important; they were given by God; they were all types, foreshadowing the realities of what we enjoy now under the New Testament. We can learn much about God and what the Creator expects from His creation by studying the lessons given to us in the Hebrew Bible.

Verse 5 quotes Exodus 25:40 to help us remember that God's revealed word is a "pattern" (I know many people don't like that word at all, but the Bible uses it often, like it or not). This verse teaches us three important things. 1.) There is a pattern. 2.) The pattern comes from God. 3.) All things have a pattern. This shows us the importance of God's word. It is a good thing, not a problem.

But the main point of Chapter 8 is to emphasize that the Old Law has been done away with and has been replaced by the New Covenant.

Verses 6-7 are transition verses from one thought to another. They are in keeping with the theme of the whole book of Hebrews, which is that everything in the new covenant under Jesus is better than anything in the old covenant under the Law of Moses. He specifies in these verses that we have a better ministry, a better covenant and better promises.

Verses 8-12 quote, in its entirety, the passage from Jeremiah 31:31-34. The Old Testament clearly predicted its own replacement with a new covenant.

There are many passages which tell us the value of studying the Old Testament. See John 5:39, Romans 15:4, and 1 Corinthians 10:6, 11. The Old Testament points people to the Messiah. It provides examples of obedience and disobedience to the Lord. It assures us that God will reward the righteous and punish the wicked. Many of the illustrations and word pictures in the New Testament cannot be understood without a knowledge of the events and people of the Old Testament.

But God's law for man today is the New Testament, the gospel of Jesus Christ (Romans 1:16). The New Testament tells us how to be saved eternally.

The Old Testament provides a pattern for how to offer sacrifices and observe special days and worship at the tabernacle and temple. The New Testament is our pattern today of worship and faithful living and teaches us how to get to heaven.

## Hebrews 9

The earthly tabernacle was a glorious structure. Its beauty is described in great detail in Exodus 25-40. It consisted of two sections, the Holy Place and the Most Holy Place. Each section contained important items for Old Testament sacrifices and worship of YHWH (or Yahweh). Physically, it was a beautiful building. Spiritually it was the temporary place where the people of Israel could meet with God. Later, it was replaced by a more permanent structure, often known as the temple or the Lord's house.

The items contained in the tabernacle are listed in these verses. In the Holy Place were located the lampstand, the table and the showbread. This section was also called "the sanctuary." Within the Holiest of All, behind the veil, were the golden censer, the ark of the covenant (covered with gold), the golden pot of manna, Aaron's rod that budded, and the tablets of the covenant (the Ten Commandment tablets written with the finger of God). Wouldn't it have been incredible to see those items from the actual tabernacle? Surely, they were an impressive display of God's power and majesty.

Jesus came to establish "the greater and more perfect tabernacle." This refers to the church, the glorious blood bought body of our Savior. The Holy Place in the tabernacle (and later, the temple) was a "type" or shadow of the church. And through the church, we can enter the Holiest of All (or the Most Holy Place), which refers to heaven itself.

As with all types/shadows, the tabernacle, as grand and beautiful as it was, was not nearly as spectacular and significant as the church and heaven, the reality of what cast the shadows. We have the reality today, the whole Bible story. They only had bits and pieces of the whole revelation that we have today. We are indeed a blessed people.

In the physical tabernacle, priests offered goats and calves as sacrifices to the Lord, as instructed in the Law of Moses. In the spiritual tabernacle (the church), we benefit from the one time for all time blood sacrifice of God's Son. When Jesus shed His blood on Calvary's cross, His death brought the New Covenant into effect, and it is said to have been dedicated with blood. We need to understand that, without the shedding of blood, there is no remission of sins.

Verse 15 teaches us that the blood of Christ flowed both ways from the cross. It not only flows toward today to cleanse the obedient from sin, but it also flowed backwards to permanently remove the sins of the faithful under the first covenant. Their sins were forgiven conditionally when various offerings for sin were sacrificed, but it took the blood of Christ, as part of God's eternal plan for human redemption, to finally and permanently take away their guilt.

The greatness of Christ's sacrifice is seen in its unique nature. Various Old Testament sacrifices were offered daily, weekly, monthly and annually. The sacrifice of Jesus was a one time event. His sacrifice was so great that it only took one time to accomplish salvation for people of all time. Just imagine in your mind that the Son of God died on the cross to save you and me, and all people who have lived, are living or ever will live on the earth. We must never become so familiar with the story about the Savior dying on the cross that we take it for granted and fail to appreciate the love and power of God that makes our eternal home in heaven possible.

Verses 27-28 remind us that "it is appointed for men to die once." The cycle of life and death was set into motion when Adam and Eve sinned in the Garden of Eden. Jesus had to die to secure our salvation. But He rose from the dead and ascended to God. He promised to come back again. When He returns, it will be to bring salvation to the faithful.

## Hebrews 10

The Old Law, in its entirety, was a "shadow of the good things to come, and not the very image of the things" (verse 1). By its very nature, a shadow (or type) is inferior to the real thing (the fulfillment or anti-type). A picture of a loved one is very nice, but the real person is much better.

The animal sacrifices of the Law of Moses were a type, which foreshadowed the sacrifice of Jesus for the sins of the world. That's the reason Jesus was called "the Lamb of God who takes away the sin of the world" (John 1:29). Some people who never study the Old Testament because we are under the New Testament today would have a difficult time understanding the imagery used by John the Baptist to describe the Messiah. Such figurative language is also found in other passages such as Revelation 5:6 where Jesus is described as "a Lamb as though it had been slain." Why would the 4 living creatures and the 24 elders fall down (verse 8) before the Lamb? Why would all creatures say (verse 13), "Blessing and honor and glory and power be to Him who sits on the throne and to the Lamb, forever and ever?" What does a simple farm animal have to do with heaven? It is all tied together in the animal sacrifices of the Old Law and the fulfillment of those types in the realities of the new covenant.

It was stated repeatedly, in the book of Leviticus, that when these sacrifices were offered by a penitent believer, his sins would be forgiven. (See Leviticus 4:20, 26, 31, 35; 5:10, 13, 16, 18; 6:7 for examples.) Yet, here in Hebrews, the author states that these sacrifices could never "make those who approach perfect" (verse 1). And that "it is not possible that the blood of bulls and goats could take away sins" (verse 4). It also says that "sacrifices and offering You (God, rh) did not desire" and "in burnt offerings and sacrifices for sin You had no pleasure" (verses 5-6). How do we reconcile these thoughts?

A Jewish brother in Christ taught me years ago that we do so by understanding the difference between forgiveness and remission.

The forgiveness of the Levitical sacrifices was conditional. This is seen in the phrase, "in those sacrifices there is a reminder of sins every year" (verse 3). The reason animal sacrifices could never take away sins (permanently) is that sin is a rebellion of humanity against God. When people, created in God's image, violate His will, that sin separates them from Him (Isaiah 59:1-2). Human death must occur to atone for that rebellion; human blood must be sacrificed for human sin. Jesus, the perfect combination of humanity and deity, bridged that gap by dying, not for His own sins (because He had none), but for the sins of others (2 Corinthians 5:17-21).

God reconciled humanity (made us friends with Him again) through Jesus Christ. This provided for us the divine atoning sacrifice, propitiation, for making us at-one with God. Atonement has been defined as simply at-one-ment-with God.

The Old Testament sacrifices were a test to show who was willing to obey God. When Jesus died on the cross, their sins were finally and forever taken away. That's what remission of sins means. On this side of the cross, because Jesus has now died for the sins of the world (John 1:29), when we repent and are baptized in the name of Christ, we have the (permanent) remission of sins (Acts 2:38).

The animal sacrifices provided a temporary forgiveness of those sins. But the Day of Atonement (the tenth day of the seventh month in the Jewish system) also brought a reminder of their past sins. Because the one time, for all time, sacrifice of Jesus brings permanent forgiveness, God says, "Their sins and their lawless deeds I will remember no more" (verse 17). Our sins are gone forever. Hallelujah, what a Savior.

## Hebrews 11

There are two, very different, kinds of faith. One is a weak faith, which when it is tested, gives up and draws "back to perdition" (Hebrews 10:39). A weak faith is characterized by a lack of confidence in God and His power. Jesus often challenged His disciples with the words, "O you of little faith!" He was trying to encourage them to grow in their relationship with the heavenly Father and trust Him more deeply.

The other is a strong faith which endures through trials and is shown by obedience to whatever God asks of us. Those with a strong, vibrant faith are the ones "who believe to the saving of the soul." This refers to those who have grown spiritually beyond the basics, the first principles of the gospel, into a richer and fuller understanding of God and His will for our lives (Hebrews 5:12-6:3).

After explaining what faith is in verse 1, the writer makes applications of it in the following parts of Chapter 11. "Now faith is the substance of things hoped for, the evidence of things not seen." This tells us that faith is not "blind," that is, without basis or foundation. It is based on "substance" and "evidence." It is real, a logical conclusion that can be drawn from facts. Some have pointed out that it takes more faith to be an atheist than to be a believer in God. I am not sure I agree with that statement, but it is true that both "views" (theism and atheism) do require faith. An open minded examination of the facts will lead one to realize that there is a God. The 1984 New International Version renders verse 1 like this: "Now faith is being sure of what we hope for and certain of what we do not see." I like that; it shows us that we can be sure and certain of our faith, not weak and wavering.

Verse 6 goes on further to remind us of the importance of faith. "But without faith it is impossible to please Him, for he who comes to God must believe that He is, and that He is a rewarder of those who diligently seek Him." This shows us that it is only an active, obedient faith that saves us. It is not mere mental agreement that Jesus is God's Son (although that is essential). Saving faith motivates and compels us to be obedient to His word.

Hebrews 11 gives us numerous examples of saving faith. It shows us specific names of Old Testament characters who persevered and how we know of their faith in God by their submission to His will. Each person is qualified by a verb (action word) which tells us what they did. Abel offered; Noah prepared; Abraham obeyed; Isaac and Jacob blessed; Moses refused, chose, forsook and kept.

Other godly people and their righteous obedience to God are left unnamed. We are told of their faith and many of the specifics seem hard to imagine. Some stopped the mouths of lions or quenched the violence of fire. Others were scourged. Still more were stoned, sawn in two (whew!), slain with swords. Some lived in deserts, mountains, dens and caves.

It is said of many of these saints of God (and of others we may have known personally) that they were people "of whom the world was not worthy." They went to their reward with complete faith and trust in God.

Their faithful example provides for us "so great a cloud of witnesses" (12:1). They remind us that anyone who determines to do so can be loyal and devoted to God. If they can serve God faithfully and be saved, so can we.

These first century disciples were encouraged to persevere, to never give up, but to continue to serve the God of heaven. Their struggles are recorded for us in this book to help us keep going.

"I have decided to follow Jesus; no turning back, no turning back."

## Hebrews 12

The Christian life is often portrayed in the New Testament as a race. It is not a 100 meter sprint, however. It is a marathon and so the author encourages us to "run with endurance the race that is set before us."

The Old Testament heroes of faith mentioned in the previous chapter are described here as the spectators who are cheering us on to successfully complete the course and not to stop short of the finish line.

In order to finish the Christian race victoriously, we must "lay aside every weight, and the sin which so easily ensnares us." Nothing must cause us to take our eyes and hearts off the goal. In the context, "the sin" (note the singular is used, not the plural) is a lack of faith and trust in God. Remember that the apostle Peter walked on water until he took his eyes off of Jesus. When he lost that focus, he sank.

There are many things we need to "lay aside" because they could cause us to lose our souls. Some of them are sinful things that we need to repent of. Some of them are not sinful, but they take up so much of our attention that we don't make time to serve the Lord as we should. (That is part of the point in the parable of the Sower; many things can be used as tools of the devil to take our attention away from serving God. Satan doesn't care if all of those things are sinful, in and of themselves, as long as we consider them to be more important than serving the Messiah.)

The important lesson we can learn from this chapter (and really, the entire book) is that we must constantly look to Jesus for salvation. Many of the original first century readers of this book had started on their marathon with the Savior, but somehow, over time, they were in danger of losing that emphasis in their daily lives. The writer has been methodically, point by point, reminding them (and, by implication, us as well) that we can never take our attention off of Him. Such an abandonment of Jesus would mean spiritual disaster.

Jesus is referred to, in verse 2, with a couple of vital titles. He is called "the author and finisher of our faith." He is the author of our faith in the sense that He is the Creator, the author of the Bible (with the other members of the Godhead), the One who purchased the church with His shed blood, and the Savior who lived a perfect life and then died on the cross for the sins of the world (1 Peter 2:24). He is "the way, the truth and the life" and no one can come to God the Father, except through Jesus. He is the only Lord and Savior there is. Secondly, Jesus is called the "finisher" of our faith. Not only did His death and resurrection make salvation possible for all people (Hebrews 2:9), but He also sent the Holy Spirit to the inspired apostles and prophets and gave us "all things that pertain to life and godliness" (2 Peter 1:3; John 16:13).

The writer, in this chapter, makes the point again that we are not under the Old Law, but are to submit to the New Covenant. He reminds us that we do not "come to" Mount Sinai, "the mountain that may be touched and that burned with fire," to learn how to serve God in the last days. Rather we come to Mount Zion, the physical mountain where Jerusalem is located. This is the place where the spiritual kingdom, the church, came into existence, on the first Pentecost after the death, burial and resurrection of Jesus, recorded for us in Acts 2, the hub of the Bible.

Verse 14 emphasizes the importance of "holiness" in our lives as Christians, and goes so far as to say that, without holiness, no one will see God. That doesn't mean we have to be perfect to go to heaven; it simply is reminding us that we are expected to live a pure and holy life, separated from sin.

## Hebrews 13

In some respects, the final chapter of this letter is a series of miscellaneous, unrelated subjects of importance to every Christian.

In other ways, this section merely concludes a lengthy appeal from its author to its original recipients encouraging them to remain faithful to their Savior. And, in delivering his last admonition to them, he reminds them of some of their new covenant obligations.

The chapter begins with an encouraging note: "Let brotherly love continue" (verse 1). It might have been tempting for those who were remaining faithful to the Lord to resent those who were returning to Judaism, which is the primary concern of the letter. We should try to restore people back to the Lord who make the decision to leave Him, but we must continue to love them and do all we can to help them make the right decision about their relationship with the Savior.

Verse 2 throws out the interesting possibility that we might have had unknown encounters with angels at various points in our lives. (Many Christians believe this verse only applies to people in the first century, but who knows for sure? We can plan to ask the Lord about that when we get to heaven.)

Verse 3 reminds them of the sacrifices that many first century believers faced due to their faith. Some were literally prisoners (remember that four of Paul's letters were called prison epistles, plus 2 Timothy, which he wrote from prison as he faced the end of his life). There have been disciples of Jesus who have been imprisoned throughout the centuries, for no other reason than their trust in God. We may or may not know any of these people by name, but God knows them, and we ought to pray for those who are persecuted around the world. It is dangerous to be a Christian in many countries of the world today and those of us who have religious freedom should be both grateful to God for it and prayerful for those who are mistreated around the world.

One of the more interesting passages in this collection of responsibilities is verse 8 – "Jesus Christ is the same yesterday, today and forever." They had already accepted Him as their Savior, obeyed His gospel, and been added to His kingdom. He would never abandon them (Joshua 1:5) and they should not fall away from serving Him.

Verses 9-16 teach us the importance of "sound teaching." We should not be drawn away by "various and strange doctrines." Jesus died for our sins "outside the camp" and we must be willing to live outside the lines of societal approval to please God in everything we do. Even if it means "bearing His reproach" and being mistreated like He was, we must offer to God the sacrifice of our lives in His service. That is not always easy, but it is always the right thing to do the right thing.

Verse 14 contrasts the trials and difficulties of this temporary earth life with the joys of the eternal home of the soul on the other side.

There is also an emphasis on respecting and obeying our spiritual leaders (verses 7, 17).

In verses 20-21, the writer confidently affirms that the God of peace, who raised Jesus from the dead, will "make you complete in every good work to do His will, working in you what is well pleasing in His sight, through Jesus Christ, to whom be glory forever and ever." Praise God for His goodness to us.

Be devoted to God. Trust in Him. Obey His will for your life, which in this age in which we live, is the New Testament. "Grace be with you all. Amen."

# The Letter from JAMES

## James 1

It was not easy to be a Christian in the first century. The Jews had been "scattered abroad" through the entire world as a result of many years of foreign oppression and captivity. At the time of this writing, Rome continued that same type of persecution (Acts 18:2) and the Jewish Christians who received the letter were included in that intense pressure. They also faced many of the same difficulties and problems in life that everyone else does.

James wrote to encourage the disciples to remain faithful no matter what the trial might be. He gave them practical advice on how to deal with life's troubles (verses 1-11).

Many (myself included) find it challenging to consider what James says about counting it "all joy when you fall into various trials" (verse 2). Most of us take no pleasure in the problems of life. Yet James speaks of benefits that can come to us through such difficulties. The end result can be a blessing. Persevering through trials can cause us to grow and develop spiritual strength (verse 3). Hardships provide us with more and broader life experiences and it has been said often that we cannot truly appreciate the good without knowing the bad (and going through it ourselves). Also, the challenges in our lives can help us to long for heaven where no such difficulties exist (Romans 8:18).

But that doesn't mean hard times are easy to take. That's why James tells us to ask God for wisdom (verse 5). Wisdom is the proper application of knowledge. The Bible often uses words and phrases like discernment and spiritual understanding to describe a mature believer's response to life's downturns. God knows our needs and will help us to learn appropriate lessons from hardships. We must ask Him for help in faith, believing that He will enable us to survive even in the worst of times.

In verses 12-18, James shifts subjects only slightly as he begins to talk about dealing with temptations in life. Someone has defined temptation as something we crawl away from, hoping all the time to get caught. If temptation were not attractive to us, there would be no desire to do wrong. Satan will try to make sin look as appealing as possible so he can catch as many people as possible.

The words "drawn away" and "enticed" are hunting and fishing terms. Temptation is the "bait" that covers up the hook or trap that will result in our being captured by the devil. And we, like the fish, often don't see the danger until it is too late.

The final section of Chapter One tells us how to practice "pure and undefiled religion" (verses 19-27). Can you imagine anything worse than standing before Christ on the Day of Judgment and having Him say that your religion was useless and then sentence you to an eternity in hell?

Some people realize they will be lost because they have never even tried to serve the Lord. But many religious people who expect to be saved will not be (Matthew 7:21-23). How sad. James discusses many important lessons we need to learn so our relationship with God will not be useless and vain.

There is much emphasis in this section of the chapter about not simply hearing what is right, but doing it. Verse 19 stresses the idea of listening to others, being careful with our words and not getting quickly angry. We must be willing to put away all forms of evil and live according to God's will (verses 21-25). It is described as "the perfect law of liberty" and offers us freedom from sin and the chance to please God with every aspect of our lives.

Often there is a great difference between what we know and what we do. We must remember to practice what God has preached in His word.

## James 2

One of the most fundamental teachings of Jesus and Christianity is that law which has come to be called "the golden rule." The Lord of glory said it this way: "Therefore, whatever you want men to do to you, do also to them, for this is the Law and the Prophets" (Matthew 7:12).

Christians are to be known by the fair and equal way in which we treat other people. Rich and poor, black and white, young and old, Jew and Gentile are all equal in the eyes of the Lord (Galatians 3:28). This section of James (2:1-13) aims at helping us learn to deal with the sin of prejudice.

There are many ways of showing prejudice toward others. It may be directed toward racial groups, or socio-economic groups, or based on someone's age, height, weight, education or other similar criteria. It is not fair to judge individuals based on some arbitrary "group" they may fit into in some way.

James gives us an example of what he means by this principle (verses 2-4). Two people come into the worship services (actually the Greek word is SUNAGOGE, which refers to a place where the church meets; this shows Bible authority for a church building). One of them is poor while the other one is rich. The rich man is treated well by providing him with a good seat (Matthew 23:6) and the poor man is mistreated by being given an inferior place to sit. There are numerous applications that can be made about how we treat guests in our assemblies today. Some are welcomed with kindness and open arms while others (for various reasons, none of them acceptable) are virtually ignored. James says that, if we are guilty of such behavior, we become "judges with evil thoughts."

Verse 5 is included here to help us never forget that, no matter what our background, culture, race, financial status, etc., a "nobody" can be an heir in God's kingdom (1 Corinthians 1:26-29). We must show mercy and kindness to all people.

Verse 10 reminds us that every sin we commit has consequences, even one that is often considered to be "no big deal." God tells us that, if we show "respect of persons" (old KJV) toward others, He is displeased with our heart and attitudes. When I was growing up, one of our Bible class teachers would often make the statement that "the ground is all level at the foot of the cross." That is an important lesson for all of us to learn.

The second major section of James 2 (verses 14-26) speaks about the balance between faith and works. This is a Bible subject that has been debated since the first century and will continue to be a major source of disagreement between sincere people who seek to serve the Lord. Many have been taught false concepts about obedience.

It is one thing to believe in something. It is an entirely different matter to have a faith that so controls your life that you will do anything you are asked to do by the Lord. That's what true walking by faith (2 Corinthians 5:7) really is, obeying anything, everything the Lord tells us to do. "Not everyone who says to Me, 'Lord, Lord,' shall enter the kingdom of heaven, but he who does the will of My Father in heaven" (Matthew 7:21).

It is not legalism or "works salvation" to say that man has a part in his eternal destiny (Philippians 2:12) and that obedience to the will of God is essential to salvation. James has a lot to say in these verses about what he calls a dead faith, which he defines as "faith without works." He wants us to know that we cannot be saved by "faith alone" (verse 24). True faith proves itself in obedience.

## James 3

The first section of Chapter Three (verses 1-12) contains many warnings about misusing the tongue.

We have already noted in our study of James that we are supposed to be "slow to speak" (James 1:19). But that's easier said than done. Once spoken, our words cannot be retrieved. We must be aware of the potentially destructive power of the spoken word.

There are many sayings about the tongue.

- "If you can't say something nice, don't say anything at all."
- "Be careful what you say or your words will come back to haunt you."
- "If your tongue weighs so little, how come you can't hold it?"

James warns us that the tongue is a dangerous part of the human body and difficult to control. He refers to the tongue with a number of startling phrases. He says the tongue is a little part of the body, yet it boasts great things. It is a little fire that sets an entire forest ablaze. It is a world of iniquity; it defiles the whole body, sets on fire the course of nature and is set on fire by hell. The tongue is an unruly evil and full of deadly poison. All of these thoughts should remind us that we need to be very careful with what we say and how we say it.

He uses two illustrations to remind us of the power of the tongue (for good or bad). He speaks of the bit in a horse bridle that can be used to control a horse and the small rudder that can determine the direction of a large ship.

There are many good uses of the tongue that can include encouraging others, comforting the broken hearted, teaching the gospel, praising God, and expressing love for others.

There are also numerous bad uses of the tongue such as gossip, lying, teaching false doctrines, cursing, taking God's name in vain and saying hurtful things to others. Marriages can be destroyed, families can be separated, friends can be alienated, churches can be split because people are not careful about how they speak to others. This is a big deal, an important theme throughout the Bible.

The second major lesson in this third chapter reminds us of the value of spiritual wisdom. James had mentioned in 1:5 that those of us who lack wisdom simply need to ask God for some. It is amazing that, with this promise from the Lord to give wisdom freely and without grudging, we still fail to do this and instead rely so much on human wisdom, which always gets us in trouble.

In James 3:13-18, the Lord reminds us that if there is one quality that more Christians could use, it is wisdom. But we must be certain that we use spiritual wisdom (the wisdom from above) and not worldly wisdom. We will get into trouble every time we try to substitute human wisdom for God's wisdom. His way is always best. James identifies some of the qualities of both worldly and spiritual wisdom.

A wise person demonstrates his wisdom by proper behavior. A wise man does the right thing. He is a "peacemaker" (Matthew 5:9) and promotes unity and harmony among all people.

A foolish person shows his foolishness by what results from his actions. His heart is filled with "bitter envy" and "self-seeking" and the result is "confusion and every evil thing." An evil person sows strife, division and conflict wherever he goes.

# James 4

This first section of Chapter 4 (verses 1-12) is a continuation of the thoughts in Chapter 3.

The wars, fights, and lust discussed here are the logical consequences of human wisdom that arise from "bitter envy and self-seeking" (3:14). It is bad enough that these things occur in the world. But it is even worse when the church ("wars and fights come from among you") is filled with such ungodliness.

Verses 1-6 describe the problem that can exist among the people of God. Verses 7-12 provide us with God's remedy for division and strife in the church.

We must rise above the level of sin talked about here by resisting the devil, submitting to God and treating one another in a righteous way. The root cause of many of the specific sins listed here is selfishness. "You lust and do not have. You murder and covet and cannot obtain" (verse 2). He says that even when we pray to God for things, we often "ask amiss, that you may spend it on your pleasures" (verse 3). Sometimes all we pray about are things that we want to go our way, even if what we want is not what God wants for us.

Verse 4 emphasizes the important Biblical principle that we cannot be friends with God while we are trying to maintain friendship with the world. "Do not love the world or the things in the world. If anyone loves the world, the love of the Father is not in him. For all that is in the world – the lust of the flesh, the lust of the eyes, and the pride of life – is not of the Father but is of the world. And the world is passing away, and the lust of it; but he who does the will of God abides forever" (1 John 2:15-17). There are just many areas of life where we must make choices. Will we do what the world (or Satan) wants us to do or will we decide to serve God?

Maybe the greatest promise in this section is that if we will resist the devil, he will run away from us. Not maybe, not hopefully, not if we are lucky, but he will flee.

Then, in verses 13-17, James speaks of the importance of using our time wisely.

People have come up with many different ways of saying similar things. They all emphasize that we only have a limited amount of time in life and we must use that time wisely.

- "Life is short. Play hard."
- "Time is money."
- "Time is the stuff that life is made of."

God said it this way: "Do not boast about tomorrow, for you do not know what a day may bring forth" (Proverbs 27:1). "See then that you walk circumspectly, not as fools but as wise, redeeming the time, because the days are evil" (Ephesians 5:15-16).

"Redeeming the time" literally means buying up every opportunity. We must be careful not to waste the time that the Lord has given us. Opportunities to do good are limited and we must take advantage of them to do the Lord's will. What I do today is important because I am exchanging a day of my life for it.

It is extremely sobering to realize that our lives are nothing more than vapor or mist and that they are here only for a little while and then vanish away. "They" say that time passes more quickly as you grow older. Of course, that is not literally so, time moves at the same pace for everyone. But it is true that, as you grow older, you realize that time marches on in a relentless manner and sometimes it is hard to realize how much of your life has flown by so very quickly.

## James 5

There may well be more warnings in the Bible about the dangers of materialism and covetousness than any other single sin. James has said much about this subject already and deals with it further in verses 1-6.

Of course, greed is not exclusively a problem of the rich. Poor people can be (and often, are) covetous as well. God's solution to the problem of covetousness for rich and poor alike is contentment.

"But godliness with contentment is great gain. For we brought nothing into this world and it is certain we can carry nothing out. And having food and clothing, with these we shall be content. But those who desire to be rich fall into temptation and a snare, and into many foolish and harmful lusts which drown men in destruction and perdition. For the love of money is a root of all kinds of evil, for which some have strayed from the faith in their greediness, and pierced themselves through with many sorrows" (1 Timothy 6:6-10).

We need to learn to be satisfied with much less than we have. God is not concerned with the amount of wealth we have, but with our attitude toward money and possessions. Have we learned contentment? Are we always dreaming about more things we want to own? Are we using the material blessings we have in a godly way?

It may be hard for poor people to believe, but rich people often are characterized by sadness and "miseries" (verse 1). They can be in constant danger of losing their wealth. They may very well be mistreated by others who are jealous of their fortune. And there is the tendency to rely on money rather than on God. (That's why Jesus warned that it is impossible to serve God and mammon, Matthew 6:24.) Verse 4 also describes the unfairness of the rich who take advantage of the poor.

Verse 4 reminds them that, in all things, we will each have to answer to the Lord Almighty (NIV). We need to keep that in mind as we interact with others, whether rich or poor.

Verses 7-12 teach us how to develop patience, endurance, persistence, or perseverance.

Remember that Christians were often persecuted, sometimes to the point of death, in the first century. They needed to be encouraged to remain faithful and never give up. James includes two Old Testament examples of this principle, the prophets and Job. Although most of us today will not be persecuted and tortured, as they were, the fact is that not everything in life will happen the way we would want. There will be problems, trials, heartaches, and disappointments. No matter what happens, we must never give up on God.

James concludes his book with a discussion of effective and fervent prayer (verses 13-20).

Prayer is the gift of God that allows us to talk with our heavenly Father. To the Christian, it is a very special privilege. In prayer, we can come boldly to God's throne and ask for His grace and mercy (Hebrews 4:16). This is perhaps the single most important part of a Christian's life. If a person has a good prayer life, it will be much easier to study, teach others, and grow as the Lord desires. One with poor prayer habits will often die a slow spiritual death. Prayer is also one of the easiest things to neglect. No one else can keep track of your prayer life. It is a personal, private matter. Prayer is a heart-felt expression of our lives toward God. There ought to be a sense of obligation and, at the same time, a sense of dependence on the Lord. "Pray without ceasing" (1 Thessalonians 5:17).

# The Letters of 1 & 2 Peter

## 1 Peter 1

First Peter was written to scattered, persecuted Christians to encourage them to remain faithful to the Lord. There are many lessons in the book that apply to our lives as disciples of Christ today.

In this initial section (1:1-12), Peter reminds these disciples of the inheritance that awaits the righteous. When one realizes the value of the reward that is promised to the faithful, no sacrifice is too great. No amount of persecution could ever cause a true follower of the Lord to give up. As a matter of fact, Peter explains that it is such trials that will prove the genuineness of our faith.

This promised inheritance was made possible by God's revelation of the gospel through the inspired prophets. That is simply another way of saying that the gospel is God's power to salvation.

1 Peter 1:3-4 introduces the one thread that stretches from beginning to end in the letter, hope. It is called "a living hope," meaning it has substance and real meaning. It is not false or imaginary. It is alive, active and vital. There is a solid basis for this hope and the inheritance promised to the faithful is genuine as well.

Peter uses that hope (called an anchor for the soul in Hebrews 6:19) as the incentive to help these Christians endure, even through severe trial and persecution. It can do the same for us.

In the second part of this first chapter (verses 13-25), Peter begins to remind the first century Jesus followers of the importance of holiness before God in their lives.

Christianity is serious business, not for the faint of heart (verse 13). The first century disciples are here warned to "prepare your minds for action" (NIV, 1984), to be serious and sober about serving God and to keep their hope until the end. Some are only serious about following the Messiah when things are going well and others only decide to do the right thing when things are difficult. We must be faithful, no matter what the circumstances of our service might bring.

Holiness in the sight of God is actually the prevailing theme of Peter's writings. Christians are to be like their Lord. 1 Peter 1:16 quotes Leviticus 11:44 because God has always wanted His people to keep themselves holy, separate from the sin and defilement of an ungodly world.

It has been said that the central message of First Peter is "Remember Who You Are." The first century disciples lived in an ungodly society, quite similar perhaps to our own. It was not easy to remain pure in an impure world. It still is not easy. Peter wrote, by inspiration, to help them and his message has been preserved for us to benefit from also.

Peter reminds them that they had been redeemed from sin by the blood of Christ and their souls had been purchased when they obeyed the truth. So they should continue to live holy and pure lives.

This chapter concludes with some important facts about the word of God. First, he reaffirms that they had purified their souls before God through their obedience to "the word of God which lives and abides forever." Second, he tells them that the word of the Lord will endure forever.

All of this means that we belong to God's family, that we are worth something (God paid for us with the life of His Son), that we are free from the slavery of sin and that we have a purpose in life as God's chosen people.

## 1 Peter 2

We begin the Christian life as "newborn babes." Through our study of God's word, we grow to spiritual maturity in our relationship with God (verses 1-3).

Part of the growth process is negative. We are to "abstain from fleshly lusts which war against the soul." These worldly desires can take over our lives and our personalities and destroy all spiritual vitality, if we allow them to do so. We must put them to death.

The other part of spiritual growth is positive. We learn God's will and strengthen our resolve in order to do what the Lord wants. The key is learning to follow in the footsteps of Jesus and to strive to live as He did in every way we can. That is true discipleship, learning and following in obedience.

The chapter begins with the negative side, things we should avoid as followers of the Messiah. We are to lay aside malice, deceit, hypocrisy, envy and all evil speaking (verse 1). We mature by starting with "the pure milk of the word" (verse 2) and gradually develop into "solid food" (Hebrews 5:12-14).

The real key to growing as a Jesus follower is "coming to Him" (verses 4-10). Jesus is the model, the perfect pattern of life that we are to strive to follow. We are compared to "living stones" (verse 5) that are built together into a spiritual house that honors and glorifies God as we offer up our lives in spiritual sacrifice to Him.

Jesus is the cornerstone of this spiritual house, the church or family of God (1 Timothy 3:15; Galatians 6:10). We are built on a solid foundation of Christ Himself. We are not alone in this task of serving God; we have our brothers and sisters in the Lord to help us survive and prosper spiritually.

Verse 9 uses several phrases to describe believers – a chosen generation, a royal priesthood, a holy nation, His own special people, and Peter reminds us that as God's people we are to proclaim His praises to a lost and dying world.

Verse 10 describes the before and after relationship we sustain in the Savior. Before we were in darkness, now we are in the light. Before we were not a people, now we are the people of God. Before we received no mercy, now we do. We owe God a tremendous debt that can never be repaid; we are to "show forth His praises" by our words and our deeds.

There are many distractions that would take our attention away from Christ, but we must always seek to live in a way that is "honorable" before the watching eyes of the world (verses 11-17). We should obey the civil authorities and laws of government ordained by God (Romans 13).

We are to live godly lives, even if it means persecution from those around us (verses 18-24). Our example in this is Jesus Himself, who was mistreated, but never used abuse from others as an excuse to behave sinfully. We are to follow His example in every way.

The word, example, is used here to refer us to our Messiah. It means a copy which is to be duplicated, a pattern, a model to follow, a template. There is no area in life in which He is not our example to imitate.

The chapter ends by reminding us that our Savior died on the cross to save us from sin and make it possible for us to live in a way that brings Him all the glory (remember Matthew 5:13-16). We were like sheep gone astray and He is the Good Shepherd who searched for us and found us.

## 1 Peter 3

In Chapter 3, Peter continues his discussion about how we should live as Christians and he begins by dealing specifically with the husband and wife relationship.

In verses 1-6, he speaks of principles concerning a wife's duties toward her husband. These principles apply to all wives, although he does make one special point about women who are married to non-Christians. His advice (by inspiration) is don't leave a non-Christian husband. Rather do all you can to convert him to Christ. He says that such a person can often (we know it doesn't always work out) bring the spouse to faith in Jesus by the faithful life and conduct of a godly wife. The best thing available for him is her righteous example, consistently living what she claims to believe.

The lessons he stresses for all wives are simple, yet powerful. Be submissive to your husband. Be a faithful loving wife. He talks about the relative unimportance of outward beauty. Don't be as concerned about outward appearances (arranging your hair, wearing lots of jewelry, wearing lots of fancy and expensive clothes) as you are about what kind of person you are on the inside (he calls it the hidden person of the heart). And he compliments a lady who possesses a "gentle and quiet spirit," one that is tranquil, at peace, calm. In other words, he is commending a woman who is not an outward showoff, but who seeks to be lovely on the inside. External beauty will often fade with time; internal (spiritual) beauty will never fade away; it is incorruptible.

In verse 7, the apostle turns to the husband. Although he only writes one verse, compared to six verses for the wives, he fills this passage with responsibilities. Honor her. Dwell with her in knowledge of her needs and the desires of her heart. Treat her as a person of value, with respect and reverence.

The most beautiful part of this text is the phrase where he describes husbands and wives as "heirs together of the grace of life." It is a wonderful, touching description of the mutual love and respect of a husband and wife who see themselves as equal partners in their service to God. As a result of that type of attitude toward God and each other, there is a wonderful promise of eternal life, where the husband and wife who have served God together in life will live forever in heaven with God.

The theme of verses 8-22 is that disciples of Jesus will suffer for their life of righteousness. After speaking in verses 1-7 to husbands and wives, the apostle Peter now turns his attention to every Christian, "all of you." Persecution that results from the disciples' faith is a major message of this book.

Peter deals here with the relationship between brothers and sisters in the church. He encourages unity, compassion, love, kindness and courtesy. Too many churches over the years have been destroyed because Christians did not treat each other as the Bible teaches us. He shows us that our relationship with God is dependent on how we treat others.

Verses 10-12 are a quote from Psalms 34:12-16. They remind us of our duties to be gentle with others, to be careful about what comes out of our mouths and through our lips. He wants us to be people of peace who pursue what is good. And he says that "the eyes of the Lord" looks with favor on the righteous and that He listens to the prayers of the faithful.

Peter also writes again on the idea of suffering persecution for our faith (verses 13-22). Sometimes life isn't fair and we are foolish if we expect others to always do the right thing. He closes this chapter with a discussion of what has united us in Christ, our baptism.

## 1 Peter 4

This chapter begins with a reminder of Christ's suffering and a word of encouragement for us to possess the same "mind" or attitude – that we are willing to likewise suffer for Him.

Peter then tells us there are two reasons why Christians may have to suffer.

First, because we don't do certain things – things that the world does (he uses the term "Gentiles" here) and things that we very well may have previously done ourselves. The victory over these kinds of temptations comes from being good stewards of the gifts God has given us to serve Him. We must be determined to leave behind the old person we used to be ("all have sinned and fall short of the glory of God") and to put on the new man, one who will still make mistakes in life, but who is trying diligently to walk in the footsteps of the Messiah.

Verses 1-6 gives us a list of many of the specific things that Christians should avoid, or, if they are already doing these things, should stop. The key to giving up sinful activities begins in verse 1 where Peter tells us to "arm yourselves with the same mind" as Christ. We will learn to avoid sin (verse 2) when we make it our life's goal to be as much like Jesus as we can be. We will always fall short but there will be increasing periods of success as we strive to continue living as He would live.

Verse 6 is a bit unusual in its wording when he refers to preaching "to those who are dead." What does that mean? It refers to the preaching that was done in the past to those who are now dead. While they were still alive, faithful Jesus followers preached the gospel to them in order to prepare them for the time when they would ultimately pass from this life. The preaching was not done after they died, rather it was done before so that they would live their lives "according to God in the spirit." Similar teaching is found in Galatians 5:16-17, 24; 6:8).

The Bible is a handbook on living the Christian life, which often includes denying former pleasures of the world. Many of these pleasures begin innocently enough, but they often grow in intensity and frequency into something that we have lost control over. They are "fleshly lusts that war against the soul" (2:11).

In verses 7-11, Peter challenges them to be good stewards of the gifts that God has given them. And again, if we arm ourselves with the mind of Christ, we will do just that. Because "the end of all things" is near, he tells us five things we should do.

- Be serious about serving God (verse 7)
- Be watchful in your prayers (verse 7)
- Have fervent love in your life for others (verse 8)
- Be hospitable and share life with others (verse 9)
- Use your talents to serve God (verses 10-11)

All of these things are to be done "that in all things God may be glorified through Jesus Christ."

The second kind of persecution comes from things we do. Peter again warns them about "the fiery trial which is to try you." His primary purpose in writing this letter is to show them how to deal with the difficulties of being a Christian in an immoral society. (This sounds much like the situation we find ourselves in today, doesn't it?)

There will be hardships (verse 12). We should rejoice in trials caused by our faith rather than despair (verses 13-14). Examine your life to determine if you are suffering for doing wrong or for doing right (verses 15-16). The apostle concludes the chapter by challenging all disciples to commit themselves fully to Him (verses 17-19). Hide your soul in the always safe and trustworthy arms of God. Never give up.

## 1 Peter 5

One of the greatest blessings God has given His people is the oversight of spiritual elders. Qualified (1 Timothy 3:1-7; Titus 1:5-9), Holy Spirit approved (Acts 20:28), esteemed highly in love for their work's sake (1 Thessalonians 5:13), these godly men watch out for our souls as those who will give account of their stewardship to God (Hebrews 13:17). They lead us, provide an example for us, feed us with God's word and protect us from spiritual harm from false teachers, just as shepherds protect their flocks from deadly wolves (or lions).

It is comforting for us to realize that God has provided for our spiritual needs in the church by supplying godly, spiritually mature men who can take care of our souls (verses 1-4). They do so as the passage indicates not for selfish reasons but for our spiritual welfare. They are not to be forced into the position of oversight, it must be a willing service, a sacrifice of their time and energy to help us (1 Timothy 3:1). They are not to desire the job for the financial benefits (I believe that many elders, perhaps most, in the first century, were paid by the church to carry out this important task, 1 Timothy 5:17-18). They are not to be power hungry, attention seekers who simply want to control others. One who simply wants the authority or prestige of being an elder is not fit for the honor.

Verse 4 emphasizes that faithful shepherds will receive a reward, a crown of glory, which may be some special mark of distinction that will identify them in heaven as one who served God in this capacity. This reward is to be given them by the Chief Shepherd, perhaps at the Day of Judgment.

And it seems touching to me that Peter has written this, not as a detached observer of elders working with local churches, but as a "fellow elder" who can personally identify with the challenges and trials inherent in watching over the souls of fellow sojourners in this earth life. It takes a special Christian, with a servant's heart, to be willing to put up with the criticism and fault finding that often is a (sad, but true) part of the responsibilities of church elders. It is hard and often heart breaking for elders to pour their heart and soul into trying to save a lost soul, only to be rejected and ignored when simply trying to help someone find room for God in his or her heart.

Inherent in our relationship with God is the need for humility, whether leader or follower in a local church. Some believe Peter is referring to church elders in verse 5 (as in the preceding four verses) while others see this as a general statement about the wisdom of learning from the experience of all older disciples. Life as a follower of Jesus can be difficult and we need to help each other to learn life's lessons to successfully navigate the trials of being faithful to God. Submit to Him; cast your cares upon Him. He cares for you and your soul (that's the good news of the gospel). It takes humility to learn to trust Him with everything.

In verses 8-11, Peter states also the reason we need spiritual oversight. He reminds us of the reality of Satan and his power. The devil is compared to a roaring lion, seeking to devour the souls of men. But he teaches us to resist his influence. That means that we can withstand his power in our lives. James 4:7 says that, when we resist the devil, he will flee from us.

Did you notice that verse 8 reminds us that Satan is our "adversary?" That means he is your enemy and wants to destroy you. In Revelation 12:9, the Bible says that he deceives the whole world. He will lie to you, steal from you, cheat you, cause people to let you down, even make you sick and then will try to make you blame God for all of your troubles. We can be victorious over the devil. God will strengthen you.

In verses 12-14, Peter encourages them to remain true to God and offers them true peace of mind.

## 2 Peter 1

Second Peter was written just shortly after First Peter. The original recipients are the same people who were blessed by the first letter (2 Peter 3:1). There are clearly more spiritual truths that the apostle wants to share with them that were not included in the first one. (Have you ever done that? Sent a letter or an email or a text to someone and realized after you sent it that there were other things you still want to say to them?)

He addresses the letter to "those who have obtained like precious faith with us by the righteousness of our God and Savior Jesus Christ" (verse 1). Ours is a faith that has value. Many place their faith in futile things or unstable people. Our faith is precious, valuable, and it is made even more so by the reality that we share it with other followers of Jesus. This binds us together as we share life's experience, both rewarding and challenging ones. We live life in common (that's what fellowship is) with others who have put their trust in the Lord.

Verses 2-4 wish us to experience God's "grace and peace" in our Christian lives. Verse 3 assures us that God has provided for us "all things that pertain to life and godliness." The "life" is eternal life in heaven with God and the "godliness" is how we are to live on earth until then. God's power has given us everything we need for both, the "here and now" and the "then."

Verse 4 reminds us that we are given "exceedingly great and precious promises." God's promises are both great (in their scope and their glory) and precious (in their eternal value). The writer of Hebrews encourages us with these words: "Let us hold fast the confession of our hope without wavering, for He who promised is faithful" (Hebrews 10:23). God has never failed to fulfill a promise and He never will.

In this chapter, Peter tells us that, through God's faithful promises, we can become partakers of the divine nature (verses 5-11). And in order to be more God-like and so that we might live a life of holiness, we need to grow as Christians. He lists in this text, what are often called "the seven Christian graces." They are virtue, knowledge, self-control, perseverance, godliness, brotherly kindness and love.

Notice that these qualities require "diligence" to become part of our character. That refers to hard work, sincerity and effort. One does not develop strong character qualities easily or accidentally. Also see that the beginning point is faith. It is our faith in God that motivates everything else we are to do.

Verses 9-11 contrast those who have and those who do not have these qualities. Those without them are "barren" and "unfruitful" in the sight of God. Those who, through the help of God and the Holy Spirit, develop these characteristics in their lives will never fall (notice that it is stated in a conditional way with the word "if"). We must make our call and election sure by doing what we can for Him, not to earn salvation, but to please Him by doing the best we can. If we do, we will have an entrance into His "everlasting kingdom."

In verses 12-15, Peter felt an urgency to remind the first century Christians of their need to develop positive Christian character. In verse 13, he says that he needed to "stir" them up. This literally means to arouse out of sleep. Sometimes, we have a tendency to forget important things. Peter wrote it for them and it is preserved for us because we need that reminder also.

Peter concludes the first chapter of this second letter by reassuring them that the word of God is trustworthy and reliable. He tells them that this is important because Christianity is real, not a hoax, myth or fable. He lists two proofs of its validity, the transfiguration and fulfilled prophecy. The Bible is not of human origin; it is an inspired message from the mind of God to all of mankind.

## 2 Peter 2

2 Peter 2 is a warning to be aware of the reality of false teachers. They were present in the first century church and, of course, they are still present today. This entire chapter deals with the motives and influence of these teachers of error.

As a matter of fact, the whole Bible contains scattered warnings about those who would seek to change the will of God into something that pleases people, not Him. They bring counterfeit truth and offer false hope that cannot save the soul. (Notice passages like Acts 20:29-30, 1 Timothy 4:1-3, 1 John 4:1-6 as examples.)

2 Peter 2:1-3 give us several descriptions of false teachers. They do much of their work in secret. Their doctrines are destructive. They blaspheme the truth. They are deceptive. They will bring swift and certain destruction on themselves. And yet, Peter warns us that "many will follow their destructive ways." False teachers always find those with itching ears to hear anything except the truth of God.

Verses 4-9 are interesting. Peter lists some godly individuals and some ungodly ones. He is teaching two things about them. First, it is possible to do right even under difficult circumstances. Some choose to do right while others make the decision to do wrong. The second thing he mentions is that there will always be a reward for the righteous and a punishment for the sinful.

On the positive side, he recommends that they recall the Old Testament accounts about Noah and Lot.

Noah (verse 5) is called "a preacher of righteousness" who was saved from the worldwide flood that destroyed all the ungodly people of the world.

Lot (verses 7-8) is listed as an example of one who survived the destruction of Sodom and Gomorrah because he was righteous and was tormented day by day by the ungodliness around him.

On the negative side, Peter speaks about the angels who sinned and were cast into chains of darkness (verse 4) and Sodom and Gomorrah, cities that were turned into ashes because of their sins (verse 6).

And he emphasizes the point that God knows the difference between the holy and the unholy. We may not always be able to tell the difference in this life, but the Lord knows (verses 9-11).

Verses 12-17 provide further descriptions of false teachers and show us the low opinion that God has of them and their wicked influence on others. If they really understood God and His power, they would not pervert His word. Peter compares first century false teachers to Balaam, a well-known, but unfaithful prophet in the Old Testament. He makes three important warnings about false teachers.

- They speak evil of things they don't understand (verse 12)
- They have hearts trained to do evil (verse 14)

- They promise great things, good things, but deliver only sorrow and misery (verse 17).

In the last part of chapter 2, verses 18-22, Peter warns them (and us) about the results of following false teachers. Those who listen to unfaithful teachers or preachers become slaves of corruption (verses 18-19), are entangled with the pollutions of the world (verse 20), and are worse off than those who have never known the truth (verses 20-22).

Sin makes wonderful sounding promises to its eager captives, but in the end, will bring only sadness and eternal destruction. Don't believe the lie.

## 2 Peter 3

In this chapter, the apostle Peter reminds them ("I stir up your pure minds by way of reminder") about the second coming of Christ. In the first part of the chapter (verses 1-9), he speaks of the reality of the second coming. He tells them of three reasons they should not doubt the certainty of the Lord's return.

- History (verses 5-7) – The scoffers said that all things had continued the same since the creation. Peter reminds them about the flood. There will someday be another major interruption; this one will be a destruction by fire (notice the similar language here to 2 Thessalonians 1:7-9).

- God's eternal nature (verse 8) – He does not measure time as we do. He is not limited by time requirements as we are. God will not forget; He will not be unable to keep this promise. He will not die before He can carry out what He said will occur. God said it will happen and it will.

- God's patience (verse 9) – The Lord is waiting for more lost souls to repent. He is not slow in carrying out His promises. He just wants more souls to be saved before the end.

In verses 10-18, he asks, how should the certainty of the second coming of the Lord change our lives?

Although the return of Christ is described "as a thief in the night," he tells us to be "looking" for it (2 Peter 3:10-13). Mark 13:32-37 says we must "watch" for His coming. This simply means that we must stay alert; there is no excuse for being unprepared. It will happen suddenly, unexpectedly and so we must always be ready just as we must prepare ahead of time so that our homes will not be invaded and our possessions stolen by a thief.

There are three things that will happen during this time of destructive power when the Savior returns to judge the people of the earth (Romans 14:12; 2 Corinthians 5:10).

- The heavens will pass away
- The elements (of the universe) will melt
- The earth will be burned up

2 Peter 3

Christians have every reason to be excited about the return of Jesus. We don't need to be afraid. Rather our citizenship is in heaven (Philippians 3:21) and this will be our chance to go home for all eternity around the throne of God.

1 Corinthians 16:22 says, "O Lord, come!" This shows the eager expectation and earnest desire of every disciple of the Lord to be with Him forever. The Bible ends in this way as well (Revelation 22:20).

There will be "a new heavens and a new earth in which righteousness dwells" (verse 13). This is another description of our inheritance in heaven. Peter began his first letter with this promise (1 Peter 1:3-5).

Matthew 24:35 says, "Heaven and earth (that's the physical universe as we know it, rh) will pass away, but My words will by no means pass away." This will be a spirit world, unlike the physical world in which we now live. See 1 Corinthians 15:50-58 and 1 John 2:2-3.

A final warning to remain faithful closes this book. It is negative (beware; don't fall away) and positive (continue to grow in Christ). Being a Christian is a constant, lifelong growing process. We must be steady and consistent as we grow in the grace and knowledge of God.

"There's a Great Day Coming." Are you ready for that day to come?

# The Letters of 1, 2, 3 JOHN & JUDE

## 1 John 1

You will immediately note the similarities between verse 1 and John 1:1. Both verses reference "the beginning" and the "Word." Both were written by the same man, the apostle John. He was a son of Zebedee and the brother of James, an apostle of Christ who was killed in Acts 12:1. John, of course, is also the author of the final book of the New Testament, Revelation.

Both the gospel of John and his 3 letters utilize similar vocabulary, emphasizing similar words like love, light, darkness, life and walking in the light of God's truth.

There will also be numerous references in 1, 2, and 3 John to those who claimed a secret and superior knowledge of truth. They were called Gnostics, from the Greek word for knowledge, GNOSIS. There were differing groups of Gnostics that began to develop around the middle to the end of the first century and the apostolic writings make subtle mention of their false teachings and their negative influence on God's work. Even some Christians were deceived by these false concepts and many left the church as a result (1 John 2:19; 4:1).

The Gnostics thought they had superior knowledge to other Christians and looked down with contempt and even hatred on those who were not a part of their sect. They would often not have fellowship with true believers and that is why John spends so much time telling them to love one another.

Because Gnostics claimed that all flesh was evil, they concluded that Jesus was merely a spirit that looked like a human being but was not really human. John begins this book with physical evidence that "the Word became flesh and dwelt among us" (John 1:14). Here he says that "we" (probably all of the apostles are being referred to) spent time with Him, heard Him, saw Him, watched Him, touched Him and knew Him to be a real flesh and blood human being. It is true that He was God, but He was God in the flesh. That is what the word, incarnation, means: that the spirit God became the human Jesus.

It is almost inconceivable to imagine that we can have "fellowship" with God. In spite of our sin, we can be in a right relationship with Him. Fellowship refers to a partnership, a joint participation, a sharing with. (For most people today, the word fellowship means coffee and doughnuts. Its real meaning is spiritual, much deeper than simply sharing a meal together with someone in a church kitchen.)

The faithful child of God has fellowship with God, the Son and the Holy Spirit, as well as with every other faithful Christian on earth. It is a wonderful thing that we can have this fellowship. John wrote so they would understand and be grateful for this spiritual relationship with God. "And these things we write to you that your joy may be full" (verse 4).

We can pray to Him and have confidence that He will hear us. We can sing to Him and believe that He is honored by our worship. We can "commune" with God as we remember the sacrifice of His Son for our sins. Fallible human beings can fellowship (again, it means to share with, partake together with, partner with) the infallible God. The creature can bow before the Creator in harmony with Him.

Through His grace, we can be forgiven. Through His mercy, we can have hope. Through His love, we can walk in the light, not in the darkness.

The idea of "walking in the light" (verses 6-7) is key to our faithfulness to God. We cannot walk in darkness (do wrong things) and please Him. It is our purpose to live as He teaches us to live in the Bible. A part of that is recognizing that we sometimes sin, even as Christians, and need to repent and confess and ask God to forgive us (verses 8-10). As His children, if we ask, He will forgive us.

## 1 John 2

John addresses his readers as "my little children" (2:1). This refers perhaps to those he had converted or to those whose faith is younger than his own. At the very least, John is older by this time (although he was perhaps the youngest of the original twelve apostles) and he speaks as a father to his children.

He makes it quite plain that his purpose in writing was to encourage them to avoid sin (verse 1). We sometimes say things like, "we are all weak and we will sin often." Perhaps that is true for some, but doesn't that tend to encourage people to go ahead and sin? Why not, everyone does it, right? John says he wants to help people to do the right thing, not the wrong.

He continues on and says that, if we do sin, (note, he says if, not when), we have an advocate in Jesus. An advocate is like a lawyer, someone who will speak (often to a judge) on our behalf. It refers to someone who will be called to help us when we are in trouble. Jesus is our Mediator in pleading our case before the heavenly Father.

In verses 1-17, John reminds us that the holy God desires that His children be holy as well. (Doesn't every parent wish that for his/her children?) And so, when we do sin, He has made provision for us to be forgiven again. Our advocate in this is Jesus, who is also the propitiation (atoning sacrifice, NIV) for our sins. And this sacrifice is available "for the whole world." This idea that Jesus died for everyone (and Hebrews 2:9 just clearly states that He did) defeats the "reformed" doctrine of Calvinism, often called Limited Atonement, that falsely claims that Jesus only died for the elect. The elect refers to those who have chosen to obey and live for God. Anyone in the "whole world" can become one of the elect. It is a personal choice we can all make.

Verses 3-5 contrast the true knowledge of believers with the false, imagined "knowledge" the gnostics claimed to have. John often uses the phrase, "that you may know" to show us that we can believe and trust God with confidence that obedience to His will pleases Him. God would have us to know Him, to keep His commandments, to walk as Jesus walked and to love our brothers and sisters (verses 6-11).

John puts all of His readers into three different groups in verses 12-14. "Little children" are the young in faith and knowledge, Christians who are just beginning their walk with God. "Fathers" are the mature, often long time followers of Jesus who have been His for some time. And "young men" refers to those who are somewhere between a baby Christian and an older one who is more mature in the faith. Most of us probably fall into the young men (or women) category.

We must not love the world or the sinful pleasures the world offers (verses 15-17). Every sin and temptation that Satan can use against us falls into one of the three areas described in verse 16. "The lust of the flesh, the lust of the eyes and the pride of life" covers all of those possibilities. John warns us that the world and its lust are passing away while "he who does the will of God abides forever."

Verses 18-29 assure us that there is always opposition to truth. From the prophets and other righteous souls of the Old Testament, to the forerunner of Christ, to Jesus Himself and to the apostles and other faithful disciples of the early church, the forces of evil have long been antagonistic to God and His holy word. This has continued through the ages since the first century and is still true today. He calls those who oppose God's truth about Jesus "antichrists" and says there were many of them in the world. The apostle John reminds the New Testament Christians of his day, and it applies to us as well, of the blessed promise of eternal life. Righteousness, even in the face of persecution, is the key to the "confidence" that we can have when the Lord returns (coupled with God's grace and mercy, of course).

## 1 John 3

Verses 1-3 speak of God's love for us. John doesn't describe God's love here or try to explain it. He just wants us to see it, to think about it and to appreciate it. We are the recipients of the greatest love ever shown to others, the sacrifice of God's Son for our sins.

The result of that love is that we can be called children of God. Someone has said that the Son of God became the Son of Man so that the sons of men might become the sons of God.

Verse 2 reminds us that those who are now the children of God will one day be changed. We are not given details about what our changed, eternal bodies will be like, but we are given some information about it (see 1 Corinthians 15:51-54; Philippians 3:20-21). It is such an eternal blessing from God that, in the afterlife, "we shall be like Him, for we shall see Him as He is."

And that hope (of being like Jesus) gives us strength and stability in this life. It helps us to purify ourselves from sin and ungodliness and iniquity (verse 3).

The only thing that destroys this relationship with God is sin (verses 4-9). There are two contrasting lifestyles described in these verses. One is a life of love, hope and righteousness. The other is a life of sin and lawlessness. The children of God seek to live a life of purity from sin.

It is not a matter of being unable to sin. The issue is desire. A child of God does not want to sin and is determined to be godly and righteous. Verse 7 encourages us to be "righteous." This word is used in three ways in the Bible. It describes the attributes of God (2 Thessalonians 1:6). It is used to speak of God's righteous plan to save man (Romans 1:16-17). And it is used in reference to the righteousness of God in man, that is, the life of one who obeys God's righteous plan. Acts 10:34-35 says we should work righteousness and 1 John 2:29 tells us to practice righteousness. That doesn't mean we earn or merit a home in heaven because we are so good; but it does tell us to submit to God's will for our lives.

Two verses in this section of the chapter tell us why Jesus was "manifested" (to make visible or clear; the NIV says this is the reason why Jesus "appeared"). Verse 5 says "to take away our sins." Verse 8 says He came to "destroy the works of the devil." We should be eternally thankful for His sacrifice on the cross for us. In other words, we are to love God (verses 4-9) because He first loved us (verses 1-3).

Verses 6 and 9 have both been misused by false teachers to promote the idea of "once saved, always saved." The verses do not say that a Christian's sins are alright; they are assuring us that one who wants to serve God has made a personal decision to follow God that will include doing our best to avoid sin. We can be forgiven by the Lord when we do wrong. That is different from saying that God just overlooks our sins. We must repent, confess and pray as Christians to be forgiven (remember 1 John 1:8-10). Satan has no power over us except what we give him (Romans 6:16). I (we) can resist him by the power of God's word. The Christian (one who is born of God) knows that he who sins is of the devil. The Savior came to destroy the devil's power (Hebrews 2:14) and the faithful disciple loves the Lord, not the world.

John shifts only slightly, in verses 10-24, to telling us to love each other. Love is not a feeling or an emotion, as much as it is a decision. It is not shown merely by words or cute sayings, but by deeds and actions (verse 18). Biblical love always seeks the best for the object of the love. This kind of love is intentional and deliberate. This love can be commanded (unlike romantic or emotional love). The world can never understand agape love, but it is vital in the life of one who has been born of God. It was modeled to perfection by Jesus, the Savior of the world, who so loved the world that "He laid down His life for us."

# 1 John 4

There have always been, and always will be, false teachers in the world (verses 1-6). In the Old Testament, they were primarily referred to as false prophets, and in the New Testament, the prominent terminology is false teachers.

In the early days of the church, the most prevalent false teachers were Judaizers. They sought to bind certain parts of the Law of Moses on New Testament followers of the Christ. Other books in the New Testament (Galatians, for example) dealt with some of their offensive teachings.

Near the end of the first century, the biggest problem for Christians was the Gnostics. They claimed superior knowledge of spiritual things. They had many erroneous concepts about good and evil and even about Jesus Himself. We must ever be on the alert for those who would pervert the Word of God.

There are several warnings about false teachers in the first century that John gives us here. The basic distinction he makes is that a true teacher from God acknowledges that Jesus came in the flesh, while a false teacher denies the humanity (or the deity of Jesus). That's why he uses the term, Antichrist. Anti means against, so this brand of false teacher speaks against Jesus (which is primarily the meaning of the word, blasphemy). It should be pointed out that John tells us that the spirit of the Antichrist was present in the first century. This is not one gigantic monster who will be revealed at the end of the world who is against Christ. He is said to be "now already in the world" (verse 3) and in Chapter Two, John told us that "even now many antichrists have come" (1 John 2:18).

John, in verses 5-6, speaks of the contrast between truth and error. He says "they" (the false teachers) are of the world and therefore, they speak of the world and the world listens to them. But "we" (the apostles and others who teach truth) are "of God." He divides everyone into two categories, the spirit of truth and the spirit of error. Numerous other New Testament passages say much the same thing, with perhaps slightly different wording (see 1 Timothy 4:1-3 and 2 Peter 2:1-3). That doesn't mean it is always easy to tell the difference (many false teachers can be quite persuasive about their views), but that's why it is so important to "test the spirits, whether they are of God" (verse 1). Error can be overcome (verse 4) but only with diligence in our efforts to do so.

Verses 7-21 begin a long section of John's writings about the importance of loving each other.

John, the son of Zebedee and brother of James, has often been referred to as "the apostle of love." Most Bible students believe that he is the person called "the disciple whom Jesus loved" in the gospel of John. John certainly had a lot to say about love in the books of the Bible he wrote, especially the gospel of John and the three epistles (perhaps slightly less in the book of Revelation).

His emphasis is always first that God loved us. Then he writes that we should love the Father in return because of all the things He did for us (through His great love for mankind). "In this is love, not that we loved God, but that He loved us and sent His Son to be the propitiation (atoning sacrifice, NIV) for our sins" (verse 10).

And finally, John teaches us that this love for God should overflow into our relationships with each other. Our responsibilities are the same as Jesus described in what He called the two greatest commandments, to love God and to love our neighbor. The Christian who has proper love for God and man in his heart will have assurance, boldness and confidence in the day of judgment. "And this commandment we have from Him: that he who loves God must love his brother also" (verse 21).

## 1 John 5

In many ways, Chapter Five is a summary of what he has already said. Repetition often helps us to remember important lessons.

John starts this section of the sacred text by reminding them of the importance of living a life of faith and obedience (verses 1-13). We show our love for other Jesus followers ("children of God") when we love God and keep His commandments (verses 2-3). And in case some felt otherwise, John emphasizes to us that "His commandments are not burdensome." There is nothing about serving the Almighty God that is unreasonable or illogical to people of faith. It is true that we will have challenges in obeying God and that the requirements of faithful discipleship will often bring about personal sacrifices in our lives. But it should be a joy to sacrifice for the Savior who loved us and gave Himself for us (Galatians 2:20).

Christians have long been tempted by "the things in the world" (1 John 2:15). James tells us that "friendship with the world is enmity with God" (James 4:4). When John 3:16 says that "God so loved the world," he was speaking of the people in the world. We should love peoples' souls as well. But "do not love the world" means the sinful, ungodly things that this world has to offer. The world is the realm of Satan and his influence. In this sense, the world refers to the same things as "the flesh." Over and over, the Bible warns us about the perpetual, daily conflict between the things of the flesh and the things of the Spirit (Romans 8:5, for example).

But John wants us to know that we can be victorious over sin and Satan and the world (verses 4-5). We can and will win this battle, although the war will be difficult at times. The victory is always promised in the same way, by focusing on the things of God through faith in Christ. The song, Faith Is The Victory, is based on the thoughts in verse 4.

The Spirit (verse 6) who bears witness of these truths is the Holy Spirit, the third member of the Godhead. He is a divine person or being, like the Father and the Son, not merely a power or force that God uses to accomplish His will. He inspired the writers of the New Testament (John 14:26; 16:13; 1 Corinthians 2:9-13) who wrote the message down so that we might know the truth and give our lives to the God of heaven (Ephesians 3:3-5). Central to God's good news is that He has given us eternal life in His Son, Jesus the Messiah (verse 11).

The Lord does not want us to go through life with doubt and uncertainty. If we have doubts, that is fine, but the Bible has the answers for those questions that might arise and He wants us to have confidence and assurance of our relationship with God and the promise of eternal life with Him (verse 13). That's why John regularly uses the phrase, "By this we know" in the book. He is giving us further promise that He loves us and wants us to live with Him forever.

This confidence then leads us to a faithful life with God (verses 15-21). We can know that God is with us and listens to our prayers to Him and we can, therefore, pray with sincere faith that God will answer us if we ask "according to His will."

Our struggle with sin is an ongoing battle and one that is not easily won. There are certain sins that do not even appeal to us and are, therefore, quickly defeated. But each of us has, in the darkest part of our souls, other sins with which we constantly wrestle. Make no mistake about it; we can overcome these temptations. But it is not easy. When we commit these sins, we must quickly and genuinely repent of our rebellion against God and determine in our hearts not to fail again. We must never forget that "we are of God" and that truth can strengthen and embolden us to live right. God will be with us and, with His help, we can and will overcome the wicked one.

## 2 John

The relationship between truth and error is a regular theme of John's epistles. This shows us that, even in the first century, Christians had to be alert. In 1 John 4:1, John told the early disciples to "test the Spirits whether they are of God; because many false prophets have gone out into the world." If one will walk according to the Lord's commandments and abide in the doctrine of Christ, he can know that he meets with God's approval. Some would suggest that truth is relative and that there is no such thing as false doctrine, as long as a person is sincere in what he believes. John would argue otherwise.

Both Second and Third John are written by one who calls himself, "The Elder." It is almost universally agreed (nothing is agreed upon 100%, is it?) that the author is John the Apostle. If these books were written near the end of the first century, which most Bible students believe to be the case, then John would have been close to 90 years old, so the term, elder, may refer to his biological age. It is also possible that he was a shepherd or overseer of a local church. You will recall that Peter the apostle was a "fellow elder" (1 Peter 5:1) and so, it is not impossible to believe that John could likewise have been serving the Lord in that way.

The original recipients of the letter are addressed as "the elect lady and her children, whom I love in truth" (verse 1; he also repeats the word, lady, in verse 5). Again, there are at least a couple of ideas about what (or whom) that could refer to. One thought is that this is speaking to a specific lady (maybe named KURIA, the Greek word found here) and her physical children. Certainly other books of the New Testament are written to individuals (Timothy, Titus, Philemon) and so this is not outside the realm of reason. Verse 13 seems to add some strength to the argument that he is talking about specific people.

The other idea is that this is an extension of references to the church as the bride of Christ, so that the elect lady may be a local church to whom John is writing with her children being the members of that congregation of God's people. Most of the "church" letters in the New Testament are named according to the geographic location of the church (Romans, Corinthians, Ephesians, Philippians), so, if that is the case here, there is some variation from the usual wording.

The use of the term, elect, however, leaves us with no other safe conclusion except that the letter was intended for Christians, either from a single family or many families together in a local church.

The letter begins, as do many of the New Testament epistles, with an urgent message on the importance of remaining faithful to God (verses 1-6). Notice the emphasis on truth and obeying the commandments of God. He is telling them how to walk in truth, which is by obeying God's commands. He was grateful that "some of your children" had been discovered who were still walking in the truth. It is always heart warming when we know people in the Lord earlier in life and then many years later learn that they and their children are still faithfully serving God. It is always heart breaking when they are not.

And, as is often the case with John, he connects two important Biblical principles, walking in truth and loving brothers and sisters in Christ. He says that to love another is something we have had "from the beginning." It has always been a significant sign of true disciples (John 13:34-35).

Unfortunately, John also has to include some warnings about false teachers (verses 7-13). He speaks of those who were denying the humanity of Jesus, "who do not confess Jesus Christ as coming in the flesh." He adds "this is a deceiver and an antichrist." He warns us that those who transgress and do not continue in "the doctrine of Christ" do not have God. This would include divergent teaching about Christ Himself and other doctrines that are not true to what He taught us to believe. We cannot support, financially or morally, those who are not faithful to the Bible in their teachings.

## 3 John

John (the Elder), also called the apostle of love, wrote much about the subject of spiritual fellowship. In his first epistle, he spoke of fellowship with the Father as we walk in the light and are cleansed from our sin by the blood of Christ. He also points out to us that when two people are both in fellowship with God, then they share a joint fellowship with each other. In the second epistle, the apostle encourages us to "abide in the doctrine of Christ" and not to have fellowship with those who teach error. In the third letter, John warns about a man who refused to have fellowship with some, with whom he ought to have had such fellowship.

There are actually three men mentioned by name in this short letter and this single chapter can be divided by the verses that speak of each of the three. (An easy memory tool: 3 John mentions 3 men.)

Gaius (verses 1-8)
Addressed to Gaius, this letter begins by John declaring his love for this brother in the Lord, "whom I love in truth." He seems to be the original, intended recipient of the letter. It is obvious as we read these initial verses (remember that the verse numbers were added later) that Gaius and John were quite close. John is historically connected to the city of Ephesus, after (and perhaps before as well) his exile on Patmos where he received and wrote Revelation. Apparently, some brothers came to Ephesus and as they spoke to John, they mentioned Gaius and reported that he was still faithful to God and His truth. That kind of news always encouraged the apostle and he wanted Gaius to know how much he loved him and his walk with God. He said, "I have no greater joy than to hear that my children walk in truth" (verse 4). He is most likely using the familial reference in a spiritual sense, just as Paul referred to both Timothy and Titus as his sons "in the faith."

In particular, John had heard that Gaius was known for his hospitality and encouragement of other Christians. He also had been gracious in helping others, whom John refers to as "strangers." This means that he was faithful to help those he knew as well as those he did not. Traveling Christians were always welcome in his home.

Diotrephes (verses 9-11)
John now turns his attention to an entirely different kind of person, one who was the polar opposite of the encouraging Gaius. Diotrephes, rather than helping others, was a church troublemaker (we have probably all known someone like him, I fear). His motive is addressed right up front, he "loves to have the preeminence among them." He wanted to be looked upon and regarded as the most important person in the church (we really don't know where he lived or what local church he was a part of). Because he desired to be first (that's what the Greek word means), he looked down on others and felt that everyone else was inferior to himself. He mistreated others in his desire for power and control and even went so far as to put others out of the church. His opinions were most important, you were either for him or against him and he wanted to punish anyone else who didn't elevate him to the important place he felt he deserved. E.M. Zerr, in his Bible Commentary said he believed Diotrephes was an elder in the church who wanted to be the first in importance, the very problem which led to the great falling away described in 2 Thessalonians 2. There is no such thing as a "head elder" in the Bible.

John warns Gaius and us about imitating those who were evil, like Diotrephes, and encourages us to do good so that we could be described as being "of God."

Demetrius (verses 12-14)
He is described as having "a good testimony from all." He is someone who was living according to truth and is one of the good examples that John commends (verse 11).

## Jude

Jude identifies himself as "a bondservant of Jesus Christ, and brother of James" (verse 1). He is widely believed to be a half-brother of Jesus Himself, called Judas in Matthew

13:55 and Mark 6:3. Early on, the physical brothers of Jesus did not believe He was really the Messiah (John 7:3-5). It would be easy to see why they felt that way. Do you think most siblings of really famous or talented people generally regard their own family members as someone who might rise to worldwide prominence? I knew a Christian who coached Michael Jordan as a child in Little League baseball and he said that he never dreamed he would grow up to be the greatest basketball player in the world. In a similar way, Jude does not call attention to himself by announcing that he grew up with the Messiah, simply that he was His bondservant and a brother of James. James was a pillar in the Jerusalem church (Galatians 1:19; 2:9) and is believed to be the likely writer of the book of James in the New Testament. After the resurrection, the brothers had all apparently become convinced about who their older brother really was (Acts 1:14). Mary must have loved all her children.

There is a short introduction to the book (verses 1-4). Jude first tells us who he is, to whom he is writing (although it is not clear to us who they might have been; he describes them in commendable ways, verse 1) and then pronounces mercy, peace and love upon them (verse 2). In verse 3, he clearly states the purpose of his letter. He had intended to emphasize some things about "our common salvation" but altered his original plan due to the rising influence of certain false teachers. He urges true believers "to contend earnestly for the faith which was once for all delivered to the saints." This shows us that sometimes we have to fight the good fight of faith as it becomes necessary for us to challenge the false teachings of the unfaithful. We battle error by sharing the truth.

Verse 4 describes the circumstance that led to his changed plan for what he felt he had to write. "For certain men have crept in unnoticed, who long ago were marked out for this condemnation, ungodly men, who turn the grace of our God into lewdness and deny the only Lord God and our Lord Jesus Christ." False teachers often do their work under the shades of darkness and secrecy until they feel confident enough to go public with their error. We must confront darkness with light.

In verses 5-19, Jude issues multiple warnings about false teachers and describes them in a variety of different ways.

The book of Jude has been referred as "the Acts of the Apostates." This epistle reminds us that there have always been those who turn God's grace into lawlessness. By implication, it teaches us that we will always face such opposition as well. Driven by their fleshly desires rather than by the Spirit, they have no hesitation to rebel against God's divine authority and defile the flesh. He gives example after example of those in New Testament times who did not serve God faithfully. They serve as warnings to us that we must do better.

Did you notice how many times in this short book Jude uses the word "ungodly?" In this section of the book, he uses terms like murmurers, grumblers, complainers, mockers, and sensual persons.

Yet, for all of that, his focus is on saving such people from themselves, as he speaks of attempts to pull them out of the fire (verses 20-25). To the inspired writers of the New

Testament, there was no one who was so bad that he didn't deserve to be saved. Everyone is created in the image of God. Everyone has an immortal soul. Everyone deserves a chance to be saved eternally. Everyone.

The final two verses of this short powerful book are a doxology, a statement of praise and honor to God

# The Book of REVELATION

## Revelation 1

The name of the book is Revelation, not Revelations. It is a singular message, unlike any other in the New Testament, encouraging the people of God to remain faithful, even under critical persecution from the powers of the world and Satan. It challenges them to hold fast to the truth, no matter what.

"The Revelation of Jesus Christ, which God gave Him to show His servants – things which must shortly take place. And He sent and signified it by His angel to His servant John, who bore witness to the word of God, and to the testimony of Jesus Christ, to all things that he saw. Blessed is he who reads and those who hear the words of this prophecy, and keep those things which are written in it; for the time is near" (Revelation 1:1-3).

The book of Revelation is not talking about events that would happen at least 2000 years later. The key issue is what it meant to these first century disciples who were struggling under heavy persecution to deny their faith in Christ and to confess Caesar as Lord. In understanding Revelation, we must consider the conditions of the day and their need for help and strength in a time of great trial. There are general lessons about faithfulness that can enable all of us, even today, to serve God in faith and hope.

Verse 3 contains three verbs that speak of what they needed to do in response to what this revelation would show them – read (listening to what God tells them), hear (in the sense of understanding its message) and keep (doing what the Lord says). That will be our challenge as well.

He opens with a greeting from all three members of the Godhead (verses 4-8).

- God the Father – "Him who is and who was and who is to come"
- The Holy Spirit – "the seven Spirits (completeness) before His throne," sharing His message
- Jesus Christ – "the faithful witness, firstborn from the dead, the ruler over kings of the earth"

John's initial vision is one of the glorious Messiah (verses 9-20).

The apostle identifies himself and states that he received this vision while on the island called Patmos, in the Aegean Sea. He tells us he was "in the Spirit," meaning that he was receiving an inspired revelation from the Holy Spirit. He informs us as well that this process began on "the Lord's Day." This refers either to the first day of the week or a day in which God punishes a nation for its sins (the phrase, "the day of the Lord," is common Old Testament prophetic language of judgment; see Joel 1:15, 2:11; Obadiah 15).

John is told to write the things he will be shown and send it to the seven churches in Asia (verse 11).

When the aged apostle looks around to see the loud voice that is speaking to him, he sees seven golden lampstands, one for each of the churches. He also sees in the midst of the lampstands "One like the Son of Man," the most common phrase Jesus used to refer to Himself when on the earth.

The description of this One (verses 13-16) includes figurative references to power, rule, priesthood, kingship, purity, eternal existence, permanence, stability, glory and majesty. When John sees this powerful being, he falls at His feet as dead. Jesus refers to His own resurrection as He raises John up (verses 17-20).

Other prophets were given a similar overwhelming vision of God's glory before they began their work for Him – Moses (Exodus 3:1-10), Isaiah (Isaiah 6:1-10), Ezekiel (Ezekiel 1), Daniel (Daniel 10:1-14). In each case, this assures them that God is in control and is ruling the whole world.

## Revelation 2

Chapters 2 and 3 contain the individual letters to the seven churches of Asia mentioned in Revelation 1:11.

All seven of the letters follow the same basic format.

- Greeting from Jesus (using the descriptive language from chapter 1)
- Praise (if any)
- Criticism (if any)
- Changes needed
- Reward for the overcomer

There are three phrases common to all of the letters.

1. "I know (your works)."
   By using this phrase, the Lord wants all Christians to realize that Jesus knows everything that is going on in every local church. Not just the larger churches in the bigger cities, then or now, He is aware of each church that is seeking to follow Him and obey His will.

2. "To him who overcomes."
   The Messiah, in each letter, promises a great reward to those who overcome. Remember the tremendous persecution of disciples in the first century under the oppression of the Roman Empire. It varied in intensity between some of the rulers, but none of them were believers who made it any easier to follow Christ in the early days of the church. The purpose of the book of Revelation is to encourage the saints to not give up, but to faithfully serve God, no matter what.

3. "He who has an ear, let him hear what the Spirit says to the churches."
   This phrase shows us the importance of listening to God's divine revelation (all of it, not just this book). Jesus often referred to those who have "ears to hear." Everyone needs to pay careful attention to the God-breathed book we call the New Testament.

Ephesus (2:1-7)
Verses 2-3 describe several admirable qualities of the church in Ephesus. They were working for God, enduring trials and difficulties from both within and outside the church. They had tested false apostles and exposed their errors, while not growing weary.

But they were no longer doing those things out of the original love they had for the Lord. It seems to have been more a matter of custom or tradition rather than fervent zeal and love for Him. Jesus calls on them to repent and "do the first works."

He promises to allow victorious Christians (him who overcomes) the right to eat from the tree of life.

Smyrna (2:8-11)
One of two churches with no criticism from the Savior, Smyrna was about to endure an intense period of persecution. "You will have tribulation ten days" is not to be understood literally but as a relatively short time of difficulty. He tells them to remain faithful, even if it means they might die for their faith and He assures them that they would not be hurt by the second death, eternity in hell.

(The rest of the letters in Chapter 2 will be discussed with those in Chapter 3.)

# Revelation 3

(We will also look at the last two churches from Chapter 2.)

Pergamos (2:12-17)
Pergamum (in many translations) is the place where "Satan's throne" was. Emperor worship, a huge problem in the first century, was common in this city. It was not easy to do the right thing under intense government pressure to refer to the Caesar as "Lord God." Christians simply would not confess to something they did not believe and many of them paid the ultimate price of their lives to be true to God (the letter mentions Antipas who was a faithful martyr).

But the church was tempted to compromise with moral impurity. Some did the right thing; some did not. Jesus promises the overcomers a white stone (of victory) and a new name (a new and better relationship with God).

Thyatira (2:18-29)
This church has some good things to commend it (Jesus does in verse 19), but also some very bad things going on (verses 20-24). Jesus encourages them to "hold fast," not to give in to moral corruption.

Sardis (3:1-6)
The warning that Jesus gives Sardis in the beginning of their letter should get the attention of every faithful Christian. They had a good reputation among other disciples, but the Master tells them plainly, "you are dead."

The Lord tells them to strengthen the good things in the church (verse 2) but they need to repent of and correct many other things (verse 3). Like most churches, they were not all bad (some had not defiled their garments), but they were not all good either. He promises the overcomers in their group that their names would not be removed from the Book of Life, but this means that some names would be blotted out.

Philadelphia (3:7-13)
This is the second church that received no criticism from the Savior. He only says good things about them. Apparently they were small in number ("you have a little strength"), but strong in spirit. He says He had set before them an open door, an expression which refers to many opportunities to preach the gospel to the lost (1 Corinthians 16:9 and Colossians 4:3). They were faithful to God's word and would not deny the Name of the Lord, even under challenging circumstances. Jesus speaks of "the hour of trial which shall come upon the whole world, to test those who dwell on the earth." His encouragement to them during this difficult test to their faith was to persevere, to never stop doing their best to serve God. He prayed for them that they might overcome.

Laodicea (3:14-22)
Laodicea is known as the lukewarm church (verse 16). In contrast to Philadelphia (no condemnation, only praise), Laodicea is the opposite (no praise, only condemnation). God's "Faithful and True Witness" (verse 14) says of this church, "So then, because you are lukewarm, and neither cold nor hot, I will vomit you out of My mouth." What

a frightening analysis from the Lord that must have been for them. He calls them to repentance and lets them know that, if they will repent, He will welcome them back. He rebukes them because of His love and prays that, even in Laodicea, there will be those who are victorious in the end.

"He who has an ear, let him hear what the Spirit says to the churches."

## Revelation 4

The chapters that are divided in our New Testament as Revelation 4 and 5 are two of the most exciting visions in all of the word of God. In these two chapters, the Lord draws back the curtain that separates heaven and earth and gives us, through a door standing open in heaven, a look into God's eternal glory. In Chapter 4, the main character is God the Father, seated on His throne, reigning from heaven over the earth beneath. In Chapter 5, the scene shifts only slightly to God's right hand, as we are blessed to see God the Son, Jesus Christ, seated on David's throne and ruling over the universe, with all authority in heaven and on earth, according to Matthew 28:18.

This is a symbolic word picture, a figurative description of the throne room of God and Christ. Chapter 4 begins with a beautiful throne, set in heaven, to reassure the persecuted disciples of the first century that God really is in control. They need not fear those who can kill the body, but who can never take a soul away from the Father.

It was hard to be a Christian during the earthly reign of the Caesars who led the Roman Empire. Most of them were ego-driven, power hungry, sensual gratification seekers who sought to fulfill their own pleasures and desired to dominate the world through force and military power. Many of them actually had what is often referred to as a "God complex." They felt so revered and adored by their citizens that, in their self-centered delusion, they considered themselves to be deity. Caligula, Nero, and Domitian, along with others before and after them, demanded to be worshiped as gods, with severe consequences for those who refused to bow down before them.

Jesus had told His followers, in passages like John 16:33, that "In the world, you will have tribulation." But He continued on to promise them that they could "be of good cheer," He said, "for I have overcome the world." That and other similar promises are easy to believe, until the time comes when a disciple is being persecuted for his faith and has to choose between living because he denies his faith in God or dying because he announces to the man holding a sword to his throat that he will not worship Caesar; he will only bow before the God of heaven. The book of Revelation, and especially Chapters 4 and 5, reminds them (and us) that God is in control and we must never lose our trust and confidence in Him.

God, in Chapter 4, is described as having an appearance like jasper and a sardius (or carnelian) stone, beautiful and valuable. There is an emerald rainbow encircling the throne, representing beauty and glory and splendor. God is on the throne, not Caesar. God is the Ultimate Ruler, the One before whom even Caesar, with all his authority, will one day bow in reverence.

In Revelation 4, God is surrounded by 24 elders, in white clothing, which symbolizes their purity and holiness. They wear crowns of gold. The Greek word here is STEPHANOS, a crown of victory and celebration, similar to the gold medals in Olympic competition.

There are also 4 living creatures, full of eyes in front and in back, reminding us that they see and know all. Nothing escapes the attention of heaven, including the persecution of the faithful by the ungodly.

All of their focus, however, is on the worship and adoration of God. Day and night, they sing His praises. Two phrases stand out in their songs. In verse 8, they never stop saying of God, "Holy, holy, holy is the Lord God Almighty, who was, and is and is to come." In verse 11, they point us to the worthy nature of God. (The word "worship" is a contraction of the idea of worth-ship.) God is worthy of all glory and honor and power. He is the One who "so loved the world that He gave His only begotten Son" to die on the cross in order that we might live through Him and with Him throughout the ceaseless ages of eternity. To God be the glory, great things He has done.

## Revelation 5

In Chapter 5, the scene shifts to the right hand of God's throne. In Chapter 4, the focus is on God the Father, seated on His majestic throne, reminiscent of the vision of Isaiah 6 as those around the throne sing, "Holy, holy, holy" to the God of heaven and earth.

But now in Chapter 5, our attention is called to God's right side, where His Son, Jesus, the Head of the church, reigns over His spiritual kingdom from the throne of David, one of His earthly forefathers (Acts 2:29-30; Mark 12:35-37).

In the right hand of God is a scroll, written inside and on the back, sealed with seven seals. This scroll contains the full will of God, which includes the destiny of these persecuted believers. Written on both the front and the back (usually scrolls were only written on the front) and sealed with seven seals, this information is complete. It contains everything they needed to know about their future (once the seals were released).

But the problem, announced by a strong angel, is finding one who is worthy to remove the seals and open the scroll. This angel himself is not worthy, nor are the twenty four elders or the four living creatures around God's throne. And the apostle John wept loudly because he knew the information in this book was vital to the faithfulness of the early disciples.

Then one of the elders announces that the Lion of the tribe of Judah, the Root of David, has prevailed to open the scroll and loose its seals. This, of course, introduces us to Jesus the Messiah, the Savior of the world. He is the One at God's right hand. He is the One who came to the earth, set a perfect example for all people of faith, and then died on the cross at the hands of the ungodly. And, on the third day, He rose from the dead, to prove that His death conquered the sin problem and that His resurrection gives us the hope of an eternity in the presence of God in heaven. The imagery of a lion is a powerful one, showing us the awesome power of the Messiah to overcome the devil, including the forgiveness of our sins and the power over death that offers us eternal life with Him.

As John continues to receive the throne scene vision, he looks and, in the midst of these heavenly beings, he sees a Lamb which, by all appearances, has been slain, yet is alive and standing up. This powerful Lion has become a humble Lamb, in His sacrifice for our rebellion against God. He has seven horns which indicate His authority (Matthew 28:18) and seven eyes, reminding us that He is all knowing (Hebrews 4:13).

Only Jesus is worthy to open the seals. Only the Savior is pure enough and powerful enough and loving enough to let these first century Christians know that He is watching over and protecting them, no matter what might happen to them in this life. Their souls were safe with this powerful Lamb of God who died to take away the sins of the world.

The response of the heavenly beings who surround the throne can be only one thing, eternal praise and worship of God and Christ. They hold harps, symbolizing songs of praise and adoration toward God, and golden bowls of incense, which represent their prayers directed up to God. Over and over, they praise God for His love and grace shared with His creation. Worthy is the Lamb who was slain.

Their number (ten thousand times ten thousand; that's 100 million) is figurative, not literal, but it impresses us with the magnitude of Christ's glory and authority. Continually they fall down before Him to worship Him, throughout all eternity. Don't you want to be in that number?

## Revelation 6

This chapter begins the part of the book where God shows the systematic punishment He will inflict on those who persecute His people, whether the Jewish people or the Roman Empire in the first century or those who would abuse His disciples in our day and time. It will begin gradually in Chapter 6 and grow in severity and intensity until it results in the complete destruction of those pernicious forces of evil and the triumph of those who remain true to their God.

Chapter 6 reveals to us the opening of the first six seals of the scroll from Chapter 5.

First Seal (6:1-2) – Military invasion
A rider comes forth on a white horse. This is either Jesus Himself (He is described this way in Revelation 19:11-16) or it is a Parthian warrior, representing Rome's most dreaded enemy. They were fierce soldiers who used the bow as their primary weapon. It is possible that this symbol represents both – Jesus, pictured as a Parthian soldier, coming to punish Rome for her treatment of Christians.

Second Seal (6:3-4) – War, bloodshed
This rider comes on a red horse (the color of blood). This represents carnal warfare that follows closely after military invasion. It is war that "takes peace from the earth."

Third Seal (6:5-6) – Famine, economic hardship
The rider on the black horse symbolizes dark days, hard times financially. The downfall of a nation or empire often begins with the collapse of its economy. It is not total; some food is still available, but there is scarcity. A bushel of wheat or barley costs an entire day's wage (a denarius). The oil and wine are not harmed, meaning that they can still be purchased by the wealthy. Economic pressure always hurts the poor more than the rich.

Fourth Seal (6:7-8) – Death
The pale horse and its rider figuratively refer to the four severe judgments of God – sword, famine, pestilence, and wild beasts (common language from the Old Testament to speak of God's punishment on the unrighteous; Ezekiel 5:17, 14:21). Only one fourth of the earth is affected (the intensity will increase as the imagery continues in later visions).

Fifth Seal (6:9-11) – Persecution of Saints
Returning to the major theme of the book, this seal finds the believers "under the altar." They are hiding, in fear and subjection; some have been slain for their testimony. They are asking how long this cruel persecution will continue, when their blood will be avenged as God judges the ungodly. Notice that there is not a cry for vindictiveness, simply vindication. It is not wrong to want justice from God. But they are not taking things into their own hands in an appeal for vigilante justice. They are asking God to judge their enemies, in thoughts similar to the imprecatory psalms of the Old Testament. They have the assurance that the God of all the earth will do right and punish the wicked (Romans 1:18; 12:19; Hebrews 10:30-31; 12:29).

Sixth Seal (6:12-17) – The Wrath of the Lamb
This seal begins to answer their question from verse 10. God will indeed punish the evildoers of the first and every century. The language incorporated here in this section is reminiscent of the language used by the Old Testament prophets as judgment warnings. Darkness, physical calamities, the whole universe being turned upside down, people hiding in caves and mountains looking for either death or relief. The wicked will find no comfort, for "the great day of His wrath has come."

## Revelation 7

The last chapter ended with a statement and a question: "For the great day of His wrath has come, and who is able to stand?" Chapter 7 answers that question.

You will recall that, during the 10 plagues on Egypt in the book of Exodus, Israel did not suffer the same fate as their enemies, the Egyptians. God protects His own, even while punishing their persecutors. This chapter illustrates that same principle of God's goodness.

In verses 1-3, four angels are sent from God, to whom it was granted to harm the earth and the sea (the whole world). But they are instructed not to begin until "the servants of God" have been sealed or protected by the Lord from the disaster that will follow.

This seal is similar to the one we read about in Ezekiel 9 where the people of God ("the men who sigh and cry over the abominations that are done in" Jerusalem) receive a mark on their foreheads. The agents of God's judgment here are told to kill the wicked, but not to harm those with God's mark on them. In Revelation 7, those who are sealed by God are not to be hurt by the coming judgment.

Verses 4-8 describe those who received the seal as 144,000 of all the tribes of the children of Israel, twelve thousand from each tribe. As they are listed, the numbering includes the tribes of Levi and Joseph, not normally considered in the twelve, but excludes the tribes of Dan and Ephraim. Remembering that the book of Revelation is written in figurative language, who do the twelve tribes represent? Using Old Testament language, which is what the book does from start to finish, they symbolize God's people on the earth, who are still suffering persecution and needing help (John 16:33; Acts 14:22; 1 Peter 4:12-16). It is not a literal number, but symbolic, like the rest of the book.

Why are Dan and Ephraim excluded? Perhaps it is because the cities of Dan (in the same tribe) and Bethel (in Ephraim) were centers of idol worship. This is where the golden calves were placed by Jeroboam in 1 Kings 12, which ultimately led to their downfall. God has never approved of sin in any form and He may be simply reminding them again of their need for purity and godliness.

It is also important for us to realize that God is not promising these disciples that they will not be killed by their persecutors. He is not telling them they will not die for Him. He is reminding them that the most important thing is their soul and that, even if they have to die physically for their faith, if they remain faithful to Him, He will protect their souls (see Matthew 10:28).

The second major section of the chapter (verses 9-17) is a picture of God's people who have survived the persecution (verse 14), not necessarily physically, but spiritually. This shows them that God's seal works.

So while the 144,000 symbolize the church on earth who are still fighting the battle, the great multitude represents the church in heaven. They are having a spiritual party, using a picture of the Jewish celebration of the Festival of Tabernacles, when they lived in tents or booths as the children of Israel did after they came out of Egypt during their 40 year desert wandering.

The church is "spiritual Israel," the people of God under the new covenant (see Romans 9:6; Galatians 6:16). They were going to be victorious if they did not give up on God. It wouldn't be easy, but this is another chapter of comfort to remind them and us to not grow weary, even in difficult circumstances.

## Revelation 8

After Revelation 7 provides transitional information between the sixth and seventh seals, Chapter 8 begins with 30 minutes of silence. It is a dramatic pause, which sets up an air of expectation for the reader. It is a delay, but not a halt, in God's judgment. With the burning of incense on the altar, there is both the enjoyment of victory of God's saints and the prayers of the faithful still in the heat of the battle, prayers to God for continued protection and safety. The message now shifts to the Seven Trumpets of judgment. God's wrath will be taken up to the next level.

The seventh seal includes the prayers of the saints (8:3-5). The trumpets are God's answer to those prayers, an assurance that God will defeat evil and Rome will fall.

Trumpets were used for various purposes in the Old Testament. In Numbers 10, they were used to call the children of Israel to an assembly before Moses or to sound the advance of the multitude from one place to another. They often were used as a symbol of approaching judgment (Joel 2:1, Amos 3:6, 1 Corinthians 15:52). Here the seven trumpets are divided into two groups:

- Trumpets 1-4 – deal with elements of nature
- Trumpets 5-7 – afflict man directly

The First Trumpet (8:7) – hail, fire, blood
The trumpet judgments seem to be modeled after the ten plagues on Egypt (see Exodus chapters 7-12). Here the land is affected (only one third, a large part, but not total).

The Second Trumpet (8:8-9) – a burning mountain
In the Bible, a mountain is a frequent symbol for an earthly kingdom. In this case, the kingdom is falling, not rising. A couple of Old Testament references may help you to understand this – Zechariah 4:7 and Jeremiah 51:25-27 (there are many others). The sea is turned to blood (which reminds us of the first plague on Egypt) and ships are destroyed (showing that commerce is affected). One of the best ways to cripple a country is to collapse its economy.

The Third Trumpet (8:10-11) – drinking water is poisoned
A falling star named Wormwood, which means bitter, poisons the nation's water supply. Water, of course, is essential to life itself and so their lives are being affected, one piece at a time.

The Fourth Trumpet (8:12-13) – darkness over the land
Reminiscent of the ninth plague on Egypt, this trumpet is designed to symbolize a "dark day" for Rome. The 12 hour day becomes an 8 hour day as a third of all light sources, sun, moon and stars, are darkened. Things are getting worse and worse for those who have made themselves God's enemies.

Verse 13 describes an angel (several translations use the word, eagle), flying through the midst of heaven, saying with a loud voice, "Woe, woe, woe to the inhabitants of the earth, because of the remaining blasts of the trumpet of the three angels who are about to sound!" Three more trumpet blasts (trumpets 5-7) will follow, each proclaiming further "woe" or judgment against the persecutors of God's people.

As a citizen in the first century, if you were to pick a winner between the church and the Roman Empire, who would you have chosen? All human logic would tell you that the Empire was far stronger and superior and would easily defeat the church. But the church belongs to God and He takes the mistreatment of His people very seriously. The Roman Empire didn't stand a chance.

## Revelation 9

The seven trumpet judgments are a part of the seventh seal. The seven bowls of wrath which will follow in Chapter 16 are a part of the seventh trumpet. Each successive set of images represents a progression of stronger and more complete punishment of Rome. Remember that the trumpets are the answer to the prayers of Christians (8:3-5), assuring them of their vindication in eternity, even if not in this life. God will prevail; evil will be vanquished. Make certain which side you are on.

The Fifth Trumpet (9:1-12) – the first woe
In verse 1, a star falls from heaven to earth and is given the key to a bottomless pit (the Abyss, NIV). In verse 11, we are told this star symbolizes Satan himself. In between, he releases a locust plague on the earth.

Of course, Satan was not literally in heaven; this represents his fall from a position of power and authority. Jesus came to destroy Satan and his control over death and the world (Hebrews 2:14; 1 John 3:8). He accomplished this by His death and resurrection. Satan remains "the god of this age" (2 Corinthians 4:4) but his power and influence are greatly diminished by the work of Christ (Mark 3:27; Luke 10:18). He will be shown in this book to be the power behind the Roman persecution of believers, but Revelation also tells us that his authority has been minimized by the Savior when He rose from the dead.

Smoke comes pouring out of the abyss, moral pollution, representing the internal, moral decay of Rome. Remember Proverbs 14:34? "Righteousness exalts a nation, But sin is a reproach to any people." All the devil has to offer the world is falsehood, perversion, ungodliness, things that offer short term pleasure but long term (eternal?) sorrow.

The locust plague he unleashes is described in symbols, some of which are difficult in meaning and challenging in precise application. Five months is a typical duration of a literal locust invasion and warns them of a period of intense destructive power, pictured by lion's teeth, wings like chariots (locusts move quickly in their destruction), stingers which wound, paralyze or kill their victims.

The name of the angel of the bottomless pit is Abaddon (Hebrew) or Apollyon (Greek). Both simply mean the destroyer. That's what Satan does. He destroys joy, happiness, and peace. He offers pain, anguish and destruction.

As a child of the 1960s and 70s in America, I must mention briefly that this chapter was used by one of the world's all-time worst criminals, Charles Manson, to believe that the Beatles, in their white album, were calling him to inflict great pain on society. Songs like Revolution #9 (Revelation 9), Blackbird and Helter Skelter were misinterpreted by

Manson in his drug fueled paranoia to bring about murder and mayhem. Satan is good at that. He often misuses scripture to confuse the gullible.

The Sixth Trumpet (9:13-21) – the second woe
This trumpet symbolizes the attack by God on the forces of evil (in the first century, Rome). A 200 million soldier army is released (verse 16), showing the overwhelming odds against the Roman Empire. Verses 17-19 describe the symbols of their fierceness and power.

The first six trumpets represent natural disasters, internal moral corruption and military invasion, all methods by which God will bring about Rome's downfall. Even with this judgment, Rome will not repent (9:20-21). God says that quite plainly and then writes three uplifting chapters of encouragement for believers (chapters 10-12). Stay tuned.

## Revelation 10

Only one chapter in Revelation is shorter (Chapter 15 only has 8 verses). This one ties with Chapter 4 as the next two shortest in the book with only 11 verses each. But it is packed full of important, spiritual meaning. Great things can come in small packages.

The chapter begins by introducing "another mighty angel." His description and clothing would symbolize his divine authority as a representative from God. The rainbow (see 4:3), the face shining like the sun (see 1:16), feet like pillars (stability – 1:15), and the voice of a lion (5:5). While there is no such thing as a weak angel, all of them are quite powerful, it is significant that this one is described as "mighty." Perhaps this indicates a level of power and authority that is greater than average. Some Bible students have suggested the possibility that this powerful angel is, in fact, Jesus Himself.

He has a "little book" in his hand, indicating a revelation from God.

He is standing with his right foot on the sea and his left foot on the land, indicating that his message is for all people.

As he speaks in a loud voice (similar to those in 1:10, 1:15, 4:1, 5:2, 6:1, 6:10, 7:2, 7:10, and 8:13), seven thunders utter their voices as well, indicating an overwhelmingly important message is about to be released.

John sets out to write down the message but is warned by a voice from heaven to seal up the things uttered by the seven thunders and not to write them.

But revealed or not, significant events are about to happen. John is going to see more visions and will indeed write many of them down in this book for us to read and understand. These things are described as "the mystery of God" (verse 7), which indicates the idea of God's truth being revealed little by little, piece by piece until it is all "finished."

Then, in verses 8-11, John is given further instructions from "the voice" out of heaven. "Go, take the little book which is open in the hand of the angel who stands on the sea and on the earth." When he does so, he is told to "Take and eat it." He is further told that "it will make your stomach bitter, but it will be as sweet as honey in your mouth."

Everything happens exactly as the angel has said, and then John is told that he has more to prophesy for God "about many peoples, nations, tongues, and kings."

Eating the book means to ingest its message, to master and understand it (read and compare Ezekiel 2:6-3:11).

There is great joy in receiving a message from God. The writer of Psalm 1 describes this kind of person as one whose "delight is in the law of the LORD, And in His law he meditates day and night" (verse 2). We should always be people who delight in God's will. We should read it often, meditate on it, understand it to the best of our ability and then apply it to our own lives and seek to teach it to others. As Psalm 19:10 states, "More to be desired are they than gold, Yea, than much fine gold; Sweeter also than honey and the honeycomb."

But often, the sweet turns bitter as we meditate on God's judgment of the wicked, His wrath to be poured out on the unrighteous. Indeed, the Bible is a two-edged sword (Hebrews 4:12), producing both joy for the faithful and sadness for the wicked.

## Revelation 11

Remember that in Revelation 9:20-21, even after God's wrath in judgment has begun to be poured out on Rome, they will not repent. This must have been very frightening to the Christians. So, God reveals to John what we read in Chapters 10-12 to provide additional assurance and comfort for them. As Chapter 11 opens, we are still learning about the Sixth Trumpet, which is also the second of three woes that will punish Rome further.

The first two verses describe a measuring rod given to John as he is instructed to "measure the temple of God, the altar, and those who worship there." This is not the literal temple; it was destroyed in A.D 70. This is speaking about the church as the temple of God (1 Corinthians 3:16-17; Ephesians 2:19-22). Using language similar to that in Zechariah 2:1-5, this symbolic language represents God's protection of His people, much like the sealing of the 144,000 in Chapter 7.

The outer court is not to be measured, which shows that unfaithful Christians (is that an oxymoron?) or non-Christians will be subject to this judgment.

This protection is needed for 42 months. There are three other "time periods" that are used to describe this imagery – three and a half years, 1260 days, and time, times, and half a time. In the numerology used in the book (where numbers have spiritual meanings), the number 7 represents fullness or completeness or perfection. If the persecution of Christians lasted 7 years, it would be completed and their opponents would fully destroy the church. Of course, the Bible tells us that the spiritual kingdom of God will never be destroyed (Daniel 2:44), so this could not happen. Here, God assures them of this by saying that the persecution would only be 42 months, three and a half years, which is meant to assure them that the church will survive this severe trial. These symbols comfort them as they represent incompleteness, the broken and limited power of Rome or imperfect oppression. That doesn't mean the church will not be hurt by the world, only that God's people will ultimately prevail.

Verses 3-14 introduce us to God's "two witnesses." They prophesy (or stand for God) during the entire 1260 days of persecution. These two witnesses symbolize the church; they are lampstands (candlesticks, KJV) or light bearers. The language used comes from Zechariah 4:1-6, 11-14. There are two of them, referring to confirmed testimony or strength. (Some Bible students suggest that this is a reference to the Old Testament and the New Testament, the fulness of God's revelation of truth.)

Verses 5-6 describe their strength in defiance of their enemies; they have the power to destroy all who oppose them.

They are killed by the beast from the Abyss (Satan), which affirms that God's people can be slowed down in the advance of truth, but then they are resurrected after three and a half (not seven) days. They ascend to heaven and great destruction in the form of a powerful earthquake kills many who have opposed their work. God's work can be harmed or damaged by the world, but it can never be destroyed or silenced. Who really wins here, the beast or the faithful? The cause of Christ and the gospel will always be resurrected in the lives of those who take up the mantle of the martyrs and continue to stand for God and His truth.

Then verses 15-19 reveal the seventh trumpet (or the third woe). The language represents a vision of victory for the people of God, while at the same time describing a trumpet of woe or disaster for the wicked. This helps us to remember the distinction made by Jesus (Matthew 7:13-14) between the narrow and challenging way of salvation (chosen by few) and the broad way of destruction (chosen by many). You must decide for yourself on which path you will walk.

## Revelation 12

Chapter 12 begins the second major section of the book of Revelation. It portrays the age long battle between God and Satan that dates all the way back to Genesis 3. The major themes of the book continue. No matter how it appears, Christians will be victorious and Rome will fall.

Jim McGuiggan, in his commentary on Revelation, says that this chapter presents Satan as a three time loser. He loses battles against a pregnant women, against a little baby, and against Michael, a messenger from God. Let's consider each of these three battles as we look into the message from Revelation 12.

The first battle described here is Satan against a pregnant woman. All of these battles are word pictures of the devil's attempts to defeat God, Christ and Christians. He will lose every time.

The pregnant woman is symbolic of God's people. The twelve stars on her head are organized religion, twelve tribes of Israel (in the Old Testament) and twelve apostles (in the New Testament). The sun and moon and stars show us that those referred to are those who stand for God's light in a world of darkness (2 Corinthians 4:3-4).

In verses 1-5, she represents God's Old Testament people, Israel. Christ, of course, came through the lineage of Abraham and it was the faithful remnant of followers which produced the Messiah (Genesis 12:1-3; Galatians 3:16-19, 29).

In verses 6-17, after the Messiah is born, she represents the church, God's people in the New Covenant. They had to flee into the wilderness for protection. This language reminds us of the forty years in the wilderness after the exodus from Egypt, a period of struggling and difficulty during which God provides for the needs of His people ("nourished" by God, similar to the manna, water and quail that God gave Israel). This hardship lasted 1260 days (verse 6) or "time and times and half a time" (verse 14), again reminding us that it was not complete destruction, only hardship that would come to an end. Verses 13-17 emphasize that God is protecting His own from the anger of the dragon.

The male child, borne by the pregnant woman, is Jesus. He rules all nations with a rod of iron (verse 5; compare to Psalm 2:7-9). Jesus is the One with all authority over heaven and earth (Matthew 28:18; Ephesians 1:20-22; Revelation 19:15-16). He is "King of kings and Lord of lords." Never forget that truth.

The great red dragon is, of course, Satan (verses 3, 9). He is the adversary, the opponent, the enemy of all that is good and right. He is "the prince of the power of the air" (Ephesians 2:2). He is a deceiver, a liar, the one who hates all good things and opposes those who seek to do right. Many have been tricked into following him to the destruction of their eternal souls.

Verses 7-13 describe a great battle in heaven. This is not to be interpreted literally, but is symbolic of spiritual warfare at the highest levels. On the heavenly level, it is God versus Satan. In our lives, it is the daily struggle between good and evil, between spirit and flesh (Matthew 26:41).

Notice that God does not even come out to fight this battle Himself. He doesn't need to. Rather He sends out a messenger (which is what the word "angel" means) and Michael defeats Satan and casts him out of this heavenly realm. Satan cannot and will not win.

Chapter 12 is another chapter of comfort. On multiple levels, God assures them that He will win and so will everyone on His side (that's us, fellow disciples). Satan will lose as will those on his side (Rome and its followers). Which side would you prefer to be on? What a mighty God we serve.

## Revelation 13

Do not misunderstand the promised victory for Christians in the book of Revelation. It was very hard to be a disciple of Christ in the first century. John, through the Holy

Spirit, is not trying to pretend that there are no challenges or difficulties in serving the Messiah. Chapter 13 presents more bad news for the Christian in the form of two beasts. Chapter 14 will tell them that the news is not all bad. On the surface, indeed things look quite bad. But Jesus wanted His followers to know and believe, beyond a shadow of a doubt, that behind the scenes, the battle has already been won by God.

The Sea Beast (verses 1-10) – Rome as a persecuting civil power

The beast that arises from the sea is a figurative word picture of a government that uses its political power to mistreat and persecute believers, in an attempt to cause them to deny their faith and abandon their God. It is similar in many respects to a modern day Communist (atheistic) government or one that is dominated by a ruthless and unbelieving dictator. (Russia, China, Cuba, Iran, Iraq, Libya are all current governments that are engaged in these kinds of activities, to varying degrees.)

The sea, here and often in the Old Testament, represents the nations of the earth and the turmoil that they cause in the world. See Isaiah 17:12-13, 57:20; Daniel 7:3ff). The 7 heads, 10 horns and 10 diadems symbolize the rule and authority of various levels of the Roman Empire in the first century.

This beast is described as having characteristics of a leopard (swiftness), a bear (strength), and a lion (fierceness). Rome is a composite of all of the worst qualities of each of these animals. The symbolism here comes from Daniel 7. The fourth world empire in Daniel 7 (and also chapter 2) is Rome. It is the same here. Satan, of course, is the power behind this beast.

One of the heads of the sea beast is mortally wounded, then healed (verse 3). When one Caesar died, he was immediately replaced by another who was just as bad or worse. There might be a temporary lull in persecution, but it would soon return.

Verse 5 does say that the mistreatment of God's people would continue for 42 months (three and one half years). This, as we have previously noted, means the persecution would be only partially successful. Verse 10 specifically reminds them God will take vengeance on their persecutors (Romans 12:19-21).

The Earth Beast (verses 11-18) – Rome as a false religious power

This beast comes up out of the earth, indicating that the religious aspect of Rome's rule (Caesar worship) is of human origin, not from heaven, which would show divine origin. This land beast is called "the false prophet" several times in the rest of the book (see, for example, 16:13, 19:20, 20:10). As a matter of fact, for the remainder of the book, these two beasts will not be described as the sea beast and the earth beast, but rather as "the beast and the false prophet."

Verse 11 tells us that the beast looks like a lamb, but speaks like a dragon. Error often sounds good, but will be deadly to the soul. Verses 12-14 tell us that the beast performs false miracles (again, wanting to appear as a legitimate religion, but in reality, is false). Verses 16-17 identifies this beast as the source of much persecution against those who refuse to worship Caesar.

Verse 18 speaks of "the mark of the beast," the infamous 666. People have speculated for years that this refers to Martin Luther, Napolean, the Roman Catholic pope, Adolph Hitler, Stalin, Castro or some other ungodly person from human history. It seems to apply contextually to the entire Roman religious system, headed by the Caesar. God is emphasizing that Caesar worship is of human origin, not divine.

## Revelation 14

Chapter 14 is another chapter of encouragement for troubled hearts.

Verses 1-5 are a picture of the victorious people of God, standing with the Lamb (Jesus the Messiah) on Mount Zion. Mount Zion is the physical mountain on which the city of Jerusalem was located. Because it is the place where the church began on Pentecost, the phrase is used to describe the church (see Hebrews 12:22-23). The church is composed of all saved people (they are added to that number by the Lord Himself, Acts 2:47). In that sense, the church has been redeemed by the blood of the Lamb, saved from sin and destruction through the marvelous grace and loving kindness of God Almighty.

Notice the similarities to the 144,000 from Chapter 7. There they are sealed by God; here they have God's name written on their foreheads. This is in contrast to those mentioned at the end of Chapter 13 who have the mark of the beast, 666, written on their foreheads. Everyone has one or the other; they either belong to God or to the devil. This is a personal choice, a decision every soul must make.

They are singing a new song, one they could not sing before they became children of God. It is a song of deliverance and salvation. No one can learn that song except those who have been redeemed from sin; only Christians can know that experience and sing about it.

Verse 4 tells us they have kept themselves pure. That is no small task, either in the first century or the one in which we live today. The world around us constantly pressures us to conform (Romans 12:2), to live like others around us, in lewdness and lust, in anger and hatred, in jealousy and strife, in rebellion and disobedience to God. The ones described here maintained their purity by following the Lamb everywhere He goes. We are to walk in His footsteps, follow His example, to serve God faithfully and with a loyal heart (1 Peter 2:21ff). Even if it means suffering persecution, we want to be godly and righteous. We are the redeemed; God expects us to be different from the world, to show them the difference that being a disciple of Jesus has made in how we live. This includes having "no deceit" in our mouths, hearts or lives as we seek to live "without fault before the throne of God."

Next we read of several proclamations made by angels of God. The first three are found in verses 6-13.

The first angel (verses 6-7) describes Christians preaching the everlasting gospel to those on the earth, to encourage them to worship God, not Caesar.

The second angel (verse 8) announces the fall of Babylon, figuratively referring to Rome's collapse. It is stated as though it has already happened. This downfall will be described in detail in chapters 17-19.

The third angel (verses 9-11) warns that emperor worshipers will be judged. He compares their fate with the eternal reward of the saints. Those who fall asleep in Christ will receive great reward and rest.

In verses 14-20, three more angels further announce Rome's downfall using the imagery of a King (having on His head a golden crown) wielding a sharp sickle with which He will punish the rebellious. "The harvest of the earth is ripe," one angel says, comparing the judgment to come to a wheat harvest, a common word picture used by John the Baptist (Matthew 3:12) and Jesus Himself (Matthew 13:24-30, 36-43). The final angel in this chapter uses the analogy of harvesting grapes, as the evil doers (the vine of the earth) are gathered and thrown "into the great winepress of the wrath of God." So much blood is spilled that it comes up to the height of a horse's bridle and extends for 180 miles (300 kilometers). The day of God's judgment is coming.

## Revelation 15

The seven bowls (vials, KJV) of wrath are also described as "the seven last plagues" (Revelation 15:1). They represent a full outpouring of God's wrath. The next section (chapters 17-20) describes the result, the complete downfall of Rome.

Chapter 15 is a reminder that the God of heaven is still in control. That was true then, in the first century. It was true during the Communist terror during the days of the USSR. It is true for those Christians who are in constant danger of death from Islamic terrorism. It is true during a global pandemic that has changed the whole world. It is true for us today. In every way, no matter what we see in the world around us, God is in control of the entire world.

Sandwiched between the sickle of God's judgment (14:14-20) and the seven bowls of God's wrath (chapter 16), we have a picture of God's heavenly temple.

Verses 1-4 describe the peace of the victorious saints. Those who have achieved victory over the beast are praising God for His power, mercy and grace. They sing the song of Moses and of the Lamb. It is a song of deliverance and celebration, joy and peace.

Verses 5-8 inform us about God's power which is prepared to pour out His wrath. The seven angels come out of the (figurative) temple, having the seven plagues, "full of the wrath of God who lives forever and ever." Smoke fills the temple, "from the glory of the Lord and from His power." It is, at the same time, both encouraging and fearful. The language is from Exodus 40:34-35 and 2 Chronicles 5:13-14.

Throughout Revelation, there are two phrases that are used over and over. They are:

- "those who dwell on the earth" (6:10; 11:10 (2x); 13:8, 12, 14; 14:6; 17:8)
- "the inhabitants of the earth" (8:13; 12:12; 17:2)

These phrases are not referring to everyone who lives in this world. They are speaking of those who are "of the world." Those who have made the wrong choice in life and are giving their lives to Satan, rather than to their Creator, the God of heaven. That decision will cost them their soul in eternity.

In John 17:14-16, Jesus mentions His followers who are in the world, but not of the world. "I have given them Your word; and the world has hated them because they are not of the world, just as I am not of the world. I do not pray that You should take them out of the world, but that you should keep them from the evil one. They are not of the world, just as I am not of the world."

1 John 2:15-17 tells us not to love the world or the things in the world. He goes on to specify what he is talking about as the lust of the flesh, the lust of the eyes and the pride of life. But He also blesses us with material things (James 1:17). He wants us to enjoy the beauty of this world and to use our physical blessings in ways that will help others and glorify Him.

But the world needs us to provide them with a living, breathing example of one who follows, trusts and obeys the Lord, one who surrenders his own will to the will of God. We are to show them that Christianity works for us and it can be what they really need, even if they don't realize how much they need the Savior.

This chapter is one more reminder that God will win and Satan will lose. Which side will you choose? May the glory of the Lord fill our lives.

## Revelation 16

In Chapter 16, we read the details of the seven last plagues. You will notice the intentional similarity between these judgments on Rome and the ten plagues that God brought upon Egypt when He was sending the clear message to stop mistreating His people and let them go free. Wicked and foolish people usually only learn the lessons of life the hard way, by experiencing personal loss or hardship. Wise and godly people will learn from the mistakes of others.

These golden bowls of God's wrath will be poured out on Rome in rapid succession (verse 1).

First bowl (16:2) – Grievous sores
This plague is poured out on the earth, that is, on wicked people who are "of the world." The symbolism here comes from the sixth plague on Egypt (Exodus 9:8-12).

Second bowl (16:3) – Sea to blood
The first of the ten plagues on Egypt is the "type" of this punishment on Rome (Exodus 7:17-20). It is also similar to the second trumpet (Revelation 8:8-9). The second trumpet judgment affected only one third of the seas; now it is complete. This would be a huge part of the economic downfall that struck the Roman Empire.

Third bowl (16:4-7) – Rivers and springs to blood
Also finding its Old Testament counterpart in the first plague, here the drinking water is now affected. In verse 6, God makes it clear that those who have shed the innocent blood of faithful disciples must now drink blood. It is an example of Galatians 6:7, the principle of reaping what you sow.

Fourth bowl (16:8-9) – Fire
The seventh plague on Egypt (Exodus 9:22-26) consisted of fire and hail. There are other Old Testament examples, as well, of fire falling from heaven as a judgment from God upon the wicked. Sodom and Gomorrah (Genesis 19) and Nadab and Abihu (Leviticus 10:1-2) are just a couple out of several instances of God's judgment in this way.

Fifth bowl (16:10-11) – Darkness and pain
This is a reference to the three days of darkness over all the land of Egypt, "darkness which may even be felt" (Exodus 10:21-29). Although the ungodly here blaspheme God because of their pain and their sores, they will still not repent, just as Pharaoh would not.

Sixth bowl (16:12-16) – The battle of Armageddon
The forces of righteousness assemble, the forces of evil gather and the war to end all wars takes place. Har-Megiddo (hill of Megiddo) is a location where good and evil fought in many Old Testament accounts (see Judges 5:19; 1 Samuel 31; 2 Kings 23, for example).

Seventh bowl (16:17-21) – It is done
The finality of God's judgment is described as Rome drinks of the cup of God's fierce wrath.

The Battle of Armageddon in its spiritual sense is God versus Satan. In our own personal lives, it is the struggle between right and wrong, between spirit and flesh. The book of Revelation is telling us that the Battle of Armageddon will be won by God and Christians, people just like us. We can win this battle and live with God forever.

## Revelation 17

Chapter 17 is a key study in the book of Revelation. It is a continuation (as are chapters 18-20) of the seventh bowl of wrath, which portrays the final downfall of the wicked city Babylon (Rome). The current situation will end in the collapse of the powerful Roman Empire, as punishment from God for their ungodly ways.

Verses 1-6 describe the scarlet woman or "the great harlot." This is Rome. Verse 6 identifies her as the persecutor of God's people. In verse 9, Rome is described as the city which sits on seven hills, which is literally true of Rome.

Rome is referred to as a great harlot, which is intended to call attention to the spiritual fornication of Rome for political, economic or social advantage.

Her description in verses 3-4 is colorful and pointed.

- Purple – royalty
- Scarlet – red (bloodshed)
- Beautiful jewelry – luxury and extravagance
- Golden cup of abominations – evil; persecution of Christians (verse 6).

Her name (verse 5) is descriptive of the vileness of all evil in the sight of God, but especially of first century Rome. Verse 18 makes it clear that all of these terms refer to a city, one which reigns over the kings of the earth. This can only be speaking of the capital city of the Roman Empire.

Then the attention turns to the seven headed beast (verse 7-11). You will recall from Chapter 13 that the beast is Rome, as a civil persecuting power. Verse 8 says that this aspect of Rome "was, and is not, and will ascend." This would likely indicate that the persecution had formerly been quite strong (probably under Nero), had subsided somewhat at the present time (not disappearing, but decreasing temporarily in its intensity) and then would rise again to its former strength (under Domitian).

The seven heads are seven kings or Caesars (verse 10). There are various possible interpretations of this.

The most popular date of writing for the book is A.D. 95 or 96. This would place the writing of the book during the reign of Domitian, who ruled the Empire from A.D. 81-96. Homer Hailey, along with many others, defended this view.

Foy E. Wallace, Jr., in his commentary on Revelation, took an earlier date for its writing (pre A.D. 70), began his count with Julius Caesar and therefore, believed that the eighth king referred to Nero.

Jim McGuiggan, in his commentary, says the five kings who "have fallen" are Augustus, Tiberius, Caligula, Claudius and Nero. The one who "is" when the book was written is Vespasian. The one who "has not yet come" is Titus and the eighth would therefore be Domitian. This view dates the book at A.D. 78-79 and states that Revelation was written to prepare Christians for the terror brought on by Domitian before it began, not at the end of his reign.

Another theory for the seven kings is that they represent the completeness or totality of Roman rule, rather than referring to specific rulers.

The ten horns (verses 11-18) refer to the leaders of the multiple Roman provinces, who persecuted believers in various localities, but who actually played a part in the final destruction of Rome (verse 16).

## Revelation 18

The major theme in Chapter 18 continues to be the fall of Rome. John is continually reminding them that, no matter how powerful the Roman Empire is, God is stronger. Historians have attributed the decline and fall of the Roman Empire to many different factors. There is probably some truth in all of those considerations. It is unlikely that any single thing caused the downfall of Rome, but rather, it was probably a combination of many different things. Ultimately, Rome fell because God said it would. He may have used multiple ways of bringing that downfall into reality, but they were doomed because of how they were treating the people of God. It was a matter of God bringing about justice for those persecuted disciples of the first century. That was one of the primary reasons for the A.D. 70 destruction of Jerusalem as well ("He came to His own, and His own did not receive Him," John 1:11).

One of the major factors in Rome's downfall as a nation/empire, used by God to accomplish this stunning collapse, was economic and that's the main idea in Chapter 18.

The first angel (in this chapter) announces the Empire's death (verses 1-3). An angel comes down from heaven with great authority from God and the earth is illuminated with his glory. He cries out mightily with a loud voice (isn't it amazing how many times that idea is found in Revelation?) that Babylon the great is fallen.

He attributes this fall to the spiritual fornication of Rome with merchants, allies and kings who lived in the lap of luxury while mistreating the Jesus followers who got in their way. James 4:4 refers to friendship with the world in two ways. First, it is described as "enmity with God." No one should want to be God's enemy. But secondly, this is described as spiritual adultery, that is, unfaithfulness to the God of heaven. Some may have snuggled up to Rome as a means of financial gain, but it was to be such only in the short term. In the long term, it meant certain judgment. Hebrews 11:25 warns us against enjoying "the passing pleasures of sin." Short term pleasure is not worth eternal punishment, not ever.

Notice that God has the angel to announce that "Babylon is fallen," as though it has already happened. That is common in prophetic language and especially in those Scriptures that are apocalyptic in nature (Ezekiel, Zechariah, and Revelation primarily, but in other passages from the prophets as well). When God decides that something is going to happen, it is certain enough for the announcement to be made in the present tense, not merely in the future tense.

In verses 4-20, a second voice from heaven reminds the people of God that they must not become entangled with evil (verses 4-5) and that Rome will now reap what she has sown (verses 6-8).

Verses 9-19 is a telling statement that those who serve Rome will be cast down when the Empire falls. There will be no market for their goods; some 30 specific items are listed (verses 11-17). Many will stand off at a distance and watch Rome's decline (verses 18-19). In verse 20, the faithful rejoice in the righteous judgment of God.

Verses 21-24 describe the destruction of the city itself. Three major sources of Rome's appeal are destroyed: entertainment, business and home life. Note that the city was not literally destroyed. Rather it was destroyed as the Christian-persecuting power of the first century. The reason for her fall? "For her sins have reached to heaven, and God has remembered her iniquities" (verse 5). Never forget that "the wages of sin is death"

(Romans 6:23). That's true of Rome and in all of our lives as well. We need to take sin seriously because God does.

## Revelation 19

Chapter 19 is, in some ways, a summary of the entire book of Revelation. Chapters 1-11 describe the struggle between Christians and the Roman Empire. Chapters 12-22 show that this is actually a battle between God and Satan. Chapters 19-20 help us to realize that this battle will be easily won by God. Chapters 21-22 conclude the book by promising us (and those first century believers) that those who choose God over Satan will be victors in this spiritual war as well.

The chapter begins with a vision of victory (verses 1-10). We see the rejoicing of the righteous as they praise God for His goodness and mercy. The word "Alleluia" (or Hallelujah), means "praise God." This is repeated by a great multitude in heaven (verse 1), the 24 elders and 4 living creatures (verse 4), an unnamed voice from the throne (verse 5) and finally, from another "great multitude" (verse 6). The first great multitude was in heaven; this one is likely all the saved people still on the earth, in the church, who have been faithful to the Lord through severe persecution and who are now pictured as being saved from the political and religious corruption brought on by the evil Roman government.

Verses 7-9 describe the beauty and joy of a wedding feast, which contrasts with 18:23, the picture of the downfall of Rome, where no marriages/weddings are taking place, only mourning and sorrow.

In verse 10, John is so overcome by joy that he falls down to worship the angel who has shown him these things. The angel reminds him that we are to worship God exclusively. "You shall worship the LORD your God, and Him only you shall serve" (Matthew 4:10; quoting Deuteronomy 6:13). We are not to worship an angel, not another human being, not Satan and not Rome or any of its Caesars. God alone is worthy of our devotion and adoration.

The final section of the chapter (verses 11-21) is a figurative description of our Lord and Savior, Jesus the Messiah.

He comes riding on a white horse, symbolizing purity and holiness. His names are mentioned several times and include Faithful and True, Word of God, King of kings and Lord of lords. He is the judge. He has eyes like a flame of fire. On His head are many crowns (the Greek word here is DIADEM, the crown of royalty). This whole description is reminiscent of the one in Chapter 1, in which we were first introduced to the majestic Messiah. Especially touching for the child of God is the explanation in verse 13 that His robe has been dipped in blood. There is no more important aspect about Christ to the Christian than to be reminded that Jesus shed His blood for our sins, paying the redemption price for our deliverance to a new life, with all of the spiritual blessings that we enjoy in Christ Jesus our Lord. He died to save us.

Verses 17-21 are one more symbolic paragraph in which God reassures His people that Rome is going to be destroyed and Christians are going to be saved to live with Him forever. Much of the language here comes from Ezekiel 38 and 39.

Of special note, in these final verses, two major enemies from Revelation 13 are defeated forever, the beast and the false prophet. You will recall that the beast (the one from the sea) is Rome as a civil persecuting government. The false prophet is Rome as a false religious power. Both are cast into the lake of fire burning with brimstone (many newer translations use the word, sulfur). This reminds the reader of the reality of an eternal fire that will never be quenched, a place of outer darkness with weeping and gnashing of teeth. This, of course, is hell, a place prepared for the devil and his angels. It is Satan's destiny to live in hell forever, but it doesn't have to be your destiny or mine. Jesus lived and died and rose again so we can live eternally in heaven.

## Revelation 20

Revelation 20 is perhaps the most difficult, and certainly the most controversial, chapter in the book. A few of the details may be obscure and challenging to interpret, but we can easily understand the overall meaning of the text. Revelation 19:20 described the destruction of the beast and the false prophet, Rome as both a persecuting civil power and as a false religion. Chapter 20 portrays the ultimate defeat of the power behind Rome, which is Satan himself.

However else you understand the other verses in this chapter, verse 10 cannot be misunderstood. "The devil, who deceived them, was cast into the lake of fire and brimstone where the beast and the false prophet are. And they will be tormented day and night forever and ever." That is crystal clear, isn't it? Satan is going to be punished and tormented forever in hell.

Here's how it is pictured, in figurative language.

John sees an angel coming down from heaven. This angel has the key to the Abyss, the bottomless pit, and he is holding a great chain. He captures the dragon (remember that imagery used in Chapter 12?), binds him with the chain and then casts him into the bottomless pit, shutting him up inside that Abyss and setting a seal on him so that he cannot escape for 1000 years. Notice that it is not God the Father or Jesus the Son or the Holy Spirit who does this to Satan, it is simply an angel from God.

The 1000 years reference has been the source of much confusion and disagreement for generations. I am convinced that it is simply another numerical symbolism that is not meant to be taken literally. It is intended to emphasize the totality of Satan's defeat. It is a perfect binding that will take him out of the picture for a long, long time.

In Psalm 50:10, God is said to own the cattle on a thousand hills. Is that literal? No, it is simply a way of expressing that they all belong to Him. It is another way of saying what we read in Psalm 24:1, that the earth and all its fullness belongs to God. In Deuteronomy 7:9, He is described as "the faithful God, who keeps covenant and mercy for a thousand generations with those who love Him and keep His commandments." Does that mean if the world stands longer than that, God will not be faithful to any generation beyond the first thousand? Of course not. It is not a specific number; it is telling us that God will always be faithful to the obedient.

In Revelation 20, God is specifically promising them that Rome will be so completely defeated that they will never again be an agent of Satan to cause the kind of turmoil they specialized in.

After the 1000 years (however long that might actually be), Satan will be released for a little while. He will still have power and influence, but never again through Rome. Sin will continue to exist, but its bondage will be broken. Our obedience to God not only frees us from the guilt of sin, but from its bondage over us also (Romans 6:1-18). Satan will be loosed (verses 7-10), but ultimately will be thrown into the lake of fire and brimstone.

The great white throne judgment that is described here is not the final judgment. It continues the previous theme in the book. It is a picture of God judging Rome and her allies. The dead are raised and judged. If they are not in the book of Life (verse 12), that is, if they are not faithful Christians, they will be lost. If they remain true to God, they will be saved. There are similarities here to the last great Day of Judgment, but this is saying that we must be certain to be on God's side, not following the Devil. It is further proof that we can overcome Satan with the help of Christ.

## Revelation 21

Beginning with chapters 15 through 20, the final downfall of Satan and Rome has been pictured. Chapters 21 and 22 portray the positive side of the picture, the reward of the faithful.

The most common explanation of these two chapters is that they describe heaven. Perhaps they do. It seems more logical, however, to believe that the reward pictured here is the church, in its triumphant state. There are two important considerations:

1.) The context of the book itself. The real point is not that the righteous go to heaven and the ungodly to hell (although we know that is true), but that in the struggle between Rome and Christians, the saints will have the ultimate victory and can find refuge and divine protection in the church.

2.) In Revelation 21:9-10, this holy Jerusalem is called "the bride, the Lamb's wife." This always speaks of the church (2 Corinthians 11:2; Ephesians 5:23-25). And this new city comes down out of heaven, rather than being heaven itself.

I believe that John uses figurative language that could be used to describe heaven as well as the church triumphant. Heaven can never be adequately described in human terms. But many of the symbolic terms could rightly be applied to both.

Chapter 21 opens up by referring to "a new heaven and a new earth," a new living environment. This is common Old Testament language referring to a new situation in life, but never refers to heaven itself (see Isaiah 65:17-19 and 66:22, for example). Remember that most of Revelation is figurative. The ungodly man's world would not be literally destroyed and the godly man's physical world would not literally become brand new.

Death is defeated by Christ so that Christians do not have to worry about it (21:3-4). Again, this language is from the Old Testament (see Isaiah 26:19; Hosea 13:14).

The city (new Jerusalem) is described with multiple words, phrases or ideas that picture for us the concept that the church is intended by God to be a taste of heaven on earth.

- Those who are ungodly are not allowed in (21:8)
- Great and high wall provides security and protection (21:12)
- 12 gates – entrance is available to anyone who wants to get in (21:12-13)
- 12 foundations – endurance and permanence (21:14)
- Foursquare city, 12,000 furlongs (1500 miles) square (21:16) – abundance of blessings for all
- The jewels (21:18-21) – beauty, splendor, glory
- The light of the city is Jesus (21:22-23)
- Nothing impure allowed in the city (21:27)

Go back and notice verse 6 one more time. "And He said to me, 'It is done! I am the Alpha and the Omega, the Beginning and the End. I will give of the fountain of the water of life freely to him who thirsts." This language of the fountain of the water of life reminds us of the statement that Jesus made in John 4 when He was speaking with the Samaritan woman at Jacob's well. When He asked her for a drink of physical water, He contrasts that water with the living water of life. "Whoever drinks of this water will thirst again, but whoever drinks of the water that I shall give him will never thirst. But the water that I shall give him will become in him a fountain of water springing up into everlasting life." Jesus came to bring this living water of everlasting life to the world. He still offers that to us today.

## Revelation 22

Chapter 22 continues the thoughts from Chapter 21 about the church. Verses 1-5 sound like a picture of Paradise, which brings up many similarities between the church and the Garden of Eden. Both of them represent the concept of an intimate personal relationship between God and His people.

We have available to us in the church today the river of water of life, as we discussed at the end of the previous chapter. We have healing from sin, as described in 1 Peter 2:24. And we have access to the tree of life (from Eden) in the everlasting life that is offered to us in the sacrifice of God's Son on the cross.

We see the Lord in the teachings of His word and His name is on our foreheads (verse 4) as we have identified ourselves with Him and "put on Christ" when we are baptized into Him (Galatians 3:27).

We have the light of His truth as we study the inspired, God-breathed message of the gospel of Jesus Christ (John 8:12; 2 Corinthians 4:4).

But if you are uncomfortable with the view that Chapters 21 and 22 describe the church, then continue to think of them as speaking of heaven. Many Bible students who know the Bible much better than I do believe these chapters describe heaven. If that thought feels better to you, then feel free to continue to be comforted by that. There are many similarities between the church and heaven when they are described in such beautiful figurative terminology.

Verses 6-21 bring this marvelous message of salvation from God to a close.

The angel reminds John that the message of the book came from God. "These words are faithful and true. And the Lord God of the holy prophets sent His angel to show His servants the things which must shortly take place."

He actually states twice that the prophecies of Revelation "must shortly take place" (verses 6 and 10), meaning that the primary application of the book dealt with their current, first century situation. There are, as we have noticed, many principles in Revelation that apply to our lives as well. And John is told again not to worship the angel (verses 8-9).

There is an interesting point that the angel makes in verse 10 when he tells John not to seal the words of the prophecy in the book. In other passages, like Daniel 8:26, the Lord has said that their teaching should be sealed; here, He makes it clear that because the time is at hand, the prophecies need to be revealed. That is why the book is called Revelation. We need to learn from it how to live for God.

"I come quickly" is stated three times (22:7,12, 20). This is not the second coming, but Jesus coming in judgment on Rome.

Notice in verses 14 and 17 that the gospel invitation is still being extended. That won't happen in heaven, but it occurs regularly in the church.

The ungodly are still outside the church (verse 15), although at times wicked people can slip in to do the work of the devil internally (Jude 4). God knows those who are His (2 Timothy 2:19) and those who are not.

There are also warnings not to change the message of the book (22:18-19). People have never had the right to change God's will. May we love His word and pattern every aspect of our lives after its teaching.

"Even so, come, Lord Jesus! The grace of our Lord Jesus Christ be with you all. Amen."

www.ingramcontent.com/pod-product-compliance
Lightning Source LLC
Chambersburg PA
CBHW050451110426
42744CB00013B/1962

* 9 7 8 1 9 6 6 9 9 2 0 2 8 *